Comparing Muslim Societies

THE COMPARATIVE STUDIES IN SOCIETY AND HISTORY BOOK SERIES

Raymond Grew, Series Editor

Comparing Muslim Societies:
Knowledge and the State in a World Civilization
  Juan R. I. Cole, editor

Comparing Muslim Societies

Knowledge and the State in a
World Civilization

Edited by Juan R. I. Cole

Ann Arbor
THE UNIVERSITY OF MICHIGAN PRESS

1995   1994   1993   1992   4   3   2   1

Library of Congress Cataloging-in-Publication Data

Comparing Muslim societies: knowledge and the state in a world
civilization/edited by Juan R. I. Cole.
     p.   cm.—(Comparative studies in society and history)
    Includes bibliographical references and index.
    ISBN 0-472-09449-1 (alk. paper).—ISBN 0-472-06449-5 (alk.
paper)
    1. Islamic countries—Civilization.   2. Islam—20th century.
I. Cole, Juan Ricardo.   II. Series: Comparative studies in society
and history (Ann Arbor, Mich.)
DS35.62.C66 1992
909'.097671—dc20   91-39981
                                                                      CIP

Foreword

For more than thirty years, *Comparative Studies in Society and History* (*CSSH*) has published articles about human society in any time or place, written by scholars in any discipline and from any country. Those articles, inevitably reflecting the changing methods and interests in their authors' specialized fields of research, have presented new evidence and new techniques, challenged established assumptions, and raised fresh questions. The series of books entitled Comparative Studies in Society and History extends and refocuses the discussions begun in some of the most stimulating essays.

The editor of each volume identifies a field of comparative study and presents contributions that help to define it, selected from among the articles that have appeared in *CSSH* from October, 1958, to the present and from scores of manuscripts currently being considered. Written by scholars trained in various traditions, some of whom were born before 1900 and some after 1960, the essays are chosen for their contribution to what the editor perceives as an important continuing dialogue. The volumes in this series are thus not just anthologies. Each contains specially commissioned essays designed to suggest more fully the potential range of the topic. In addition, the articles taken from *CSSH* have been revised by their authors in light of the larger project. Each volume is, therefore, a new work in the specific sense that its chapters are abreast of current scholarship and, in its broader purpose, a cooperative enterprise reconsidering (and thereby reconstructing) a common topic.

Having established a theme and identified scholars to address it, the editor then invites these colleagues to join in exploring the ramifications of their common interest. In most instances this step includes a conference in Ann Arbor, attended by contributors and other scholars, where issues of conceptualization, interpretation, and method can be debated. Sometimes the volume's topic is made the basis of a graduate course, with contributors giving a series of lectures in a seminar lasting a term or more and attended by a variety of interested specialists. The book, which started from an indirect dialogue in the pages of *CSSH,* thus takes form through direct encounters among scholars from different disciplines and specializations. In open-ended and lively discussion, individual manuscripts are criticized and new suggestions tested, common concerns identified and then matched against the criteria of different disciplines and the experience of different societies. Reshaped by the community it has created, each volume becomes a statement of the current state of scholarship and of questions raised as by-products of the process in which general problems are reformulated while individual essays are reconsidered and revised.

By building from discussions conducted over the years in *CSSH,* this series extends the tradition represented by the journal itself. A scholarly quarterly is a peculiar kind of institution, its core permanently fixed in print, its rhythmic appearance in familiar covers an assurance of some central continuity, its contents influenced by its past yet pointing in new directions. *CSSH* seeks to create a community without formal boundaries—a community whose membership is only loosely determined by subject, space, or time. Just as notes and references embed each article in particular intellectual traditions while stretching beyond them, so the journal itself reaches beyond editors, contributors, and subscribers, speaking in whatever voice unknown readers respond to whenever and wherever they turn its pages. The resulting dialogues are not limited to any single forum, and the journal changes from within while balancing between venturesomeness and rigor as old debates are refined and new problems posed.

The books in this series further the aspirations acknowledged in the opening editorial of *CSSH,* in which Sylvia Thrupp declared her belief that "there is a definite set of problems common to the humanities, to history, and to the various social sciences." Changes in the way these problems are conceived and in the vocabulary for expressing them have not lessened the determination to reject "the false dilemma" between "error through insularity and probable superficiality." Insistence upon thorough, original research has been the principal defense against superficiality, emphasis upon comparison the means for overcoming insularity. Many of the articles published in *CSSH* are systematically comparative, across time and between societies, and that is always welcome; but many are not. Each published article is chosen for its scholarship and imagination as well as for its broad implications. For the contributors to and readers of that journal, comparison has come to mean more a way of thinking than the merely mechanical listing of parallels among separate cases. Articles designed to speak to scholars in many disciplines and to students of different societies are recognized as instrinsically comparative by the nature of the problem addressed, structure, and effect.

Every piece of research deserves to be seen in many contexts: the problems and concerns of a particular society, the immediately relevant scholarly literature with its own vocabulary and evidence, the methods and goals of a given discipline, a body of theory and hypotheses, and sets of questions (established, currently in vogue, or new). It is also impossible for any prescription to delimit, in advance, how far subsequent comparisons of similar problems in different contexts may reach. For the past twenty years, *CSSH* has placed articles under rubrics that call attention to a central comparative theme among related studies. In addition, an editorial foreword in each issue notes other sets of connections between current articles and earlier ones, inviting additional comparisons of broad themes, specific topics, and particular problems or methods. A variety of potential discourses is thus identified, and that open-ended process has culminated in this series of books. Some of the volumes in the series are built around themes for comparative study that have always been recognized as requiring comparison, some address topics not always recognized as a field of study, creating a new perspective through a fresh set of questions. Each volume is thus an autonomous undertaking, a discussion with its own purposes and focus, the work of many authors and an editor's vision of the topic, establishing a field of knowledge, assessing its present state, and suggesting some future directions.

The goal, in the quarterly issues of *CSSH* and in these books, is to break out of received categories and to cross barriers of convention that, like the residual silt from streams that once flowed faster, have channeled inquiry into patterns convenient for familiar ideas, academic disciplines, and established specialties. Contemporary intellectual trends encourage, indeed demand, this rethinking and provide some powerful tools for accomplishing it. In fact, such ambitious goals have become unnervingly fashionable, for it no longer requires original daring or theoretical independence to attack the hegemony of paradigms—positivism, scientism, Orientalism, modernization, Marxism, behavioralism, and so forth—that once shaped the discourse of social science. Scholars, however, must hope that the effort to think anew also allows some cumulative element in our understanding of how human societies work. Thus, these books begin by recognizing and building from the lasting qualities of solid scholarship.

As a subject of study, Muslim societies raise special difficulties, not just because of the profound uncertainty about what it is they have in common or because of the fascinating complexity of the societies themselves but because of the noise surrounding them. An Olympian tone cannot protect scholarship from the prejudice, propaganda, diplomacy, and wars that kindle interest. The long histories and vast geographical range of these societies defy any single treatment, and this book rejects such an effort as a matter of principle; yet the essays gathered here treat Muslim societies from the Middle Ages to the Iranian revolution and from Morocco to Pakistan. Using comparison to illustrate the diversity among Muslim societies and the ways in which each of them is similar to some non-Muslim societies, the chapters introduce students and members of the general public to worlds often misunderstood in their very naming. Pernicious and persistent stereotypes are rejected not by labored attack but by analysis that renders them impossible, revealing adaptive change as well as continuity and emphasizing the importance of other factors, from geography to social experience, in the role of religion. For specialists, too, the critical perspectives developed here suggest additional questions; and the accompanying bibliography invites all readers to further exploration. These studies begin with specific societies carefully set in time and place rather than from assumptions about the nature of Islam. They neither formulate nor test some single schema but probe the intersections of technology, politics, class, gender, ideology, and learning in particular Muslim societies.

Juan Cole reflects on many of the trends and controversies of current scholarship in the introduction, and his striking assessment of types of comparison demonstrates their usefulness. Comparison also works in another direction, enabling us to learn about ourselves and the matters that most concern us, as well as about the societies we study. Most of the issues considered here are universal. Themes about that transformation once unself-consciously called modernization run through all these chapters. So, of course, do discussions of religion; and anyone interested in the intersection of politics and religion will want to read the chapters by Charles Lindholm, Ellis Goldberg, and Shahrough Akhavi. Intellectuals, always interested in intellectuals, will find much to ponder in the chapters by Lindholm, Dale Eickelman, and Charles Smith. For students of technology in Europe, Africa, or Asia, there are challenging issues in Nikki Keddie's chapter. There is much to be learned about schooling and education throughout the world in Eickelman's study, about legal systems and the nature of colonial rule in Allan Christelow's chapter, and about gender studies in Deniz Kandiyoti's chapter. Once the Other is no longer alien, the familiar cannot go unquestioned or be assumed simply to be natural. Each of these imaginative and learned chapters, with its carefully constructed arguments, offers its own rewards, and that is not the least of the many reasons for welcoming this collection of studies on a set of important and complex societies.

Raymond Grew

Acknowledgments

This book, the first in a series, brings together new chapters and revised versions of important essays that earlier appeared in *Comparative Studies in Society and History*. Most of the authors attended a conference in Ann Arbor on October 13-15, 1989, sponsored by the journal and the Horace H. Rackham School of Graduate Studies of the University of Michigan. The original essays were (sometimes heatedly) discussed by colleagues at the conference, and then the authors went home to revise them, bring them up to date, and make them into book chapters. Many authors have recast classic essays or expanded them in scope. In addition, two authors (Lindholm and Kandiyoti) were invited to submit new chapters that have not appeared elsewhere.

In general, transliteration follows the system employed in the *International Journal of Middle East Studies*. Given the wide cultural range covered by these chapters, I have not attempted to impose absolute uniformity in regard to transliteration. Thus, several technical terms are given in Dale Eickelman's essay in colloquial Moroccan Arabic, and take forms slightly different than those they would take in modern standard Arabic. So be it. I have, on the other hand, attempted to ensure that key words deriving from Islamic practices or ideas and that have been adopted into English are transliterated in the same way throughout. For the sake of quick reference, a short glossary appears at the end of the book.

I am grateful to Raymond Grew, the editor of *Comparative Studies in Society and History,* for suggesting that I undertake the task of bringing these essays together in book form. I also want to thank Grace Fredkin, Shah Hanifi, and Eric Hanne for helping in technical matters related to the book or to the conference, and Joyce Harrison at the University of Michigan Press for her patience and helpfulness.

Grateful acknowledgement is given to *Comparative Studies in Society and History* for permission to reproduce the following articles in revised form:

Chapter 2 appeared originally in *CSSH* 26:709-35 as "Material Culture and Geography: Toward a Holistic Comparative Study of the Muslim Middle East."

Chapter 4 appeared originally in *CSSH* 20:485–515 as "The Art of Memory: Islam, Education and Social Reproduction."

Chapter 5 appeared originally in *CSSH* 24:3–24.

Chapter 6 appeared originally in *CSSH* 22:413–33 as "The Intellectual and Modernization: Definitions and Reconsiderations: The Egyptian Experience."

Chapter 7 appeared originally in *CSSH* 33:4–35.

Chapter 9 appeared originally in *CSSH* 25:195–221 as "The Ideology and Practice of Shi'ism in the Iranian Revolution."

Contents

Introduction

Juan R. I. Cole

The essays in this volume all deal, in one way or another, with the consequences of living in societies where the majority of the population is Muslim. All the authors wrestle with the problem of how important Muslim culture has been in areas such as politics, social movements, the place of women, and education. The book premises that comparison, as a set of strategies, offers many advantages in arriving at an answer to such questions. Comparison also helps us avoid essentialism and reification in the way we pose the questions. This strategy clarifies the manner in which we are confronted not with a monolithic phenomenon, Islam, but with a range of exceedingly diverse societies in which a variety of peoples has adopted a Muslim identity through editing the Great Tradition and combining it with elements of local traditions. In some areas of social life, being Muslim matters more than in others. Often it is Islam *and* something else that must combine to endow it with that importance. Some authors argue that class or technology or state policy is as important as Islam per se in understanding, say, the position of women or intellectuals or the economy in Muslim-majority societies. Others focus on elements of Muslim identity within culture, where the importance of religion is less problematic.

Here I should clarify what I mean by "Muslim societies." I do not mean "Islamic societies." I do not mean to suggest that, in countries where most persons are Muslim, most persons are pious or pray very frequently or obey Islamic law closely (or even necessarily know much about it). I mean, instead, societies that share a cultural heritage influenced by Islam. In short, I mean Muslim as a marker of ethnicity and broad culture, not necessarily as a marker of religion. Such a usage is defensible, I think. In Yugoslavia, for instance, secular intellectuals from a Muslim background demanded the right to be classed as "Muslims" just as Serbs were classed as Serbs. For all its genuine importance, Islam as religion is overused as an interpretive tool in studying the Middle East. My use of Muslim, however, encompasses a cultural heritage, an ethnic construction of identity, and means to say nothing about religious belief. I think most of the authors represented here would share this view of things, and feel that their analyses, as historians and social scientists, of Muslim societies in this sense make their chapters original and exciting.

Even if this proposed usage is found useful and legitimate, the question remains of whether it matters all that much. The combination of indigenous Middle Eastern rhetoric about the importance of Islam with the practicalities of area studies training for academic research, along with the "unnatural" or nongeographic nature of the Middle East as an idea, may have conspired to make "being Muslim" seem more important than it is. How should we decide, one way or another? Here, I would argue, the importance of comparison becomes paramount. Only by looking at a broad range of societies characterizing themselves as Muslim, and only by comparing Muslim societies with non-Muslim ones, could we hope to assess more sensitively the place of the Muslim heritage in various spheres of life.

The argument between the Orientalist heritage in Middle Eastern studies and its challengers in the social sciences and the New Left, which I will discuss subsequently, possesses momentous implications for our understanding of a civilization. I find in these essays a fresh set of perspectives on this debate, a series of intellectual excursions that pose new questions in the search to solve this and other, more specific problems. They often provide an exit from the by-now sterile debate over Orientalism versus class analysis by pointing to key factors that both approaches have tended to slight: technology, tribalism, and the state. Their use of comparison is also key to breaking down artificial ideas about Self and Other that have impeded Western understanding of the Middle East.

There is no such thing, of course, as "the comparative method." Comparison is more a tactic than a method. Here I want to explore several sorts of comparison and their implications for our understanding of Muslim societies. I see four poles connecting intersecting lines. The first is internal comparison, the comparison of one Muslim society with another as a means of determining whether they share some common trait that could be called "Muslim." The second is external comparison, the juxtaposition of a Muslim society or group with, say, a European or Chinese one, as a way of illuminating what might be distinctive or unexceptional about a Muslim phenomenon. The other axis has to do, not with tactics, but with focus. The third pole is ideal culture, the role of symbol in the construction of human meaning. The fourth is social structure and its material bases. Thus, an author might compare the social structure of two Muslim societies as a way of testing theories about the relative explanatory weight of class alliances in shaping forms of polity. Or an author might compare symbolic conceptions of authority in one Muslim and one Buddhist society. These four poles do not exhaust the possibilities for comparison, of course, but I believe they do account for all the chapters of this book.

What forces have been most important in the shaping of Middle Eastern and other Muslim societies? Few contemporary Western intellectuals would any longer hold either an extreme Hegelian idealism or an extreme Marxist materialism. Rather, the question for most observers is how to weight the material and the symbolic in explaining human behavior and the growth of institutions. Here, at the outset, I have juxtaposed two chapters in part 1. One makes a wide-ranging argument for the importance of geography and technology in forming Middle Eastern institutions and ways of life. Technology has not been as fashionable an area of social explanation as class formation and struggle, perhaps because academics feel they lack the technical expertise to investigate it. Clearly, from the camel stirrup to Iranian underground irrigation canals and from carpet looms to gunpowder, local technology and its geographic context have powerfully influenced styles of life in the Middle East. The second chapter focuses on the symbolic issue of the conflict within a Muslim society between a widespread ethos of equality and a reality of hierarchy. Questions of social norms concerning equality and hierarchy have been topical in modern social thought since the French Revolution, from de Tocqueville on America through French anthropologist Louis Dumont on the Hindu caste system. How have Islamic societies dealt with these conflicting social imperatives? These first two chapters neatly explore the four poles of analysis I have outlined, giving us an external comparison (Europe and the Middle East) of a social-structural issue (material culture), and an internal comparison (Morocco and Pakistan) of a symbolic one. They thus set the stage for what is to come.

Part 2 of the book focuses on the place of symbols in political and intellectual culture. How have Muslim clergy and intellectuals been affected by, and responded to, the challenges of Western imperial domination and cultural influence in the twentieth century? What has colonialism meant for clerical institutions and training, and how have Muslims appealed to Islamic symbols in facing Western hegemony? What has Islam meant for modern intellectuals, a group that, in the West, has often been strongly associated with secular ideologies?

Finally, part 3 turns to essays that are more broadly structuralist in orientation and that bring the state in as an important variable in the analyses. Are there similarities in the conditions under which Muslim fundamentalism has developed in the contemporary Middle East and those under which Calvinism emerged in early modern Europe? More especially, was the transition to a new sort of regime-type important in both instances? What produces the vast difference in the status and treatment of women across Muslim societies, from Tunisia to Pakistan? Is Islam, or is state policy, the primary variable here, and what role do internal political coalitions play in affecting that policy? Contemporary Iran affords us the only view of what a state ruled by the Muslim clergy would look like. Certainly, symbol and culture have heavily influenced the shape of the Islamic Republic. Yet this state, like its Pahlavi predecessor, depends heavily on petroleum revenues and uses them to distribute patronage to corporate groups within Iranian society. What role do rentierism (the state's dependence on a lucrative, state-owned export commodity for its revenues) and corporatism play in Islamic Iran, as opposed to Islam as a set of symbols, practices, and institutions, in influencing the shape of polity?

The question of the place of Islam in their analyses is one with which all the authors had to wrestle, and it has been a central problem for the study of the Middle East. Many Westerners think that being Muslim matters in the Middle East in a way that being Christian is no longer centrally important in France or Germany. The study of religion is also more central to the tradition of research on the Middle East than it is to research on China or sub-Saharan Africa. Some commentators have an annoying habit of referring to Middle Eastern and other Muslim areas as "Islam," and Islam is not a neutral term as used in the West. The Muslim civilization surpassed that of Europe in the early medieval period, and rivalled that of Europe until the early modern period. It constituted the nearest neighbor to Europe among world civilizations, allowing a long history of both conflict and cooperation. This rivalry has left a legacy of negative images concerning Islam in Western cultures that is unlike the image most Europeans and North Americans have of, say, Buddhism. Ironically, from a Buddhist point of view, Islam and Christianity appear as perhaps little more than two branches of the same Abrahamic faith, and maybe this sameness-with-difference partially underlies the antipathy of the two religion's adherents toward one another. Each looks into the other and sees what appears to be a distorted image of the Self. The philological, textually based approach to Muslim societies was promoted by Europeans in particular, and it had an impact in the United States during and after World War II as such European Orientalists as G. E. von Grunebaum immigrated and helped found academic centers for the study of the Middle East.

On the other hand, observers from the Left often assert that most ordinary persons in the Middle East, workers and peasants, place no great importance on religion, and that class is more significant as an analytical idea. Ironically, during the 1960s and 1970s, the Centers for Middle Eastern studies founded or expanded by European Orientalists helped train a new generation of American area specialists, many of them shaped politically by opposition to the Vietnam War and by the rise of the New Left. The influence of Middle Eastern leftist movements was also felt in this period. Exciting books appeared about the social origins of members of radical political parties such as the Baath in Iraq or the Communists in Iran. The new generation also made excursions into the relatively underwritten areas of Middle Eastern labor history or gender relations. Revisionist scholarship on the Middle East has made enormous contributions to our understanding of the region, and has given a voice to workers, women, and peasants whom the old Orientalist tradition had tended to ignore in favor of textual analysis (most texts having been produced by elite males). It has also had some failures, as in the leftist literature on Pahlavi Iran in the 1970s, which signally failed to see the potential significance of the Shi'ite clergy as national leaders.

The preoccupation with Islam in the study of the Middle East has several roots. First, Middle Easterners themselves often insist on its importance. The rulers of Saudi Arabia proclaim that their country has no constitution save the holy Qur'an itself; Iran is an Islamic republic ruled primarily by Muslim clergymen; the Islamic Republic of Pakistan has had bouts of Islamization in law and public affairs. In countries such as Tunisia, Jordan, and Egypt, the most important opposition parties identify themselves as Islamic. Most states in the Middle East send their foreign ministers to meetings of the Islamic Conference Organization. Now, Western European states do not send their foreign ministers to meetings of a Christian Conference Organization. Peasants in the Middle East may not consider Islam the most important thing in their daily lives, or know much about Islamic law, but the religion has a constitutional and political importance in their countries unlike the position of religion in contemporary France or China. Peasants in Malaysia may attempt to avoid paying the poor tax (*zakat,* 2.5 percent per annum on liquid assets to be used to help the indigent), but it is not without significance that some of their taxation takes this traditional Islamic form. Women factory workers in Egypt may not pray five times a day (though some no doubt do), but laws about the status of women in that country are often framed with reference to medieval Muslim juridical codes.

As I have suggested, the importance of Islam and Muslims in the study of the Middle East may further derive from the lack of a geographic or linguistic substratum that might lend the area an illusion of naturalness. Major specialists in the study of the Middle East write essays entitled "Is There a Middle East?" and conclude that there may not be.[1] China scholars seem seldom to agonize about whether there is a China. One can always say the field is geographically coterminous with the areas now overseen by the formidable apparatus of the Chinese bureaucracy. The Middle East suffers from having no obvious geographic correlate or even a consistent definition. It consists, as usually defined, primarily of modern successor-states to the medieval Muslim Abbasid Empire, stretching from North Africa to Afghanistan and Pakistan, with the addition of modern Turkey. The heritage of Muslim state making and the influence of Arabic language and Muslim religion help give the region a broad cultural unity. Area studies specialists who master that heritage can often deal with some aspects of a Southern Asian country such as Muslim Pakistan more ably than South Asianists with a narrow training in Sanskrit and Hinduism. Pakistani law increasingly bases itself upon the Hanafi Muslim juridical corpus in Arabic, and the millions of Pakistanis who have worked in the Middle East as guest workers have often come under the influence of the conservative Islam of the Arabian peninsula, into which most specialists in Hinduism have relatively few insights.

The need for comparative studies of the Muslim Middle East has been augmented by debates between the philologists and the revisionists that have led to an acute crisis of Orientalism. The Western study of the

Middle East, and of Muslim societies in general, has been controversial and contested for a long time, of course, but during the past two decades the intensity of the conflicts has increased. With much critical writing by intellectuals such as Abdullah Laroui and Anwar Abdel Malik, the major broadside against the tradition of Middle Eastern studies in Europe was Edward W. Said's influential *Orientalism*.[2] Said's work ingeniously combined neo-Marxism and poststructuralism with a dazzling survey of scholarship and literature, focusing upon the manner in which one culture decisively defines another as "the Other" in a "racist, imperialist, and almost totally ethnocentric" manner.[3] Said presents a Faustian story of how Western scholars, who thought themselves to be building up a body of objective knowledge, were spiritually suborned by the power that Europe gained over the East, and by the close networks that linked academics, travelers, diplomats, and colonialists.

Said brews a potent mixture of Italian Marxist Antonio Gramsci's theories with those of poststructuralist Michel Foucault. Can these two thinkers, these two approaches, really be melded successfully? Gramsci was concerned with the subtle dominance (hegemony) that the bourgeois ruling class gains over the exploited classes of workers and peasants through the schools, through public discourse, and through quiet censorship, in short, through less direct and formal institutions than the army and police. In Said's transcription, Western academics, travelers, and authors become the exploiting "bourgeoisie," attaining "hegemony" over the exploited Orient. Like the Marxist bourgeoisie, the Saidian Orientalists represent the exploited even to themselves (so that an Arab intellectual studying Middle East history at a U.S. university becomes a badge of hegemony).[4] For these purposes, academics, travelers, and authors are amalgamated to the imperialist and neoimperialist ruling classes who most directly benefit from exploitation of the Orient by the West. For Said, the original sin that precipitated the fall for academics and thinkers was an identification with the state.

Over this metaphor of class domination by means of cultural manipulation Said laid a framework of Foucauldian discourse analysis. For Foucault, discourse was to text as a medieval commentary was to the work on which it commented. Discourse represented something else, in such a way as to substitute for it and to make one forget that it had done so.[5] Orientalism, Said argued, constituted a discourse that represented the Orient and tried to make the reader forget that it could be represented in any other manner. Foucault saw each epoch as dominated by a particular way of knowing and expressing, which he called an "episteme," but the ages he discussed turned out to be more or less the Renaissance, the Enlightenment, and other periods that previous historians had already demarcated. More interested in power than in class, Foucault, unlike Gramsci, does not address whether this episteme governs discourse among all the social classes in a particular epoch or whether it pervades the entire society. I believe the latter would have been his view. Foucault's approach has been seen by some as nihilist. He denies the importance of the individual as active agent, and his conception of disjuncture challenges the idea of historical causality. On the other hand, he does see power as capillary, as present even among the weak and oppressed, which may be one ray of optimism in his system.

The conflation of Gramsci and Foucault effected by Said—and by many others as "discourse" history has become popular and postmodernism has come to replace, or meld itself with, New Left thinking—holds certain dangers, it seems to me. From a Marxist approach, we would expect that Said should distinguish among the authors he treats in their class background, their relationship to the means of production, and their political sympathies. What we get is Disraeli, Flaubert, Massignon, Lord Curzon, Goethe, and H. A. R. Gibb, all jumbled together as though they constituted a seamless web. Presumably they can all be addressed together, not because they represent the same class, but because the same discourse speaks through them. By substituting Western culture for Gramsci's bourgeoisie, and by conflating Gramscian hegemony with Foucault's conceptions of discourse and episteme, Said takes the focus off fine analytical distinctions among thinkers, whether of an intellectual, class, or political nature. Gramsci thought there were ways to escape hegemony, for intellectuals to build alternate visions of society. Said's analysis of Orientalism seldom exhibits that sort of optimism. The Hegelian fallacy lay in thinking that we cannot know anything without first knowing everything. Despite denials and qualifications, Said's work, in practice, comes close to saying that all representation of another culture is misrepresentation, that all knowledge in a powerful society is corrupted by that power. Most historians no longer adhere to a positivist view of their work, and it would come as no surprise to them that their writing is influenced by their context.[6] But Said seems often to be saying something more, to be employing terms such as *hegemony* and *discourse* to insist on not simply contextual influence, but an almost inescapable dominance over Western academic writing about the Middle East by imperialism and neoimperialism.

Said did put forward some positive role models, but one is hard put to know why he exempted them from his general opprobrium. He rightly praises French Marxian scholar Maxime Rodinson, though Rodinson, it should be noted, does not agree with Said's wholesale rejection of the Orientalist enterprise.[7] Said also praises Clifford Geertz, the anthropologist of Indonesia and Morocco, though it seems unlikely he would agree with Said's (or Rodinson's) perspective on most things. Both these figures are committed secularists with, self-admittedly, little sympathy for Muslim modernism. Was Said attempting to suggest that humanist Marxism (Rodinson) and symbolic anthropology (Geertz) are better at representing the Muslim Orient than other approaches? If so, it should be noted that much of the academic writing now done on the Middle East is heavily influenced by one or the other of these methodologies.

Said has challenged those who write about the Middle East and Muslims to reexamine their epistemology, to reconsider how they think they know what they know. He has usefully drawn attention to the problem of essentialism, of formulations about Muslim societies, such as "Islam is antimodern," that take no account of specific social and chronological context. Most of the negative images that nineteenth-century Europeans produced about the Middle East derived from a contrastive approach. Europe was rational, the Orient irrational; Europe was orderly, the Orient in disarray; Europe was virile, the Orient effeminate; Europe was dynamic, the Orient stagnant. The construction of an Other depends on contrast as its basic intellectual gesture, on delineating the manner in which the Other differs from Self. Yet to think one can employ contrast alone in pairing two objects is, at the least, an error of some magnitude. Comparison and contrast are inevitably coupled. To admit difference without admitting likeness in any comparison constitutes a critical moment of bad faith, an escape from oneself. To the extent that a "bad" Orientalism existed and exists in Said's terms, its faults lay, at least to a large degree, in this closed contrastive gesture. Even when the Europeans who denigrated the Middle East or Muslims deployed a comparison, it was actually a reflexed contrast; for sober, Protestant, British colonial officers, Muslim festivals and attendance at shrines recalled Roman Catholic practice. British Prime Minister Anthony Eden rather madly read Egyptian President Gamal Abdel Nasser as Mussolini, again equating the enemy outside Europe with the enemy inside Europe.

Restoring the "absent present" of comparison to the comparison-and-contrast dyad offers one way out of the bad Orientalist temptation. It cannot resolve all the problems that beset Middle Eastern studies as a field, of course, but it seems one promising strategy for dealing with the problem of depicting the Other. This set of strategies helps put things in perspective, but requires an enormous amount of empathy. It requires that one think of the ways in which different cultures are like one's own at the same time that one gives them their due for the manner in which they have enriched the common human heritage by their distinctiveness. An example might help make my point more concrete. Westerners often hold stereotypes of Arabs in Africa as slave traders. On the one hand, this image does a great injustice to the cultural contributions Arab civilization made in Africa. On the other, it ignores the predominant European and U.S. role in the slave trade from the early modern period until the early nineteenth century, and the ways in which European plantation slavery compared unfavorably with Middle Eastern household slavery as an institution. The long-term historical consequences of large-scale slave importation in persistent patterns of racial discrimination also seem less severe in the Muslim world than in a society such as the United States. Posing such questions comparatively raises issues about the differences between Western and Middle Eastern slave holding and bonded labor that might be answered structurally, and provides an important exit from mere stereotyping on either side.

One way to test generalizations about the Middle East and about Muslim societies, then, is through comparison. Although the comparative approach enjoyed a vogue in the nineteenth century, its practitioners ranged so widely, in such an undisciplined manner, that later scholars often avoided this approach. German sociologist Max Weber, for instance, was capable of citing biblical evidence alongside travelers' reports from the Middle East in his time to make a point about the structures of society in non-European regions. Some scholars continued to envisage a more rigorous sort of comparison as a basis for generalization. A breakthrough in this regard occurred when Sylvia Thrupp, the historian of medieval England, founded *Comparative Studies in Society and History* in the late 1950s, an enterprise that became a major academic success story. One of the first books published in the United States to revive an interest in comparison as a way of studying Muslim societies was Clifford Geertz's *Islam Observed,* which compared and contrasted the leadership styles in the early modern and modern periods of Morocco and Indonesia.[8] Geertz, a proponent of symbolic anthropology, focused on the ways Muslims in these two countries thought about power and charisma. Although he paid attention to the material culture and geography of the two places, his primary concern remained the way a culture elaborates its symbols of authority over time. One also has the impression that, in the end, Geertz did not think Islam as a religion united Moroccans and Indonesians very much culturally. It was and is, he seems to say, a vague, universalistic umbrella under which thrives a great variety of vigorous localisms. Moreover, in his depiction, the latter are probably more important than the former. Nor is he sanguine about the prospects for a successful Muslim modernism that could hope to achieve greater cultural unity within the Muslim ecumene. In short, Geertz's book appears to answer an unspoken question, "Is there such a thing as universal Islamic style of leadership?" and to answer it in the negative. A concern with understanding or even deconstructing Muslim societies through comparing two such societies might be called "internal comparison."

The other primary manner in which scholars have employed comparison to study Middle Eastern and Islamic societies concerns social structure. The pioneering general works in this area included Barrington Moore's *Social Origins of Dictatorship and Democracy* and Eric Wolf's *Peasant Wars of the Twentieth Century.*[9] These authors premised that political forms, such as democracy or military dictatorship, had historical roots in broad class alliances. They expressed their conclusions in almost mathematical form, for example, alliance of bourgeoisie with medium peasants against aristocracy equals liberal democracy. Moore considered Mughal India and its successor-states but did not treat the Middle East, and Wolf looked only at the North African country of Algeria among Middle Eastern states. Theda Skocpol, whose book *States and Social Revolutions* treated the French, Russian, and Chinese revolutions through a structural comparison, also subsequently wrote about the Iranian Revolution of 1978–79. She suggested that it differed from the other social revolutions she studied because it came in reaction to a rentier state, one where petroleum income led to the state's political and economic isolation from its own people. She also reversed herself in her essay on Iran, accepting the independent causal role of ideology, in the form of Shi'ite Islam.

Recently, specialists in the study of the Middle East, notably Lisa Anderson and Haim Gerber, have attempted to reconsider Middle Eastern history with premises drawn from the Moore school of social-structural analysis. Anderson stressed the importance of nineteenth-century forms of state (bureaucratic or tribal) for the development of modern Middle Eastern states. She suggested that Tunisia's formidable state apparatus had roots in the bureaucracy of the nineteenth-century Ottoman beyli-cate, whereas Libya's Muslim Trotskyism grew up against the background of a tribal society unsubdued by Ottoman or colonial bureaucracy. Gerber argued that the Middle East, unlike China, experienced relatively few peasant revolts because it lacked a permanent class of large landowners. The prevalence of peasant small-holding and the impermanence of mil-itary feudal overlords worked against the emergence of major peasant revolts against landlords. By the mid-twentieth century, of course, a class of large landowners had grown up in places like Iraq and Syria, but military coups in the 1950s forestalled potential peasant unrest by imple-menting some form of land reform.[10] Note that the structuralists most often favor external comparisons among major regions of the world— thus the importance of the contrast with China for Gerber or the dis-similarity of the Iranian revolution to the other social revolutions she had studied for Skocpol. Still, the structuralists can employ other tactics. Anderson builds a structural comparison-and-contrast on an internal comparison of two Middle Eastern polities, Tunisia and Libya.

These two approaches to comparative studies, the symbolic and the social-structural, differ in the weight they give ideal factors. Clearly, symbolic anthropologists are interested in ideas and culture, and, what-ever they think of its long-term prospects, they tend to give at least the local version of Islam much attention in their studies of contemporary Muslim societies. For Geertz, religious ethnicity is primordial, a given with which one is born. One can escape into the more artificial and self-conscious identity of a modern political party, of course, but one's religious ethnicity is more a heritage than a constructed artifact in this view. The agrarian structuralists in the mold of Barrington Moore, on the other hand, appear not to think ideal culture matters very much. They believe, rather, that the development of long-term political alliances between a set of social classes as defined by their material bases explains the political culture that develops in a country, without much reference to the authority of symbols rooted in primordial identities.

Both these approaches, the structural and the symbolic, are present in this book, though often in a nuanced manner that challenges the absolute distinction between the two. I have deliberately begun the book by juxtaposing the work of two authors who focus, in turn, on material culture and then on ideals and norms. The first chapter treats factors such as geography, climate, and technology in the shaping of Muslim societies. The impact of the Middle East's aridity on its economic development, for instance, is a crucial and often overlooked issue. Could Egypt, without coal or wood and lacking in foreign colonies for most of its modern history, have hoped to industrialize in the way that coal and wood–rich England did? Aridity also created large tracts of marginal land unsuited to agriculture but exploitable by pastoral nomads raising sheep. About one-third of Iraq's population in the first half of the nineteenth century consisted of pastoral nomads, and the proportion was higher in Iran. Pastoralists, in turn, are highly resistant to taxation and cannot easily be dominated by the central state. The emergence of strong, centralized states in early modern Europe was not paralleled in the Middle East to nearly the same degree, and I would suggest that pastoralism and tribalism were so widespread in some parts of the Middle East as to retard state formation of the sort that occurred in Europe. I bring up such points to underscore how significant geography and technology are for a comparative understanding of the economic and political development of Europe and the Middle East. The second chapter examines the contradictions in two Muslim societies between an ethos (with Islamic and tribal roots) of the equality of all the Muslim tribesmen and a social reality that admits of hierarchy and inequality, whether of power or wealth. This issue possesses an importance far beyond the tribal communities of the Muslim world. Most contemporary fundamentalist Muslim movements have the same sort of commitment to an egalitarian ethos as do Pukhtuns and Berber clansmen. The former president of Iran, Bani-Sadr, argued that the very conception of Islamic monotheism implied social equality among Muslims. Authors writing in this vein aver that the unity and undifferentiated nature of God implies the unity and egalitarian status of human beings, His deputies on earth. In fact, of course, wealth, power, and status have always been distributed unevenly in the Middle East, and urbanization and capitalism have led to even greater stratification of wealth in modern Muslim societies. How to deal with the contradiction between ideal and reality? This issue, like that of the impact of technology, has pervasive implications for our understanding of Muslim societies and for their self-understanding. The issue has implications for understanding non-Muslim societies where the same tension exists between an ethos of individual equality and a social structure based on differentiation and domination.

Unlike the Barrington Moore school, Nikki Keddie pays attention, not only to social classes and class alliances, but also to geography and material culture. Some have argued that the cultural isolation of Muslims from Western Europe helps explain their failure to adopt many technical innovations from the latter and their later backwardness compared to the North Atlantic states.[11] Keddie poses the question of why Muslims, possessors of the leading civilization along with China before 1200 C.E., were thereafter overtaken by Western Europe economically and technologically. She seeks the answer primarily in the geographical, material, and class conditions of the Muslim Middle East, rather than simply in a cultural attitude of standoffishness. She points out that the Marxist conception of the mode of production requires attention to both the means of production and the relations of production, but that most analysts coming out of this tradition have preferred to focus on class formation and struggle, rather than on material culture. She notes that "a historian who does not feel intimidated by Sigmund Freud, Michel Foucault, or Louis Althusser . . . will often black out at the simplest discussion of textile looms." She underscores the importance of the new archeology for the development of history from below; of the study of agricultural technique and innovation for medieval social history; and of manufacturing and transportation techniques for understanding the marginal advantage that Western Europe developed over its rival. She suggests that research into the roles of extremely large and important premodern populations, such as women and nomads, who until recently have been little studied by historians as social groups, can be enhanced by attention to material culture. Clearly, she says, the urban history of the Muslim world could also profit from use of archaeological techniques. Keddie does not by any means discount the importance of symbol or ideal culture to the formation of Muslim civilization, but she does believe greater weight should be given in social explanation to material culture, which she thinks has been insufficiently explored. We may take her chapter as sounding many keynotes for the later ones that focus on structural or material explanations for features of Muslim societies, especially those in part 3.

A different sort of approach, still comparative, may be found in Charles Lindholm's "Quandaries of Command in Egalitarian Societies." Like Geertz, Lindholm is primarily interested in values and symbols. Pastoral nomadic tribes, as Keddie pointed out, have been hugely important in the history of the Muslim world. Arab tribes were among the earlier and more important converts to Islam, and were crucial in carrying out the seventh- and eighth-century conquests that established the first Muslim empire. As the North African inventor of sociology Ibn

Khaldun pointed out, pastoral nomads came to play a key and recurrent role in state formation in the Middle East. As late as 1800, perhaps half the inhabitants of Iran were tribal nomads. The ethos of the tribes, most of them raisers of livestock, thus remained important in the historical memory of Muslim civilization, although most Muslims, and certainly most Muslim writers and preachers, were sedentary. Nowadays, of course, pastoral nomads constitute only 1 or 2 percent of Muslims, though the number of persons in tribes is greater, since many nomads retained their tribal kinship organization when they settled in villages as peasants during the twentieth century. Lindholm addresses the contradiction in Muslim societies between an egalitarian ideology, wherein all believers are equal before God, and the highly unequal class societies in which Muslims have lived and still live. He does not attempt to discuss Muslim culture in general, but focuses on the tribal peoples of Swat, in northern Pakistan, and the Berbers of Morocco. He sees a good fit between Islam, a religion with egalitarian values, and the "ordered anarchy" of tribal societies. Lindholm sees the ruler among the Pukhtuns to be the first among equals, not in wealth or actual power, but in status. Such a ruler typically lacks any profound Weberian legitimacy, but is simply a capable man able to take power, and tribesmen are loyal to him only as long as he proves successful in that role. Authority also could be had in such a system by saintly personages who were not perceived as part of the secular, competitive, egalitarian Pukhtun or Berber society. Yet when such figures did become rulers, over the period of their dynasty they were pulled toward an identification with the secular, egalitarian society of the tribespeople. When saints, they had the awe of their followers, but not necessarily, Lindholm argues, their respect. He not only compares the Pukhtuns with the Berbers as Muslim tribespeople, but both to U.S. citizens, another people with a hierarchical society but a highly egalitarian ethos, and he argues that they often deal with this contradiction in similar ways.

Keddie and Lindholm give us very different paradigms for pursuing a comparative study of Muslim societies. Ironically, Keddie's more universalistic concern with technology leads her to stress features that were unique to the Muslim Middle East, whereas Lindholm's symbolic approach, so amenable to a concentration on local knowledge, leads him, instead, to compare his tribespeople with de Tocqueville's Americans. Both techniques can lead away from a hostile alterity in the depiction of Muslim societies. Keddie's emphasis on geography and material culture suggests reasons for difference and otherness that are not essentialist or intrinsic to Islam or Muslims. Lindholm appeals to an image of his tribespeople, not as an inscrutable Other, but as possessors of an ethos that resembles in some ways the contradictory individualism and conformity, anarchy and order, of Americans themselves. Islam with a capital *I* is not center stage in either chapter, though it is a major presence in both. Even the ethos identified by Lindholm, although bound up with Islamic values, clearly has a great deal to do with the specific social organization of tribal peoples.

The second part of the book, dealing with the Muslim intelligentsia in the modern period, has perhaps most in common with Lindholm's approach. Like him, the authors concern themselves with Weberian questions of values and beliefs, a defensible approach in dealing with intellectuals to whom such questions meant a great deal. These chapters all explore the cultural tensions and conflicts among the Muslim literate classes that resulted from their experience of Western colonialism and secular ideas. Yet they do so in a challenging and revisionist manner. The authors draw attention to several stock assertions about Muslim clerics and intellectuals in colonial Orientalism and in modernization theory. Western observers, from colonial officials to the usually sympathetic University of Chicago historian Marshall Hodgson, have taken a dim view of the emphasis on memorization of texts in Muslim seminary education. They have seen it as deadening to the analytical faculties, a substitution of rote learning and passive transmission of tradition for analytical understanding. Few predicted a bright future for this sort of pedagogy, or for the seminaries in general, convinced that they would be left behind in the wash of a speeding modernization and secularization. Many observers have also taken the marginalization of Muslim institutions (such as judgeships) under colonial rule as a natural outcome of imperial subjection. They have assumed that colonial officials inevitably deprive indigenous peoples of a voice in government and create frustrations that eventually explode into bitter movements for liberation. If the literature has tended to see the Muslim clerics as increasingly shunted aside by modernity, it has depicted modern, Western-educated Muslims as a vanguard of secularization. Agnostic novelist, literary critic, and educator Taha Husayn of Egypt or Marxist, Buddhist, Existentialist novelist Sadiq Hidayat of Iran (d. 1951) were seen as emblematic of the new class emerging in the Middle East during the twentieth century. Yet the modernization theorists' prediction of an elective affinity between the intellectuals of the new middle class and secularism failed often and decisively. Muslim seminaries now help produce the political elite of Iran and are newly involved in staffing the judiciary of Pakistan, since the addition of Islamic-law benches to the federal and provincial courts there. Although their functions have changed, they have hardly disappeared. Many intellectuals in Muslim societies are secularists, of course, whether socialists on the Left or, for example, Kemalists on the Right. Yet some very important lay thinkers have advocated a religious solution to society's ills, despite their secular education. Those who thought religion and religious institutions were doomed soon to die out have not found much comfort in developments in the late-twentieth-century Middle East.

Dale Eickelman begins his essay on Moroccan seminary education by suggesting that higher schooling, in complex societies, transmits deeply valued patterns of language and thought, rather as religion functions in simpler societies. He argues that Muslim seminary or madrasa education stands at the intersection of oral and written cognitive styles, given its emphasis on memorization. On the other hand, he is not willing to concede the often-voiced Western complaint that such mnemonic learning does not teach "understanding"; rather, his question is what sort of understanding it teaches. He deals with the period from 1912, when the French and Spanish colonized the country, through the 1930s, when French education decisively shunted aside the madrasa, or seminary, system. He argues that the seminarians came from the notable class and constituted the country's "secondary elite," those who allow the rulers to rule. Eickelman cannily discusses memorization, learning circles, and the formal emphasis on the pure transmission of tradition, pointing out that the way the teacher stressed certain words could endow them with contemporary significance. The process was one, he concludes, not of the passive handing down of rote learning, but of the active appropriation of cultural capital with a shrewd appreciation of its presentist implications. Eickelman's discovery of the importance of peer learning, something that was evident in his interviews, is of great importance for our understanding of how madrasa training worked, since the biographical dictionaries produced by Muslim learned men de-emphasized peer interaction in favor of a concentration on intellectual lineages leading through senior professors. Also important is his stress on the madrasa experience as a means of building a social network of contacts and influence in the wider society for the prospective merchants, politicians, and others who passed through it.

Eickelman traces the decline of the Muslim seminaries in Morocco to French interference in them as well as to an increasing conviction among urban families that a French education was the passport to a successful future. The seminary students from the late 1930s increasingly came from poor, rural backgrounds, a decisive social shift. In this revised version of his classic essay, he suggests that the rise of modern, mass education constituted a further disjuncture with the older seminary and Qur'an-school forms of pedagogy. He also candidly confesses that the 1978–79 Islamic revolution in Iran has put a different light on the fate of madrasa education, which now functions in that country to produce the political elite. The persistence of the madrasa, and the new uses to which it is now being put, however, only underline the importance of this chapter. Eickelman's essay employs comparison subtly, as when he points out that mnemonic technique characterized European education during some eras, or when he cites Bourdieu's comparison of the formalism of a Sorbonne training with that of the Bororo. He also suggests that the Moroccans prized a very long period of memorization (15 years) more than did, say, the Tunisians, and (implicitly) that the fate of seminary education may have been different in Muslim countries not colonized by Europeans.

Allan Christelow shows that indigenous institutions such as Muslim judgeships had different meanings in the French colonies of Algeria and Senegal. In both places, even anticlerical, Republican France allowed the judgeships to function, as a nod to local law and custom. In Algeria, he argues, land was the most important form of wealth, and the Muslim judge was thus a powerful and controversial figure, since he adjudicated personal status cases that often had implications for the disposition of landed wealth. Conflicts emerged between French mayors and local qadis, between the Algerian Muslim community and the immigrant communities of French *colons* (colonists) or of Mzab merchants from the interior oases. In the tribal areas, the French refused to recognize qadis, preferring to appoint French magistrates who made their decisions based on Kabyle customary law. Since the Kabyles or tribes believed themselves Muslims, the Algerians perceived this French privileging of customary law among the tribespeople as a means of dividing and ruling, or perhaps as a step toward their de-Islamization. The colonial state and the local Muslim urban notables finally struck a bargain in which the French grudgingly retained the qadis in urban areas, at least, and the Muslims gave up claims to wider political rights. That generation of urban Muslim notables felt the qadis were enough to protect their property rights, family mores, and religious beliefs, their main concerns in the late nineteenth century. This bargain came back to haunt the Algerian Muslims, as they found themselves locked out of participatory politics and left only with the qadis, now minor French officials, as spokesmen for the community. Christelow suggests that as the Algerian Muslims came to perceive the bargain as a bad one, they began moving toward involvement in a bloody conflict with France in the 1950s and early 1960s. Was this invidious colonial policy, declining role for the old-style Muslim intelligentsia, and increasing anger and frustration among the disenfranchised indigenous Muslims, Christelow asks, a structural feature? Did the European colonization of Muslims simply tend to work that way?

Christelow offers, in answer, a counterexample, that of Senegal. In that West African country, where trade was more important to the urban elite than land, the qadi had little economic importance, since commercial cases went to the French courts. He functioned as a mediator between the Muslims of Dakar and the French administration, and local Muslims resisted later French attempts to abolish the post. The Muslims of Dakar also could vote, making the Muslim judge an alternate means of articulating grievances rather than the sole voice of the community. Christelow sees a symbol for the relatively good relations that obtained throughout the twentieth century between France and Senegal in the willingness of the colonial authorities officially to sanction both the Muslim vote and the Muslim court. In the end, he stresses the contingency of such colonial arrangements. The spaces between colonial authority and Muslim subjection formed arenas for contention, for the articulation of intercommunity relationships. In Senegal, unlike Algeria, the French authorities allowed both electoral politics and Muslim courts to institutionalize such contention, reworking it into renewed political bargains. In Algeria, the bargain was struck once and the French there never saw it as subject to renegotiation, producing a political logjam that eventually broke with thunderous force.

Charles D. Smith examines a different sort of Muslim thinker, Muhammad Husayn Haykal (1888–1956), contributing to the continuing debate over the role of intellectuals in modernization. Unlike the figures discussed by Eickelman and Christelow, Haykal was a modern intellectual and lacked seminary training, though he went on to write a biography of the Prophet Muhammad. From a village notable background, he became a large landholder and leader in the conservative

Liberal Constitutionalist Party. Modernization theory might lead us to guess that Haykal, an elite, European-educated lawyer living in the first half of the twentieth century, would become an advocate of secular values, and Smith shows how that expectation proved only half correct. Haykal did, in fact, adopt a positivist, nationalist view of the world early in life, but his fear of the masses drove him in a different direction after the early 1930s. He became an advocate of what he called "Islamic socialism," which was an elaboration of the village paternalism with which he grew up. He saw Islam instrumentally, as, potentially, a means of restraining unreasonable demands by the masses for redistribution of wealth and social equality. Within an Islamic community, he became convinced, bonds of belief could eliminate class conflict and replace it with class harmony and organic community such that those with large property would engage in philanthropy, while those of limited means would be satisfied with their lot. He thought the blind passion of the masses, like that of women, could only be controlled by an appeal to the Islamic heritage of normative values.

In this revision, Smith compares Haykal to Ali Shari'ati, an Iranian intellectual from a clerical family, active in the 1960s and 1970s. Shari'ati studied philology in Paris and took an interest in French sociology and philosophy, in Fanon and Sartre. Unlike Haykal, he was a true believer and a social revolutionary, but like him he advocated a leading role in the contemporary Islamic community for the modern intellectual. These two twentieth-century Muslim intellectuals had very different orientations, the one secular and the other sincerely religious, the one a conservative politician, the other a fervent revolutionary. Yet both advocated Islam as a means of creating or maintaining an organic Muslim community in the face of the alienation and division characteristic of modern society, and both promoted the new class of modern intellectuals as the natural leaders of this community. Modernization theorists would not have predicted this embrace of religion by modern intellectuals. The manner in which these themes have a universal import beyond the Middle East was underlined by the aftermath of the revolutions of 1989 in Eastern Europe. The marginality and alienation of the modern intellectual, often caught between local culture and more universal or cosmopolitan ideas, drive many to bridge this gap by an appeal to nativist themes, exalting provincial ethnicity or ancestral religion.

We take away from part 2 an appreciation of the ironies of the colonial situation for literate Muslim culture. The supposedly hidebound pedagogy of the madrasas had left many spaces for individual understanding, for nuance and shrewd allusions to contemporary conditions. As the French reformed this institution into insignificance, they brought with them a "modern" educational system that advertised itself as aiming at the inculcation of understanding, yet was the carrier of hidebound colonial values. In both instances, Eickelman observes, the literate classes saw schooling not only as a means to understanding, but also as a venue for the formation of social networks that might later be useful to their mercantile or political careers. Christelow shows that the colonial relationship to indigenous institutions such as the Muslim qadi was contingent upon the meaning and implications of these institutions in each setting. The French tolerance of various forms of Muslim representation in Dakar contrasted with the colonial demotion of the Muslim judgeship in Algeria. The difference derived, in part, from the variable importance of landed wealth in the two countries and the presence in Algeria of a huge population of French *colons*. Smith suggests that theories of the role of intellectuals in modernization have in common a tendency to place intellectuals in the vanguard of power and leadership; not unsurprisingly, these theories have been developed by intellectuals. His examples challenge the theoretical premise that modernization necessarily entails secularization. He says that we ought to be wary when intellectuals describe society as a community in danger of falling apart and present their class as its most promising saviors, whether they do so as Western social scientists or as Middle Eastern publicists.

Part 3 of the book brings the state back in as an explanatory variable in its own right, and so evokes a major concern of recent social theorists.[12] These essays give more weight to structure than to symbol, though they remain vitally concerned with the ways in which symbol and structure interact. Much theorizing about the state has depicted it as an arena for the struggle of social classes. Theda Skocpol and others in the past decade have been influential in arguing for a different conception, of the state as an actor in its own right. This approach has been criticized for reifying "the state," as if it were not an abstract noun referring to a congeries of individual human beings and institutions. Nevertheless, the point that state elites often have interests of their own that are not always congruent with those of the bourgeoisie or of other social classes seems unexceptionable. The Middle East in the early modern period and into the twentieth century was largely characterized by weak states. The Qajar shah in Iran lacked a strong, standing army, and could stay in power only by playing one group of tribespeople, or one official or city quarter, off against another. Since World War II, however, the leverage of state elites over the rest of society in most Muslim countries has increased a great deal. Decolonization left a vacuum of power that local governmental elites eagerly sought to fill, and it allowed them to reappropriate key sources such as petroleum revenues and the mass media. Since most Middle Eastern states rejected democratic forms, the strengthening of state elites raised profound questions of their legitimacy. The new incursion of state power into spheres of society formerly considered private, such as ownership of the means of production, religious observance, and the status of women, has created explosive conflicts. Oddly enough, most discussions of such issues in Muslim societies have not put much weight on the actions of state elites as an explanatory variable. The authors in this part seek to fill this gap.

Ellis Goldberg brings together several problems in understanding Islamic activists in modern Egypt by bracketing them with the Calvinists of Reformation Europe. He points out that Islamic radicalism in Egypt, of the sort that led to the assassination of President Anwar El-Sadat, has often been blamed on relative deprivation and wants to explore the validity of this explanation, keeping Calvin's Geneva in mind all the while. Goldberg's essay is an excellent example of the manner in which comparison can help break down absolute distinctions of the sort that underpin typical constrasts between Self and Other. Deniz Kandiyoti, writing about the place of women in modern Muslim societies, notes that theorists of this issue have either blamed Islam for inculcating patriarchal values or attempted to reinterpret Islam as emancipatory of women in essence, despite the religion's subversion by patriarchy in history. She complains that those engaged in this debate have tended to agree in privileging Islam as an explantory idea and in concentrating on culture and ideology to the exclusion of social and state structures. Her riposte involves an ambitious survey of the women's issue in Muslim societies from Egypt to Bangladesh, taking into account state structures and policies. Shahrough Akhavi also objects to the 1980s rash of articles and books that overstressed the revolutionary characteristics of Islam, "as though 'Islam' is a monolithic actor in international history." Akhavi, while not wishing to play down the importance of Shi'ite ideology in the Islamic Republic of Iran, draws attention to the importance of corporatism and the rentier state in understanding the development of modern Iran under both the Pahlavi dynasty and the Islamic Republic.

Goldberg begins by presenting the Calvinists of the Reformation period as especially concerned, not only with individual salvation, but also with the community maintenance of values, which required that they reject a separation of church and state. In short, he sees the independence of the state from Calvinist control as a problem for Calvinists living in France and England. He then turns to religious ideas of the Muslim Brotherhood, as formulated by Hasan al-Banna and Sayyid Qutb, showing their concern with what they saw as the un-Islamic governments, or Pharaohs, of their day. Goldberg then turns to explanations for the rise of Islamic radicalism in Egypt. Especially in the 1970s and 1980s, Egyptians suffered high inflation, urban crowding, and low productivity, and theorists have seen this stagnant economy as the breeding ground for the Islamic fundamentalists. With his comparison to Calvin's Geneva in mind, he challenges this explanation, suggesting instead that the Muslim Brotherhood and other groups were reacting to a strengthened state. He finds that an increasingly strong state able to invade areas of society previously more autonomous constituted one motive behind the Islamic radicals' disaffection. This finding has the advantage of explaining the fundamentalists' strength even in times of increased prosperity and among a constituency that was "middle class in origins and prospects."

In her study of women in the Muslim world, Deniz Kandiyoti also insists on the centrality of the state to any analysis of this issue. Many writers have suggested that women are repressed, by current Western standards, in Muslim societies, and that Islam is peculiarly and tenaciously patriarchal. Kandiyoti believes that Muslim women face about the same patriarchal limitations as do Afro-Asian women generally, whether in Hindu India or Buddhist Thailand. She goes on to show that an actor other than cultural norms helps decide the status of women, and that is the state. She shows that state policy often has a great deal more to do with the precise status of women than does the Muslim cultural heritage, and that these policies differ enormously from Muslim country to Muslim country.

Kandiyoti shows how the local community, which helps structure family life, could resist the premodern state in the Middle East more successfully than similar communities could do in Europe, given the former region's small urban populations and vast rural hinterlands. Yet in the twentieth century, the state in most Muslim societies has increasingly extended its reach into most of society. With decolonization during and after World War II, Middle Eastern elites attempted to articulate new bases for state building, and often they legislated a new place for women as part of their authoritarian programs of reform. Local communities and sectarian groups that developed grievances toward the state's distribution of resources or that resented increased state interference frequently made the issue of women central to their political symbology. The international state system also had an impact on women, and Kandiyoti draws a fascinating picture of the manner in which Western aid donors fight for women's souls with ultraconservative Muslim oil states in arenas such as Bangladesh, one of the poorer and more overpopulated countries in the world. She finds, ironically, that local women often find spaces within these arenas of contention to form their own movements and projects. In exemplary fashion, her chapter applies internal comparisons, within the Muslim world, to demonstrate how diverse it is and to suggest structural reasons for that diversity that go beyond the invocation of Islam as a monolithic explanation.

Shahrough Akhavi analyzes the Iranian Revolution of 1978–79, and the Islamic Republic that grew out of it, not simply as an expression of Islamic zeal, but as resulting, to a large extent, from a volatile mixture of a rentier state with a corporatist social system. The rentier state is one, like the petroleum-producing members of OPEC, that receives large amounts of external income from a state-owned primary commodity. This income gives the state a great deal more independence of its own citizens than that possessed by ordinary states that must raise revenue by taxes. Akhavi sees the Pahlavi state in Iran from 1955 onward as having based itself on an authoritarian form of governance called "exclusionary corporatism." In this system, the state structures the population into various "corporations," large social groups that depend on the state and are incapable of challenging it. State elites thereby avoid the creation of a civil society full of independent organizations that could lobby the state for their interests, but they achieve this elite autonomy at the price of large-scale coercion.

Akhavi notes that many "corporations," including, for instance, the bazaar guilds, regained some autonomy from the state in the mid-1970s and employed that autonomy to challenge the regime. Prominent among these corporations was the religious institution, which had been among the victims of the Shah's policies. He concludes that Iran's Muslims employed Shi'i symbols to articulate their grievances against the Pahlavi system of exclusionary corporatism, but that lay, popular Shi'ism initially played as large a role as clerical leadership. Once Khomeini's new state established itself, it gradually became even stronger than the old regime. Ironically, the Islamic Republic denied real autonomy and representation to most of the same groups excluded from power by the Shah. Although a bit more inclusionary in its approach, the revolutionary government, ruling without an organized political party, has continued the exclusionary corporatism of the old Pahlavi regime in many ways. The populist regime's commitment to a safety net for the poor has made it difficult for it to promote the private sector vigorously, and the Islamic Republic has remained a rentier state primarily dependent on petroleum revenues.

The final chapters, then, move decisively away from an essentialist view of Islam as a sui generis explanation for social change in Muslim societies. The organization of fundamentalist opposition groups, the bargaining over the place of women in society, and even the establishment of an Islamic Republic, are all revealed to be intertwined with issues in state formation. The intrusion of the modern bureaucratic state into new arenas of social life, according to all three authors, helps explain Muslim radicalism, revolution, and concern about the place of women. On the other hand, these chapters take Muslim doctrines and symbology seriously, and seek not to reduce Islamic activism to an aspect of state making, but to locate the problems they address in the interaction between structure and ideology. They give more weight in the end, it seems to me, to structure.

The intellectual climate in the late twentieth-century United States is increasingly propitious for the growth of comparative studies of regions of the world such as the Middle East. First, disciplinary boundaries have become more fluid. When historians treated mainly political history within the framework of a single country, comparative studies held little appeal. The growth of social history in the past thirty years to a position of dominance within the discipline has led to a focus on social groups such as women, laborers, slaves, urban dwellers, peasants, and enthusiasts of popular religion. The social position of most of these groups can be effectively investigated through comparison, and historians' appropriation of theory from anthropology and sociology often makes them more open to comparison as a strategy. Historical anthropology and historical sociology have also flourished, with social scientists comparatively exploring a variety of historical phenomena, from revolutions to colonialism. The historical turn has been followed in the 1980s by a linguistic one, as philosophers of language such as Wittgenstein,

Foucault, and Derrida have provoked scholars in many fields to reexamine their epistemologies, the ways they thought they knew what they knew. In the 1960s and 1970s it was a breakthrough to recover the history of the working class; in the 1980s it became important to listen to the metaphors and rhetorical devices by which workers constructed their worlds. The concern of the postmodernists, as this tendency has become known, with conceptions of Self and Other also lends itself to comparative concerns. Scholars studying Muslim societies have already been influenced by these wider tendencies and seem likely to make a significant contribution to the emerging debates. Whereas academic specialists in Islam and in Middle Eastern studies often held their posts in a Department of Near Eastern Studies in the past, the contemporary practice is more often for historians of the Middle East to be in history departments, and anthropologists in Departments of Anthropology. This diaspora has had the salutary effect of encouraging Middle East area specialists to engage in a more sustained debate with colleagues in other fields. This institutional arrangement, in turn, seems likely to promote comparative concerns more than did the old concentration of area specialists in a single department.

If the intellectual climate may have shifted in favor of comparative studies, the need for such work has become even more desperate than ever. A series of major crises in relations between Western powers such as the United States and Middle Eastern states such as Iran and Iraq began in the late 1970s, and have recurred in some form ever since. The Middle East contains some of the few states in the Southern Hemisphere that have the financial and demographic means to challenge the Northern Hemisphere's dominance over the world's resources. With the end of the cold war, the North Atlantic states have lost their most powerful image of the Other. The crises centering on states around the petroleum-rich Persian Gulf region have impelled the Western mass media to create another icon of the external enemy as Middle Eastern, building on conventions within Western culture that may well go back to the crusades. Such demonization of another civilization within the mass media and in popular culture, however pernicious, is extremely difficult to combat. Serious students of the Middle Eastern and Muslim worlds can scarcely afford to ignore this new and debased Orientalism. A cheeky insistence on comparison as well as contrast seems a serviceable weapon.

This book sums up the state of the field in comparative studies of Muslim societies. My pragmatic, inductive approach to this introduction has led me to see the essays as divided broadly into symbolic studies akin to the work of Clifford Geertz, and social-structural studies centering especially on the state in the tradition of Moore and Wolf. The chapters are concerned with both difference and similarity. For instance, North Atlantic and Muslim societies are both similar and dissimilar. The profound differences among them are depicted here, not in an essentialist manner, but as growing out of technological arrangements, place in the world system, or bargains struck with the state. The comparative method, employed judiciously as it is here, brings us away from some traps of the Orientalist debate. We are no longer concerned simply with the Western depiction of an Other. Rigid antinomies break down in these chapters. Akhavi discerns a remarkable resemblance between the political economy of the Islamic Republic and that of its predecessor, the "Westernizing" Pahlavi state. Lindholm's Pukhtuns, with their contradictory devotion both to individualism and to tribal solidarity, come to sound strangely like U.S. corporate entrepreneurs. Goldberg's Egyptian fundamentalists have many of the same concerns as the early modern Calvinists that have become, through Weber, central to the founding myth of the modern West. Even my attempt to divide these essays into ones concerned primarily with symbol and ones more concerned with structure does injustice to them, since most address issues in both spheres. This blurring of boundaries, even between Self and Other, is surely an appeal of comparative studies in the postmodern world.

NOTES

1. Nikki Keddie, "Is There a Middle East?" *International Journal of Middle East Studies* 3 (July, 1973): 255–71.

2. Anwar Abdel Malik, "Orientalism in Crisis," *Diogenes* 44 (Winter, 1963); Abdullah Laroui, *The Crisis of the Arab Intellectual,* trans. D. Cammell (Berkeley and Los Angeles: University of California Press, 1976); Edward W. Said, *Orientalism* (New York: Vintage, 1979).

3. Said, *Orientalism,* 204.

4. Ibid., 323.

5. Michel Foucault, *The Order of Things: An Archaeology of the Human Sciences* (New York: Vintage, 1973), 79.

6. Peter Novick, *That Noble Dream: The "Objectivity Question" and the American Historical Profession* (Cambridge: Cambridge University Press, 1988).

7. Maxime Rodinson, *Europe and the Mystique of Islam,* trans. Roger Veinus (Seattle: University of Washington Near Eastern Publications, 1987).

8. Clifford Geertz, *Islam Observed* (New Haven: Yale University Press, 1968).

9. Barrington Moore, Jr., *Social Origins of Dictatorship and Democracy* (Boston: Beacon Press, 1966); Eric Wolf, *Peasant Wars of the Twentieth Century* (San Francisco: Harper Torchbooks, 1973). For the social-structural approach to comparative studies, see Charles C. Ragin, *The Comparative Method* (Berkeley and Los Angeles: University of California Press, 1987).

10. Theda Skocpol, *States and Social Revolutions* (Cambridge: Cambridge University Press, 1979); Theda Skocpol, "Rentier State and Shi'a Islam in the Iranian Revolution," *Theory and Society* 11 (1982): 265–83; Lisa Anderson, *The State and Social Transformation in Tunisia and Libya, 1830–1980* (Princeton: Princeton University Press, 1986); Haim Gerber, *The Social Origins of the Modern Middle East* (Boulder, Colo.: Lynne Riener, 1987).

11. Andrew C. Hess, *The Forgotten Frontier: A History of the Sixteenth-Century Ibero-African Frontier* (Chicago: University of Chicago Press, 1978).

12. Peter B. Evans, Dietrich Rueschemeyer, and Theda Skocpol, eds., *Bringing the State Back In* (Cambridge: Cambridge University Press, 1985).

Part 1
Structure and Symbol

Material Culture, Technology, and Geography: Toward a Holistic Comparative Study of the Middle East

Nikki R. Keddie

Why Study Material Culture?

The study of material culture and geography is relatively new and under-developed in most fields of history. This underdevelopment is acute for the history of the Middle East since the rise of Islam. Although most serious historians no longer ascribe nearly everything in Middle Eastern history to Islam, and there is a growing awareness of socioeconomic factors, discussions of these factors often overstress trade or center almost exclusively around dependent relations with the West, virtually ignoring specific internal developments in Middle Eastern material culture and ecology that help explain Middle Eastern history. This chapter will draw attention to some important conclusions drawn from works written on these subjects. It will show how the study of material culture can illuminate phases of development and decline in the Middle East and suggest some reasons why the West overtook and passed the Middle East economically. It will indicate methods that might be used to bring our understanding of the Middle East nearer to the level of our knowledge about the West, and will suggest the importance of material culture and technology in East-West interaction. The chapter will concentrate mainly on the premodern period, when the gaps in knowledge are the greatest.

To begin with definitions, *material culture* here encompasses both technology and objects produced or adapted, often using technology, for human use. *Geography* is interpreted broadly to include changes over time in landscape and climate, due both to natural factors and to changes in human use. Although these factors are not always considered to be part of the same spectrum, they do go together in forming material strata present in all societies and affecting, in different degrees, all individuals within a society. Some of these factors have only recently begun to be studied seriously. It is becoming increasingly clear that no general holistic understanding of history is possible without considering them and learning much more about them than we now know.

The important technological component of Marx's key, and still much-cited, concept of *mode of production* is often neglected by those who use this concept. For Marx, a mode of production involves a relationship between the *means of production,* chiefly the technology used in production, and the *relations of production* between classes. Changes in both elements are important. Class relations have largely engaged recent Marxist or Marxist-influenced historians to the virtual exclusion of the study of technological developments or geographical factors that affect the mode of production. Most Marxist-influenced historians and theorists deal overwhelmingly with class struggle, trade, exploitation of the Third World by the West, and dependency, to the neglect of the indigenous material and technological factors operating within the societies they discuss.[1] Although there have been attempts to bring technology into a generally Marxist view of history, more of the important work on material culture and ecology in history has been done by non-Marxists, especially by members of the *Annales* school in France, and by U.S. scholars working individually, such as William McNeill and Lynn White. The prominence of China in the history of technology is mainly owing to the monumental work of Joseph Needham, working with excellent associates. Although Needham is often classed as a Marxist, it would be equally plausible, surveying his view of history as expressed in his first volume, to characterize him as a non-Marxist.[2]

For the Middle East, too, studies of material culture and ecology have been done mainly by non-Marxists, and more has been done by non-historians than by historians—notably by anthropologists, archeologists, geographers, and art historians. Such scholars often command techniques and training that most historians do not, but historians have been too willing to be intimidated by the technical knowledge they imagine is required for studies of material culture and geography. Good historians have been able to do excellent studies in these fields without great technical expertise.[3] The understanding of archeological techniques and methods does require training, but the historian does not need a training sufficient to lead an archeological expedition—only to understand methods used by professional archeologists to place and date their finds and decide where they fit into a general pattern of cultural development.

This is not to deny that it would be highly useful for many historians to acquire training in archeology, anthropology, geography, or the history of technology, architecture, and restoration. Similarly, people in those fields could often use more training in history and languages. This kind of cross-fertilization could bring both groups closer to the ideal of understanding history as a totality than is now the case.

Historians of the Middle East have not gone as far as they should into other disciplines. As with many non–Middle East historians, their interdisciplinary efforts are generally limited to fields seen as closely allied with history and that, like history, rely heavily on the written word. These include sociology, political science, economic history, simple economics and demography, written anthropology, written literature, and even philosophy and psychology. The gap between what C. P. Snow calls the "two cultures"—the scientific culture and the literary one—exists even for simple technology and material culture, however. A historian who does not feel intimidated by Sigmund Freud, Michel Foucault, or Louis Althusser, however little he or she may really understand them, will often black out at the simplest discussion of textile looms, and will know far more about alienation than about how warp threads are controlled on a simple loom or why plowing is necessary to long-term cultivation. This means that most historians have no way to judge the significance of the artifacts described by archeologists, anthropologists, and art historians, and are not equipped to consider questions such as: What was the historical and economic significance of the development and spread of underground water canals (qanats) in Iran and elsewhere? Were Middle Eastern textile inventions generally directed toward producing elaborate textiles, while medieval and modern European inventions emphasized productivity, and, if so, what is the significance of this difference? How did Middle Eastern climate and terrain influence the spread of nomadism there, and did such factors as increasing salinization of the soil and deforestation encourage a decline in settled agriculture and a rise in nomadism? Indeed, stressing such questions often leads to charges that one is a "geographical determinist" or a "technological determinist," whereas many historians can, and do, ignore such questions without being charged with distortion.

Historians should learn to handle unwritten sources whose deciphering requires methodologies different from those for written ones. Archeologists have long since learned to make potsherds, walls, burial sites, and other remains speak, but their methods are rarely understood, much less emulated, by historians. Even without digging, one may view the many medieval Muslim towns and monuments that have remained uncovered, and the work of art historians, architects and city planners, and geographers is available to help historians develop a methodology for understanding the structure and function of what they see. Anthropologists who discuss technology (found more in France than in the United States) also provide ways to understand the functions of different technologies in different cultures. Probably, however, historians will have to develop further their own methodologies and even their own excavations (assuming archeological training) if they are to answer their own historical questions, as their questions and methods are usually different from those of other disciplines.

As to the recent interest in "making the silent masses speak," the study of material culture is one of the best means for arriving at that goal. Whereas written documents, the stock-in-trade of historians, tell us most about the literate, wealthier classes, this is not true of material remains. Many buildings, even great monuments such as mosques, were used by rich and poor alike. Excavated dwellings can tell us about the lives of all classes and of women, and the "new archeology" provides an approach that emphasizes the lives and dwellings of ordinary people. Artifacts, tools, and irrigation networks can similarly tell us much about the lives of ordinary people, including, in many cases, the lives of women, who did much of the weaving and many other tasks in the cities and countryside. The roles of peasants and nomads in history are impossible to understand without further such studies.

Studying material culture does not mean avoiding written documents, many of which tell about material culture. One must realize, however, that, as Oleg Grabar has shown, a material object or monument may contradict a written document, and that this often means that the document is idealized or in error.[4] An extensive study of material culture thus helps to control or correct our written accounts.

Perhaps the main contribution that material culture and geography can make to historians of the Middle East is to indicate the interplay of material and socioeconomic factors in creating the economy and society of the cultures they study, and hence give us a more accurate understanding of the rise, development, and sometimes decline of those cultures. An excellent example of this use of material culture and geography is Andrew M. Watson's book, *Agricultural Innovation in the Early Islamic World*. Watson discusses the spread of numerous crops, mainly from tropical areas further east, throughout the Muslim world in the early Middle Ages, and the technological and organizational transformation of agriculture that allowed far more fruitful, varied, labor-intensive, and irrigated production than before. Watson ties this in with social changes, such as widespread de facto free ownership of land, diffused among different classes; the growth of trade, cities, transportation, and possibilities for agricultural specialization; and free communication within the Muslim world and beyond. Similarly, the decline in agricultural production that began in about the eleventh century is tied to overcrowding of the land, soil exhaustion arising from certain agricultural practices, a decline in free, small ownership, the growth of landholding systems that were more class divided and less flexible than before, and the invasion, occupation, and rule by nomadic tribes and other military conquerors.[5] Although not all of Watson's conclusions are universally accepted, his is, without doubt, a seminal work.

Watson's book and some of the other studies I will discuss contribute to our understanding of the different courses of development taken by the Middle East and the West, with the Muslim Middle East being more technically and economically developed in the early Middle Ages, while the originally "backward" West overtook it thereafter. Many items of material culture of various origins found their way to the West via the Middle East, but, as Watson and others have shown, diffusion can occur effectively and lead to something new only if a socioeconomic system is ready to exploit, and develop further, the item diffused.

This chapter will suggest what has been achieved and what remains to be achieved in the study of material culture and geography; it will also suggest ways in which such study could be tied to a general socioeconomic and holistic study of the Middle East, thereby helping to explain the different rhythms of historical change and development in the Middle East and the West.

Examples of What Can be Learned from Studies of Material Culture

In reviewing significant contributions to the knowledge of the Middle East made by studies of material culture, I will give a few examples of how these studies have added to our understanding of Middle Eastern history, suggesting areas where further study can make significant contributions. Islamic archeology, Middle Eastern technology, and other areas of Middle Eastern material culture have just begun to be explored. Even these bare beginnings, however, suggest the crucial importance of this research and the need to develop it further. The areas discussed will include both subject matter areas (like technology) and methodological ones (like archeology), both of which can add to our knowledge of the socioeconomic history of the Middle East and provide a firmer basis for comparisons with other societies.

Technology and the Production of Goods

The standard accounts of technology and production are much sketchier for the Muslim Middle East than for either the Far East or Europe, and this has been a weak area in knowledge of Middle Eastern history. Pre-Islamic Middle Eastern irrigation techniques such as animal-powered wheels for raising and distributing water and the underground qanat, a device of Iranian origin that conducts water to the surface at a desired point, are known to have become much more widespread during the Islamic period; however, despite numerous technical studies, neither the causes nor the agricultural and economic effects of this diffusion and of other changes in irrigation technology have been well studied.[6] Contrary trends toward the decline in use of irrigation channels and in the production and population dependent on them are only vaguely known, and Robert McC. Adams's documentation, partly through aerial archeology, of such a decline in one area from the Islamic period, remains a unique, large-scale study.[7] Although older views that declines in irrigation and agriculture were overwhelmingly due to catastrophic events like the Mongol conquest are no longer widely held, they have not been replaced by detailed studies of why, where, and when irrigation works did develop and decline. Such techniques as aerial archeology, which in Europe has revealed Roman and medieval field patterns and can be used to show old irrigation networks, have scarcely been used in the Orient except by Adams. Given the aridity of the Middle East and its dependence on irrigated agriculture, we could learn much more about the extent and density of settlement in different periods by studying old irrigation networks, as suggested by Adams's work and articles by a few of his followers. The dependence of the Middle East on fragile irrigation meant its agriculture could suffer long-term damage from the increase of warfare and nomadic raiding after the tenth century.

Still in the area of agricultural production, Andrew Watson, in two important articles and the book discussed previously, has argued that the early centuries of Islam saw what might be called an "agricultural revolution" in the Muslim world in which the wide dissemination of new crops and techniques greatly increased agricultural quantity and variety.[8] Watson traces the history of a number of these innovations that, partly because of the early Pax Islamica and easy communication throughout the Islamic cultural area, could be diffused much more rapidly than they were in earlier periods. Contacts with India and the Far East brought in additional crops and techniques. The complex cultivation of the new crops was tied to an expanding economy, widespread landownership, and population growth. With changed circumstances, including the rise of nomadic and other military conqueror-rulers, there was a decrease in agricultural production, which may be seen as part of a general economic decline in the late medieval Muslim world. Although some scholars have found Watson too enthusiastic about agricultural progress in the first centuries of Islam, his general view seems far more convincing than that of E. Ashtor and others who, relying on literary sources for a few areas or attributing Islamic developments to pre-Islamic times, think that the Muslim conquest was, from the first, harmful to agriculture.[9] For a more complete picture of agricultural trends, it will be necessary for scholars to supplement literary evidence, as Watson does, with more use of archeology and ecological and chemical evidence than heretofore, and many more areas must be subjected to both literary and nonliterary scrutiny. Given the paucity of past studies, however, those of both Adams and Watson are major achievements. Both are significant in that they use new methods to explore past agricultural developments and declines, elements of crucial importance to the total history of the Middle East.

One aspect of the study of material culture that, for now, must be partially inferential is nonetheless so important as to demand consideration. This concerns the nomadic and other military conquests in the Middle East and North Africa from the eleventh century on, which were followed by military rule and a kind of quasi feudalism, with land grants being conditional on military or other service. To what degree were these developments rooted in material conditions? One kind of material cause for these events could have been an increased military superiority of nomadic and slave military forces over other forces, due either to technical or organizational improvements. So far no evidence of any dramatic change has been found, but, as there has been little serious research, this negative conclusion may not be decisive. William McNeill suggests that the movement of Iranian landlords from countryside to cities made them less prepared to fight steppe nomads. Another material cause could be an internal crisis in the settled agrarian system of the Middle East that made it easier for nomads to conquer, and also easy for them to remain nomads after conquest instead of settling, as many earlier Arab nomads had done. Watson suggests agricultural weaknesses before conquest.[10] Any such hypothesis must consider the interaction of social and material factors: social elements in the past have received some attention, however inadequate, but material ones hardly any. It seems that the influence of long-term factors of material decline may have combined with factors of socioeconomic decline. Among long-term trends was deforestation, which the Middle East could afford much less than heavily forested Europe and which had been going on since ancient times. The fact that large parts of the Middle East had known settled agriculture and dense populations earlier than other parts of the world eventually put the Middle East at a disadvantage, as man-made damage had operated over a longer period. The nomads, who became widespread in the Middle East from the eleventh century on, did make appropriate use of lands that were, or were becoming, unsuited for settled agriculture; but nomadic raids and overgrazing by nomad herds, particularly goats that uprooted plants, also contributed to deforestation and agricultural decline (although there is disagreement about how important this was).

Another factor influencing the decline of agriculture may have contributed as well to the spread of nomadism and to decreases in production and population: salinization of the soil, a frequent result of large-scale irrigation works, makes soils less productive or completely unproductive, and it is difficult, and often impossible, to reverse. There may also have been a drying of the climate down through the eleventh century and again in the thirteenth century—periods that in Europe were dry and warm. This would have hurt Middle Eastern agriculture and encouraged nomadism.[11] A combination of literary sources, aerial archeology, techniques for the study of past climate and vegetation, and cooperation by various kinds of scientists may be needed to establish even a rough chronology and geography for the trends mentioned above, but if we do not take such trends into account, our view of Middle Eastern history is likely to be mistaken. (In Iran in the 1970s, for example, overuse of tractors and deep wells resulted in a lowered water table and a reduction in grazing areas and in meat production. It raised the possibility of flooding as lowering the water table and plowing the topsoil into rivers caused the level of the land to sink and that of the rivers to rise.) While older technologies could not be as quickly disastrous as modern ones, over the centuries the overuse of wood, overgrazing, salinization, and waterlogging, among other processes, resulted in the decline of settled agricultural production. Watson believes the new agriculture was fragile and overextended and easily put into a cycle of decline by nomadic incursions.[12] Certainly the growing presence and power of nomads in the Middle East from the eleventh century acted to curtail agricultural production.

The question, why did capitalism develop indigenously only in Western Europe, is of great interest, and attempted answers generally say little about material factors, especially in agriculture. While not enough is known to make a good comparison between the medieval Middle East and Western Europe regarding this question, some differences may be noted. In general, the geography and climate of the Middle East were suited to encouraging the earliest development of settled agriculture but not to making use of the more advanced agricultural technologies developed in medieval Europe, which permitted increased agricultural productivity and a wider range of settlement. Specifically, the great unforested river valleys of Egypt and Iraq encouraged river-based irrigation and an easy production of crops, while more difficult areas could also produce, if somewhat less fruitfully, with modified versions of ancient technology. But the centuries-long processes of deforestation and soil salinization eventually brought a decline in production, and there were no major technological developments dramatically to reverse this trend. Western, and particularly northern, Europe was originally harder to cultivate because of its heavy soils and forests. But once technologies to clear trees and stones appeared—especially metal tools for clearing and the heavy, wheeled plow and improved horse harnesses appropriate to cultivation of heavy soils and thick topsoil—productivity could grow more in Europe than in the Middle East, where light soils rendered inventions like the heavy plow worse than useless. While the history of agrarian technology in the Islamic Middle East has scarcely been studied, what has been done generally supports the view of technological conservatism since ancient times, with few radical improvements. Even scholars who stress development, such as Watson, Henri Goblot, and Thomas

Glick, point more to the dispersion of old technologies than to inventions in Islamic times.[13] Improvements may have been very difficult, given the nature of local agriculture, or social factors may have discouraged them; most likely, a combination of these factors was at work. The same centuries that witnessed an overall decline in production and population over most of the Middle East saw a general rise in these elements in the West. The medieval West entered a cycle of technological development in agriculture and industry at about the same time as innovation was waning in the Middle East. These inverse technological patterns were part of a more pervasive developmental difference between the West and the Middle East, with innovation and development strongest in the Middle East from the seventh to the early eleventh centuries, and thereafter in the West. Even periods that go against these trends, such as the early Ottoman empire or the fourteenth century in the West, do not reverse the general trends.

Manufacturing techniques are scarcely better studied than agricultural ones, and some of what exists was written by art historians as an adjunct to studies on textiles, pottery, and the like, and is difficult to comprehend for those who do not understand the techniques and terminology of the arts. Nonetheless, there is much to be gained from reading such works, as they often contain important material not to be found elsewhere.[14] While comparatively few medieval looms, potters' wheels, and so on have come down to the present, we do have some literary sources and pictorial representations of medieval machines, and it is sometimes also possible to infer how an object was made from its appearance and structure. In addition, many old methods are still in use, as recorded in such works as Wulff's *Traditional Crafts of Persia* or Digard's published thesis on techniques of the Bakhtiari tribe.[15] Medieval techniques can often be understood from a careful study of existing ones. Although little study has been done, it appears that whereas medieval Middle Eastern productive techniques were often quite sophisticated, much of this sophistication was directed toward producing more complex or artistic products rather than toward increasing production. This is another contrast with medieval Western Europe, where the textiles and other articles produced were generally less sophisticated than in the Middle East but where, from the twelfth century on, tools and machines to maximize productivity were developed. The Middle East was increasingly known for the complex production of luxury goods, while the West mechanized the production of goods for a relatively wide domestic and early foreign market. These differences probably reflected different social structures in the late medieval period, as the Middle East moved away from its earlier, more egalitarian phase, and manufacturing was increasingly controlled by rulers and the wealthy.

To take one example of this difference, in the textile field, the Middle East, with Iran in the lead, developed and perfected a wide range of techniques that culminated in such sophisticated and complex products as the cut and voided Safavid velvets, which combined an intricacy of pattern and color with the difficulties of weaving velvet, cutting it at different levels, and often the incorporation of gold and silver threads (beaten metal wound around cloth thread). This and other elaborately patterned fabrics require a draw loom, which some scholars believe was a Middle Eastern, pre-Islamic invention, although most opt for China, which also knew it early. Complex woven patterns depend on the raising and lowering of different warp threads, changing with every weft. This cannot be done by one weaver, so a drawboy, usually working from a platform above the loom, pulls strings attached to loops that raise the appropriate warp threads. (Through a series of modifications, this loom was later developed into the Jacquard loom, which used punch cards, the ancestor of computer tape—material for an article, "From Draw Loom to Computer.") The draw loom, like the later Jacquard loom, was a complicated invention that permitted a vast expansion in the *types* of patterned cloths that could be produced. It did not, however, speed up the production of cloth, and its operation is much slower than that of simpler looms producing simpler cloths. This example seems fairly typical—most medieval artisans of the Middle East sought to perfect their products rather than to increase their production. It seems likely that socioeconomic causes may be found to account for this, especially in later medieval times when distinctions between elite and mass grew, and the vital bourgeoisie ceased to expand in most regions. Also, much Middle Eastern production was luxury production controlled by courts rather than being oriented to expanding markets.

In contrast, recent authors have stressed the technological innovations of the European Middle Ages, and one claims that, when it comes to directly productive inventions, medieval Europe surpassed even China, which is generally said to have been ahead of the West in inventions, without considering particular types, until about 1450.[16] (To be sure, the term *productive invention,* meaning one that helped produce goods, is not always precise: clocks and infrastructural inventions produce nothing, but do facilitate production. Europe was early ahead in these, also.) The importance for historians of productive inventions goes beyond simple comparison. The economic relations of Europe and the Middle East were apparently affected by European inventions and their productivity much earlier than has generally been thought. Ashtor notes that Middle Eastern technology stagnated or declined in several fields at the same time as European productive technology was advancing. Textiles were especially important. Late medieval Europe developed the modern spinning wheel. Earlier spindle wheels and treadle looms diffused from China, but were made more efficient in the West. Fulling mills were among the many devices run by waterwheels in the medieval West, and, like the others, they produced more goods with fewer workers than could be done with human power alone. Thus, while the Western weavers could not yet compete with the quality of the fabric from Middle Eastern draw looms, they could and did produce larger amounts of simpler cloths at a lower price.

Using eyewitness accounts and trade documents, Ashtor demonstrates that the direction of the East-West textile trade began to change as early as the thirteenth century. Whereas Egypt and the Levant had been net exporters of textiles, they became net importers of European goods that were based on more efficient production methods. Ashtor shows that similar developments took place in sugar manufacture and in paper-making, where Europeans first learned from the Middle East but then moved ahead of the East technologically. Ashtor's account suggests that the Middle East did not quickly adopt European advances; if this is so, some explanation should be sought.[17] Possibly a combination of military and bureaucratic elites who had little interest in production, a long-term decline or stagnation in the Muslim bourgeoisie, and a growth in the gap between the elegantly attired rich and the poor who bought little meant there was insufficient interest in increasing the production of simple goods. Most significant for those who study comparative development, however, is that European primacy in manufactured exports, and its role in undermining manufactures elsewhere, began far earlier than is usually thought. Whereas, in the case of agriculture, geographical conditions may have been important in Europe's growing leadership and inventiveness, geography seems less central in manufacturing, where the difference is probably more to be accounted for by social, economic, and possibly ideological factors. To be sure, Middle Eastern agricultural decline and the rise of nomadism also reduced the market and increased the difficulty of transporting goods, and the dearth of wood and water greatly limited nonhuman sources of power. Conversely, European agricultural development encouraged market development.

The change in textile import-export patterns has also been shown in relation to the sixteenth- to eighteenth-century Ottoman silk production in studies by O. L. Barkan and by Halil Inalcik.[18] In this period, the Ottoman empire, which had been a major center of silk manufacturing, was hit by the competition of cheaper or more fashionable European, especially Italian, silk, and Ottoman production of silk cloth declined in quality while exports of raw silk and silk thread rose. Scholars note that the Italians began to mechanize silk manufacturing as early as the thirteenth century, replacing human power with animal and especially water power. It was no accident that silk was the first fabric to employ mechanized production, as silk reeling and throwing are simpler processes than cotton or wool spinning. The original silk thread is a continuous fiber wound in a cocoon and over a kilometer long. All other natural fabric fibers are very short and must be spun together to form a thread; in the case of silk, however, the process involves removing the fiber from the cocoon (usually by opening the cocoon in boiling water), unwinding it onto a reel, and doubling or quadrupling the thin fiber by twisting ("throwing") fibers together. Because the fiber is very long and even, the obstacles to mechanization are fewer than with other fabrics. On the other hand, as silk was an expensive textile lacking a mass market, its mechanization could not change a national or international economy as cotton mechanization did later. Mechanization of silk production in early modern Italy was widespread, as demonstrated by Carlo Poni. This mechanization, as noted earlier, undermined the Ottoman silk industry, although Inalcik disagrees with those who see a major decline before the eighteenth century.[19] The emphasis on the novel import-export or "dependency" effect of the industrial revolution should not be discarded entirely because of the examples cited here, since it is clear that Western exports after the industrial revolution were quantitatively much greater than before, and these manufactures undermined the crafts much more rapidly than before. We do, however, need other studies along the lines of Ashtor's and Barkan's to cover additional countries, periods, and branches of manufacturing, in order to construct a more satisfactory picture of the history of Middle Eastern manufacturing and trade. The sophisticated preindustrial technology of the Middle East, which supplied local needs and exports and contributed to later inventions, also requires further study. Differences in manufacturing trends between East and West early affected economic relations between them.

A related point is that medieval Europeans were generally more inclined than were Middle Easterners to use nonhuman sources of power. In the case of water mills, which were far more abundant in Europe than in the Middle East and were progressively used for new purposes, the cause lies partly in the relative scarcity of water in the Middle East and its abundance in Europe. But Europeans traveling in the Middle East after 1100 noted that available water resources were not exploited for mills as much as they should have been, although water-powered mills were known. Windmills with horizontal sails are considered an Afghan-Persian invention (with possible Tibetan cultic origins), but they apparently did not spread, and their European invention seems independent. Wind power aside, Europe's endowment with sources of power such as wood and water was much superior to that of the Middle East. This superiority, however, does not completely account for the tendency of medieval Europeans to use mechanical equipment and nonhuman energy sources.[20]

Like other economic sectors that manifested an inverse pace of development in the Middle East and in Europe, mills and manufacturing were affected by Middle Eastern declines in population and in free peasants and bourgeoisie, with the resultant drop in local markets. A rise of nomadic and military ruling classes more distant from the population and their productive activities than in early Islamic times was an additional problem in the Middle East, as was a growth in the gap between elites and direct producers. Past scholars have often stressed factors such as a rigidification within Islam, but recent scholars generally see this as more a result than a cause of socioeconomic decline. Such factors as the increasing control of education and its curriculum by orthodox religious leaders, from about the eleventh century on, probably did have an effect on economic life and inventiveness, but were not the primary causes of the changes under discussion.

Allied to the technology of production were developments in commercial transport, which also have been little studied. Richard Bulliet's important book, *The Camel and the Wheel,* shows that, even before Islam, wheeled transport had largely disappeared from the Middle East, primarily because camel transport was more economical once an efficient method of camel harnessing had been developed.[21] The absence of wheeled transport in Middle Eastern cities influenced the contours of those cities. Once wheeled carts were no longer in use, it became unnecessary to have even a few broad, straight roads crisscrossing towns, and it became practical to reduce the effects of sun, heat, and wind by building narrow, irregular streets with shade coming from houses on several sides. These were also useful to slow down invading or marauding bands. Bulliet gives figures to prove that camels were significantly cheaper than carts for transport, but he or someone else should perhaps also try to calculate the economics of donkey transport as, for short-distance and in-town transport, donkeys are more important than camels in most parts of the Middle East. The domestication of the camel and its proper harnessing clearly increased the area of dry territory that could be crossed by caravans. Although the other chief mode of transport for international trade, the ship, has been the subject of some specialized work, there has been no general book on the scale of Bulliet's, and this is another area that needs further research. Needed, too, is more detailed study of the nature and economics of the caravan trade, which carried goods across huge distances within and outside the Middle East for centuries.[22]

Comparisons over time between the Middle East and Europe are even more rare for trade and transport technology than for productive technology. There has been some comparative study of ships, but little study of either a monographic or a comparative nature of overland transport. Clearly, further investigation of Middle Eastern transport over the centuries can tell us much more about social history and about the nature of Middle Eastern society as compared to the West.

Many topics, including transport and manufacturing, are covered in S. D. Goitein's magisterial *A Mediterranean Society,* based mainly on documents of the Cairo Geniza.[23] The medieval Middle East is poor in archival and other documents, so that historians must rely heavily on literary sources such as histories, geographies, and biographical dictionaries. Traditional Jewish reluctance to throw away papers with writing on them, based on the idea that these might contain the name of God, resulted in the deposit of such documents in rooms, often attached to synagogues, and from the Cairo storehouse a wealth of such medieval papers remained until modern times. Using these letters, accounts, and records, Goitein reconstructed the socioeconomic life of the Jewish community in Cairo and beyond, and showed that it paralleled closely that of its Muslim neighbors. His first and fourth volumes are very rich on material culture. Volume 1 discusses the different branches of manufacturing—especially textiles— and notes how peripatetic the merchants were. From these details of everyday life and of the domestic economy (of both men and women) there emerges a picture of a pious yet cosmopolitan and production- and trade-oriented society, with a full rendering of the lives and thoughts of men and women who might otherwise remain unknown.

Although it may be impossible ever to describe medieval Muslim society in similar detail, further investigations of trade, technology, and manufacturing, which could continue the use of European and Middle Eastern archives and employ more archeology, could give a far more complete picture than is now available of the socioeconomic life of the later Middle Ages. Such studies could also add to our knowledge of groups about whom traditional sources and studies tell us little, such as workers and women, both of whom are well covered by Goitein's account of the details of everyday lives, occupations, and wages.

Women and Nomads

A pioneering study of the Muslim community, exploiting both literary and material sources, including archeological finds, is Ahmad Abd ar-Raziq's work concerning women in Mamluk society.[24] Despite the ideological bias of this book, which, like several other Middle Eastern works, tries to blame decline on foreigners—here, the Ottomans—and exaggerates the high position of Egyptian women before the Ottoman conquest, it does manage to bring together a variety of sources, including the *Thousand and One Nights* (put into final shape in Mamluk times), in order to reconstruct the life of several categories of women. (The widespread view that Turks spread the practice of veiling in Egypt and elsewhere in the Arab world is mainly based on the fact that Turks veiled more than Arabs simply because a great proportion of Turks in Arab countries were upper class, and *upper-class* Muslims veiled more than did other classes until recently.)

The example of Goitein and Abd ar-Raziq indicates the potential utility of material culture in studying the poorly documented lives of the popular classes and of women, who together make up a great majority of society. The study of relationships between men and women shows the interweaving of the social and the material, and yet the material evidence of the nature of such relationships has rarely been well studied, nor has evidence from existing societies been applied to the past in any systematic way. It is known from both Near Eastern and other societies that the adoption of settled agriculture, and especially plowing, tended to make men the dominant figures in agriculture—they controlled the plow and irrigation. The development of metal smelting and hammering and of the pottery wheel created a similar dominance, as men came to be in charge of these instruments (as they did of more advanced looms). Nonwheel pottery, the simpler looms, and many other textile processes remained in the domain of women. The technology controlled by men was both more advanced and more market oriented, while women's production was primarily in home industry and subsistence agriculture. Although women continued to work hard, especially in the rural areas where the great majority of premodern populations lived, there evolved an urban elite ideal that limited women's labor, particularly outside the home. In many Mediterranean and Far Eastern cultural areas, women came to be kept in or near the home, and access to premenopausal women was restricted to family men, mainly in order to guarantee a bride's virginity and a wife's fidelity, and hence the paternity of the husband. In Muslim and Indian societies, veiling reinforced these restrictions.[25]

Studies of Middle Eastern women's historic relationships to technology and of their dress and domicile, including veiling and seclusion, are few and far between, although there is existing evidence in the form of architecture, art, legal records, and other texts. An unexpectedly active role for some women in owning and using means of production has been revealed for Mamluk Egypt and for the Ottoman empire before the period of its economic decline.[26] Urban architecture (and even rural houses and nomadic tents) displays evidence of degrees of female seclusion. Blank walls onto the streets and heavily latticed shutters are partially designed to prevent strangers from seeing women of the household, and, in turn, allowed the women some comfort in moving about much of the house and courtyard unveiled. Tribal and rural carpets and many textiles and handmade pots are living records of women's creativity and cultural concepts.

Changes in veiling practices over time and space have scarcely been studied, but the Qur'an does not mention, much less enjoin, veiling, which was picked up and extended by the Arab Muslims from the Byzantines and Iranians, after which Muslim scholars read it back into the Qur'an. Both paintings and texts show that there has been great variation in veiling and, indeed, in women's dress. Renaissance Italian travelers to Iran write of the shockingly revealing dress of Iranian women(!)—and there is evidence that the coming of Westerners to such countries as

Egypt and Algeria caused, for a time, an increase in veiling as a protective reaction. Except among the recent, modernized elite, veiling has been widely regarded as a sign of status, showing that the husband and wife can afford for her not to work; thus, veiling and seclusion have spread in this century, as has been widely attested, especially in rural areas and in the provinces, and with more recent Islamic movements, again in cities.[27]

One example of the complexities of veiling comes from North Yemen, where, as in Egypt but with as little foundation, it is widely said that the Ottoman Turks introduced veiling. The standard biography of the first ninth-century Zaidi Shi'i imam to rule in Yemen, written by a contemporary, notes that the imam used to walk through the marketplace and, among other things, enforce veiling upon unveiled women, its strictness variable according to the women's ages.[28] Here, it is clear that veiling had begun centuries before the Ottomans, that it was not universal, and also that a strict religious ruler thought it important to enforce it. An item that probably *was* actually connected to the Turks is the particular form of all-covering black outfit called the *sharshaf,* which the imams' family traditionally restricted to themselves. After the 1962 revolution, however, it spread like wildfire, so that it became ironically known to some as "the flag of the republic." This is not the only case where the spread of veiling, or a style of veiling, had a "democratic" significance; the Westernized elite often abandons veiling just as it spreads among the popular classes.

Clearly, the implications of women's dress, and also of men's, both of which have attracted much twentieth-century legislation and concern in the Middle East, deserve more attention than they have received among historians. So, too, do the material and other aspects of women's productive and domestic activities.

The links between various forms of urban architecture and relationships between the sexes may be studied from old buildings or archeological remains, and yet little of this has been done. The fact of female seclusion and the nature of female domestic activity may often be inferred from building style, preferably in combination with other evidence. In addition, the kinds and amounts of objects owned and used by women may be judged from both remains and from legal documents, particularly those dealing with inheritance or division of property. There are scattered references from the time of Muhammad's first wife, the trader Khadija,

down through the Ottoman empire that show women as occasional owners of material technology, and more written evidence of this surely exists.

A more speculative question, for which material culture can provide
only part of the answer, concerns whether the relatively unsecluded position of women in medieval and early modern northern Europe, as compared to the Middle East and Asia, had any connection with northern
Europe's economic primacy from about 1500 onward. Although no
answer to this question can be attempted in a chapter on material culture,
questions about the degree to which the status of women affects the
development of society as a whole deserve to be asked more than they
are, and evidence from material culture can contribute importantly to
telling us what that status was, in reality, in different social classes and
groups.

Although women, workers, and peasants are all relatively neglected
in historical works about the Middle East, as in most of the relevant
written sources, the group whose productive activities and material life
in the past is perhaps the most neglected is the nomads. Nomads appear
in Islamic histories mainly as conquerors or raiders, but rarely are we
given an internal picture of the nomadic life and economy or of their
interrelationships with settled peoples; for the Middle East, there is still
no book that has the theoretical sophistication of Owen Lattimore's *Inner
Asian Frontiers of China.* Anthropologists and historians of tribes have
begun to study the material culture and economy of nomads, but, with
a few exceptions, one feels that even most historians of tribes (a new
subspecies) are hindered by a lack of adequate understanding of technology, geography, ecology, and economics. On the other hand, we do
now have quite sophisticated and convincing discussions, mainly by
anthropologists, of such matters as the differences between the Central
Asian nomads, who have two-humped camels and live in colder climates,
and the southern nomads, who have one-humped camels, as well as of
goat- and sheep-herding nomads. In addition, the picture of nomadic
economies has become much more complex than formerly, with authors
not only stressing the various mixes of animals and migration patterns
characteristic of different groups and regions, but also noting that nearly
all nomads depend, to some degree, on agricultural activities carried out
by themselves or others or both. Some authors find these mixed patterns
so involved and varied that they wish to abandon such terms as *pure
nomad, seminomad,* and *transhumant,* but these terms have at least a

classificatory convenience, and it has not yet been proven that nomads do not tend to cluster in groups that can be so classified, however complex some borderline groups may be. Regarding historians, what may be noted is how little they have applied advances in anthropological theory and knowledge to the task of illuminating the past. Indeed, one can name historians of the Middle East who virtually ignore nomads, although an intelligent grasp of the course of that area's history since its beginnings, and especially since the eleventh century, requires a knowledge of the role of nomads, not only as conquerors and raiders, but also as soldiers, producers, frequent rulers, and persons who engaged in trade and other relationships with non-nomads, providing meat products and serving as camel drivers. Whereas, as in the case of women, peasants, and workers, scholars are inclined to believe that sources on nomads are limited, the few historians who have set out to study nomads have found sources and have been able to put together convincing and important works, even though they might have benefited from more study of technology.[29]

Less speculative than the comparative impact of the status of Middle Eastern and European women is the impact on the Middle East of the large-scale nomadic presence since about 1050 C.E. Although nomadism is a good adaptation to arid lands, nomadic raiding and migration can harm agriculture and trade. The downward agricultural trend since the eleventh century had many causes, but the spread of nomadism was important among them. Nomadic tribal organization encouraged local autonomy and discouraged the economic and political unity of sizeable territories. The spread of nomadism was due not only to nomadic conquests but also to the growing aridity that made agriculture less feasible in many areas.

Military Technology and Organization

Although military technology in the Middle East is far from having been adequately studied, it has been examined more satisfactorily than has productive technology. I will here name a very few works as examples of what has been done in this field.

The reasons for the rapid military success of Muhammad and of the early Muslim armies, which lie not only in Muslim strength but in Byzantine and Sasanian weakness, have long been an area of scholarly concern, and some discussion of them can be found in the important postwar books on Muhammad and early Islam.[30] Bulliet's *The Camel and the Wheel* emphasizes the development of the North Arabian camel saddle as a technological advance that enabled camels to be used successfully in war, thus giving the Arab armies advantages over their opponents. More generally, it may be said that mobile pastoral and nomadic groups accustomed to riding and raiding make superior fighters and that this helps account both for the Muslim conquests and for later nomadic conquests in the Muslim world. Ideological and socioeconomic factors were, of course, involved in the Muslim conquest, but this is not the place to discuss them.

Advances in military technology in medieval Islamic times have not been adequately studied, although some have been discussed by Claude Cahen.[31] Cahen believes that advances were slow and without dramatic changes. It remains to be studied, however, whether there were technological reasons beyond the general military superiority of nomads that help explain their increasing military success in the Muslim Middle East after the eleventh century.

More adequately studied have been firearms, although more work could be done. The Ottomans adopted firearms from the West quickly and efficiently, but this was not true of most other Middle Eastern states. In a classic monograph, David Ayalon has demonstrated the unwillingness of Egypt's Mamluk ruling elite to have anything to do with firearms, even after it became clear that they were losing battles because of this.[32] They finally let blacks and low-class soldiers use them, but the elite Mamluks disdained these weapons. This was a major factor in the Ottoman conquest of the Mamluk state by Sultan Selim I in the early sixteenth century (and presumably also in other Ottoman victories in the Middle East at this time). Very possibly not only Ottoman conquests everywhere but also the efficiency of early Ottoman rule owed something to the mastery of firearms and of the military organization appropriate to them. The Mamluk counterexample is a reminder that a study of technological advance and diffusion must often also be a study of nonadvance and resistance to diffusion. Often, as in the Mamluk case, such resistance has both a class and an ideological basis—certain arms, like certain occupations, have been and often still are disdained as suitable only to the lowest classes.

A second stage in the history of firearms and their social consequences has recently been opened to study. Inalcik and a few others have shown that, whereas early firearms (cannons and inefficient handguns) strengthened the central state, which was the only body capable of manufacturing and effectively utilizing such weapons, the development of better hand-guns often strengthened local dissidents against the state, since these guns were available to all. Inalcik ties this to the development of major local revolts in Anatolia in the seventeenth century. Similarly, one scholar has suggested that the rise of local tribal power in eighteenth-century Iran was partly due to the spread of handguns among the tribes at that time.[33]

A recent study of ships and naval warfare is similarly suggestive of the interaction of military technology and society.[34] In both naval and land warfare, Europe surpassed the Ottomans by the late seventeenth century, and it is striking that the military technical gap developed much later than other technical gaps, probably because the Ottomans felt more sharply the need to borrow Western technology in the military sphere than elsewhere. Also, restructuring the military is easier than trying to reshape the whole economy.

Cities and Buildings

Muslim cities, especially large cities, have been a popular topic of schol-arship, and they have attracted far more scholarly work than any other unit of settlement. Several American and English symposia on Middle Eastern cities have been published, as well as numerous books and articles devoted wholly or in part to individual cities.[35] Little of this work, however, has stressed the physical or material aspects of cities. Some of the recent work on Islamic cities has provided salutary correction of the myths of a previous generation. The idea that there was a distinctively Islamic city pattern and type has been attacked; on the one hand, Muslim cities in different parts of the world have been found to resemble sur-rounding cities more than any ideal Muslim pattern, while on the other hand, many Muslim Middle Eastern patterns, such as narrow, winding streets and alleys and the concentration of crafts in particular quarters, have been traced to pre-Islamic times and found to have material, rather than ideological, causes. Another effectively refuted view, that of Louis Massignon, is that there were trade guilds in the early medieval Middle East, and that these guilds had ties to the Ismaili sect. Cahen, S. M. Stern, Goitein, and Gabriel Baer have shown that Massignon had no real evidence for these views, that guilds were a late phenomenon in the Muslim world, and that they did not have the autonomous status they often had in the West.[36] Aside from this, most of the recent urban literature has stressed the sociopolitical organization of the Middle Eastern city and, except for some work by nonhistorians—archeologists, geographers, art historians, and architects—has been light on its physical and material aspects.

In the field of archeology and art history, outstanding work on cities and structures, especially their development and social significance, has been done by Oleg Grabar, who stresses the sociohistorical context and meaning of the art objects he discusses. He has studied the evolution of the mosque and other structures not only as art and architecture, but also from the viewpoint of function and ideology, and he sees that these different aspects of design should not be separated.[37] A similar social approach to monuments and cities is taken in articles and monographs by a number of younger scholars, including Renata Holod, Lisa Golombek, Ülkü Bates, and Priscilla Soucek. Grabar may be said to build on the urban studies of Jean Sauvaget and on the pioneering sociohistorical study of buildings carried out in Italian by Ugo Monneret de Villard. Monneret de Villard's most important book, far less technical than its title implies, deserves an English translation, even though some of its main ideas have, with acknowledgment, been presented in English by Grabar.[38] In addition to their work on monuments, cities, and bazaars, social historians of art have discussed the social and economic significance of the development of certain crafts, such as pottery and textiles, an area where much remains to be done.

Urban studies have been notably interdisciplinary. In addition to historians such as Ira Lapidus, André Raymond, and Jacob Lassner, there have been geographers such as Paul English, Michael Bonine, and several French and German scholars; sociologists such as Janet Abu-Lughod; anthropologists such as John Gulick; archeologists such as David Whitehouse; art historians; and architects such as Eugenio Galdieri who have shed light on urban history and often on its material aspects.[39] English's book on Kirman, Iran, uses a social geographer's insights to show the degree to which Kirman has dominated the economic and social life of its hinterland, thus pointing to a pattern of urban dominance that English takes to be typical of Middle Eastern cities. Bonine has shown the functionality of street patterns that often follow water channels and/or field patterns. Abu-Lughod includes a convincing discussion of the changing patterns of construction and urban life in Cairo in modern times. Whitehouse has headed excavations at the southern Iranian port city of Siraf, and has published his results in successive issues of the

British journal *Iran*. Like many archeological reports, his accounts have been (at least thus far) limited to good descriptions of major finds. It is clear both that Islamic archeologists should be encouraged to put their discoveries into a general historical context and that historians must become sufficiently knowledgeable in archeology to be able to make use of archeological reports as well as of that majority of excavated objects whose significance and exact provenance are never published.

The work of Galdieri and the other architect-restorers and archeologists who worked with the prerevolutionary Iranian government on the study and restoration of Isfahan's major monuments, and have done similar work in Afghanistan and elsewhere, deserves special notice. Italians have been at the forefront of the most recent trends in restoration; they insist both that restorers be trained architects, archeologists, or artists (depending on their specific functions) and that they make use of primary sources and secondary studies in developing an adequate understanding of the particular monument and its history. Galdieri led the work on the site in Isfahan, with special responsibility for the study and restoration of its great Masjid-i Jum'a. Over several seasons, he and his workers unearthed a whole series of reconstructions and additions to the mosque, starting with an early Arab-style mosque, which André Godard had considered destroyed, and going on through major changes in the Buyid, Seljuk, and later periods. Here there is a living history of mosque development unparalleled anywhere in the world, a fundamental source for historians of the structure and function of mosques.[40] Others have done similar work elsewhere in the Middle East.

Architects have also begun to study the structure and function of non-monumental and even humble traditional buildings. Hassan Fathy is among those attempting to stop the expensive and frequently impractical rush to imitate Western styles, showing the functionality of simple, traditional architecture, often of mud-brick construction. In Iran and Iraq, Susan Ross Rauf and Michael Bonine have studied mud-brick houses and passive (nonenergy-using) cooling systems such as ice houses and the wind towers of Yazd. A serious examination of the history and function of ordinary houses, including the homes of peasants and nomadic tents (studied especially by Peter Andrews), can add to our knowledge of the life of this silent majority and, hence, of the social history of the Middle East.[41]

An important addition to the study of the material aspects of a Middle Eastern city is Heinz Gaube and Eugen Wirth's *Der Bazar von Isfahan*.[42]

Wirth has been one of the rare vocal advocates of the increased study of material culture in its broadest sense to achieve a fuller understanding of Middle Eastern civilization. In urban studies as elsewhere, useful comparisons may be made between the Middle East and the West. Older comparisons were based on a view that inaccurately characterized Middle Eastern cities as disorganized; the time has come to compare what are actually the different forms of urban organization found in the Middle East and the West.

How Can We Increase Our Knowledge of Material Culture?

Some suggestions, intended mainly for historians, have been made in the paragraphs above; here they will be augmented and grouped together. Most important is that historians need to appreciate the role of material culture in explaining the life of the past, and particularly the lives of those who left few written records. Historians should also understand that technology is not a hopelessly complicated subject.

In addition, more historians should seek technical training in relevant fields—whether archeology, art history, anthropology, or architecture. In the Middle Eastern case, the most pressing need appears to be for archeologist-historians. It is not enough for historians to rely on existing archeological work. Joint graduate programs in history and archeology should be encouraged. It is sometimes said that the historian is busy enough without taking on another entire discipline, but historians like André Raymond have successfully participated in archeological expeditions, and the archeological training suggested need not reach the point of making one a professional archeologist. Andrew Watson's book indicates what can be done by a historian with archeological knowledge.

A similar interdisciplinary approach is easier to achieve in art history, given the existence of Islamic art historians already oriented toward social history. The average historian rarely or never uses evidence from the crafts (especially not from tools), from buildings, or from iconography (except numismatics), although these objects are available and could add to our knowledge of people's lives. Art historians concerned with social history have developed means for using such things as evidence, and these are rarely difficult to learn.

Anthropologists, too, have developed ways to understand the functioning of technology and society among popular groups and classes, and much of what they find in the present goes back far into the past.

The tents and weaving techniques of nomads, for example, can be shown from old products and pictures to have had a long prior existence. Many historians, including the present writer, have found it useful to spend some time living among groups, such as the nomadic tribes, who resemble the groups they study in the past. An understanding of traditional techniques and material culture is among the benefits gained from such residence and its opportunity to question and observe.

Finally, such aids as books on the history of technology or architecture, visits to technical and ethnographic museums, and appropriate ethnographic films can contribute to the historian's understanding of the functioning of technology and material culture.

Historians have often been put off by technological works that appear either forbiddingly or purely descriptive. Lengthy, usually ethnographic theses that describe the minutiae of local material culture but do not tell how it functions dynamically in society and archeological reports that catalog finds without saying how they affect our view of history are difficult for a historian to use; such works tend to encourage historians to think of the study of material culture as a study of disembodied things that can be cataloged but are difficult to put into the stream of important historical developments. Recent books and articles that concentrate on technology and its interaction with other historical forces show, however, both that it is possible to understand this field and that it is a field of great historic importance. Particularly for the study of the silent classes, of women, of socioeconomic change, and of comparisons between societies the investigation of material culture has revealed much that is new and important and promises much more in the future.

NOTES

This chapter is intended to suggest the importance of work in a field in which the author has done little primary research. The works cited are examples of what can be learned by historians from the study of material culture; the chapter is not a comprehensive bibliographical essay. Some important works, especially in foreign languages, have been omitted.

Oleg Grabar has written to me noting that a number of Soviet scholars use material culture in important ways. Among them are V. V. Barthold, K. A. Inostrantzev, and B. I. Marshak. Grabar's 1978 letter also names Jean Sauvaget as "the first one to see history and 'things' together," and "as much the founder of that attitude as Monneret de Villard." Additions suggested in letters from

Halil Inalcik have been incorporated into the text, as have comments from Michael Bonine, Richard Bulliet, Edmund Burke, William McNeill, Carlo Poni, and Peter von Sivers. Profound thanks for his help and ideas are also due my former assistant, Jean-Luc Krawczyk, who is working on Middle Eastern and European technology, and on tribal history. Ken Mayers checked my notes, and Andrew Newman helped with proofreading. Where this chapter differs from the 1984 article, this version is to be preferred.

1. For example, among the very intelligent works that stress class or trade and underplay technology, see Robert Brenner, "Agrarian Class Structure and Economic Development in Pre-Industrial Europe," *Past and Present* 70 (1976): 30–75; also see the discussion of Brenner's article in subsequent issues of *Past and Present,* now brought together in T. H. Ashton and C. H. E. Philipin, eds., *The Brenner Debate: Agrarian Class Structure and Economic Development in Pre-Industrial Europe* (Cambridge, 1984); Immanuel Wallerstein, *The Modern World-System* (New York, 1974). More coverage of technological, geographic, and climatic factors is given in Georges Duby, *The Early Growth of the European Economy,* trans. Howard B. Clarke (Ithaca, 1974).

2. See Joseph Needham, *Science and Civilization in China* (Cambridge, 1954–).

3. Lack of such technical expertise has been confessed to me by such pioneering authors as Richard W. Bulliet, author of *The Camel and the Wheel* (Cambridge, Mass., 1975); Lynn White, Jr., author of *Medieval Technology and Social Change* (Oxford, 1963) and numerous articles on technology; William McNeill; and Carlo Poni, author of important works on agricultural and silk technology in Italy.

4. Oleg Grabar, "The Architecture of the Middle Eastern City," in *Middle Eastern Cities,* ed. Ira Lapidus (Berkeley, 1969) 26–46.

5. Andrew M. Watson, *Agricultural Innovation in the Early Islamic World* (Cambridge, 1983).

6. The most complete study is that by an engineer, Henri Goblot, *Les qanats: une technique d'acquisition de l'eau* (Paris, 1979). Goblot shows the spread of qanats from Iran, and thinks there were only a few places of independent origin in Europe. He also says that qanats could only have emerged as a by-product of the runoff water from mining. The diffusion of qanats occurred mostly in Islamic times, but Goblot does not, as does Watson, tie this diffusion and the later decline of some qanats to more general agricultural and economic developments. On qanats and irrigation, see also Robert McC. Adams, *Land behind Baghdad: A History of Settlement on the Diyala Plains* (Chicago, 1965); P. Beckett, "Qanats-Persia," *Journal of the Iran Society* 1 (1952): 125–33; C. Cahen, "Le service de l'irrigation en Iraq au debut du XIe siècle," *Bulletin d'études orientales* 13 (1949–51): 117–43; G. S. Colin, "La noria marocaine et les machines hydroliques dans le monde arabe," *Hesperis* 14 (1932): 22–60; Thomas F. Glick,

Irrigation and Society in Medieval Valencia (Cambridge, Mass., 1970); Glick, *Islamic and Christian Spain in the Early Middle Ages* (Princeton, 1979); F. Krenkow, "The Construction of Subterranean Water Supplies during the Abbaside Caliphate," *Glasgow University Oriental Society Transactions* 13 (1947–49): 23–32; A. Smith, "Qanats," *Journal of the Iran Society* 1 (1951): 86–90. See also P. W. English, "The Origin and Spread of Qanats in the Old World," *Proceedings of the American Philosophical Society* 112, no. 3 (1968): 170–81; H. E. Wulff, "The Qanats of Iran," *Scientific American* 218, no. 4 (1968): 94–105. A short analysis of Middle Eastern irrigation is in Arnold Pacey, *Technology in World Civilization* (London, 1990), chap. 1.

7. Adams, *Land behind Baghdad.* A partial critique of Adams's methods and conclusions is in Watson, *Agricultural Innovation,* 206 n. 14.

8. Andrew M. Watson, "A Medieval Green Revolution: New Crops and Farming Techniques in the Early Islamic World," in *The Islamic Middle East, 700–1900: Studies in Social and Economic History,* ed. A. Udovitch (Princeton, 1981); Watson, "The Arab Agricultural Revolution and Its Diffusion, 700–1100," *Journal of Economic History* 34, no. 1 (March 1974): 8–35; and especially, Watson, *Agricultural Innovation.*

9. See the discussions of agriculture in E. Ashtor, *A Social and Economic History of the Near East in the Middle Ages* (London, 1976). Watson, *Agricultural Innovation,* includes critiques of writers who ascribe Islamic advances to pre-Islamic times or overgeneralize from a few cases of decline. Also stressing agricultural productivity is Peter von Sivers, "Riverine Realms: Iraq, Egypt, and Syria during the Classical Islamic Period," *Newsletter of the American Research Center in Egypt,* no. 124 (Winter, 1983): 12–18.

10. William McNeill, *The Rise of the West* (Chicago, 1963), 487 n. 3, citing works by W. Barthold. Also see Watson, *Agricultural Innovation,* pt. 5.

11. The probable importance of medieval climatic change in the extension of nomadism was suggested to me in conversation by William McNeill, who has dealt with the climatic factor in his writings on world history. On the history of European climate (using and describing methods that could also be used in the Middle East), see Emmanuel Le Roy Ladurie, *Times of Feast, Times of Famine: A History of Climate since the Year 1000* (Garden City, N.Y., 1971). The same medieval warm climate trends that helped Europe may have hurt the Middle East. On medieval eras of aridity and high temperatures and their probable special impact on areas that were agriculturally marginal, see T. M. L. Wigley, M. J. Ingram, and G. Farmer, eds., *Climate and History* (Cambridge, 1981). Medieval climate and geographical issues relevant to comparisons with the Middle East are also discussed in Duby, *Early Growth of the European Economy,* especially chap. 7; and E. L. Jones, *The European Miracle: Environments, Economies and Geopolitics in the History of Europe and Asia* (Cambridge, 1981).

12. Watson, *Agricultural Innovation,* pt. 5.

13. See, for example, H. Rabie, "Some Technical Aspects of Agriculture in Medieval Egypt," in Udovitch, ed., *Islamic Middle East.* Books by Glick, Goblot, and Watson are cited in notes 5 and 6.

14. Iran, perhaps because of the sophistication and esthetic appeal of its crafts, has been well served with descriptive books and articles on crafts, and much of what is said about Iranian technique is applicable to other countries. The most comprehensive descriptions of craft processes and products are in Arthur Upham Pope, ed., *A Survey of Persian Art from Prehistoric Times to the Present,* 6 vols. (London, 1938–39); H. Wulff, *The Traditional Crafts of Persia* (Cambridge, Mass., 1966); J. Gluck and S. Gluck, eds., *A Survey of Persian Handicraft* (Tehran, 1977). See also the very important unpublished paper by Dorothy G. Shepherd, "The Textile Industry in Medieval Iran," and N. A. Reath and F. B. Sachs, *Persian Textiles and Their Technique* (New Haven, 1937).

15. Wulff, *Traditional Crafts;* J.-P. Digard, *Techniques et cultures des nomades baxtyari d'Iran* (Paris, 1981).

16. On the high rate of invention in the Middle Ages, see White, *Medieval Technology;* White, "Expansion of Technology 500–1500," in *The Fontana Economic History of Europe: The Middle Ages,* ed. Carlo M. Cipolla (N.p., 1972); Jean Gimpel, *La revolution industrielle du Moyen Age* (English trans., *The Medieval Machine*) (Harmondsworth, 1977); S. Lilley, *Men, Machines, and History* (London, 1965). Although some of White's and Gimpel's generalizations have been criticized, their demonstration of rapid and cumulative technological development in the West during the Middle Ages seems irrefutable. The amazing range of early Chinese invention is shown in Joseph Needham's multivolume *Science and Civilization in China;* see especially vol. 5, pt. 9 by Dieter Kuhn on textile technology.

17. Ashtor, *Social and Economic History;* see especially Ashtor, "Levantine Sugar Industry in the Late Middle Ages—An Example of Technological Decline," in Udovitch, ed., *Islamic Middle East.*

18. Omer Lutfi Barkan, "The Price Revolution of the Sixteenth Century: A Turning Point in the Economic History of the Near East," trans. Justin McCarthy, *International Journal of Middle East Studies* 6, no. 1 (January, 1975): 3–28. See also Halil Inalcik, "Bursa and the Commerce of the Levant," *Journal of the Economic and Social History of the Orient* 32, no. 2 (1960); *Encyclopedia Islamica* (1971), s.v. "Harir" [silk].

19. Carlo Poni, "Archeologie de la fabrique: La diffusion des moulins a soie . . . ," *Annales* 27, no. 6 (1972): 1475–96; Inalcik, "Bursa."

20. Lynn White, Jr., *Medieval Religion and Technology* (Berkeley, 1978), 47–50, discusses windmills. On the importance of medieval Europe's superiority in water and wood, see J. L. Krawczyk, "Environment, Constraints, and Technology: The Middle East and Europe in the Middle Ages," manuscript; F.

Braudel, *Capitalism and Material Life,* trans. M. Kochan (New York, 1973). In an unpublished colloquium (1960), Claude Cahen noted the relative lack of Muslim inventions and said it might be tied to the easy availability of slaves.

21. Bulliet, *Camel and Wheel.*

22. Thanks are due William McNeill for suggesting the importance, and need to study the economics, of the caravan trade.

23. S. D. Goitein, *A Mediterranean Society,* 5 vols. (Berkeley and Los Angeles, 1968–88).

24. Ahmad Abd ar-Raziq, *La femme au temps des Mamlouks en Egypte* (Cairo, 1973).

25. Nikki R. Keddie and Lois Beck, "Introduction," in *Women in the Muslim World,* ed. Lois Beck and Nikki R. Keddie (Cambridge, Mass., 1978); Nikki R. Keddie, "Introduction," in *Women in Middle Eastern History,* ed. Nikki R. Keddie and Beth Baron (New Haven, 1991). See especially the articles by Erika Friedl and Deniz Kandiyoti in *Shifting Boundaries.*

26. Ian Dengler, "Turkish Women in the Ottoman Empire: The Classical Age," in Beck and Keddie, eds., *Women,* and the Introduction and articles on Mamluk Egypt in Keddie and Baron, eds., *Women in Middle Eastern History.*

27. See Beck and Keddie, eds., *Women,* and the various references to women in Nikki R. Keddie, *Roots of Revolution* (New Haven, 1981).

28. This account is translated twice in *San'a: An Arabian Islamic City,* ed. R. B. Sergeant and R. Lewcock (London, 1983), with the better translation that of Martha Mundy (535), saying Imam Hadi used to inspect the streets and "if he saw a woman he ordered her to wear a veil, and if she was past menopause, he ordered her to wear a cloak. He was the first to bring the *burqu'* face-veil to Yemeni women and he ordered them to adopt it."

29. See, particularly, the historical articles on tribes by Gene Garthwaite, James Reid, and John M. Smith in the special issue of *Iranian Studies, State and Society in Iran* (January, 1979), ed. A. Banani. These authors have also done other work on tribal history. The impact of nomads on Middle Eastern history in Islamic times is also very well analyzed in various works by Claude Cahen. See also Lois Beck, *The Qashqa'i Confederacy of Iran* (New Haven, 1986); Gene R. Garthwaite, *Khans and Shahs* (Cambridge, 1983); Pierre Oberling, *The Qashqa'i Nomads of Fars* (The Hague, 1974).

30. See M. Rodinson, *Mahomet* (Paris, 1961) (published in English as *Mohammed,* trans. Anne Carter [London, 1971]); W. M. Watt, *Muhammad at Mecca* (Oxford, 1953); Watt, *Muhammad at Medina* (Oxford, 1956); Claude Cahen, *L'Islam: Des origines au debut de l'Empire Ottoman* (Paris, 1970). Cahen's book is also published in German, Italian, and Spanish translations.

31. Claude Cahen, "Les changements techniques militaires dans le Proche Orient medieval et leur importance historique," in *War, Technology, and Society in the Middle East,* ed. V. Parry and M. Yapp (London, 1975). See also the

discussion of medieval military technology in William McNeill, *The Pursuit of Power* (Chicago, 1982), and the superbly illustrated survey of Muslim military technology and organization in E. Bosworth, "Armies of the Prophet," in *The World of Islam,* ed. Bernard Lewis (London, 1976), 201–24.

32. David Ayalon, *Gunpowder and Firearms in the Mamluk Kingdom,* 2d. ed. (London, 1978).

33. Halil Inalcik, "The Sociopolitical Effects of the Diffusion of Firearms in the Middle East," in Parry and Yapp, eds., *War.* Robert McDaniel, who is studying the Iranian military, told me this conclusion about tribal power.

34. J. F. Guilmartin, Jr., *Gunpowder and Galleys* (Cambridge, 1974). See also *Encyclopedia Islamica* (1960), s.v. "Barud" [gunpowder].

35. See L. Carl Brown, ed., *From Madina to Metropolis* (Princeton, 1973); Lapidus, ed., *Middle Eastern Cities;* A. Hourani and S. M. Stern, eds., *The Islamic City* (Oxford, 1970).

36. The crucial refutations are C. Cahen, "Y a-t-il des corporations professionelles dans le monde musulman classique," and S. M. Stern, "The Construction of the Islamic City," in *Islamic City,* Hourani and Stern, eds., 51–63, 25–50. Recently, some writers, including André Raymond, have spoken and written of "Arab cities" as an entity. This seems to me no improvement over "Muslim cities" because city types no more follow linguistic lines than religious ones, and many eastern Arab cities resemble those in Iran and Turkey more than they do Moroccan or Yemeni cities. On the material basis of derivation of urban street patterns from patterns of water channels and fields, see M. E. Bonine, "The Morphogenesis of Iranian Cities," *Annals of the Association of American Geographers* 69, no. 2 (June, 1979): 208–24.

37. See Oleg Grabar, "Architecture," in *Middle Eastern Cities,* ed. Lapidus; Grabar, *The Formation of Islamic Art* (New Haven, 1973); Grabar, "Islamic Art and Archaeology," in *The Study of the Middle East,* ed. L. Binder (New York, 1976).

38. Ugo Monneret de Villard, *Introduzione allo studio dell'archeologia islamica: Le origini e il periodo omayyade* (Venice, 1966). A recent application of archaeology to history is R. Hodges and D. Whitehouse, *Mohammad, Charlemagne, and the Origins of Europe* (Ithaca, N.Y., 1983).

39. The chief works on urban topics by these authors are: I. Lapidus, *Muslim Cities in the Later Middle Ages* (Cambridge, Mass., 1967); A. Raymond, *Artisans et commercants au Caire au XVIII siècle* (Damascus, 1974); J. Lassner, *The Topography of Baghdad in the Early Middle Ages* (Detroit, 1970); P. English, *City and Village in Iran: Settlement and Economy in the Kirman Basin* (Madison, Wis., 1966); J. Abu-Lughod, *Cairo: 1,001 Years of the City Victorious* (Princeton, 1971); J. Gulick, *Tripoli: A Modern Arab City* (Cambridge, Mass., 1967); and the series reports on work at Siraf by David Whitehouse that appeared in the journal of the British Institute of Persian Studies, *Iran* 6–12 (1968–74). For

Eugenio Galdieri, see note 40 and Renata Holod, ed., *Studies on Isfahan* (Boston, 1974); for article references see the bibliographic survey in Michael F. Bonine, "From Uruk to Casablanca: Perspectives on the Urban Experience of the Middle East," *Journal of Urban History* 3, no. 2 (February, 1977): 141–80. Among the books that I have not cited and are relevant to material culture are: Robert McC. Adams, *The Evolution of Urban Society* (Chicago, 1966); T. E. Downing and M. Gibson, eds., *Irrigation's Impact on Society* (Tucson, Ariz., 1974); Xavier de Planhol, *The World of Islam* (Ithaca, N.Y., 1959); S. D. Goitein, *Studies in Islamic History and Institutions* (Leiden, 1966); G. Baer, *Studies in the Social History of Modern Egypt* (Chicago, 1969); Edward W. Lane, *The Manners and Customs of the Modern Egyptians,* 5th ed. (London, 1871); R. Le Tourneau, *Fès avant le protectorat* (Casablanca, 1949); K. L. Brown, *People of Salé: Tradition and Change in a Moroccan City* (Cambridge, Mass., 1976); Holod, ed., *Studies on Isfahan.* There are numerous studies of individual cities, especially in English, French, and German, mainly by geographers.

40. See E. Galdieri, *Isfahan: Mağid-i Ğum'a* (Rome, 1972–74); G. Zander, *Travaux de restauration des monuments historiques en Iran* (Rome, 1968).

41. See P. A. Andrews, "The Felt Tent in Middle Asia: The Nomadic Tradition and Its Interaction with Princely Tentage" (D. Phil. thesis, University of London, 1980). On mud architecture and passive cooling systems, see Michael E. Bonine, "Aridity and Structure: Adaptation of Indigenous Housing in Central Iran," in *Desert Housing: Balancing Experience and Technology for Dwelling in Hot Arid Zones,* ed. K. N. Clark and P. Baylore (Tucson, 1980); M. N. Bahadori, "Passive Cooling Systems in Iranian Architecture," *Scientific American* 238, no. 2 (1978): 144–54.

42. Heinz Gaube and Eugen Wirth, *Der Bazar von Isfahan* (Wiesbaden, 1978).

Quandaries of Command in Egalitarian Societies: Examples from Swat and Morocco

Charles Lindholm

This chapter is built upon the Weberian hypotheses that belief systems motivate actors, and that there is an elective affinity between moral codes, social roles, and orientations toward action. I begin by outlining some of the taken-for-granted norms, habits, and values—Bourdieu's "habitus," Geertz's "system of meaning," or what old-fashioned anthropologists simply called "ethos"—that provide a pattern for the moral life among the people of Swat District in Northern Pakistan. I then use this model, and its underlying ambiguities, to help explicate some real-life problems in the representation and implementation of authority, making comparisons with tribal Morocco, which has a similar value structure and social system and, therefore, similar quandaries in the conceptualization and enactment of hierarchy.[1] The emphasis is thus not on specifics and exceptions or on historical contingencies, but on discovering the social processes that flow from the logic and contradictions of fundamental premises about reality at work beneath cultural variation.

The Ethos of Egalitarian Individualism

The Swat Pukhtun of Northern Pakistan, among whom I did anthropological fieldwork, exist within a social and ecological world very far removed from the modern West: Swat is a rural world where devout Muslims use bullock-drawn plows to work the land, the inhabitants live in what most Westerners would consider dire poverty, and rivalries and amities are organized by a relatively rigid patrilineal and patriarchal kinship structure that is subdivided into warring factions. Instead of police and courts, feud and self-help remain the main instruments for maintaining order, and the traditional values enshrined in the Swati code of honor—hospitality, refuge, and revenge—continue to motivate people's actions and beliefs.[2]

Yet when I lived in Swat and began to know its people, I was continually impressed by the resemblances between the self-conceptions and essential values of Swatis and U.S. citizens. I found that in Swat, as in the United States, persons are assumed to be essentially independent actors, each separately responsible for his or her own fate and endowed with a God-given potential for free choice and agency. Moreover, in both societies, each separate individual is believed to be motivated by a desire for self-aggrandizement and the maximal accumulation of what economists call "utility functions."

A second similarity between the ethos of the United States and that of Swat is the shared faith that all men (though not women) are equal before God and the law and have an absolute intrinsic value as members of the participatory social group. This affirmation of equal rights exists despite actual differences in power; indeed, at the time of my first fieldwork in 1969, Swat had a king (who was deposed a few months later), and there were marked discrepancies in wealth, power, and influence among ordinary tribesmen—so much so that Talal Asad characterized Swat as a class society dominated by a cohesive and self-interested group of oppressive landlords[3]—much as the United States has been portrayed as dominated by the interests of wealthy capitalists.

The extraordinary thing, however, is that these distinctions of rank are not evident in daily interaction in either society. Instead, it is very difficult to discern superiority and inferiority from overt behavior in both Swat and the United States. Of course, Swati society does have some internal distinctions, particularly in the polite respect offered by juniors to elders. But standardized deference behavior can be overridden by the exigencies of the moment, and, in general, Swati men show no obvious subordination to anyone else; this lack of deference is very typical of many North African and Middle Eastern peoples, but is in marked contrast to Hindu South Asia, or to Muslim culture in adjoining Punjab, where haughtiness and a matching obsequiousness are a deeply ingrained part of daily social interaction; it even differs from Europe, where class and status remain elaborately coded and relatively rigid. In this respect, then, the people of Swat are far more "American" than South Asian or European, since, in the United States, hierarchical discriminations in terms of accent, dress, and so on are the object of considerable ambivalence and even derision, as befits an egalitarian society where the overwhelming majority of persons unhesitatingly define themselves as "middle class" and where social and geographic mobility have blurred economic and regional distinctions.

Like North Americans, the people of Swat are extremely proud of their self-proclaimed equality and independence; they often speak contemptuously of the invidious distinctions made among men by their southern neighbors and heartily concur with the Pukhto writer Ghani Khan's aphorism: "A true democrat, every Pukhtun thinks he is as good as anyone and his father rolled into one."

As is evident from this aphorism, the lack of differentiation and the ideology of egalitarianism among the Pukhtun and their clients should not be taken to indicate an absence of intense competition and rivalry. As Ghani Khan tells us, "The Pukhtun have not succeeded in being a great nation because there is an autocrat in each home who would rather burn his own house than see his brother rule it."[4] The pervasiveness of intense internal rivalry is indicated in Swat by the word for patrilateral cousin (*tarbur*), which also means "enemy."[5]

The seemingly counterintuitive intertwining of equality and hostility found in Swat is not unique; it has, in fact, been classically explored by Alexis de Tocqueville, who argued in *Democracy in America* that the egalitarian ideals and ideologies of personal liberty in the United States coincided with an absence of ascribed social positions and a social world of status anxiety and competitiveness.[6] He reasoned that, within such a mobile social setting, individuals were forced to struggle continually to make their own positions secure; thus, egalitarian individualism fosters, rather than precludes, competition. In the United States this competition is primarily in the marketplace, but in Swat, where the market is undeveloped, competition is a political battle for ephemeral domination over coequals.

Yet, despite differences in the way conflict is waged, every Swati, like every North American, can and does make a claim to be worthy of respect by all other members, with God-given inalienable rights and characteristics. Consequently, in the egalitarian societies of Swat and the United States, all individuals—the poor and the rich, the landless and the landowner—may eat side by side, speak among themselves with an absence of abasement or insolence, and look one another directly in the eye. In sum, beneath distinctions of economy, religion, politics, and culture, the citizens of Swat, like the citizens of the United States, envision themselves to be what Charles MacPherson has called "possessive individuals," that is, free and separate agents, essentially similar to other agents, acting rationally to realize personal self-interest against the competing interests of rivals.[7]

These values are hardly peculiar to Swat and the United States. They exist, in fact, as articles of faith in the great religion of Islam that the Swati follow; a religion marked, more than any other faith, by the "pursuit of the egalitarian ideal and consequent emphasis on the dignity of the individual believer."[8] In Islam, the Prophet makes no claims to be a God; instead he affirms himself to be an ordinary man, one among the Muslim brethren—albeit one who is exemplary and inspired. Furthermore, in the Islamic world, any man who follows the urging of his own heart and mind and accepts the message of Muhammad is equal, in principle, to any other of the faithful.

The doctrine of masculine equality and choice is carried through in the organization of the religion as well as in its ideology. Muslims in the tradition of scriptural Islam proclaim their faith to be lacking an ordained clergy, a church structure, and an ecclesiastical hierarchy. Organized spiritual bureaucracies that do exist have historically been established by states, such as the Ottoman empire, rather than developing to meet purely religious needs. Except in sectarian versions of Islam such as Sufism and Shi'ism, little stands between individual Muslims and their relationship with Allah. Thus, as Patricia Crone writes, in classical Muslim thought "God's community was envisaged as an egalitarian one unencumbered by profane or religious structures of power below the Caliph."[9]

However, the theological rejection of ascribed authority and the confirmation of the individual actor as master of his own fate that is part of Islamic doctrine can be overshadowed by other factors that favor antithetical norms. We can see this, for example, in most of India, where cultural values of caste and the realities of power combine to inculcate patterns of deference and inferiority, even among Muslims.[10] Instead, the abstract values of egalitarianism and individualism have an "elective affinity," Weber would say, to a social formation that lacks set ascribed statuses and is highly mobile and competitive. Such fluidity and uncertainty existed in early America, as Tocqueville showed, but was and remains characteristic, too, of Swat, which only developed an ephemeral central authority in the last century, and where, as I have noted, the main battles for domination continue to be fought between close agnates and coequals.

Of course, as the reader probably recognizes, the fluid and competitive Swati social formation, with its affinity for an ideology of egalitarian individualism, is not unusual in the Islamic world. In fact, it is quite characteristic of the hinterlands of North Africa, the Middle East, and southwestern Asia where we find the multitude of "tribal" societies that anthropologists have called areas of "institutionalized dissidence," "organized acephaly," or "ordered anarchy,"[11] and which indigenously are designated as the "wild" tracts (siba in Morocco, yaghistan in Pakistan) in opposition to the "tame" lands (makhzan or hukumat) where people are taxpayers and citizens of the state.

Typically, in siba or yaghistan, independent-minded social groups are located within sparse or remote ecological settings. Lacking an overarching authority structure, these peoples universally espoused a pugnacious and "heroic" warrior ethic that sanctioned their fierce struggle over scarce resources.[12] Whether nomads or farmers, these groups organized themselves, as in Swat, by reference to an ideology of patrilineal kinship, partible inheritance among coequal brothers, a polity based on self-help, and social relations of structured antagonism between segments crosscut by intense factionalism.[13] As Paul Dresch argues, they regularly evolved a social system in which "formally equal elements are defined by contradistinction, and formal inequality is admissible only in terms of the inclusion of subsets in larger sets."[14]

Though differently articulated and practiced among the vast array of "tribal" peoples across this wide range of territory and culture, these values pervasively militated against the acceptance of institutionalized secular hierarchy and favored, instead, a faith in personal, contested opposition against other actors. Thus, we find any number of ethnographies of Arabia, North Africa, and Iran agreeing that "each kin group, not accepting exclusive control of resources, fundamentally considers itself the equal of others in regard to prestige, honor, state and in rights." Even poverty "indicates only a lack of material goods at the present time, nothing more. Though regrettable, it does not reflect unfavorably on one's character."[15] These statements apply equally well both to Swat and to Moroccan highland tribes.

Nor is the egalitarian individualism of siba and yaghistan confined solely to the margins of the state. Indeed, the elective affinity between tribal values and the Islamic dogma of egalitarianism and individualism carries even into the heart of the realm, where Islamic tenets about the equality of believers help to validate the ideals of urbanized "tribesmen" despite the objective reality of obvious status distinctions. For instance, in urban Morocco, ethnographers find "a fiercely egalitarian society" in which each person makes "claims to independence" despite "great and manifest discrepancies of wealth and power, prestige and rank."[16]

But although the ideals of equality and independence are unmistakably articulated and believed both in Islamic theology and in the ethic of Muslim tribesmen and their urban counterparts, the salience of these values for understanding society has been questioned, just as U.S. egalitarianism has been questioned, on the grounds that these convictions are actually masks used by the oppressors to delude the oppressed. As evidence, a long history of central rule is cited, as well as the many objective distinctions of wealth, status, and power to be found in even the most remote areas.[17]

Furthermore, although Islam declares itself the religion of equality, in actual fact religious practitioners, by claiming a holy geneaology or special mystical powers or knowledge of the Qur'an and hadith, have sought for themselves the right to decide questions of morals and law among the faithful. Inasmuch as these affirmations are accepted, a de facto hierarchy of sacredness has been imported into the leveling revelations of the Prophet: a hierarchy disclosed in the ranked (though often disputed) claims of sacred authority found among categories of Sayyid, sufi, or 'ulama.'[18]

That significant distinctions of rank occur in the secular and religious realm of Muslim societies cannot be denied. But this is not really any surprise, since inequalities must appear within any complex social formation. What is interesting and worth discussion is the indisputable fact that these differences of rank coincide with an ideological framework that, unlike the South Asian caste belief system, is decidedly opposed to accepting them. The logical question, then, is not whether hierarchy exists, or who gains advantage from charades of egalitarianism, or even how such unrealistic beliefs came to be held, but, as Dale Eickelman asks: "How can the tenet of . . . equality before God be reconciled with the implicit notion of hierarchy?"[19]

Secular Authority in Egalitarian Systems: Validating Inferiority

One theorist who has dealt with this question, albeit in a very different context, is Louis Dumont, who, in his book *Homo Hierarchicus,* reverses

Tocqueville's portrait of America to account for Hindu society where rank, rather than equality, is at the core of the culture's vision of itself. His claim is that, in India, relations of equality and autonomy can only be covertly expressed because they counter the prevailing value system of hierarchy and subordination. By extension, Dumont then argues that wherever the primary ethos of a culture favors egalitarianism and independence, distinction and subordination can likewise appear only in a disguised and distorted manner.

Dumont does not test his hypothesis in the Muslim world, but focuses on North America, maintaining that the pervasive color prejudice in the United States is an indigenous way of understanding and legitimizing difference and inferiority in a cultural system that has no place for these distinctions. From this perspective, via its claim that a dark skin color is a genetic and, therefore, true sign of subhuman character, racism makes "natural" what cannot be justified within the prevailing ethos; people of color are thus regarded as "naturally" bestial and not qualified for inclusion as human beings and coequals.

Is there a similar logic for justifying inferiority in Swat? Indeed, a Dumontian "naturalization" of permanently subaltern roles does occur there as subject categories of person (barbers, leatherworkers, musicians, etc.) are attributed "innate" characteristics that condemn them to servitude.[20] In a metaphor used to validate all forms of inferiority, these subordinate groups are viewed as equivalent to women and children; like women and children they are "naturally" incapable of judgment and honor and so deserve to be dominated by the Pukhtun warriors, who possess the "natural" qualities of coequal adult men.[21]

Similar images of masculine warrior adults "naturally" dominating female and childish underlings are common among other egalitarian Muslim tribal groups. For instance, the Berbers of Morocco believe the lower orders of serfs, smiths, and musicians have wayward or effeminate characters that contrast with the steady, manly personalities of the tribesmen. Similar patterns of the naturalization of the inferiority of subordinate groups are to be found in ethnographies of the Kabyle, the Daghara Arabs, the Marri Baluch, and the Tuareg—among others.[22] The imputation of inferiority can take on castelike proportions in practice, as intermarriage and even commensality may be prohibited between the manly warrior elite and the debased effeminate inferior—despite the stated values of Islam that all Muslims are brothers.

The same idiom of stigma is used externally as well as internally to express the inferiority of the tribesmen's lowland cousins, who are obliged to pay taxes and homage to the state. For the Pukhtun, those who are subjected in this manner are considered to have become "naturally" lower because they have given up their masculine assertion of autonomy and equality. This is interpreted as feminization or castration, and those who submit are conceived of as "gelded," no longer fit to claim themselves to be true men. Similar imagery holds in Morocco, as well. The Berbers of siba, as Ernest Gellner writes, see themselves as wolves permitted to prey upon "the sheep who have submitted to authority, thereby betraying a loss of moral fibre that might make them royal, and losing it ever more completely through the habits of submission."[23]

Historically, the imagery of gelding and taming was more than a metaphor. Within Swat, the short-lived imperial system lasted only two generations, and never developed all the elaborations of other states, but nonetheless the servants of the state were primarily those whom the local warriors held in contempt for their blemished identities. For instance, the first ruler's shadow and messenger was a Sikh convert to Islam; his two vazirs were sons of a Chitrali servant; his administration was staffed by imported, lowland clerks. All of these categories—convert, Chitrali, servant, lowlander—are despised as innately inferior by the Pukhtun.

In more developed courts elsewhere in North Africa, Arabia, and southwestern Asia, the tendency to recruit those with degraded identities as minions of the state was carried much farther, and underlings were often remade to fit the cultural concept of the "natural" inferior. Thus, throughout Muslim imperial systems, the retinue of a ruler were treated as children ("sons of the house"), enslaved, and regularly emasculated.

Ibn Khaldun was the first to argue that this pattern of enslavement, adoption, and castration is a rational effort by the king to rid himself of encumbering kinship ties and establish a client bureaucracy loyal only to him.[24] This interpretation is not in dispute here; clearly the rivalry of the king's kinsmen and coequals provides the social base from which the metaphors of subordination arise. But what I wish to stress is the manner in which dependence is imprinted. By actually enslaving and emasculating and symbolically infantalizing and feminizing underlings, the rulers made subordination "natural" within the idiom of an Islamic and tribal discourse that equates independence and equality with virility and adulthood.

From this perspective, the manner in which rulers throughout this region deeply and concretely impressed their retinues with identities that are thought to be inherently inferior and dependent is, at least in part, a correlate of the pervasive cultural axioms of equality and autonomy that these assertions of power seek to subvert. I would argue that it is precisely in a society with such an all-embracing egalitarian ethic that the pressure is greatest for a ruler to differentiate himself from his fellows and potential rivals by rendering his supporters not only completely dependent, but also symbolically subhuman. It is for this reason that these societies are unique in the world in the attention paid to the enslavement, castration, and metaphorical infantalization of the ruler's retinue.[25]

Secular Authority in Egalitarian Systems: Validating Superiority

Even if the ruler can impress signs of natural inferiority onto the persons of his entourage, he cannot do so to the whole subject population of the realm. This incapacity leads us to a critical problem in the analysis of egalitarian societies that is not discussed by Dumont, whose concern is solely with the way inferiority is covertly expressed and ratified via the idiom of "naturalization." This leaves out the question of the manner in which superiority is conceptualized, instated, and accepted by persons who believe in the premises of equality and independence, who are not stigmatized by "natural" marks of inferiority—castration, enslavement, infantalization—and who yet are objectively subordinate to a leader.

One way in which this is accomplished by those directly subject to imperial rule is for authority to be understood as a kind of natural catastrophe, like a flood, that must be borne if necessary, escaped if possible. The state, like a deluge, has no warrant except the brute fact of its ability to destroy all who oppose it. From this stance arises the motto common in Swat and throughout the tribal Muslim world that "all Rulers are usurpers." Those who are caught up in the compulsions of government can thus see themselves as hapless victims of disaster, not deserving the disrespect of those fortunate enough to have been delivered, by the Grace of God, from the plague of taxes and other indignities heaped upon its victims by a malignant and overwhelming central power.

The disdain for any moral claims made by the state to validate its rule coincides with tribal and Islamic values of egalitarianism and autonomy. This attitude gains further religious confirmation because, as Roy

Mottahedeh asserts, after the fall of the Caliphate, Muslim states were unable to "pose as the instrument of salvation for their subjects," leading the most scrupulous men "to set political ambitions aside." Patricia Crone writes that it was exactly this "moral gap" that led to the unprecedented rise of slave dynasties in the central Islamic states: illegitimate rulers were appropriate in a society where imperial power had itself become "illegitimate in the most literal sense of the word," and where, as we have seen, men of reputation, fearing emasculation and the taint of inequality and dishonor, would not deign to enter government service.[26]

It follows, then, that since "there is no reason in principle for the subject Muslim to prefer any particular Muslim ruler to any other," the ruler's authority is more often than not acknowledged purely because of its factual reality—he leads because he can attract and hold followers by whatever means he has at his disposal, including bribery, persuasion, or coercion. He himself has no special "calling" to rule, and no need to seek rationalization for his authority beyond the actuality of power itself.[27]

This was certainly the case in Swat, where, as Fredrik Barth comments, "It is the fact of effective control and ascendancy—not its formal confirmation or justification—that is consistently pursued." The Swati ruler thus did not have legitimacy in the Weberian sense. Authority carried no sacred quality; it was based purely on the pragmatic grounds that the leader held power and could command and punish others. Authority did not serve a higher purpose beyond the exercise of command. In this context, Swat was, as Barth writes, a polity of "complex decisions without equally elaborate goals" in which the followers were "an instrument of the Ruler"; when the leader lost the capacity to command, he lost his followers' respect and loyalty as well.[28] Similar pragmatism is nicely captured in the frank words of a soldier abandoning an unsuccessful commander during the rise of the Buyids: "If you become powerful again, we will return to you."[29]

This vision of leadership as a matter purely of power and benefits has a wide resonance; many readers will recognize the realistic and disenchanted attitude toward government from anthropological accounts of the Maghreb, where "there was an absence of legitimate political authority" and, according to standard ethnographies by Ernest Gellner and Clifford Geertz, the state was thought to serve only to monopolize "large-scale injustice," and was spoken of as a "machine less for the governing of men...than for the amassment and consumption of the material rewards of power."[30]

Because of the pervasive cultural distrust of authority, within Swati society all claims to secular leadership at every level were continually resisted and subverted—a stance typical of individualistic warriors who consider a leader to be simply first among equals, soon to be deserted when he fails to produce tangible results. In Swat, then, in every situation, strong men compete for secular power, but the actual power of an individual is transient, undermined by the resistance of peers and by the institution of the jirga, which speaks for the assembly of all the tribesmen and can overturn a leader's orders and plans.

Similarly, in Moroccan tribal regions, we find "institutions of policy making by consensus in a situation where policy making by leadership would have been far more efficient."[31] And here, too, the secular leadership that does arise is normally an ephemeral matter of primus inter pares, as leaders are selected by rotation from qualified candidates and are regularly replaced by their competitive coequals. Even in Moroccan cities, despite the long-term presence of the centralized state, there is a parallel absence of permanent hierarchy on the local level, and we find, as Clifford Geertz tells us, "a constantly rearranging kaleidoscope of political constellations, centering around rising and falling strong men."[32]

But it is especially in the unstable world of yaghistan and siba that we discover another mechanism for justifying inferiority to a secular leader that is quite different from the "victim of disaster" imagery often found among those of hukumat and makhzan, who are directly and reluctantly subject to the coercion of the state. Where the polity is fluid and real power over others is difficult to gain and hold, as is the case among the Pukhtun and in Moroccan tribal areas, the successful secular leader is simply regarded as an individual whose *personal* characteristics inspire the allegiance of those who hold themselves to be his coequals.

The qualities that verify the leader's right to command are the obverse of the traits of inferiority used to justify subordination, and include such "manly" virtues as foresight, intelligence, courage, ruthlessness, pride, generosity, rhetorical skill, pragmatism, forcefulness, and adherence to the warrior code of honor. Men with these characteristics are believed to gain advantage in the perpetual internecine competition to become the heads of factions because they "naturally" inspire the confidence and (momentary) submission of their coequal cousins and allies.

What is remarkable and of theoretical interest is that these attributes are exactly the traits believed to be the normal characteristics of every able adult man. The ability to be a secular political leader is, in fact, thought to be an essential quality of a true male member of the tribe. Thus, in Swat, the highest praise and ultimate criterion for a leader is that he is a "real Pukhtun."

The merger of the leader and his "natural" capacities with the qualities of the ordinary tribesmen serves two purposes. In the first place, it distinguishes leader and follower from their inferior clients, thereby providing a degree of solidarity among the ruling group. But even more important, it offers a solution to the predicament of justifying inferiority among a society of ideological equals. If the leader is an exemplar of all Pukhtun, he is, thus, just like his followers and is regarded simply as a person who has managed to assert his typical tribal character to achieve the universal goal of power. His superiority is, therefore, in no way otherworldly or awesome; he is only a man who has displayed the traits central to everyman's vision of himself and who has temporarily won the political game that all men play. His authority is a prize to be contested, not an essence to be accepted.

Under these circumstances, each man hopes someday to gain power for himself—if not over the village, at least over his cousins—and feels no great moral horror at another man's enactment of his own desire. Even the landless peasant does not easily ally himself with his oppressed fellows, nor does he greatly resent the power of his oppressor. Instead, he wishes to maintain the content of authority relationships and assume the dominant role for himself. As a poor laborer once told me, "The landlords sit upon the necks of the poor. God grant that I may become a landlord!"

In these circumstances, as Fredrik Barth notes, "Independence and personal sovereignty were highly, perhaps inordinately, valued; but they were conceptualized as goods for each to seek for himself, not as rights for all, to be collectively safeguarded by all."[33] Those who manage to dominate others are admired and followed or, if they become too powerful and threatening, avoided, allied against, and fought. But they are not held to have any unique or unusual qualities whatsoever, nor are their actions reprehensible.[34]

Within this ideological framework, it is difficult for the Pukhtun and his tribal brethren in Morocco and elsewhere to generate an argument against the unrestrained use of power by anyone, although invaders or heretics who threaten the social fabric can inspire the tribesmen to temporary unity in opposition. This laissez-faire attitude toward the exercise of might by those within the tribal system paradoxically fosters a relative inability to resist domination when it does occur, as witnessed in the independent Swati tribesmen's seemingly counterintuitive willingness to accept the imposition of a central authority for much of the last century, when they were ruled by two authoritarian dictators—the famous Badshah, and his son, the Wali.

How did this occur? Historically, the Swati polity consisted of a welter of constantly shifting factions gathered around pragmatic, power-seeking political entrepreneurs, out of which no one person could gain ascendance for any length of time. As in Smith's economic theory, which underpins Western entrepreneurship, within the Pukhtun marketplace of political manipulation the "unseen hand" of free competition historically maintained a relative balance of power.[35]

But one family did manage to gain authority in Swat toward the end of the nineteenth century, and ruled until deposed by the Pakistani state in 1969. The circumstances of their rise are too complex to relate at length,[36] but, in short, ascendancy was gained because the dynastic founder, the Badshah, was elected as temporary war leader of the tribesmen during a period of invasion. This position was justified because he was a brave man, an able leader, and a "real Pukhtun," and also because he was a descendant of a great spiritual leader and could, therefore, justify his role as leader and mediator between rival segments on theological and genealogical grounds.[37] Once in power, however, the Badshah did not wish to give it up. He managed to retain authority not only because of British support (they wanted a central figure to negotiate with and found the Badshah an amenable partner), but also because he manipulated the tribal political system through unremitting support of weaker parties in disputes.

The Badshah's technique, which relied upon the tensions of the egalitarian tribal ethos, helped keep the Pukhtun from joining together to resist him effectively. Rivals did arise bound together by a desire to acquire power for themselves, but other Pukhtuns could not accept pretensions to authority by any one of their coequals. Instead, they enlisted the ruler as mediator in local disputes, where he undermined anyone who had gained a substantial following—much to the glee of weaker local parties. In this instance, the maintenance of the center was not primarily derived from coercion; instead, it was power held due to the leader's ability to play upon the disarray and rivalry of the subjects, who, following the ethos of egalitarian individualism, could not unite against a dictator arising from within and instead spent their energy on struggles with personal rivals—struggles the leader could mediate to his own advantage.

Though of far greater duration and complexity, an analogous situation pertains in Morocco, where the present dynasty and its immediate predecessor arose in times of social collapse and invasion. Claims to spiritual genealogy coupled with brilliant political manipulation permitted the ascent of central rulers who held power primarily through playing off rival groups against one another. In the Moroccan situation, as Megali Morsy writes, "the state is largely derived from and dependent on the institution of arbitration." Centralized power is thus a result of the sultan's "manipulation of the arbiter network and manipulation of the tribal pattern (notably through an extension of segmentary opposition)."[38] Once again, the ruler attains authority among the tribes because he can exploit their ethos of possessive individualism, with its endemic rivalry, its need for arbitration, and its relative incapacity to unite against internally generated tyranny.

To better understand this seemingly perverse turn of the egalitarian ideology in which autonomous individualists accept authoritarian rulers, Tocqueville may again be of use. He warned Americans that men concerned with their own particular freedom might progressively withdraw from the public world of obligation and cooperation and retreat into the realm of capitalistic self-aggrandizement. They might, therefore, submit willingly to the rise of a tyrant if he would provide them with a space for economic entrepreneurship. In a similar manner, the Pukhtun tribesmen and their Moroccan cousins accepted the yoke of a ruler so long as they could continue their own factional rivalries.[39]

However, even a successful tyrant who manages to dominate his fellows in an egalitarian social system is limited in his actions by the strong pressure toward conformity implicit in the cultural ethos. The apparently paradoxical relationship between the individualistic struggle for domination and an accompanying rigid conformity has again been classically explicated by Tocqueville in his analysis of America. He was struck by the anxious adaptiveness of remorselessly profit-seeking entrepreneurs, and attributed the high degree of U.S. conformity to the absence of clear status markers within the society. This absence stimulates not only competition, as mentioned earlier, but also a deep fear of appearing out of place and a subsequent compulsive accommodation of the self to the social surround. This insight was later extended by David Riesman and his colleagues in the famous paradigm of the modern, "other-directed" man.[40]

Such other-directedness may be found in Swat as well, where the popular wisdom is that "the Pukhtun are like rain-sown wheat—they are all the same" and that "the bravest man dare not go against custom." Here, conformity and status anxiety are pervasive. Under these conditions, the leader, too, is obliged to act according to given social mores and not to overstep his connection with tribal beliefs and local understandings of Islam. In consequence, he must continually enact the part of the "real Pukhtun" in order to retain his own self-esteem as well as the authority grudgingly granted him by his subjects, who identify with him as an archetype of themselves. This means he must not only show the virtues of strength, cunning, and ruthlessness, but he must also embody values of generosity, hospitality, and piety. In this manner, tyranny is limited by the very configuration of values that also helps to make leadership a matter of the pursuit of naked and desacralized power.[41]

Sacred Authority in Egalitarian Systems

There is, however, a second logical possibility for validating authority within a cultural ethos of equality and autonomy—one intimated earlier in my short discussion of hierarchy in Islam and in the claims made by the Badshah and the Moroccan sultan to spiritual legitimacy. This alternative is the acceptance of the leader as sacred and, therefore, divinely exalted above the realm of common men. The idiom of saintliness is the mirror of the image of innate inferiority, and allows subjects to convince themselves that obedience, far from being degrading, is a holy act.[42] But to be convincing, the sacred leader, in contrast to the secular leader, must not be an exemplary everyman; instead he necessarily exhibits characteristics quite distinct from the qualities of persons in general—a necessity that, as we shall see, entails certain ambiguities in the identities of holy men and in the attitudes of their tribal clientele toward them.

In Swat and Morocco, such figures did indeed exist and stood symbolically removed from the tribal world of independent, amoral competition between coequals. A great deal has been written about these religious practitioners (known generally as the *stanadar* in Swat, the *igurramen* in Morocco) and there is much variety in the way they displayed their supramundane sanctity, including control over the sacred knowledge of the Qur'an, a display of mystical virtuosity, or perhaps a demonstration of austerity and an ostentatious emulation of the life of the Prophet. All of these patterns, and more, appeared throughout the Muslim tribal world in myriad configurations and combinations, and their proponents have been indigenously categorized in many ways—as Sufis, Pirs, Mullahs, Malangs, Sayyids, Marabouts, Mahdis, and so on.

Academics have also exercised themselves in constructing categories for local religious practitioners. The "Doctor" and "Saint" distinction between those men displaying scriptural knowledge and those exhibiting exemplary revelation—famously propounded by Ernest Gellner—is one instance.[43] These categories, however, were historically not mutually exclusive. In mainstream Islam, the case of al-Ghazzali is the most obvious example of a scholar cum mystic, but al-Ansari and al-Qadir, precursors of the "scripturalism" of modern Islam, were also themselves Sufis.[44] Furthermore, even though we assume that writing and mystical inspiration are opposed, we should recall that literacy—the mark of the scholar—was seen in tribal areas as a kind of magical and holy capacity. Scribes, like other Muslim men of God, were thus thought to have a mystical character, and, like ecstatics and magicians, could travel in the tribal areas of Morocco, Pakistan, and elsewhere without armed escort, and could fill the saintly role of spiritual exemplar and mediator demanded by the tribesmen.[45]

So, for the purpose of this chapter, I will combine all rural religious practitioners under the catchall rubric of "saint," which I take to signify a unifying theme, that is, an effort by the religious man to assert a special quality of sacredness for himself that sets him apart from ordinary mortals, regardless of whether the source of this sacredness is Qur'anic knowledge or mystical enlightenment or holy genealogy. I cannot comment here on the causes and correlates of the diversity of sacred assertions of self, but will simply make the general argument that the potential spiritual leader among tribesmen generally (though not always) comes from a nontribal lineage and often (though not always) makes claims to some form of descent from the Prophet Muhammad. He usually lives in the interstices between tribal segments and often serves as an arbiter in internal disputes and, when the need arises, as a rallying point for his tribal clients in resistance to invasion or in wars of expansion. Such figures, whatever their type, also claim membership in a sacred hierarchical structure that validates their pretensions to leadership.

For instance, the founding saintly ancestor of the rulers of Swat was a non-Pukhtun who left the Valley to seek spiritual instruction. He underwent rigorous instruction as a disciple at a Sufi school in India where, under the tutelage of recognized spiritual masters, he learned not only Qur'anic knowledge, but also techniques of meditation and self-discipline. In Swat, he impressed the tribesmen with his seemingly super-human asceticism and scholarship and was awarded the religious title of Akhund. Simultaneously, rival holy men rose and fell in the region, ranging in type from Sayyids demanding leadership roles because of their evident piety and elevated lineage, to ecstatic magicians claiming to be the Mahdi sent to redeem the faithful from disaster. However, the Akhund's knowledge of local custom, his fairness as a mediator, his ability to interpret holy teachings, and his austerities won him many local disciples who eventually called upon him to be their symbolic leader in a war against invading colonial forces. After the war, the Akhund gave up his leadership role and was satisfied to continue as a religious mediator—but his grandson, the Badshah, was more ambitious and, as we have seen, converted a similar situation into a position of permanent secular power.

Comparable varieties of saintly practitioners existed in Morocco as well, gaining adherents by virtue of their training and revealed sacred capacities; in peacetime offering mediation, solace, and a personal link to the divine for their tribal clients; and sometimes acting as candidates for secular power during periods of crisis. As in Swat, it is from this cadre that the eventual ruling dynasties of the state arose, bringing the warring factions together under their aegis.

Of course, some lineages and groups are more prone to gaining an elevated spiritual status that can be translated into secular dominion: the members of the Prophet's genealogical line are prime candidates, as are those whose fathers and grandfathers have been recognized as schol-ars or saints. But such descent is by no means a necessary precondition for becoming a religious leader, and members of "sacred" lineages can easily become as mundane as anyone else. Religious claims need to be proved to be accepted; the saint has to appear beyond the realm of the ordinary in order to win acolytes. This can be achieved primarily by a transformation of identity entailing a loss of one's own "natural," manly self through immersion in the practices and dogmas of a spiritual teacher.

For instance, among the Sufis, who are very often the founders of saintly lineages in the hinterlands, training of a student (a *murid*) by his master (the *murshid* or shaykh) requires strict discipline in which, as Ira Lapidus writes, "all behavior must be channeled into revealed and correct forms that eliminate idiosyncratic irrational expressions of feeling."[46] The required suppression of personal impulse and individual character is achieved by "cadaver obedience," as the Sufis call it—the disciple is "cut off from humanity for God's sake" and becomes dead to the willful self through cultivating passive and unquestioning devotion to the master. As a Sufi manual puts it:

> He should always obey the *shaikh* and he should serve him with his life and property. Nothing is achieved without love for the *shaikh,* and obedience is the mark of love. . . . He should not object to anything that the *murshid* says or does. . . . He should believe that the *shaikh*'s mistake is better than his own virtue.[47]

In a like manner, orthodox Qur'anic scholarship requires the seeker to submit completely to the domination of a specific master whose rule is absolute. In both Sufic and Qur'anic schools the disciple was removed from his family and community; complete self-abnegation and unconditional subordination to the spiritual teacher were demanded, and, thus, the expression of personality was prohibited. The recognition of spiritual achievement was given not as a result of a rationalized test, and occurred only after the disciple had shown that he had given up his personal will.[48]

Therefore, despite differences in training and outlook, both scholar and mystic ideally became "slaves of God" who achieved "closeness" to the deity by means of rigorous suppression of the self, devotion to an exemplary mentor, and withdrawal from the mundane world of family and kin. As a direct result of their shared experience of absolute subordination to a master and their subsequent self-loss and inner transformation, Sufi and scholar alike were believed by the populace, and by themselves, to have become conduits for sacred power, and to be part of a spiritual pyramid of holiness.

Obviously, the submission and deindividuation demanded of the religious practitioner is the absolute antithesis of the model of Pukhtun and Moroccan tribal secular leadership where, as Ibn Khaldun wrote, "he who has been ruled is not fit to rule." As we have seen, in tribal society, the value of subordination is totally denied in favor of the free and forceful demonstration of the prospective leader's innate, "natural," manly qualities of bravery, pride, cunning, generosity, and the like. In contrast to the religious man, in exercising his power to rule, the tribal leader is not transformed, nor is his separate identity lost in the pursuit of command; instead he asserts what he and others take to be his essential character. In other words, the religious acolyte gains status and authority through *passive acquiescence* to a divine force that uses him as a vessel and locates him within a sacred hierarchy; in contrast, the tribesman seeking to dominate others gains his power through *active expression* of his own inner and personal capacities in competition with his coequals.

Ambiguity of Sacred Authority

Because they achieve validation within a supramundane, sacred hierarchy, religious figures have a potential for legitimate leadership that is denied the ordinary tribesman. Sacralized bureaucracies of saints and their disciples standing at the interstices of tribal territory and between the tribes and the central state offer an alternative mode of authority and mediation to the competitive and egalitarian warriors, who find it difficult to accept one of themselves as anything more than a temporary superior. Precisely because of his distinctiveness and his sacred legitimacy within a spiritual hierarchy, a saint can stand apart and bring the warring tribal kinsmen together in times of distress. From this point, it is only a small step for the saint's descendants to claim permanent leadership status—as occurred in Swat and Morocco.

But sanctified authority imposes a great burden of ambiguity upon those who aspire to hold it. This is because the religious figure contradicts, in his essential identity, the basic assumptions of the tribesmen he lives among. For them, leadership is a result of manifesting the transient natural power common to all equal adult male members of the group; conversely, the religious leader claims permanent elite status due to the training, genealogy, and special experiences that have allowed him to be close to the magical powers of the supernatural. But these powers are a result of being "bound," a slave to God and, more directly, an obedient servant of a master, and therefore contradict the local, secular values of independence and equality.

Because of these tensions, deep suspicion, as well as awe and attraction, are felt by the tribesmen for the religious figures who walk among them. This ambiguity is evident in myths and legends that, in terms of function, have much in common with the metaphors used to justify the "natural" inferiority of certain groups. But the symbolism here is more convoluted, since the saint is recognized as in some ways superior due to his connection with the divine, obliging the tribesman to rationalize his own subordination. I have argued that, in the case of secular authority, this could be done either by imagining the dominant authority to be a kind of natural disaster with no legitimacy beyond the power to coerce or by "naturalizing" and desacralizing the leader's role so that he becomes just like everyone else, only more so. However, neither of these strategies can work for the saint, who is neither illegitimate nor an ideal everyman.

What we see instead are images of saints that show both their extraordinary power, but also reveal the dark and disreputable side of that power—at least from the tribesman's viewpoint. The saint is thus both given respect and simultaneously denigrated as unmanly. In Pukhtun stories, for instance, potent local spiritual figures (pirs) are by no means the benevolent characters we might imagine from a reading of Christian hagiography. Instead, they are portrayed as dangerous, arrogant, and jealous individuals who often use their powers malevolently. In the lightest, and very typical, incidents, the saint is depicted as a trickster: train conductors who demand a fare from him find their trains suddenly immobilized, their watches stopped—but all comes right again when abject apologies are made. But in other cases, the power of the saint is far more frightening: those who disturb the holy man, even unintentionally, are cursed, and die miserably; the wandering malang (Sufi beggar) is feared for his evil eye, and so on. Saints do give favors, but generally they are unpredictable and menacing, and the Pukhtun would agree with the Moroccan proverb that "God's mercy comes from visiting a Saint and going away soon."[49]

The ambivalence of the sacred is also seen in appearance. The saint, representing himself as the wife of God, may look effeminate; in Swat and elsewhere the wandering ecstatic malangs may dress in women's clothes and speak of their relationship with Allah in explicitly sexual terms. These mystics, and their more orthodox counterparts, are thought by the tribesmen to be driven by insatiable sexual appetites and to seduce the chaste tribal women who go to them for spiritual help. In Swat, men with birthmarks on their faces are pointed out as the products of their mothers' illicit unions with these erotic religious figures. Similarly ambivalent sexual powers are expressed in the High Atlas in the ritual celebrations presided over by the "goat man," who has breasts on his chest, genitals on his back, who can fertilize barren women, and who is likened to a saint, and also, significantly, to a Caid.[50]

Holy men are also often accused of hypocrisy. "Any fool can grow a beard," the Pukhtun say, and believe that many religious practitioners pretend piety while hiding vices under their virtuous disguises. This accusation gains its force because, in this system, the authority of the saint does not spring from his essential core, but from his training; he therefore has the potential for being false, whereas the naked ability of the secular leader is thought to spring from his natural manhood and to be transparently real and immediate. No one can pretend to be brave and manly while immersed in the daily struggle—but a pretender to piety is not so easily found out.

Thus, partially because of their heritage of passive acceptance of hierarchical domination, which is totally opposed to the secular tribal value system, the holy man, though feared and venerated, is also perceived as all that the Pukhtun would like to believe that he is not: hypocritical, sexually ambivalent, childishly enslaved by desire, servile, cowardly; in the worst scenario, he is a kind of witch, gaining magical power through betrayal of his own masculinity.

In Morocco, too, we find an equivalent distaste for the holy man among the tribal peoples clearly expressed in Westermarck's voluminous work *Ritual and Belief in Morocco.*

> The same sorts of places—rocks, caves, springs, the sea—as are haunted by *jnun* (a malevolent spirit) are also associated with Saints— so much so that there is often some doubt whether a certain place is connected with a Saint or merely haunted by *jnun.* . . . The relationship between Saints and *jnun* is often of a very intimate character. Many Saints . . . rule over *jnun,* who act as their *huddam,* or servants, and in the so-called *jenn* Saint the borderline between Saint and *jenn* is almost obliterated. . . . There are no doubt Saints and *shereefs* who have been habitually and notoriously guilty of great crimes without losing their reputation for sanctity.[51]

In Morocco, as in Swat, these ambiguities and fearsome saints were believed by the populace to have magical powers of flight and shape changing, as well as a frightening ability to curse and destroy all who irritated them. They showed the same arrogant desire for power and a potent but polymorphous sexuality, so that the religious man was often feminized in dress and appearance, but also was reputed to have sexual domination over his acolytes, and it was even believed that, as Westermarck reports, "a boy cannot learn the Koran well unless a scribe commits pederasty with him."[52]

The truth or falsehood of the beliefs held by the common tribesman about saints is irrelevant for the argument made here. What is of interest is the symbolic counterposition made between religious figures—the "bound"—and the warriors—the "free."[53] From the point of view of the putatively autonomous and egalitarian warrior, the Sufi or the scholar, with his claim to descent from the Prophet and to special sacred knowledge, is a man whose potency and sanctity is venerated insofar as he reveals his extraordinary powers, but only with a marked degree of ambiguity and denigration, as signaled by imagery of enslavement, feminization, and infantilization that is attached to him—the same sorts of negative symbolism that are attached to the minions of the central state and the inferior members of the tribal society.

In reaction to this negative imagery, many saintly lineages in Swat, including the old royal lineage, now claim themselves to be the equivalent of the Pukhtun who surround them. They act in a manner fully comparable to their combative countrymen, accepting the values of Pukhtunness, relinquishing all rights to spiritual distinction, and competing with the tribesmen for secular domination on the grounds of their "natural" exemplary character.[54]

This is certainly an appropriate mode of deportment when the social system is not under stress, and the tribal virtues of equality and competitive individualism are unchallenged. In these circumstances, men of a holy lineage are not in demand for their services as the node for tribal unity, and the negative aspects of their identity may come to the fore if they attempt to claim leadership status. Without the power to coerce or suborn a following, men of religious lineage and political ambition may then wish to align themselves with the tribesmen who surround them, avoiding the moral ambivalence that attends the assertion of sacredness. Clearly, this has occurred in Swat, as the descendants of the ruler have become fully secularized. Even the tomb of the saintly ancestor of the clan has lost its sacred appeal to pilgrims, who now patronize the tombs of saints whose descendants have not attempted to wield secular power.

In Morocco, however, a different trajectory occurred, one that led to the permanent empowerment of the 'Alawite dynasty. The crisis in

Morocco that led to the rise of holy lineages in the central state during the sixteenth century was of long duration, and involved the nearly complete breakdown of secular authority and a collapse of the economy, accompanied by plagues and invasion. Here, unlike Swat, the entire culture was under threat. In the absence of secular successes of warrior rulers, there was an increased focus on Islamic values and, in particular, a stress on holy descent as a requirement for leadership.

Under these pressing circumstances, the rise of the sherifian Sa'di dynasty, and later the 'Alawite, was, as Elaine Combs-Schilling argues, "a means of selecting a supreme political authority in the absence of military victory or economic florescence. . . ." In this instance, "super-structural strength compensated for infrastructural weakness"; an emphasis on sacred ritual masked the general failure of the social system in a government that was "rich in political identity and weak in bureaucratic power."[55]

As Combs-Schilling shows, the Moroccan state solidified itself not only through the manipulation of segmentary opposition between rival groups, but also through the astute centralization of major rituals, which were focused on the sherifian ruler, and identified him as a ceremonial representative both of the Prophet and the people. Tribesmen recognized the king as a legitimate inheritor of the Caliphate and as the symbolic center of a threatened society; they were willing to use him as a mediator in their disputes, as a legitimator of their own local authority, and as a war leader against the infidel. This did not mean, however, a willingness to pay taxes or submit to a state bureaucracy. Nor did it mean a complete absence of ambivalence toward the ruler, who traditionally was mocked at his wedding ceremony, and who was sometimes regarded as a "mighty wizard who had the ability to perceive hidden realities."[56]

Furthermore, even in this highly ritualized and sacralized central bureaucracy, there was a tendency toward secularization of the kingly role over time, as is seen especially in the ruler's symbolic enactment of the sacrifice at Eid, where he takes the part of the paradigmatic male head of household. Nor does he try to set himself off from his secular brethren by appearance or acts. This is in marked contrast to earlier rulers, who cultivated an effeminate look, used many elaborate devices to indicate high status, and held audiences from behind veils. Instead, the present king, Combs-Schilling says, is portrayed as the "archetypal man" whose legitimacy "does not rest on abstract clusters of criteria that categorically distinguishes the Ruler from all other men . . . but rather depends on the Ruler being like every other man only more exemplary, the best-of-category-representative."[57]

Conclusion

In this chapter I have made some rather large arguments about an intersection between values of equality and autonomy, with their implicit contradictions and tensions, and the forms in which authority is conceptualized and enacted in Swat and in Morocco, with a few references to another well-known egalitarian culture, the United States. I have used ethnographic detail to illustrate the modes in which distinction and hierarchy are manifested in societies where equality and independence are valued above all else.

Essentially, I have reasoned that the ethos of egalitarianism and autonomy in Swat and in Morocco correlates with several ways in which authority is expressed and symbolized. In its secular form, rule may be seen as a cataclysm and the ruler as a coercive brute; in more fluid systems, the ruler, instead, is conceived to be expressing the "natural," manly power to command that is thought to be an essential characteristic of the followers themselves.

Following Tocqueville, I argued that this symbolic system implies a minimum of moral outrage by subjects at the raw exercise of power by a locally generated leader, but also requires the leader to conform to a limited range of behavior. For subjects, the legitimacy of such leaders is justified, I have argued, solely on the grounds of expediency and strength, and loyalty evaporates rapidly when there is a fall from power. In reaction, leaders in this moral universe are impelled to create absolute dependents who are impressed with visible signs of "natural" inferiority, that is, emasculated and enslaved. In a parallel manner, inferiority is "naturalized" in the tribal environment by attributing effeminate and childish characteristics to those who are dominated.

The contradictions and tensions implicit in this strongly secularized and pragmatic political ethos generate their logical opposite in the rise of sacred authority figures who claim power not because of "natural" strength, but through the magical potency they have achieved via passive discipleship to a spiritual master. This affirmation of sacred power allows the tribesmen to accept an authority that stands outside and above their own competitive and individualistic value system as legitimate, and provides them as well with much-needed mediators to mitigate their endemic internal disputes.

But, as Dumont noted, the manifestation of a counterideology in any society is always deeply problematic and dangerous. In Swat and Morocco, the assertion of sacralized superiority by the saint is met with considerable ambivalence, since the holy man poses a very real threat, both symbolically and in political terms, to the egalitarian values of the tribesmen. A complex web of symbolism, therefore, surrounds the saint, who is portrayed both as powerful and as degraded and unmanly.

The tribal social formation, with its familiar ethos of equality and autonomy, is thus caught in a dilemma. Power that is secular is fleeting and weakly legitimized, while power that is sacred is held by ambiguous religious figures who excite both awe and repulsion. There seems, on the evidence of these two cases, to be a strong tendency for religious dynasties to gradually secularize their rule and to fashion their representatives into semblances of "ideal everymen"—warriors instead of saints. But then they, too, must cope with the inevitable crisis of legitimacy and the rivalry of coequals that such desacralization implies.

NOTES

1. The comparability between tribesmen of North Africa and Northern Pakistan may seem minimal, but the peoples actually have much in common in terms of social structure, ecology, economy, ideology, and in their relationship to the central state. Pukhtun who have met Berbers have been struck as well by their affinity, and have told me the Berbers are "like us." David Hart has made an explicit anthropological comparison between the two regions. See David Hart, "Les Ait 'Atta du Sud-Centre Marocain: Elements d'Analyse comparative avec les Pakhtuns (Afridi) du Nord-Ouest Pakistanais," in *Islam: Société et communauté,* ed. Ernest Gellner (Paris: Centre National de la Recherche Scientifique, 1981); Hart, *Guardians of the Khaibar Pass: The Social Organization and History of the Afridis of Pakistan* (Lahore: Vanguard Books, 1985). I should also make clear here that other basic values may also exist alongside, or even in opposition to, those I discuss. For an argument in favor of an alternative value system in Morocco, see Dale Eickelman, *The Middle East: An Anthropological Approach* (Englewood Cliffs, N.J.: Prentice-Hall, 1981), which considers the fundamental beliefs there to consist of a faith in God's will, reason, obligation, propriety, and compulsion.

2. For standard studies of Swat and the Pukhtun in general, see Olaf Caroe, *The Pathans* (London: Macmillan, 1965); Fredrik Barth, *Political Leadership*

among Swat Pathans (London: Athlone Press, 1965); Akbar Ahmed, *Millenium and Charisma among Pathans* (London: Routledge and Kegan Paul, 1976); Ahmed, *Pukhtun Economy and Society* (London: Routledge and Kegan Paul, 1980); Charles Lindholm, *Generosity and Jealousy: The Swat Pukhtun of Northern Pakistan* (New York: Columbia University Press, 1982).

3. Talal Asad, "Market Model, Class Structure, and Consent: A Reconsideration of Swat Political Organization," *Man* 7 (1972): 74–94.

4. Ghani Khan, *The Pathans: A Sketch* (Peshawar: University Books, 1958), 46–47.

5. The violence in Swat is structured by kinship alliances and localized factional confederations based in large measure on the rivalry between close patrilineal cousins for prestige and for control over land. For more on this subject, see Charles Lindholm, "The Structure of Violence among the Swat Pukhtun," *Ethnology* 20 (1981): 147–56; Fredrik Barth, "Segmentary Opposition and the Theory of Games: A Study of Pathan Organization," *Journal of the Royal Anthropological Institute* 89 (1959): 5–21.

6. Alexis de Tocqueville, *Democracy in America* (Garden City, N.Y.: Doubleday, 1969).

7. Charles MacPherson, *The Political Theory of Possessive Individualism* (London: Oxford University Press, 1962).

8. H. A. R. Gibb and Harold Bowen, *Islamic Society and the West* (London: Oxford University Press, 1957), 1:77.

9. Patricia Crone, *Slaves on Horses* (Cambridge: Cambridge University Press, 1980), 63.

10. For a discussion of the relationship between caste and Muslim values, see Imtiaz Ahmad, ed., *Family, Kinship, and Marriage among Muslims in India* (New Delhi: Manohar, 1976); Ahmad, ed., *Caste and Stratification among Muslims in India* (New Delhi: Manohar, 1978); Ahmad, ed., *Ritual and Religion among Muslims in India* (New Delhi: Manohar, 1981); Charles Lindholm, "Caste in Islam and the Problem of Deviant Systems: A Critique of Recent Theory," *Contributions to Indian Sociology,* n.s. 20 (1986): 61–73.

11. I use the word *tribal* advisedly as a shorthand designation for named and relatively self-reliant social units outside the direct control of the state.

12. Michael Meeker, *Literature and Violence in Early Arabia* (London: Cambridge University Press, 1979); Meeker, "The Twilight of a South Asian Heroic Age: A Rereading of Barth's Study of Swat," *Man* 15 (1980): 682–701.

13. These characteristics have been the object of debate because of the high degrees of variation found in many settings. Nonetheless, I continue to hold these factors as central. For a statement of my argument about the ubiquity of these characteristics in the North African, Middle Eastern, and Southwest Asian tribal context, and for a discussion of the distinctiveness of this vast region in comparison to central Asia, see Charles Lindholm, "Kinship Structure and

Political Authority: The Middle East and Central Asia," *Comparative Studies in Society and History* 28 (1986): 334–65. In the context of this chapter, the historical and structural roots of a cultural stance of egalitarian individualism in these regions need not be debated, only asserted as a starting point for the argument.

14. Paul Dresch, "The Significance of the Course Events Take in Segmentary Systems," *American Ethnologist* 13 (1986): 321.

15. Henry Rosenfeld, "The Social Composition of the Military in the Process of State Formation in the Arabian Desert," *Journal of the Royal Anthropological Institute* 95 (1965): 174; Paul Rabinow, *Reflections on Fieldwork in Morocco* (Berkeley: University of California Press, 1977), 116.

16. Lawrence Rosen, "Social Identity and Points of Attachment: Approaches to Social Organization," in *Meaning and Order in Moroccan Society,* ed. Clifford Geertz, Hildred Geertz, and Lawrence Rosen (Cambridge: Cambridge University Press, 1979), 48; Rabinow, *Reflections on Fieldwork,* 49; Vincent Crapanzo, *Tuhami: Portrait of a Moroccan* (Chicago: University of Chicago Press, 1980), 80.

17. For a standard statement of this position, see Jacob Black, "Tyranny as a Strategy for Survival in an 'Egalitarian' Society: Luri Facts versus an Anthropological Mystique," *Man* 7 (1972): 614–34. A similar case for Swat is made in Asad, "Market Model."

18. Some of the contradictions and implications of sacred hierarchy will be discussed later in the chapter.

19. Eickelman, *The Middle East,* 229.

20. Unlike race and caste, however, some upward mobility is recognized as possible—demonstrating the deep egalitarian ethic of the society. Formerly, for example, a demonstration of the quintessential Pukhtun virtue of bravery could lead to a grant in land and the acquisition of Pukhtun status by acclamation. Nowadays, the accumulation of wealth allows some members of subaltern groups to purchase land and to make claims to be the equals of Pukhtun warriors, but these newcomers are not so widely accepted. Downward mobility was more prevalent, and many despised individuals and groups claim elite ancestry.

21. For a discussion of these metaphors, see Charles Lindholm, "Leatherworkers and Love Potions," *American Ethnologist* 9 (1981): 512–25. See also Barth, *Political Leadership,* on the place of inferiors in Swat.

22. On the Berbers, see Carleton Coon, *Caravan: The Story of the Middle East* (New York: Holt, 1953); David M. Hart, *The Aith Waryaghar of the Moroccan Rif: An Ethnography and History* (Tucson: University of Arizona Press, 1976); Hart, *Dadda 'Atta and His Forty Grandsons: The Sociopolitical Organization of the Ait 'Atta of Southern Morocco* (Outwell: MENAS Press, 1981); Abdullah Hammoudi, "Sainteté, pouvoir, et société: Tamgrout aux XVII et XVIII siècles," *Annales—Économies, sociétés, civilisations* (1980): 615–41. On the Kayble, see Jacques Berque, *Structure sociales de Haut Atlas* (Paris: Uni-

versitaires de France, 1955). On the Daghara Arabs, see Richard Fernea, *Shaiykh and Effendi* (Boston: Harvard University Press, 1970). On the Marri Baluch, see Robert Pehrson, *The Social Organization of the Marri Baluch* (New York: Wenner-Gren, 1966). On the Taureg, see L. Briggs, *Tribes of the Sahara* (Boston: Harvard University Press, 1960).

23. Ernest Gellner, *Muslim Society* (Cambridge: Cambridge University Press, 1981), 30. This distinction was, however, impermanent, and a tribe could regain honor if it freed itself from the grip of the state or if, as has occurred in Saudi Arabia, the tribe becomes the military arm of the government. The image of the masculine world of the independent tribesman is presently greatly challenged as more and more tribal groups are integrated into an increasingly potent state structure. But the power of the central state to overwhelm and encapsulate the periphery is a very new phenomenon, a result of central control over an unprecedented technology of war. Previously, the state was noted for its chronic instability and fragility, and the tribes had far stronger hands to play. On the interplay between center and periphery in the Maghreb, and the literature on Swat for analogous patterns in the region, see Yves Lacoste, "General Characteristics and Fundamental Structures of Medieval North African Society," *Economy and Society* 3 (1974): 1–17; David Seddon, "Economic Anthropology or Political Economy (II): Approaches to the Analysis of Pre-Capitalist Formation in the Maghreb," in *The New Economic Anthropology,* ed. John Clammer (New York: St. Martin's Press, 1978).

24. See Ibn Khaldun, *The Muqaddimah* (Princeton: Bollingen Press, 1967); Patricia Crone, *Slaves on Horses;* Daniel Pipes, *Slave Soldiers and Islam* (New Haven: Yale University Press, 1981).

25. The prevalence of slave dynasties in the region does not invalidate this point. See Crone, *Slaves on Horses;* Lindholm, "Kinship Structure"; and subsequent discussion in this chapter for more on the intertwining between the illegitimacy of secular authority and the rise and acceptance of slave dynasties.

26. Roy Mottahedeh, *Loyalty and Leadership in an Early Islamic Society* (Princeton: Princeton University Press, 1980), 187; Crone, *Slaves on Horses,* 63. There are clear exceptions to the general illegitimacy of Muslim rulers, particularly in social formations influenced by sectarian Sufism and Shi'ism, the most recent being the rule of Khomeini in Iran. This propensity correlates with a general theological orientation toward the acceptance of authority among Sufis and Shi'ites that is, in many senses, the reverse of the attitude of Sunni Islam (see Henry Munson, *Islam and Revolution in the Middle East* [New Haven: Yale University Press, 1988] for a recent study on this topic). Among Sunnis, the most long-lasting kingship with undoubted legitimacy is the 'Alawite dynasty in Morocco, who have made a claim to incarnate the Caliphate. I will discuss these religious claims and their ambiguities in the next two sections. But, for the moment, I hope the reader will allow my blanket statement to stand.

27. Peter Hardy, "The Authority of Muslim Kings in Mediaeval South Asia," in *Islam and Society in South Asia,* ed. Marc Gaborieau (Paris: Editions de l'école des hautes études en sciences sociales, 1986). It is interesting to note that, despite a similar egalitarian ideology, the approval, or at least tolerance, of the pursuit of pure power in the political realm is not found in the U.S. context. There, the revelation of raw political power is muted by a legitimizing and sacralizing ideology that political leaders are not superior, but are subordinate to the electorate; the possession of political power is thereby hidden beneath a rhetoric emphasizing the influence of the voters, so that the senator is called a civil servant at the command of his or her constituency. This imagery does not permit any claims to raw power by the political elite—such claims must always be posed on the grounds of pursuing the legitimate interests of the voters the power-holder represents under the precepts of the hallowed Constitution. When the pursuit and exercise of raw personal power does become evident, the office-holder may be voted out of office, charged with being "corrupt," power hungry, self-seeking, and the like.

28. Fredrik Barth, *The Last Wali of Swat* (New York: Columbia University Press, 1985), 175, 181, 168.

29. Mottahedeh, *Loyalty and Leadership,* 80.

30. Meeker, *Literature and Violence,* 235; Gellner, *Muslim Society,* 28; Clifford Geertz, "Suq: The Bazaar Economy in Sefrou," in *Meaning and Order in Moroccan Society,* ed. Clifford Geertz, Hildred Geertz, and Lawrence Rosen (Cambridge: Cambridge University Press, 1979), 141.

31. Meeker, *Literature and Violence,* 219.

32. See Ernest Gellner, "Political and Religious Organization of the Berbers of the Central High Atlas," in *Arabs and Berbers,* ed. Ernest Gellner and Charles Micaud (Lexington, Mass.: Lexington Books, 1972); Gellner, *Muslim Society*; Hart, *The Aith Waryaghar;* Hart, *Dadda 'Atta;* Geertz, "Suq," 239. For a discussion of the objective limitations on the pool of potential leaders in the tribal regions, see Hammoudi, "Sainteté, pouvoir, et société."

33. Barth, *Last Wali of Swat,* 169.

34. The equivalent ideology appears in the United States not in relation to politics, which is ideologically sacralized via the invocation of the Constitution, but in the realm of economic competition, where there is little or no notion of cooperative action for the larger public good, where the wealthy are thought of as "just like everyone else," and where ruthlessness in the pursuit of money excites no great moral horror among a population that, itself, hopes to become wealthy and admires those who have succeeded at reaching the cultural goal.

35. On some of these mechanisms, see Barth, "Segmentary Opposition"; David Hart, "Clan, Lineage, Local Community, and the Feud in a Rifian Tribe," in *Peoples and Cultures in the Middle East,* ed. Louise Sweet, vol. 2 (New York: Natural History Press, 1970).

36. See Barth, *Political Leadership;* Ahmed, *Millenium and Charisma;* Lindholm, *Generosity and Jealousy.* For autobiographical narratives by the Badshah and the Wali on their methods for gaining and wielding power, also see Barth, *Last Wali of Swat;* A. Wadud, *The Story of Swat as Told by the Founder* (Peshawar: Ferozsons, 1962).

37. The contradictions implicit in the assertion of spiritual power will be explored in the next section.

38. Megali Morsy, "Arbitration as a Political Institution: An Interpretation of the Status of Monarchy in Morocco," in *Islam in Tribal Societies,* ed. David Hart and Akbar Ahmed (London: Routledge and Kegan Paul, 1984), 52, 54. As Bryan Turner notes, similar patterns of a weak state holding power by "playing one section of the community off against another" are typical of the Middle East in general; see Bryan Turner, *Weber and Islam* (London: Routledge and Kegan Paul, 1974), 101.

39. Of course, the situation in Swat is quite different from that which Tocqueville warned against, since the Pukhtun emphasis on self-assertion finds its expression, as we have seen, in the pursuit of political power, rather than in the economic realm. This means that the Pukhtun, far from withdrawing from public life, are instead actively seeking public recognition and power. But the parallel remains that the Swati political world is similar in composition to the economic sphere in the West, in that there are no formal or ideological structures supporting cooperation, nor is there any ethic of public service.

40. David Riesman, Nathan Glazer, and Ruel Denny, *The Lonely Crowd* (New Haven: Yale University Press, 1961).

41. Once again, there are, of course, substantial differences in the manner in which conformity is engendered and enacted in the Swati context and in the United States. In the West, it is manifested within a world where roles are amorphous; anxiety is thought to be a product of this lack of definition. In Swat, on the other hand, there is a very specific and clear image of appropriate masculine behavior, one that every man must seek to enact. Thus, while U.S. citizens may suffer alienation from society, the Pukhtun may suffer from too great an integration into society—they call it being "narrow." But, in both cases, there is no possibility of breaking stereotypes and ignoring the opinions of neighbors. The modern Westerner may, therefore, be searching for the appropriate model for action, while the Pukhtun knows quite well how to act; but each is haunted by the fear of being shamed and suffers from the tension of being obliged to find one's own way in a fluid and antagonistic social world.

42. For an interesting discussion of this model, see J. Katz, "Deviance, Charisma, and Role-Defined Behavior," *Social Problems* 20 (1972): 186–202.

43. Gellner, *Muslim Society.*

44. Gellner, *Muslim Society;* George Makdisi, "Hanbalite Islam," in *Studies in Islam,* ed. Merlin Swartz (New York: Oxford University Press, 1981).

45. For examples of the types of holy men among the Pukhtun, see Barth, *Political Leadership;* Ahmed, *Millenium and Charisma;* Ahmed, "Islam and the District Paradigm," *Contributions to Indian Sociology* 17 (1983): 155–83. For North Africa, see Ernest Gellner, *Saints of the Atlas* (1969); Gellner, *Muslim Society;* Dale Eickelman, *Knowledge and Power in Morocco: The Education of a Twentieth-Century Notable* (Princeton: Princeton University Press, 1985); M. Brett, "Mufti, Marabout, Murabit, and Mahdi: Four Types in the Islamic History of North Africa," *Revue de l'Occident Musulman et de la Méditerranée* 29 (1980): 5–15; Hammoudi, "Sainteté, pouvoir, et société." For a general, process-oriented portrait of the movement from ecstatic saint to a bureaucratic school, see J. Trimingham, *The Sufi Orders of Islam* (Oxford: Oxford University Press, 1971). For a case of a school that saw itself as completely scripturalist, but was interpreted by the surrounding tribesmen as saintly, see E. Evans-Pritchard, *The Sanusi of Cyrenaica* (London: Oxford University Press, 1949).

46. Ira Lapidus, "Knowledge, Virtue, and Action: The Classical Muslim Conception of *Adab* and the Nature of Religious Fulfillment in Islam," in *Moral Conduct and Authority: The Place of Adab in South Asian Islam,* ed. Barbara Daly Metcalf (Berkeley: University of California Press, 1984), 57.

47. Quoted in Mohammed Ajmal, "A Note on *Adab* in the *Murshid-Murid* Relationship," in Metcalf, ed., *Moral Conduct and Authority,* 241.

48. For more on the training of Islamic scholars in North Africa, see Dale Eickelman, "The Art of Memory: Islamic Knowledge and Its Social Reproduction," in this volume; Eickelman, *Knowledge and Power in Morocco.* For Sufi training, see Trimingham, *Sufi Orders of Islam;* Gerhard Bowering, "The *Adab* Literature of Classical Sufism: Ansari's Code of Conduct," in Metcalf, ed., *Moral Conduct and Authority;* Ajmal, "A Note on *Adab.*"

49. Quoted in Edward Westermarck, *Ritual and Belief in Morocco* (London: Macmillan, 1926), 1:228.

50. Abdullah Hammoudi, "Authoritarianism and Cultural Models in North Africa," lecture delivered to the Center for Middle Eastern Studies, Harvard University.

51. Westermarck, *Ritual and Belief* 1:389, 228, 238.

52. Ibid., 1:198.

53. Westermarck touches on this opposition when he notes that Moroccans have told him "those who regularly say their prayers are weak, whereas those who never pray are strong as wild boars" (Ibid., 1:226).

54. The intermingling between religious hierarchy and that of the state is evident in the Arabic word *wali,* which was the title of the first Swati ruler. The term means "close to God," but was also conflated with *walaya,* "governance." Elsewhere in the region, saints and secular authorities are known by the same titles (for instance shaikh or shah) and, in India, the shrines of saints are called *dargah,* "royal courts." Saints, like secular rulers, also have territories, and

struggle with rivals over spiritual control over disciples. Such saintly power can easily shift to secular power, as occurred in Swat and Morocco.

55. M. E. Combs-Schilling, *Sacred Performances: Islam, Sexuality, and Sacrifice* (New York: Columbia University Press, 1989), 137, 132, 183.

56. Ibid., 143.

57. Ibid., 385.

Part 2
Symbol and Habitus

The Art of Memory: Islamic Education and Its Social Reproduction

Dale F. Eickelman

To complex societies, the study of education can be what the study of religion has been to societies variously characterized by anthropologists as "simple," "cold," or "elementary." Recognizing this potential, sociologists and social anthropologists have indicated a renewed interest in the study of how schooling, especially higher schooling, implicitly defines and transmits a culturally valued cognitive style, "a set of basic, deeply interiorized master-patterns" of language and thought on the basis of which other patterns are subsequently acquired.[1] To place such a concern in the context of more traditional anthropological interests, Bourdieu compares the cognitive style implicitly learned at the Sorbonne to that transmitted by Bororo elders. He sees the verbal maneuvers learned by students preparing for the *leçon* at the Sorbonne as furnishing "a model of the 'right' mode of intellectual activity" for the French context. The dualistic method of the *leçon,* in which the traditional "two views" on any subject are established, is subsequently applied to discussion of a wide range of intellectual problems to the exclusion of alternative, less culturally valued approaches. Bourdieu compares this cognitive style to Bororo cosmology as interpreted by dominant elders to form the pattern for the dualistic spatial layout of their villages and the distribution of their houses.[2]

Bourdieu characterizes the cognitive style learned at the Sorbonne and that of Bororo elders as equally "formal and fictitious."[3] His use of these terms carries significant implications for one of the principal problems of the sociology of knowledge—how symbolic representations of the world relate to the social order. For Bourdieu, there is no inherent relation between a specific pattern of thought and the social contexts in which it is found. Each may be in significant tension with the other, but never fully congruent. Bourdieu's notion of fictitiousness stands in sharp contrast to an earlier anthropological tradition that presumed a direct, one-to-one correlation between ideology and social action.[4]

However questionable such an assumption of correspondence may be when applied to "simple" societies, it is decidedly inadequate when applied to those that are complex, internally differentiated, and historically known.[5] Emile Durkheim clearly recognized this in his largely neglected *Evolution of Educational Thought,* which is why I refer to a renewed interest in the study of education. Durkheim's more widely known studies on education stress its integrative or "correspondence" aspects. The analysis in *Evolution,* in contrast, suggests a side of Durkheim's thought that has been largely ignored until recently because it was out of step with prevailing sociological currents.[6] In this study, Durkheim argues that changes in ideas of knowledge in complex societies and the means by which such ideas are transmitted result from continual struggles among competing groups within society, each of which seeks domination or influence. Durkheim considered educational systems, like other social institutions, to be tied to prevailing social structures but did not regard such ties as determinate. Thus, the forms of knowledge shaped and conveyed in educational systems are partially autonomous and must be seen in relation to the social distribution of power. Such assumptions began to be considered in the study of specific educational systems only in the 1970s.[7]

This chapter explores the alternatives to correspondence theory through description and analysis of the cognitive style of Islamic learning, the institutions of higher learning, and the social context of both, as they existed in Marrakesh in the 1920s and 1930s, just before the effective collapse of traditional educational institutions there. The relatively sudden decline of traditional higher learning in Morocco during this period makes it a particularly appropriate setting for considering the specific and variable links between concepts of knowledge, the institutional context in which such concepts are conveyed, and the adaptation to change of each of these elements. In particular, Islamic education in Morocco was, in some ways, intermediate between the oral and written systems of knowledge transmission. Its key treatises existed in written form but were conveyed orally, to be written down and memorized by students. This chapter considers how "intellectual technology," or the forms of transmission of knowledge in a society, shape and accommodate social and cultural change. By so doing, I suggest ways to refine further the debate over the "great divide" in modes of thought, or cognitive styles, between societies that possess systems of writing and those that do not.[8]

A complementary goal is to place the comparative study of higher education in a broader context than that of Europe and North America, the locus of most such studies.[9] With the expansion of European hegemony over most of the world in the last two centuries, non-Western institutions of higher learning have collapsed or have been eclipsed by their Western-based counterparts, so that comparative studies dealing with non-European institutional forms have necessarily been relegated to social historical analyses.[10] This study is no exception, but because it deals with a relatively recent period, it has been possible to complement printed and manuscript sources with intensive interviews of persons who were in the milieu of traditional learning in the 1920s and 1930s. These interviews have been especially important in the Islamic context. The principal written sources, including teaching licenses (ijazas) and traditional biographies and autobiographies of men of learning, follow highly stylized conventions that are, themselves, a product of Islamic education and severely limit information on how the educational process actually worked.[11]

Islamic Education: Recent Political and Historical Contexts

Although the exact timing of decisive European influence has varied, traditional Islamic education had been drastically altered in most regions since Bonaparte's invasion of Egypt in 1798. For this reason, it is important to specify the historical context in which such education is described. In some cases, such as Algeria, the colonial power deliberately destroyed the financial base of Islamic education so that all that remained of higher education by the 1880s were a few schools of poor quality. Graduates of such schools were ill prepared to assume positions of significance in colonial Algerian society, so Islamic education became increasingly regarded by Algerian Muslims as inferior to that provided in official, French colonial schools.[12]

In other countries, Islamic education was not as directly undermined, yet the establishment of European-style institutions, at first only for specialized military training, had an equally detrimental impact. Such schools quickly attracted more ambitious students and those from the more privileged social strata, leaving Islamic schools to students of a modest and usually rural origin.[13] To meet the threat of European-style institutions, many centers of Islamic learning were compelled to introduce such Western devices as formal curricula, new subjects, entrance and course examinations, formally appointed faculties, and budgets subject to external governmental control. Such "organization" *(nizam)*—the use of terms implying "reform" was deliberately avoided—was imposed upon the famous Azhar mosque-university of Cairo between 1872 and 1896.[14] As a means of weakening the political strength of Islamic men of learning ('alim; pl. 'ulama') in Egypt, the revenues from pious endowments upon which Islamic education depended were undermined earlier in the century.[15] Consequently, descriptions of "reformed" institutions cannot be taken as reliable indicators of the nature of Islamic education prior to "organization" or "modernization," although such studies provide insight into the contradictions involved in attempts at reform.[16]

In contrast, Islamic education in Morocco survived relatively intact until the 1930s. The "organization" of the Qarawiyin mosque-university in Fez occurred under French auspices in 1931, while the counterpart of the Qarawiyin in Marrakesh, the Yusufiya mosque-university, was subject to "organization" in 1939. Moreover, Moroccan students who went to Europe to study in the nineteenth century found themselves largely ignored and isolated on their return; the needs of the expanding precolonial government were met instead by students educated at the Qarawiyin or the Yusufiya, which led to a temporary reinvigoration of these institutions.[17] Similarly, the colonial administrations established by the French and the Spanish in 1912 were nominally based upon indirect rule that at first drew heavily upon the traditionally educated elite to fill the ranks of the judiciary, to implement the rural tax, and to act as scribes in other sections of the local and central administrations.

Despite the sudden decline of mosque-universities in the 1930s, many who were students in this period remained socially and politically active as what Mosca calls a "secondary elite"—those who allow the rulers to rule—through the 1970s. The social networks of influence and patronage formed, in part, by such persons have remained relatively intact. This is particularly true for Marrakesh and its hinterland, where former Yusufiya students continue to exercise an administrative, political, and economic hegemony.[18]

The Idea of Islamic Knowledge in Morocco

The cultural idea of religious knowledge has remained remarkably constant throughout the regions of Islamic influence. Writing specifically of medieval Islamic civilization, Marshall Hodgson notes that education was "commonly conceived as the teaching of fixed and memorizable statements and formulas which could be learned *without any process of thinking as such.*"[19] The italicized phrase raises the issue of the meaning of "understanding" associated with such a concept of knowledge. The "static and finite sum of statements"[20] conveyed by education constitutes the religious sciences, the totality of knowledge and technique necessary in principle for a Muslim to lead the fullest possible religious life. They also constitute the most culturally valued knowledge. The paradigm of all such knowledge is the Qur'an, considered literally to be the word of God; in Morocco its accurate memorization in one or more of the seven conventional recitational forms is the first step in mastering the religious sciences through *malakat al-ḥifẓ* (mnemonic possession).[21] The memorization of key texts, just as the Qur'an is memorized, is also the starting point for the mastery of the religious sciences. To facilitate this task, most standard treatises are written in rhymed verse.

Historians and sociologists have tended to take at face value the ideological claim of the fixed nature of religious knowledge in Islam. Consequently, little attention has been given to how such a system of knowledge is affected by its mode of transmission and its linkages with other aspects of society. Educated Muslims consider all bodies of knowledge that elucidate the *al-klām al-'alī* (high words) of the Qur'an and the traditions of the Prophet to comprise the religious sciences. Normatively speaking, the emphasis in transmitting this knowledge is conservational, especially in Morocco. Even Ibn Khaldun (d. 1406) noted that the role of memory was stressed more in Morocco than elsewhere in the Islamic Middle East. It took sixteen years to acquire sufficient mastery of texts to teach on one's own in Morocco, owing to the necessity of memorization, but only five in Tunis.[22] Thus it is not surprising that contemporary Muslim and European scholars expressed extreme opinions about Moroccan traditional education. Writing with a first-hand knowledge of the Qarawiyin of sixty years ago, a distinguished French historian and Arabist noted the "astonishing" (to a European) domestication of the memory involved in Islamic higher education. He claimed that it deadened the student's sense of inquiry to the point that the knowledge and comportment of twentieth-century men of learning could be assumed "without fear of anachronism" to be exact replicas of four centuries earlier.[23] Another Western scholar has written of the "stifling dullness" of Islamic education[24] and a third, perhaps indicating an impatience with the unfamiliar principles upon which traditional Islamic education is based, claims that it "defies all [sic] pedagogical technique."[25] Islamic education fares no better in the hands of Western-educated Muslims, who write of it as a "purely mechanical, monotonous form of study."[26]

Two general propositions can be made concerning the form of Islamic knowledge. The first is that an intellectual tradition emphasizing fixity and memory, as is characteristic of many traditions of religious knowledge, can still be capable of considerable flexibility. In practice, there is considerable variation throughout the Islamic world concerning the exact bodies of knowledge to be included in the religious sciences. Even during the "classical" period of Islamic civilization, learning could be characterized as "prismatic": interpretation and elaboration of the religious sciences shifted constantly.[27] Once this shifting is recognized, the circumstances under which redefinitions of the "proper" scope of the religious sciences can be recognized. The hyperbolic assertion of an earlier generation, that Islamic education deadens all sense of inquiry, is hard to reconcile with such transformations. In Morocco, for example, grammar, rhetoric, jurisprudence, and, to a lesser extent, the prophetic tradition (hadith) were among the most central of the religious sciences until the early twentieth century, although subjects that began to be emphasized (or reemphasized) after the 1920s as components of a "new" orthodoxy included Qur'anic interpretation (tafsir), theology (*kalam*), and a knowledge of pre-Islamic and early Islamic poetry. If the compass of religious studies appears unduly narrow, it is no more so than the products of the English public school in the Victorian era, with its emphasis on Greek and Latin, or the result of a classical training in France. Former students of the Yusufiya and the Qarawiyin have become scholars, but also politicians and ministers of state who have played important roles in Morocco and merchants and financiers capable of dealing with contemporary economic and entrepreneurial activities.

The second proposition is that the cognitive style associated with Islamic knowledge is tied closely to popular understandings of Islam in Morocco and has important analogies in nonreligious spheres of knowledge. This formal congruence has enhanced the popular legitimacy of religious knowledge and its carriers in Morocco, but, at the same time, it has limited the pace and range of change in Islamic education and the ways in which changes are perceived. Thus, the notion of Islamic law (shra') encompasses religious law in its jural sense and law as a code for personal conduct. A Moroccan judge (qadi) explained this by drawing two parallel lines on a sheet of paper—another word derived from the same root as shra' means "path"—saying that everything within the two lines was shra'. All activities not within the body of knowledge encompassed by the lines constituted innovation (*bida'*). Some innovations are contrary to Islamic law, but others, such as religious brotherhoods or certain governmental reforms, are tolerated as long as they do not contradict the principles of Islamic law. Most Moroccans do not possess exact knowledge of this law but assume that religious knowledge is fixed and knowable and that it is known by men of learning.[28]

Ma'rifa is the term used to refer to knowledge not encompassed by the religious sciences; it includes knowledge related to commerce and crafts, including music and oral poetry. In form, these have significant parallels with the religious sciences and are also presumed to consist in fixed, memorizable truths. As Clifford Geertz notes, popular oral poetry in North Africa takes this shape, just as effective public speech involves both the skillful invocation of Qur'anic phrases and the mundane but memorizable stock of knowledge drawn from poetry and proverbs.[29] A further parallel lies in the model for the transmission of knowledge. The religious sciences throughout the Islamic world are thought to be transmitted traditionally through a quasi-genealogical chain of authority that descends from master or teacher (shaykh) to student (talib) to insure that the knowledge of earlier generations is passed on intact. Knowledge of crafts is passed from master to apprentice in an analogous fashion, with any knowledge or skill acquired independent of such a tradition regarded as suspect.

These analogues suggest how Islamic education is to be evaluated. Marshall Hodgson, by characterizing it as not involving "any process of thinking as such," implicitly evaluated Islamic education in terms of Western pedagogical expectations. In contrast, the measure of "understanding" appropriate to Islamic knowledge is its use, often creative, in wider social contexts than the milieu of learning itself or by the abstract manipulation of memorized materials in "classroom" situations.

The Qur'anic Presence: The Social Paradigm
of Understanding

Any analysis of Islamic education must convey a sense of how many were educated and who they were. Until 1930, literacy in rural Morocco necessarily implied religious schooling, although schooling did not necessarily imply literacy. The first years of study consisted of memorizing and reciting the Qur'an; only at later stages did students learn to read and write, and then usually outside the context of the mosque school. Contemporary literacy is difficult to measure, let alone the literacy rates of earlier periods, but estimates are essential to indicate the scale of traditional education. For the 1920s and 1930s, it appears reasonable to assume that no more than 4 percent of the adult male rural population was literate, allowing for regional variations, and perhaps 10–20 percent of the adult male urban population.[30]

Religious learning was popularly respected, yet Qur'anic schools were characterized by a high rate of attrition. Virtually every urban quarter and rural local community maintained a mosque school, as is still the case, with a teacher (fqih) contracted on an annual basis to teach and to perform certain other religious services for the community.[31] Most Moroccan males and a fair number of females, at least in towns, attended Qur'anic schools long enough to commit to memory a few passages of the Qur'an, but the majority left before they acquired literacy, and few students remained the six to eight years required to memorize the entire Qu'ran.[32]

The formal features of Qu'ranic schools have been frequently described,[33] although the consequences of their form of pedagogy on modes of thought have only begun to be critically explored.[34] The Islamic emphasis upon memory, for example, is not unique, as has been implied by some scholars: elaborate mnemonic systems existed in classical Greece and Rome to facilitate memorization through the association of material with "memory posts," visual images like the columns of a building or places at a banquet table.[35] Accompanying such techniques was the notion that mnemonic knowledge was "purer" than that communicated through writing.[36] What is remarkable about memory in the context of Islamic education in Morocco is not the performance of "prodigious" mnemonic feats—such feats were fully paralleled in Europe.[37] It is the insistence of former students that they employed no devices to facilitate memorization. Nonetheless, these same students recall visualizing the shape of the letters on their slates and the circumstances associated with the memorization of particular verses and texts. Wagner suggests that patterns of intonation and rhythm systematically serve as mnemonic markers.[38]

A typical fqih (in this context, Qur'anic teacher) had between fifteen and twenty students, ranging in age from four to sixteen. No printed or manuscript copies of the Qur'an were used in the process of memorization, partly because of the lack of printed or manuscript books, but also because of the cultural concept of learning implicit in Islamic education. Each morning the fqih wrote the verses to be memorized on each student's wooden slate (luh), and the student then spent the day memorizing the verses by reciting them out loud and reciting the verses learned the previous day. Memorization was incremental, with the recitation of new material added to that already learned (i.e., a, then a, b, then a, b, c,). Students were not grouped into classes based on age or progress in memorization.

Two features associated with Islamic education are its rigorous discipline and its lack of explicit explanation of memorized material. Both these features are congruent with the essentially fixed concept of knowledge that is at the base of Islamic education and, in the Moroccan context, the associated concept of 'qal (reason), which is conceived as man's ability to discipline his nature in accord with the arbitrary code of conduct laid down by God and epitomized by acts of communal obedience, such as the fast of Ramadan.[39] A firm discipline in the course of learning the Qur'an was thus regarded as an integral part of socialization. This popular attitude toward learning is one reason why it is inappropriate to view Islamic education as a "high tradition" grafted onto or independent of a more implicit understanding of religion and society, as was the case with an earlier tradition of scholarship.

When a father handed his son over to a fqih, he did so with the formulaic phrase that the child could be beaten. Such punishment was considered necessary for accurate Qur'anic recitation. Former students explained that the fqih (or the student's father, when he supervised the process of memorization) was regarded as the impersonal agency of punishment, which, like the unchanging word of God itself, was merely transmitted by him.[40] Students were also told that the parts of their bodies struck in the process of Qur'anic memorization would not burn in hell. The same notion applied to the beatings apprentices received from craftsmen (m'allmin dyal l-harfa), including musicians, since music is popularly considered to be a craft.[41] In practice, students were slapped or whipped only when their attention flagged or when they repeated errors, although the children of high-status fathers appear to have been struck much less frequently than other children.

Former students emphasize that they asked no questions concerning the meaning of Qur'anic verses, even among themselves, and it did not occur to them to do so. Their sole activity was memorizing proper recitation. Because the grammar and vocabulary of the Qur'an are not immediately accessible to speakers of colloquial Arabic, and even less so to students from Berber-speaking regions, former students readily admitted that they did not comprehend what they were memorizing until fairly late in their studies.[42] *Fahm* (understanding) was not measured by ability explicitly to "explain" particular verses, since explanation was considered a science to be acquired through years of study of the exegetical literature (tafsir). Any informal attempt to explain meaning was considered blasphemy and did not occur. Instead, the measure of understanding consisted in the ability to use Qur'anic verses in appropriate contexts.

In the first few years of Qur'anic school, students had little control over what they recited. They could not, for instance, recite specific chapters of the Qur'an, but had to begin one of the sixty principal recitational sections. Firmer control was achieved as students accompanied their father, other relatives, or occasionally the fqih to social gatherings, where they heard adults incorporate Qur'anic verses into particular contexts and gradually acquired the ability to do so themselves, as well as to recite specific sections of the Qur'an without regard to the order in which they had been memorized. Thus, the measure of understanding was the ability to make practical reference to the memorized text, just as originality was shown in working Qur'anic references into conversation, sermons, and formal occasions. Knowledge and manipulation of secular oral poetry and proverbs in a parallel fashion is still a sign of good rhetorical style; the skill is not confined to religious learning.[43]

The high rate of attrition from Qur'anic schools supports the notion that mnemonic "possession" can be considered a form of cultural capital.[44] Education was free aside from small gifts to the fqih, yet most students were compelled to drop out after a short period to contribute to the support of their families or because they did not receive familial support for the arduous and imperfectly understood process of learning. In practice, memorization of the Qur'an was accomplished primarily by children from relatively prosperous households or by those whose fathers or guardians were already literate. Nonetheless, education was a means of social mobility, especially for poor students who managed to progress through higher, post-Qur'anic education.[45]

The notion of cultural capital implies more than possession of the material resources to allow a child to spend six to eight years in the memorization of the Qur'an; it also implies a sustained adult discipline over the child. Many contemporary, Western pedagogical concepts treat education as a separable institutional activity, but this idea is inappropriate to learning in the traditional Islamic context. Students' fathers, elder brothers, other close relatives—including women in some cases[46]— and peers, especially at later stages of learning, were integrally involved in the learning process. All provided contexts for learning to continue, since formal education did not involve being systematically taught to read and write outside the context of the Qur'an, even for urban students from wealthy families. Students acquired such skills, if at all, apart from their studies in Qur'anic schools, just as they acquired an understanding of the Qur'an through social situations.[47]

A student became a hafiz (memorizer) once he knew the entire Qur'an; this set him apart from ordinary society even without additional studies. In the precolonial era, fqihs and students often were the only strangers who could travel in safety through tribal regions without making prior arrangements for protection. In larger towns throughout Morocco, students wishing to pursue "higher" studies began by sitting with the circles of men of learning and their disciples who met regularly in the principal mosques.[48] In rural areas, most advanced students continued their lessons at one of the numerous madrasas (place of studies) located throughout the country until the early decades of this century.[49] Often the level of learning at rural madrasas and religious lodges (zawyas) compared favorably with the education obtainable in major urban centers. They were an essential intermediate stage when Arabic was a student's second language. In some regions madrasas were only clusters of tents; others were village mosques with adjoining lodgings for the shaykh and his students—who were supported by gifts of food from villagers and tribesmen. Most students attended madrasas (often several in succession) within their region of origin. The three to five years spent in this all-male environment, partially removed from their families and communities of origin, was an intense socializing experience. Students frequently developed close ties with their shaykhs, who could introduce them to scholars elsewhere in Morocco, and with their fellow students.

There was no fixed progression of studies, although serious students advanced their knowledge of Arabic and memorized basic commentaries on grammar and jurisprudence.[50]

The Yusufiya: A Profile of Higher Islamic Learning

Traditional higher education was considerably more restricted in scale than Qur'anic education. In 1931, the year of the first reliable census in the French zone of Morocco, there were approximately 1,200 students in Morocco's two mosque-universities. The country's total population (including estimates for the Spanish zone of influence) was 5.8 million, so that mosque-university students constituted 0.02 percent of the population.[51] Since most students left their studies after a few years to become merchants, village teachers, notaries, and the like, only a limited number could claim to be men of learning.

The Yusufiya was smaller in scale than its Fez counterpart, and for most of its existence it tended to attract students and scholars from the hinterland of Marrakesh and the southern part of Morocco. Marrakesh emerged as a major center of learning in the twelfth century, when it rivaled Seville and Cordoba in Muslim Spain. In the following centuries, its reputation as a center of learning rose and fell with the political fortunes of the city itself. Thus, it thrived early in the nineteenth century and again became prominent with the sultan resident there almost continuously from 1895 to 1901. In the late 1920s and early 1930s, the period of immediate concern to this study, the Yusufiya contained roughly 400 students. Six to eight shaykhs met daily with students in ten lesson circles (*halqa*s).[52]

The Yusufiya, like the Qarawiyin, constituted an institution in the sense of a field of activity whose members shared subjectively held ideas and conventions about how given tasks should be accomplished. Although students and, to a limited extent, their teachers were transient members of the community of learning, most participated in the mosque-university milieu long enough to give it stability in terms of its participants and their relations with wider society.

The mosque-university's use of space indicates its lack of sharp separation from the rest of society. The activities of the Yusufiya, like those of its counterpart in Fez, were concentrated in space shared with the wider community for worship and other gatherings. Lesson circles of teachers, students, and onlookers met regularly in the Yusufiya mosque, one of the largest and most central in Marrakesh, as well as in smaller mosques, religious lodges, and at least one shrine, that of the principal marabout of Marrakesh, 'Abd al-'Aziz at-Tabba'. Only the hostels for rural students were reserved exclusively for student use.

The Yusufiya had no sharply defined body of students or faculty, administration, entrance or course examinations, curriculum, or unified sources of funds. In fact, former teachers related with amusement the efforts of French colonial officials to determine its "responsible" leaders and to treat it as a corporate entity analogous to a medieval European university. Although teachers did not act as a formal collectivity, several older and respected shaykhs served as informal spokesmen for their colleagues on various occasions. Because of their recognition by the wider community, these individuals also controlled the distribution of gifts given by wealthy or powerful individuals to the community of learning. The ability of certain men of learning to control such distributions and to exercise influence on other occasions did much to consolidate their reputations.

Activities of higher learning were integrally related to and limited by the values and expectations of wider society in numerous ways. Teachers were not formally appointed, although some held royal decrees (zahirs), which provided them with recognition and specified emoluments. Younger shaykhs began to teach after they were assured of the sponsorship of established men of learning. The lack of a formal appointment meant that shaykhs of lesser reputation had to be scrupulous in their comportment and in commenting on texts in expected ways. Recognition brought most teachers small stipends from pious endowments, in addition to occasional gifts of grain, olive oil, and clothing from pious townsmen, tribesmen, the sultan, and his entourage.

The publicly accessible activites of the mosque-university did not provide the full range of knowledge, including poetry, history, and literature, or training in the rhetorical style essential for men of learning. The formal speech of men of learning alluded to classical texts and used stylistic conventions far removed from ordinary speech—the rhyming of words and phrases and the use of a classicized diction that avoided colloquial or "common" ('ammi) syntax or phrases. Another quality prized by men of learning was the ability to compose verses for particular occasions, and these verses circulated constantly in oral and written form. Most such poetry drew upon stock formulas, which still had to be learned and were expected of educated men.

As in any educational system with diffuse, implicit criteria for success and where essential skills were not fully embodied in formal learning, the existing elite was favored. Moreover, the attribute of "student" did not form much of a basis for meaningful collective action, at least after the late 1920s. Students became known through their comportment and through acceptance by the community of learning, not through formal procedures. Each student had to discern independently the persons and ideas that were significant in the world of learning and create the necessary personal ties. Students from Marrakesh, especially those from wealthy or powerful families, had initial advantages in securing useful ties, for they continued to be enmeshed in their families' networks of kinship, friendship, and patronage. Since these students continued to live at home, those from wealthier and more prestigious families were in a position to invite shaykhs to their homes and to arrange for formal or informal tutoring. They often only irregularly attended the public lesson circles of the mosques and shrines.

Rural students were at an initial disadvantage. They were readily distinguished from townsmen by their clothing and what townsmen judged as their awkward comportment. In the 1920s, most students of rural origin shaved their heads and, as a sign of humility toward their shaykhs, did not wear turbans. This practice had virtually disappeared among younger townsmen, many of whom adopted the fez as a sign of modernity. Nonetheless, some rural students, especially those from families of learning, attained scholarly distinction by the most exigent urban standards. Two of the most influential reformist shaykhs of the early twentieth century in Morocco, Bu Shu'ayb al-Dukkali (1878–1937) and Mukhtar al-Susi (1900–63), were of rural origin, as were several other leading shaykhs of the Yusufiya.

Students acquired the knowledge and personal contacts necessary to achieve reputations as men of learning through three overlapping spheres of activity: lesson circles, peer learning, including participation in student literary circles; and sponsorship by established men of learning. The first and third spheres are familiar elements in accounts of Islamic education. Peer learning is not, since traditional Arabic sources have stylistic conventions that render them almost entirely silent on informal patterns of learning. Thus, when several Moroccan men of learning were asked to prepare autobiographies (tarjamas), they mentioned only learning derived from their shaykhs, in conformity with explicit assumptions concerning the proper acquisition and transmission of learning. Yet in interviews and discussions, the importance of peer learning was repeatedly stressed.

Lesson Circles

The spatial and temporal setting of formal learning is highly significant in suggesting the relation of religious knowledge to society at large. Almost all daytime lesson circles were held in the Yusufiya mosque and concerned the most traditional and accepted texts of jurisprudence, grammar, and rhetoric. They were conducted by shaykhs regarded as the most senior and conventional. Evening lesson circles were usually held in shrines, religious lodges, and smaller mosques. They tended to be devoted to less established subjects and texts and were generally conducted by reformist shaykhs and those of reformist sympathies, although a few were conducted by shaykhs who also lectured at the Yusufiya.

The conduct of lesson circles in public settings, where they were accessible to nonstudents at all times, indicated popular support of and respect for learning but imposed constraints upon what was learned. Leading shaykhs were treated with deference as they walked through the streets; their hands were kissed, and it was not unusual for gifts to be offered them by pious townsmen and villagers. Many merchants and craftsmen regularly attended lesson circles for the religious merit they felt such participation would bring, despite the fact that few could follow the classical Arabic. Nonetheless, their presence restricted the introduction of unfamiliar material, informal discussions between teachers and students, and anything that deviated from what was considered proper for such activities.

Propriety of form obliged shaykhs to adhere to the rhetoric of classical Arabic and to comment only upon the texts of others. The necessity to do so, no matter how urgent some considered the political issues of the day, constrained reformist and traditionalist shaykhs alike to stress that they spoke as transmitters of a fixed body of knowledge.[53] As Bloch has observed, at a high level of rhetorical formality, the content of speech and the order in which material is arranged are not seen "as the result of the acts of anybody in particular, but of a state which has always existed."[54] This is, of course, congruent with the paradigm of mnemonic (and popularly legitimate) learning. The same level of formality is apparent in the preparation of tarjamas. Their impersonal nature, where the third person is used both for biographies and autobiographies, reinforces the ideological conviction that religious knowledge is transmitted from generation to generation without alteration by persons or events. But while the words may be the same, meaning could shift, and the use of particular texts could be used to make a statement on contemporary events.

Shaykhs could—and did—introduce a wide variety of material into their commentaries, but the base of the educational process was still a set of texts that took years to memorize and even longer to use actively in discourse. The form of commentaries did not limit innovation in subject matter and adaptation to change, except that it deflected attention from historical and contextual transformations.

Lesson circles also conveyed the notion of the fixity of knowledge by minimizing active student contributions and by providing no checks upon what students understood. Only the student chosen as reader (*sarid*) took an active role, and as this task was rarely rotated, few students acquired this experience. The shaykh interrupted the student's reading only to correct errors of vocalization and to deliver his commentary. At the same time, such interruption could signal important points, and verbal emphasis could communicate more than a written text could convey. Thus, the introduction of printed texts after 1865 had minimal impact on the form of the lesson circles.[55] Students rarely took notes or made annotations in the printed texts and no questions were asked during the sessions. Former students explained that deference toward their shaykhs prevented them from directly raising any issues. Questions were raised indirectly, usually in private, as the shaykh prepared to leave, so as not to suggest a public challenge to his scholarship.[56] Informal contact with shaykhs to discuss textual matters was exceptional, so there were few opportunities for students to use the concepts or materials they sought to learn under the guidance of their shaykhs.

A parenthetical comment is essential here. There is no reason to assume, as many scholars have, that latter-day Islamic higher education in Morocco was a "decayed" remnant of earlier periods. Intra-Islamic differences noted by Ibn Khaldun for earlier centuries have already been mentioned. In Morocco, for example, the education process was never fully encompassed within the public activities of lesson circles, while in other countries lesson circles were sometimes arenas for long-term dialogues between teachers and students.[57] There were several patterns of Islamic education, of which the Moroccan emphasis upon mnemonic possession is but one realized form. This pattern has often incorrectly been seen as normative for the entire Islamic world.

Reformist shaykhs sought to introduce new material into lesson circles and to draw students into questioning the relation of Islam to contemporary society.[58] Former students spoke enthusiastically of the reformist shaykhs as liberating (*harrar*) them from commentaries on a narrow range of subjects that had remained unchanged for three or four hundred years. Reformist teachings, in fact, fit well within the prismatic nature of Islamic learning: lists of texts commented on from the late nineteenth to the early twentieth century indicate variation in both subjects and texts.[59]

The principal achievement of the reformers of the 1920s was to introduce material into lesson circles that men of learning had privately acquired in the houses of the elite: Qur'anic exegesis, theology, history, classical poetry, and literature (*adab*). The reformers argued that these topics were as much a part of the religious sciences as subjects that had been previously taught in Morocco.[60]

Despite reformist efforts to instill a new critical approach, however, knowledge continued to be legitimized by how it fitted within the established religious sciences. It also had to be conveyed in classical Arabic, limiting its accessibility to the same select few who participated in traditional Islamic education. Reformists did make some use of colloquial Arabic, an immensely popular innovation, but mostly on religious holidays.

Nonetheless, even reformist shaykhs lectured in expected places and times, primarily to give legitimacy to their teachings. The fact that they lectured only after the sunset prayers, a time set aside for the more peripheral religious sciences, and in religious lodges and smaller mosques signaled that their teachings were not as central as the religious sciences taught during the day at the Yusufiya. Yet within the restricted group of mosque-university students, reformist shaykhs enjoyed a considerable following, despite the opposition of more traditional shaykhs, who were frequently backed by the public and by political authorities. In the context of the lesson circles, however, the reformists did little to make their teachings accessible to a wider audience or to change prevalent understandings of the forms in which valued knowledge was conveyed.

Peer Learning

Peer learning has been neglected in the study of many educational systems, including Western ones, probably because it is informal. In Morocco, it provided what public lesson circles could not—an active engagement with basic texts. For most rural students, peer learning had special importance, since they were usually more cut off than their urban counterparts from informal contacts with their shaykhs, especially during the early years of their studies.

An interview with a retired judge, who was sixteen when he arrived at the Yusufiya in 1928, indicates the significance of peer learning. The qadi was from a rural family that had produced several judges and men of learning. One was an elder brother who had entered the Yusufiya several years earlier and thus was able to arrange introductions to his former teachers. At the house of one of these shaykhs, the qadi-to-be encountered the man who later became his roommate.

[My roommate] was a great man of learning who never spoke unless it was necessary. The Quran was always on his lips. He lived from the daily bread given rural students and from the daily eight francs he received for reciting [the Quran] at a mosque. I observed his conduct for some time. Finally, I spoke to him and said that I was a beginner [in the religious sciences] and wanted someone to live with me who could help me in my studies. So I gave him the key to one of my rooms and said it was his. I wanted nothing in return except the opportunity to speak with him about the books I was reading.

What I had been doing until I met him was memorizing books, but without understanding what I read. We worked alone for the first several months that we lived together. Then, although I was a newcomer to Marrakesh, students who had been there for years asked *me* to read with them. They saw that I was a serious student and wanted to study with me.

For seven years I lived with [him]. . . . This was the real learning that I did in my years at the Yusufiya. Of course I learned much at the lesson circles, but it was in reading texts with [my roommate] and with other students and in explaining them to each other that most of the real learning went on.

Knowledge of basic texts, however, was qualification only for modest positions as notaries or village teachers, though it was the terminal stage of learning for all but a few students. The additional knowledge essential for men of learning and the practice necessary for developing a competent rhetorical style took place in another form of peer learning—the small, ephemeral literary circles to which large numbers of successful students

belonged. These literary circles flourished with the rise of the protona-
tionalist movement of the late 1920s, but similar groups existed in earlier
periods and were not unique to Morocco.[61] Participants in the circles
read and discussed Moroccan literary magazines (e.g., *Majallat al-Maghrib*
and *Majallat al-Salam*), Moroccan newspapers and those of the Arab
East (banned by the French), books on subjects such as history (including
that of Morocco), geography, poetry, and their own compositions.

As was the case with other aspects of higher Islamic education, student
literary circles were weak in organizational form and dissolved frequently.
Most were relatively small, with a dozen or so members, and usually
met daily, after sunset prayers. They provided a training ground for
debating, speaking, and writing within the conventions of formal Arabic.
Relations among the members of the circles approached equality, so
participants took turns delivering speeches, which were subjected to the
criticism of the group.

One former student showed me a notebook containing a speech he
presented in 1932. His aim had been to rebut the charge that Marrakesh
was not a major cultural center because so many of its inhabitants were
Berber-speakers and because it had a smaller community of learned men
than Fez. In alliterative, rhymed prose, the student described Marrakesh's
physical beauty and its poets and men of letters, both past and present.
The speech enumerated the major marabouts *(salihun)* associated with
Marrakesh, confirming the lack of a sharp dichotomy in the early 1930s
between a reformed-minded Islam and a more popular form in which
local maraboutic beliefs were considered an integral part of Islam.[62]
Most of the speech consisted of conventional platitudes, but its content,
diction, and syntax reflected a style mastered only by those with traditional education.

Some literary circles, particularly those influenced by reformist ideas,
were concerned with undertaking political action for the benefit of the
wider Islamic community. Carriers of religious knowledge regarded themselves as spokesmen for Islam and were popularly regarded as such. This
was especially true after the Berber Proclamation of 1930, by which the
French formally extracted certain Berber-speaking regions of Morocco
from the jurisdiction of Islamic law courts. This had repercussions
throughout the Islamic world as a symbol of European colonial attempts
to weaken Islam. The influence of men of learning, sharply circumscribed
since the advent of colonial rule, reemerged temporarily with this event.
In some Moroccan cities, including Fez, protests against the proclamation

were overtly political and occasionally violent.[63] In general, however, protests took traditional and nonviolent forms—for example, public communal prayers as would be prompted by drought or other natural disasters. Many prayers were organized by literary circles. In Marrakesh, which was firmly under the control of its Pasha, Hajj Thami al-Glawi (1879–1956), demonstrations were rapidly quelled. Students with ties to urban and rural notables were warned by relatives to stay removed from the "troubles," but participants in several literary circles took action that could be construed as nonpolitical. One such action was for students individually to approach (to avoid suspicion of organized group activity) men who gathered each evening in the town's mosques and persuade them to recite the Qur'an in unison instead of separately, as had been the practice, to symbolize the unity of Islam.

The narrow range of political actions undertaken by participants in lesson circles suggests the restricted vision of public responsibility associated with the Islamic tradition of "gentlemanly" education elaborated in Morocco. The primary responsibility of a man of learning was to acquire religious knowledge and to use it in prescribed ways, not to attempt to alter the shape of society. Reformist Muslim intellectuals in North Africa, stimulated, in part, by European political dominance, challenged many aspects of Islam as locally understood, but they fell short of offering ideological and practical alternatives to the existing social order. Their teachings did not question the accepted popular notion of social inequality as a "natural" fact of the social order and they did not elaborate a notion of social responsibility to men of learning other than that of perfecting their understanding of religious knowledge and communicating it to relatively restricted circles.[64]

Sponsorship

Students remained in the milieu of learning for as long as they chose or were able to. Just as there were no formal markers of entry, there were none upon leaving it. Only a few managed to acquire reputations as men of learning. There were no explicit criteria by which recognition could be achieved, so education could not assume the function of certification associated with modern Western institutions.

One means of signaling the completion of studies was for a student to ask each of his shaykhs for a teaching license *(ijaza)*, which specified the texts or subjects studied. Throughout the Islamic world, teaching licenses were only as good as the reputations of their writers and the facility with which their bearers could use them.[65] As one former student remarked, one sought ijazas from those shaykhs who "had God's blessings in the religious sciences and feared God the most, those who were older and more powerful and who always had their hands kissed in the street." In practice, many students did not ask for such documents; since many were prepared as courtesies for educated rural notables, claiming not to possess one could sometimes be a mark of higher status. What counted was sponsorship, the active recognition of established men of learning, and the use to which an individual could put such ties with other persons of influence.

Since the world of learning was not a closed community, support in nonlearned environments could also be decisive in acquiring a reputation for learning. Moroccan men of learning in the 1930s had significant ties to each other, created in part through common schooling, but these ties were not exclusive and overlapped with social bonds created on other bases. In Morocco, men of learning constitute a social type rather than a group with sharply defined boundaries or one that acts collectively.[66]

The majority of students rarely used religious knowledge in more than an iconic fashion, a marker of participation in the milieu of learning. When I asked former students about the fact that most left their studies prior to acquiring scholarly recognition, there was often a formal expression of regret but no indication of failure. Most emphasized the opportunities the years at the mosque-university created for ties to persons within and without the community of learning, which were often useful in facilitating subsequent commercial, political, and entrepreneurial activities. The mention of such ties was frequent enough to suggest a shared conception of career, although not in the occupational sense of the term. When I asked former students their goals at the time of their studies, most replied that they were concerned primarily with the acquisition of the religious sciences. This was to be expected, given the cultural emphasis upon such knowledge. Acquisition of religious knowledge also implied participation in social networks with persons of different backgrounds and from other regions of Morocco, and thus with access to a wide range of centers of power. No other preparation, except perhaps association with the sultan's entourage, enabled a person to acquire such a wide range of potential associations. Knowledge of the religious sciences was, of course, essential at some level in order to function as a qadi, a notary, a scribe with the government, or a teacher in the religious sciences. Acquiring such knowledge provided the consociational base from which a wide range of extralocal political, economic, and social activities could be undertaken, so long as there were no major alternatives to Islamic higher education.

Knowledge and Social Change

When alternatives to the mosque-university developed on a wide scale in the 1930s, higher Islamic education quickly lost its vitality. Its decline can be attributed to a relatively straightforward conjunction of events. First was the French "organization" of Morocco's two principal mosque-universities, the Qarawiyin in 1931 and the Yusufiya in 1939, ostensibly undertaken to improve the standard of learning. These "reforms" came in the wake of major protests against French rule, in which the mosque-universities had played a role.[67] Those faculty members who were retained became salaried civil servants subject to governmental control and they suffered a significant loss of popular prestige. Gifts by pious Moroccans diminished. After 1931, several of the Qarawiyin's leading teachers left for other parts of the country, including the Yusufiya or to mosques in smaller towns. A similar exodus occurred from the Yusufiya when organization was imposed upon it in November, 1939.

A second major factor was the increasing availability of government schools run by the French, which siphoned off the children of Morocco's elite beginning in the 1930s. In a context analogous to what Colonna has described for Algeria, Islamic institutions became the least attractive option to Moroccan Muslims in colonial society. Moreover, significant numbers of Moroccan graduates from French schools began, by the 1930s, to fill posts in the colonial bureaucracy and to play key roles in colonial society that remained open to Muslims. Study in a mosque-university ceased to be an effective means of social advancement.

The consequence was that mosque-universities were attended primarily by poor students of rural origin. Contemporary estimates at the Qarawiyin indicate the significance of these changes. In 1924, 300 students were from Fez, whereas 419 were from outlying and predominantly rural regions.[68] By 1938, only 100 students were from Fez, and 800 were of rural origin.[69] Although exact figures are unavailable for Marrakesh, former students estimate that there were about 400 students at the Yusufiya in the early 1930s, of whom approximately 150 were from Marrakesh. The number of urban students had dropped to a handful by 1935, and almost none were from prominent rural or urban families. Islamic education began to be regarded with disdain, even by those who took part in it during earlier periods, because of its lack of "analysis and synthesis" in style and content.[70] Such criticism implicitly compared the style and content of Islamic education with that presumably available in schools provided by the French.

In the decade after colonial rule was established, concerned members of the Moroccan bourgeoisie sought to meet the challenge of French-controlled education through the establishment of Free Schools that adopted some European subjects and pedagogical methods to provide an alternative education, primarily in Arabic.[71] As important as such schools were as an ideological expression of those who backed them, their long-term educational impact was minimal. Moroccan notables saw their children's futures increasingly tied to the training and certification that only French schools could provide.

A more interesting, and difficult, question is why the collapse of Islamic higher education had no direct impact on the paradigm of valued knowledge as fixed and memorizable, especially since, in principle, the social reproduction of such knowledge was necessary for making the word of God available for the guidance of the Islamic community. Why did the effective collapse not result in any major action, or reaction, on the part of men of learning? The answer to this question lies in the relation of knowledge to society in the Moroccan context and the way value is placed on various bodies of knowledge and its carriers.

Traditionally educated Moroccan intellectuals were acutely aware of the major transformations their society was experiencing as a consequence of colonial rule. In practical terms, the principal response of reformist intellectuals to perceived crisis was to seek to persuade those who possessed an understanding of the religious sciences to accept the "new orthodoxy" they advocated. Yet many of these individuals sent their sons and daughters to French-run schools rather than to mosque-universities or even the independent Free Schools. A partial explanation for the inaction of men of learning is that colonial rule posed no direct threat to their interests. As with their nineteenth-century counterparts in India,[72] Morocco's men of learning concluded that there was little effective resistance they could make against foreign rule, and they sought instead to maintain their religious integrity. From the inception of the protectorate, the French sought to engage elite support by assimilating them into a system of indirect rule, a system that functioned with a high measure of success in the first two decades of colonial rule, especially under Lyautey.[73] Unlike neighboring Algeria, where the influence of the traditional elite was systematically destroyed, the Moroccan traditional elite was given administrative and political preferment, and their children were given access to French education. Thus, despite radical political and economic transformations, the elite managed to confer its status on their descendants.[74]

Taken by itself, however, an explanation based on material interests is insufficient. It does not account for the continued respect enjoyed by men of learning. In a study of rural notables in Morocco in the 1960s, a French scholar notes the preponderant influence of traditional men of learning who, in spite of their "confused ideal of social justice,"[75] retained popular support while a "modern" bureaucratic elite exposed to Western education and influenced by cosmopolitan Western life-styles failed to do so.

The ideal of social justice held by traditional men of learning is confused only when analysts consider it in Western terms. Two implicit premises of the worldview of traditionally educated Moroccan intellectuals have already been cited—the notion of inequality as a natural fact of the social order and a highly restricted sense of social responsibility. These premises are most effectively delineated through comparison with two contrasting traditions of "gentlemanly" education, English and Chinese, which also embodied notions of social inequality. Students of public schools in Victorian England were inculcated with a sense of equity or "fair play," leadership, and public spirit, which had its analogues in political life, whereas in China men of learning were thought to possess moral virtues that suited them for positions of authority.[76] There was no expectation in Morocco, however, that men of learning should constitute an ideological vanguard, even in times of major social upheaval. They could serve as iconic expressions of popular sentiment on occasion, but there was no tradition to shape these sentiments or guide the direction of social change.

The affinity between popular conceptions of valued knowledge and those conveyed in Islamic education explain their continuing authority and the legitimacy, at least in principle, of its carriers. What of the limitations of form of Islamic knowledge and its associated intellectual technology? The notion that the most valued knowledge was fixed by memorization limited the number of texts any individual could "possess" thoroughly, as did the notion that valued knowledge was accessible to all men of learning. New materials could be introduced by men of influence in the area of religious learning, but there was no value placed upon specialization of knowledge, and innovations suggested by outsiders had little chance of taking hold. As a result, innovations of content suffered the same fate as innovations in societies without developed traditions of writing. This tradition stifled the proliferation of specialized knowledge, such as the attempt to introduce mathematics and military technology in the nineteenth century.[77] While the body of valued knowledge shared by men of learning shifted over time, it did not become more elaborate in form. There was no room in this tradition for disciplinary competencies to be carved out and elaborated by smaller, specialized communities. Moreover, since knowledge was considered fixed and memorizable, the central ideological problem was that of justifying any change of form or content in terms of its essential replication of past forms, instead of allowing an elaboration of form and content autonomous from accepted conventions.

Major changes in educational systems take a long time to have a widespread impact. The concept of knowledge as fixed and memorizable truths is still demonstrated by Moroccans who have memorized the Qur'an and its proper recitations, and associated texts are still mnemonically carried by the last generation of traditionally educated men of learning. Yet the number of individuals who demonstrate "possession" of such knowledge is rapidly diminishing. Older men of learning consider their younger counterparts ignorant of Islamic law, their knowledge limited to bilingual French and Arabic handbooks prepared by the Ministry of Justice. The accuracy of this appraisal is not at issue here, but the implication that younger judges and teachers are merely bureaucratically appointed specialists who lack the authority and sense of legitimacy that had been possessed in the past is a notion that appears to be popularly shared.

The shift of religious knowledge from that which is mnemonically possessed to material that can only be consulted in books suggests a major transformation in the nature of knowledge and its carriers. This shift may not be consciously recognized, just as many Muslim intellectuals believe that the French colonial experience had little impact on the belief and practice of Islam, which, from a sociological point of view, is decidedly not the case.[78] One consequence is that socially recognized carriers of religious learning are no longer confined to those who have studied traditionally recognized religious texts. A long apprenticeship under an established man of learning is no longer a prerequisite to legitimizing religious knowledge. Printed and mimeographed tracts and the clandestine dissemination of "lessons" on cassettes have begun to displace the mosque as the center for disseminating visions of Islam that challenge those offered by the state, particularly when the state exerts control over what is said in the mosque. In the modern era, those who can interpret what Islam "really" is can be of more varied social status than was the case when mnemonics were an essential element in the legitimacy of knowledge. The carriers of religious knowledge are now those who can claim a strong Islamic commitment. Freed from mnemonic domination, religious knowledge is delineated and interpreted in a more abstract and flexible fashion.

Epilogue

Writing of ties of dependence in feudal Europe, Marc Bloch wrote that new social forms were not consciously created by successive generations, but were created "in the process of trying to adapt the old."[79] Much the same could be said of "authoritative" religious knowledge in Morocco. In retrospect, my original, 1978 account depicted how traditional Muslim schooling in Morocco produced "hegemonic" forms of learning and thinking in the 1920s and 1930s and how alternative schooling provided by the colonial authorities displaced the authority and prestige of Islamic higher education and its carriers. However, like most accounts of religious learning and thinking written prior to the 1978–79 Iranian revolution, my 1978 account did not sufficiently stress the subsequent issue of where madrasa-trained men of learning stood with respect to the increasingly evident political activism of more recent years.

The primary goal of my original essay was to stress how ideas of Islamic learning and tradition were shaped by the contexts in which they took place, even as the carriers of this tradition maintained that they were transmitting it unaltered from earlier generations. My essay was intended as a first step toward making Muslim education amenable to comparative studies with traditions of learning elsewhere. Few accounts of the social contexts of traditional Muslim education and the influence of these contexts upon the transmission of ideas of learning and its cultural forms were available at the time. I referred to variations in classical and contemporary forms of traditional Muslim learning but elaborated upon its working in Morocco alone. Because of the emphasis upon the social context of learning, I emphasized the ordinary experience of students rather than the distinguished intellectual accomplishments of scholars at the pinnacle of traditional learning and deliberately discussed contexts more than texts and their internal logic.

My *Knowledge and Power in Morocco* (1985) further explored the social context of religious learning, using the biography of a provincial judge I came to know in the late 1960s as a narrative vehicle. The biographical form seemed appropriate because it allowed me to combine short essays on related themes—the implementation and disintegration of colonial rule, the role of "intellectuals" in traditional societies, taxation, responses to drought and famine, learning and literacy in rural and tribal societies, ideas of social justice, and family support for religious studies—that conveyed the world of traditional learning in rural Moroccan society more effectively than separate monographs. In the introduction to *The Death of Woman Wang,* Spence explains that he deliberately sought to keep his narrative "rural and local" as well as biographical to counter the "almost inevitable" depersonalization that occurs in describing peoples and localities remote in time and space.[80] A desire to offset the similarly depersonalized and decontextualized accounts of traditional Islamic learning, a tendency offset only recently in studies of legal and religious scholarship, provided added motivation to approach the subject through biography.[81] Possibly for similar reasons, Mottahedeh wrote a biography of a fictionalized mullah, Ali Hashemi, to convey the world of Iranian religious learning,[82] and Mardin used the vehicle of a biography to convey the role of religion in Turkey.[83]

Since the late 1960s in Morocco, but earlier elsewhere in the Muslim world, a text-based religious activism, in which religious authority is no longer based on the mastery of traditional texts but upon a commitment to religious and political activism, has become increasingly evident. This development is noted in the 1978 article and again in my subsequent book but is not highlighted as the dominant contemporary trend.[84] In a book also published in 1985, Mottahedeh is similarly uncertain about depicting the future of Iranian religious learning or alternative codes of knowledge.[85]

Today I would place greater stress on how modern mass education, not just colonial state schools, constitutes a significant break with earlier forms of traditional religious learning. While Islam, on the one hand, is considered to transcend all spheres of life, on the other hand, it is taught as one subject among many in modern schooling and is increasingly considered a discrete, "objectified" body of thought and doctrine. Indeed, fundamentalist thinkers such as Sayyid Qutb use terms such as *curriculum* (*minhaj*) to describe Muslim doctrine, which they see as a system of closely related beliefs and principles. Such a pervasive notion of system is a new element in modern religious thought. Despite the claims of Sayyid Qutb and others that Islam is self-contained, the notion of system facilitates the incorporation of outside elements into Muslim beliefs.[86] It also facilitates an awareness of internal differences within the Muslim community. In some parts of the Muslim world, catechisms are now being published to provide a glossary of key religious events, personalities, and theological terms so that Islamic doctrines can be "correctly" represented.[87]

Yet older, dominant forms of knowledge are not inexorably displaced by earlier ones. Their influence often continues in altered forms. Many elements of madrasa education continue to have contemporary significance. In Morocco, for example, the models of peer learning in madrasa education and in religious brotherhoods have been taken over by religious activists, often obliged to meet surreptitiously because of state sanctions against them. The monarchy, for its part, uses the Qarawiyin mosque-university to train senior administrators in the religious sciences in an effort to accord the state greater legitimacy, and religious lessons (*dars*), often with the monarch in attendance, are broadcast nightly throughout Ramadan.[88] In some parts of rural Morocco, wealthy Muslims sponsor small madrasas in which men of learning congregate to study religious texts and are fed and lodged at their patron's expense. Colonna has observed that in the Gourara region of southern Algeria, known for its tradition of religious learning, Qur'anic schooling in 1972, more than a decade after Algeria's independence, was still considered by the local population to be better adapted to their needs than the schooling provided by the state.[89] Madrasas in Iran now serve as places for training the political elite, a reversal from their role prior to the 1979 revolution, when many madrasa students were dropouts from the higher levels of secular education in Iran, where at each level they were progressively screened out by exigent entrance examinations.[90] Elsewhere, as in the Arabian peninsula and in an Islamicizing Pakistan, highly modified forms of traditional Islamic education serve to train jurists and teachers of the religious sciences for all levels of state education. When put to such uses, however, the popular authority of "traditional" scholars often declines rapidly, much as it did in an earlier era in Morocco.

"Great transformations" in ideas of learning occur incrementally. Only in retrospect can they be seen to constitute sharp breaks with the past. Mass education and the objectification of religious experience that comes with treating Islam as one subject in a curriculum alongside others may facilitate a decentralization of religious authority, shifting away from an earlier pattern of authoritative scholarly interpreters of tradition. Greater access to religious texts (or tracts) facilitates an awareness of variations in how authoritative texts are interpreted. Ironically, it also enables sectarian lines to be demarcated more clearly than they often were in the past. This objectification of religious experience, more than the rise of Muslim fundamentalism, may prove to be the key element in shaping new and emerging forms of religious authority.[91] This development is not unique to the Muslim world and appears to have its parallels in other religious traditions, including the Hindu and Buddhist.[92] What is certain is that key elements of the structure of traditional Islamic learning, often in unexpected ways, continue to inform contemporary ideas of learning and authority.

NOTES

The author thanks Thomas R. Trautmann, Deborah Hodges, and participants in the conference, "Dialectics of Tradition and Modernity in Muslim Societies," held at the University of Michigan, October 13–15, 1989.

1. Pierre Bourdieu, "Systems of Education and Systems of Thought," *International Social Science Journal* 19 (1967): 343; see also Michael Cole, John Gay, Joseph A. Glick, and Donald W. Sharp, *The Cultural Context of Learning and Thinking* (New York: Basic Books, 1971).

2. Bourdieu, "Systems of Education," 338–39, 350.

3. Ibid., 339.

4. See, e.g., Mary Douglas, *Natural Symbols* (New York: Vintage Books, 1973); Emile Durkheim, *The Elementary Forms of the Religious Life,* trans. Joseph Swain (London: Allen and Unwin, 1915); E. E. Evans-Pritchard, *The Nuer* (Oxford: Oxford University Press, 1940); Godfrey Lienhardt, *Divinity and Experience: The Religion of the Dinka* (Oxford: Clarendon Press, 1967); Marcel Mauss, "Essai sur les variations saisoniéres des sociétés eskimos: Etude de morphologie sociale," in *Sociologie et anthropologie,* ed. Marcel Mausse, 389–477 (Paris: Presses Universitaires de France, 1966).

5. Dale F. Eickelman, "Time in a Complex Society: A Moroccan Example," *Ethnology* 16 (1977): 39–55; Eickelman, "Ideological Change and Regional Cults:

Maraboutism and Ties of 'Closeness' in Western Morocco," in *Regional Cults,* ed. Richard P. Werbuer, 3–28 (New York: Academic Press, 1977).

6. Emile Durkheim, *Evolution of Educational Thought,* trans. Peter Collins (London: Routledge and Kegan Paul, 1977).

The fact that *Evolution* was the last of Durkheim's major works to be translated into English is indicative of its neglect, as is the omission of all reference to it in E. K. Wilson's introduction to the English translation of *Moral Education* (1973). See also Mohamed Cherkaoui, "Socialisation et conflit: Les systèmes educatifs et leur histoire selon Durkheim," *Revue française de sociologie* 17 (1976): 197–212.

7. See, e.g., Basil Bernstein, *Class, Codes, and Control,* 2d ed. (London: Routledge and Kegan Paul, 1977), 3:174–200; Pierre Bourdieu, "Cultural Reproduction and Social Reproduction," in *Knowledge, Education, and Cultural Change,* ed. Richard Brown, 71–112 (London: Tavistock Publications, 1973); Pierre Bourdieu and Jean-Claude Passeron, *Reproduction in Education, Society, and Culture* (Beverly Hills, Calif.: Sage Publications, 1977); Fanny Colonna, *Instituteurs algériens, 1883–1939* (Paris: Presses de la Fondation Nationale des Sciences Politiques, 1975); Michael F. D. Young, ed., *Knowledge and Control: New Directions for the Sociology of Education* (London: Collier-Macmillan, 1971).

8. Jack Goody, ed., *Literacy in Traditional Societies* (Cambridge: Cambridge University Press, 1968); Goody, *The Domestication of the Savage Mind* (Cambridge: Cambridge University Press, 1977); Goody, *The Logic of Writing and the Organization of Society* (Cambridge: Cambridge University Press, 1986); Goody, *The Interface between the Written and the Oral* (Cambridge: Cambridge University Press, 1987).

9. Lawrence Stone, ed., *The University in Society* (Princeton: Princeton University Press, 1974).

10. See, e.g., Max Weber, "The Chinese Literati," in *From Max Weber: Essays in Sociology,* ed. H. H. Gerth and C. Wright Mills, 416–44 (New York: Oxford University Press, 1958); Rupert Wilkinson, *The Prefects: British Leadership and the Public School Tradition* (New York: Oxford University Press, 1964); Wilkinson, ed., *Governing Elites: Studies in Training and Selection* (New York: Oxford University Press, 1969); Ronald P. Dore, *Education in Tokugawa Japan* (Berkeley and Los Angeles: University of California Press, 1965).

11. George Makdisi, *The Rise of Colleges: Institutions of Learning in Islam and the West* (Edinburgh: Edinburgh University Press, 1981).

12. Colonna, *Instituteurs algériens.*

13. See, e.g., Donald M. Reid, "Educational and Career Choices of Egyptian Students, 1882–1922," *International Journal of Middle East Studies* 8 (1977): 351, 357.

14. Pierre Arminjon, *L'Enseignment: La doctrine et la vie dans les universités*

Musulmanes d'Egypte (Paris: Felix Alcan, 1907), 13–18; J. Heyworth Dunne, *An Introduction to the History of Education in Modern Egypt* (London: Frank Cass, 1968), 395–405.

15. Albert Houran, *Arabic Thought in the Liberal Age* (Oxford: Oxford University Press, 1970), 52.

16. See, e.g., Michael M. J. Fisher, *Iran: From Religious Dispute to Revolution* (Cambridge, Mass.: Harvard University Press, 1980).

17. Edmund Burke III, *Prelude to Protectorate in Morocco* (Chicago: University of Chicago Press, 1976), 218. A number of excellent ethnographic accounts depict higher education in Morocco from the late nineteenth century through the 1930s. These include Gaëtan Delphin, *Fas, son université et l'enseignement supérieur Musulman* (Paris: Ernest Leroux, 1889); A. Perétié, "Les medrasas de Fès," *Archives marocaines* 18 (1912): 257–372; E. Michaux-Bellaire, "L'enseignement indigène au Maroc," *Revue du monde musulman* 15 (1911): 422–52; Paul Marty, "L'université de Qaraouiyne," *Renseignements coloniaux, supplément de l'Afrique Française* (November, 1924): 329–53; Jacques Berque, "Dans le Maroc nouveau: Le rôle d'une université islamique," *Annals d'histoire économique et sociale* 10 (1938): 193–207; Berque, "Ville et université, aperçu sur l'histoire de l'école de Fes," *Revue historique de droit français et étranger* 27 (1949): 64–117; Berque, *Al-Yousi: Problèmes de la culture marocaine au XVIIème siècle* (Paris: Mouton, 1958); Berque, "Lieux et moments du réformisme islamique," in Jacques Berque, *Maghreb: Histoire et sociétés* (Paris: Editions J. Duculot, 1974), 162–88; Muhammad ibn 'Uthman, *al-Jami'a al-Yusufiyya bi Marrakush* (Cairo: Economical Press, 1935); Mukhtar as-Susi, *al-Ma'sul* (Casablanca: al-Najah Press, 1961). Islamic education without competing institution forms survived in the Yemen until the 1950s. Snouck Hurgronje, *Mekka in the Latter Part of the 19th Century* (Leiden: E. J. Brill, 1931), 153, 212, provides a brief ethnographic account of higher education in Mecca in 1884–85. For a general survey of sources on Islamic education, see Jacques Waardenburg, "Some Institutional Aspects of Muslim Higher Education and Their Relation to Islam," *Numen* 12 (1964): 96–138.

18. Rémy Leveau, *Le fellah marocain: Defenseur du Trône* (Paris: Presses de la Fondation Nationale des Sciences Politiques, 1976), 93, 116. The terms *primary* and *secondary* elite in this context refer to function rather than to any organized group or class. The primary elite is today almost exclusively constituted by Moroccans bilingual in French and Arabic; see Gaetano Mosca, *The Ruling Class: Elementi di scienza politica,* trans. Hannah D. Kahn (New York: McGraw-Hill, 1939).

19. Marshall Hodgson, *The Venture of Islam* (Chicago: University of Chicago Press, 1974), 438; italics added.

20. Ibid.

21. This is the contextual meaning of the term among contemporary Moroccan

men of learning. Its meaning differs in other sociohistorical contexts. For instance, in psychological treatises of the 'Abbasid period the term implies "the faculty of memory." I am grateful to Roy Mottahedeh for pointing out this earlier usage. See also Franz Rosenthal, *Knowledge Triumphant: The Concept of Knowledge in Mediaeval Islam* (Leiden: E. J. Brill, 1970).

22. Ibn Khaldun, *The Mugaddimah,* trans. Franz Rosenthal, 2d ed. (Princeton: Princeton University Press, 1967), 430–31.

23. E. Lévy-Provençal, *Les historiens des chorfa* (Paris: Librairie Orientaliste Paul Geunther, 1922), 11.

24. Leon Carl Brown, "The Religious Establishment in Husainid Tunisia," in *Scholars, Saints, and Sufis,* ed. Nikki Keddie, 71 (Berkeley and Los Angeles: University of California Press, 1972).

25. Jacques Berque, "Lieux et moments," 167.

26. Nefissa Zerdoumi, *Enfant d'hier* (Paris: Maspéro, 1970), 196; also see Taha Hussein, *The Stream of Days,* trans. Hilary Waymont (London: Longman, Green, 1948).

27. Roy Mottahedeh, personal communication, November 19, 1973.

28. See Dale F. Eickelman, *Moroccan Islam: Tradition and Society in a Pilgrimage Center* (Austin: University of Texas Press, 1976), 130–38.

29. Clifford Geertz, *Local Knowledge* (New York: Basic Books, 1983), 94–120.

30. David Montgomery Hart, *The Aith Waryaghar of the Moroccan Rif: An Ethnography and History* (Tucson: University of Arizona Press, 1976), 183; Hildred Geertz, "A Statistical Profile of the Population of the Town of Sefrou in 1960: Analysis of the Census," in *Meaning and Order in Moroccan Society,* ed. Clifford Geertz, Hildred Geertz, and Lawrence Rosen, 470–87 (New York: Cambridge University Press, 1979); Kenneth Brown, "The Impact of the Dahir Berbère in Salé," in *Arabs and Berbers,* ed. Ernest Gellner and Charles Micaud, 107 (London: Duckworth, 1973).

31. Eickelman, *Moroccan Islam,* 97, 111–12; Eickelman, *Knowledge and Power in Morocco* (Princeton: Princeton University Press, 1985), 60–61; Fernando Martínez Valderrama, *Historia de la accion cultural de España en Marruecos (1912–1956)* (Tetouan: Editora Marroqui, 1956), map opposite 155.

32. Dan Wagner and Abdelhamid Lotfi, "Traditional Islamic Education in Morocco: Sociohistorical and Psychological Perspectives," *Comparative Education Review* 24 (1980): 241.

33. See, e.g., E. Michaux-Bellaire, "L'enseignement indigène."

34. See Dan Wagner, "Memories of Morocco: The Influence of Age, Schooling, and Environment on Memory," *Cognitive Psychology* 10 (1978): 1–28; Wagner, "Indigenous Education and Literacy in the Third World," in *Child Development and International Development: Research Policy Interfaces,* ed. Daniel A. Wagner, 77–86 (San Francisco: Jossey-Bass, 1983); Wagner and Lotfi, "Traditional Islamic Education," 238–51.

35. Frances A. Yates, *The Art of Memory* (Chicago: University of Chicago Press, 1966), 2–7.

36. James A. Notopoulos, "Mnemosyne in Oral Literature," *Transactions and Proceedings of the American Philological Association* 69 (1938): 478.

37. Yates, *Art of Memory*.

38. Wagner, "Memories of Morocco," 14.

39. Eickelman, *Moroccan Islam,* 130–38.

40. as-Susi, *al-Ma'sul,* xiii, 35–36, 101, 168; Hamidou Kane, *Ambiguous Adventure* (New York: Walker, 1963), 3–38.

41. Philip D. Schuyler, "Music Education in Morocco: Three Models," *World of Music* (Berlin) 21 (1979): 22–27.

42. Hart, *The Aith Waryaghar,* 85; John Waterbury, *North for the Trade: The Life and Times of a Berber Merchant* (Berkeley and Los Angeles: University of California Press, 1972), 32.

43. Geertz, *Local Knowledge,* 112–13.

44. Bourdieux, "Cultural Reproduction," 80.

45. Cf. Arnold Green, "Political Attitudes and Activities of the Ulama in the Liberal Age: Tunisia as an Exceptional Case," *International Journal of Middle East Studies* 7 (1976): 218–21.

46. See, e.g., Waterbury, *North for the Trade,* 31–32. Such notions have also hampered the study of education in Western historical contexts. For colonial America, see Bernard Bailyn, *Education in the Forming of American Society* (New York: Vintage, 1960).

47. Berque, "Lieux et moments," 167–68.

48. See Abdallah Laroui, *Les origines sociales et culturelles du nationalisme marocain (1830–1912)* (Paris: Maspéro, 1977), 196–97, 199–201; Kenneth Brown, *People of Salé: Tradition and Change in a Moroccan City (1830–1930)* (Cambridge, Mass.: Harvard University Press, 1976), 77. Like other technical terms, *hafiz* is subject to contextual variation. Among highly educated Moroccans, it refers only to the most outstanding scholars of any generation.

49. Auguste Moliéras, *La Marox inconnu,* vol. 1, *Exploration du Rif* (Paris: Librairie Coloniale, 1895) and vol. 2, *Exploration des Djebala* (Paris: Augustin Challamel, 1899); Michaux-Bellaire, "L'enseignement indigène," 436; Waterbury, *North for the Trade,* 30.

50. Berque, *Al-Yousi,* 12; Eickelman, *Moroccan Islam,* 39, 60, 222, 249; as-Susi, *al-Ma'sul;* Edmond Doutté, *En tribu* (Paris: Paul Geuthner, 1914), 269; Moulieras, *Le Maroc inconnu,* 1:76, 124, 187, and 2:49, 583.

Until the late nineteenth century, students also made collective visits to surrounding villages each year after harvest to collect donations of grain and animals. With these donations, students then camped together and feasted for a week or longer. This practice ceased with the disorders that accompanied increasing European penetration. The urban counterpart to these outings were the

"Feasts of Students," sanctioned by the monarch. See Eugene Aubin, *Morocco of Today* (London: J. M. Dent, 1906); Michaux-Bellaire, "L'enseignement indigène," 437; Eickelman, *Knowledge and Power,* 4–5, 88–90.

One of the most commonly memorized texts was the *Ajarumiya,* a concise treatise on grammar. The title is an adjectival form of the name of its author, Ibn Ajarum (d. 1324). Memorization began by writing the *Ajarumiya*'s verses on the lower part of a student's slate before he completed memorization of the Qur'an. Another text that was frequently studied was the *Alfiya* of Ibn Malik (d. 1274), a grammar of 1,000 verses, so compact that its comprehension requires elaborate commentaries. Finally, there was Ibn 'Asim's (d. 1426) *Tuhfat al-Hukkam,* a handbook of practical law with 104 chapters and 1,679 verses.

51. Daniel Noin, *La population rurale du Maroc* (Paris: Presses Universitaires de France, 1970), i, 30, 32. In comparison, French secondary education for Moroccan Muslims accounted for 505 students in 1924–25 and 1,618 students in 1930–31.

52. Burke, *Prelude to Protectorate,* 42, 59. The Qarawiyin had 700 students in the early 1920s, with roughly 40 lesson circles meeting regularly, given by 25 shaykhs.

53. Berque, "Lieux et moments," 174–75.

54. Maurice Bloch, "Introduction," in *Political Language and Oratory in Traditional Society,* ed. Maurice Bloch, 16 (New York: Academic Press, 1975).

55. Muhammad al-Manuni, *Mazahir yaqza al-Maghrib al-hadith,* pt. 1 (Rabat: Omnia Press, 1973), 207–13.

56. See also Delphin, *Fas, son université,* 28.

57. See, e.g., Hurgronje, *Mekka,* 190; Fischer, *Iran,* 61–103; Makdisi, *The Rise of Colleges.*

58. Ali Merad, *Ibn Badis: Commentateur du Coran* (Paris: Librairie Orientaliste Paul Geunther, 1971).

59. Delphin, *Fas, son université,* 30–41; Michaux-Bellaire, "L'enseignement indigène," 434–49; A. Péretié, "Les medrasas de Fès," *Archives marocaines* 18 (1912): 334–45; Paul Marty, "L'université de Qaraouiyne," 345–47; Berque, "Ville et université."

60. as-Susi, *al-Ma'sul,* ix, 167–68.

61. Delphin, *Fas, son université,* 27, 53; Heyworth Dunne, *An Introduction,* 13, 40, 66.

62. See Eickelman, *Moroccan Islam,* 211–30.

63. See Brown, "The Impact of the Dahir Berbére," 201–15; Brown, *People of Salé,* 198–206.

64. Merad, *Ibn Badis,* 193–227; Eickelman, *Moroccan Islam,* 126–30.

65. Cf. Heyworth Dunne, *An Introduction,* 67–69; Makdisi, *The Rise of Colleges.*

66. Brown, *People of Salé,* 75–81; Burke, *Prelude to Protectorate,* 218;

cf. Eickelman, *Moroccan Islam,* 89–91, 183–89; Richard Bulliet, *The Patricians of Nishapur* (Cambridge, Mass.: Harvard University Press, 1972); Roy P. Mottahedeh, "Review of Bulliet, *The Patricians of Nishapur,*" *Journal of the American Oriental Society* 95 (1975): 491–95; Mottahedeh, *The Mantle of the Prophet* (New York: Simon and Schuster, 1985).

67. 'Allal al-Fassi, *The Independence Movements in Arab North Africa,* trans. Hazem Zaki Nuseibeh (Washington: American Council of Learned Societies, 1954), 128–29, 133–35.

68. Marty, "L'université de Qaraouiyne," 337.

69. Jacques Berque, "Dans le Maroc nouveau," 197.

70. Berque, "Lieux et moments," 173–79.

71. John Damis, "Early Moroccan Reactions to the French Protectorate: The Cultural Dimension," *Humanioria Islamica* 1 (1973): 15–31.

72. Barbara Daly Metcalf, *Islamic Revival in British India: Deoband, 1860–1900* (Princeton: Princeton University Press, 1982), 87–88.

73. Daniel Rivet, "Lyautey l'africain," *L'histoire,* no. 29 (December, 1980): 17–24.

74. Rémy Leveau, "The Rural Elite as an Element in the Social Stratification of Morocco," in *Commoners, Climbers, and Notables,* ed. C. A. O. van Nieuwenhuijze, 226–47 (Leiden: E. J. Brill, 1977); John Waterbury, *The Commander of the Faithful* (New York: Columbia University Press, 1970); cf. Bourdieu and Passeron, *Reproduction in Education.*

75. Leveau, *Le fellah marocain,* 93.

76. Wilkinson, *The Prefects;* Max Weber, "The Chinese Literati."

77. al-Manuni, *Mazahir yaqza,* pt. 1.

78. Dale F. Eickelman, "Islam and the Impact of the French Colonial System in Morocco," *Humaniora Islamica* 2 (1974): 215–35.

79. Marc Bloch, *Feudal Society,* trans. L.A. Manyon (Chicago: University of Chicago Press, [1939] 1961), 148.

80. Spence, *The Death of Woman Wang* (New York: Viking Press, 1978), xi.

81. See, e.g., Brinkley Messick, "The Mufti, the Text, and the World: Legal Interpretation in Yemen," *Man,* n.s. 21 (1986): 102–19; Rosen, *The Anthropology of Justice: Law as Culture in Islamic Society* (Chicago: University of Chicago Press, 1989).

82. Mottahedeh, *Mantle of the Prophet.*

83. Serif Mardin, *Religion and Social Change in Modern Turkey* (Albany: State University of New York Press, 1989).

84. Eickelman, *Knowledge and Power,* 174–88.

85. Mottahedeh, *Mantle of the Prophet,* 390.

86. William E. Shepard, "Islam as a 'System' in the Later Writings of Sayyid Qutb," *Middle Eastern Studies* 25 (1989): 45–46.

87. Dale F. Eickelman, "National Identity and Religious Discourse in Con-

temporary Oman," *International Journal of Islamic and Arabic Studies* 6 (1989): 11–12.

88. Dale F. Eickelman, "Religion in Polity and Society," in *The Political Economy of Morocco,* ed. I. William Zartman, 91 (New York: Praeger, 1987).

89. Fanny Colonna, personal communication, 1975.

90. Yann Richard, personal communication, 1987.

91. Eickelman, "National Identity," 1–20.

92. Amanda E. Wood, *Knowledge Before Printing and After: The Indian Tradition in Changing Kerala* (Delhi: Oxford University Press, 1985).

The Muslim Judge and Municipal Politics in Colonial Algeria and Senegal

Allan Christelow

Outside Islam's cradle, the Hijaz, there has seldom been a completely Muslim society. Rather, Muslim communities have always lived, up to the modern era, side by side with non-Muslim communities in varying proportions, often, but not always, exercising political domination. The various phases of European domination, from the establishment of capitulatory regimes to protectorates, to colonization or annexation, undermined or destroyed Muslim political domination, but perpetuated and further complicated the plural character of these societies.

The plural character of predominantly Muslim societies and the doubly plural character of these societies under European domination have entangled the process of building modern states in the Muslim world in complex debates over whether and how religious communities could maintain distinct identities within an integrated national polity. In some independent states of Africa, in particular Nigeria and Sudan, the problem continues to be a source of intense conflict.[1] With Muslim migration to Europe, this type of debate has spread to the former colonial metropolises.[2] The key question has been law: to what extent can religious groups retain their distinct legal practices and still claim the same political rights as other members of the society? Is the right to be different—or the fact of being different—compatible with the right to equality?

The builders of European national institutions from the French Revolution onward assumed a negative answer to this question. National unity, they believed, needed the solvent of secular law applicable to all citizens. Modernizing Muslim statesmen always advanced the cause of secular law, though they usually hesitated to attack the shari'a's last stronghold in personal status law. The common practice of statebuilders became the axiom of Western scholars studying modernization in the Muslim world who, by and large, would concur with Bryan Turner's formulation: that Muslims have been unable to solve the problem of "how to get into the modern political world with one's spiritual credentials intact."[3] Even such apparent attempts to reverse the process of secularization as one finds in Iran or Sudan do not challenge the axiom of the incompatibility of legal difference and political equality. Islamic regimes have simply substituted their versions of Islamic law for Western model secular law as the solvent for legal unity.[4]

The wide applicability of the axiom has unfortunately discouraged both inquiry into the social and political dynamics that underlie it and the exploration of exceptions to the rule. Indeed these two tasks are closely interrelated, for the exceptional case can serve as a foil to explore the forces that generate the norm. This chapter is concerned with an exceptional case in the colonial Muslim world where the maintenance of separate Muslim legal status did not constitute an insuperable obstacle to political equality—the colonial cities of Senegal—and with a dramatic illustration of the axiom of difference/equality incompatibility, colonial Algeria. In Algeria, the deadlock over this issue helped set the stage for one of the twentieth century's most violent civil conflicts, the revolution of 1954–62.[5] In contrast, the early admission of indigenous Senegalese to the French political arena helped pave the way for a peaceful transition to independence and, moreover, helped to lay foundations for France's continuing important, postcolonial role in sub-Saharan Africa.[6]

The search for an explanation of why the same issue was resolved differently in Senegal and Algeria leads through the underbrush of local history to an investigation of the role of the Muslim courts in the politics of colonial municipalities, and it also leads to a study of the connections between law and another broad issue with a close bearing on political rights—military conscription.

The Contexts

The qadi, or Muslim judge, strikes one as an anomalous figure in the contexts of colonial Algeria and Senegal, areas better known for their mahdilike resistance leaders, quietist Sufi shaykhs, and strongly assimilationist colonial regimes. In both cases, there were, in fact, attempts to eliminate the Muslim courts—in Algeria in the 1880s and in the communes of Senegal in the early 1900s.[7] While the two court systems were rather different, it is striking that the eventual crises had similar dynamics and that both occurred just as indigenous urban elites were beginning to seek an active role in politics. A comparative study of the two cases should not only help to put the problem of Islamic law in colonial settings into wider perspective, but also shed light on the antecedents of some well-known, twentieth-century political developments.

To put the matter in theoretical terms, the problem of the Muslim courts might be viewed as one aspect in the development of a peculiar hybrid, the French colonial–Muslim city, in which the simultaneous presence of a French mayor and a qadi evokes two contrasting principles of urban social and political organization. The mayor represents the French conception of the municipality as a unified polity embracing different classes and interest groups, and the qadi the Muslim conception of the madina as a protected physical space shared by autonomous communities, each internally articulated by its religious courts and schools.[8] Because so much of the research on the colonial period in Algeria and Senegal has been based on central government archives and is thus focused on relations between the colonial state and its subjects, little work has been done in this area. Yet the conflict concerning the courts is crucial to understanding the origins of the Algerian revolution.

Of the municipalities in question, only a few—Algiers, Constantine, and Tlemcen—had strong elements of the classical Muslim city. The Senegalese communes and numerous Algerian provincial towns had been founded by the French. But these settlements, like the older Algerian cities, came to be regarded as part French, part Muslim, and the Muslim court was central to this conception. Whether honorably traditional or a colonial innovation, it helped give the Muslim urban community a sense of autonomy and identity, especially as long as that community was barred from effective participation in municipal politics.

During the Second Empire, French and Muslim urban systems managed to coexist without serious friction because the colonial state served as a mediator. But with the collapse of the empire in 1870 and the return to open electoral politics, the colonial state's effectiveness as a mediator was severely reduced, and, thus, the different communities within the colonial municipality had to confront more directly the incompatibility of their political and social conceptions. Additional pressure developed in the 1880s, when proposals for military conscription of natives in Algeria and the Senegalese communes were debated before the Chamber of Deputies. The reason for considering these proposals was France's acute need for military manpower in the wake of her defeat by the Germans.[9] Although these measures failed to pass at the time, it had become clear that assimilation could ultimately involve not just land, laws, and institutions, but also people, transforming them into full-fledged participants in politics.

The question was thus raised: How was the Muslim (or, in Senegal, the predominantly Muslim) community to be adapted to the colonial municipality? In Algeria, no viable, long-term solution was found. Rather, there developed a stalemate in which the principle of political equality was not explicitly denied, but the price for that equality—loss of social and cultural autonomy through loss of Muslim personal status— was all but prohibitive. The Muslim court crisis of the 1880s had an important part in establishing that stalemate. In Senegal, however, the adaptation was comparatively successful. The African urban community there was encapsulated by the colonial city, as that community found its place within the city as a competing interest group. The *originaires* of the communes were able to retain the Muslim courts for their personal status affairs, even though their citizenship rights were confirmed in 1915. But in Algeria, the question of religious law remained a stumbling block to campaigns for greater political rights up until 1945, in spite of military conscription.

The common elements of these two cases are numerous: the same political institutions were involved, the same legal theories could be invoked, the same issues—political rights and military conscription— were linked to the court question. In seeking an explanation for the disparate outcomes, one needs to look at differences between the court systems themselves, their social and economic settings, and at the political significance of the courts, both within the colonial state and within the colonial municipality.

Though the original Senegalese court, established in 1857 at Saint-Louis, can be considered an offshoot of the Algerian Muslim courts, substantial differences subsequently developed. By the 1870s, the Muslim courts in Algeria had acquired a supralocal character as part of a countrywide, centrally controlled judicial bureaucracy.[10] In Dakar—a city that formed its habits under the Third Republic—when the qadi first appeared on the scene in the 1890s, he was clearly marked as an electoral agent, beholden to the mayor. Thus, a central question is: How did the bureaucratization of the Algerian Muslim judiciary affect the dynamics of local politics?

In the analysis of social and economic settings, one encounters a problem. The territorial unit of Algeria and the enclaves of the Senegalese communes are incommensurable. However, there is a useful contrast within Algeria itself, between the old precolonial cities and the new provincial towns. The principal urban centers, Algiers and Constantine, were old and well-established Muslim cities, whose traditional elites of scholars and merchants stood as elements of continuity in their histories.[11] Under colonial rule, these two cities continued to serve as commercial and administrative centers and, in this respect, they were similar to Saint-Louis and Dakar. (The latter, however, lacked precolonial commercial and urban traditions.) Algerian provincial towns, especially those of the interior such as Sétif and Orléansville, began as military outposts and then came to serve as economic centers of an export-oriented colonial agriculture.[12] They resembled not Tours or Poitiers, but their contemporary creations in such places as Kansas and California, towns whose lifeline was the railway that carried their produce to market. In these towns, the Muslim communities were often smaller and of more recent establishment than the European ones.

Since northern Algeria came to be treated as a homogeneous political unit, the provincial towns, and the colon agricultural interests who dominated them, developed considerable influence and weight in Algerian politics. But in Senegal, the commercial and administrative centers of Saint-Louis and Dakar remained insulated from political forces in the countryside. The importance of these differences will emerge in the analysis of the two court crises.

Underlying Assumptions

Before venturing into the development of the Muslim courts in colonial Algeria and Senegal, it is necessary to review certain assumptions pertinent to the role of qadi that were held by the various parties involved, among both the colonizer and colonized.

As for the French colonial authorities, though the qadi might seem a stranger to their well-known assimilationist vision, one must realize that the formative period of Algerian Muslim judicial policy occurred during the Second Empire in France and was affected by the background of the Tanzimat period of Westernizing reforms in the Ottoman Empire.[13] General Faidherbe, who laid the foundations for France's West African empire in this period together with many of his fellow officers, saw Islam as a sort of intermediate step on the road from tribal anarchy to civilization. And since their chief enemies were rural religious leaders, they understandably saw urban Islam, with its emphasis on law and book learning, as a progressive force.[14] One might also point out that a certain conception of the qadi can harmonize well with Napoleonic ideas: the office was one that the state had not only the right but the obligation to fill with its own chosen candidate, and qadis could be seen as judicial bureaucrats, administering a uniform code of law.

It was after the fall of the Second Empire—which coincided with the decline of the Tanzimat reformers in the Ottoman Empire and the rise of Pan-Islam—that aspects of French colonial thought that are now more familiar to us came to have a considerable role in shaping both Islamic and judicial policy. One aspect was assimilation, the judicial corollary of which was the "unification of jurisdictions," in which Islamic or customary law was still applied, but by French magistrates. The other was a combination of Islamophobia and racism.

Colon politicians had often harped on the Islamic threat, sometimes out of deep-seated insecurity, sometimes as a convenient way to achieve a short-term end.[15] It was mainly among colonial administrators that an important new attitude began to take hold in the 1870s, as they came to see the promotion of ethnic consciousness, be it Kabyle or Bambara, as the surest way to stem the tide of Islamic fanaticism. Another way was to win the cooperation of Sufi shayks with administrative favors and financial rewards.[16] Ideologically, such policies were presented as separating religion from politics and promoting a local, indigenous Islam to counter the universalist Islam of eastward-looking urban dwellers.

Too, the late nineteenth century saw a widespread movement toward the codification of law and the establishment of secular national court systems, in Egypt and the Ottoman Empire and as far away as Japan. This surely had a marked influence on top-level Algerian judicial officials, as it did on those in Indochina. However, by the early twentieth century, serious criticisms of this trend were to develop among colonial administrators and jurists, who began to recognize their own shortcomings as experts on native law and language and to regret their having undercut the power of local mandarins.[17]

At the root of arguments both for and against codification and the unification of jurisdictions—which went hand-in-hand since French colonial magistrates could not effectively judge without a French-language code organized and indexed according to their own legal concepts—was a phenomenon common to the Afro-Asian world. In the last half of the nineteenth century, internationally linked domestic markets developed rapidly in many parts of Africa and Asia, giving impetus to legal rationalization in settings where traditional values, often running at cross-purposes to the development of the market, retained considerable force.

In short, by the 1880s, changing assumptions tended to create a climate of French colonial opinion hostile to the qadi, but there were important qualifications. Colon hostility tended to be shallow and instrumental, in spite of its vociferousness. And the arguments of French judicial officials in favor of the unification of jurisdictions were vulnerable at several points. Given the limited abilities of most French colonial judges, one could make the case that the qadis could more effectively reconcile the demands of an expanding market and those of social and cultural continuity. Moreover, the Algerian qadis could invoke bureaucratic rationality in their own defense. And by the 1890s, the infusion of Islamic modernism into the Algerian madrasas, the government-run, higher Islamic schools, would help consecrate the position of respectability preserved by the qadis through the Islamophobe onslaught of the 1880s.[18]

A basic element in the Muslim consideration of the judicial question was the conceptual division between politics and religion. Politics, it was understood, had to do with the exercise of physical constraint or compulsion, religion with moral constraint or compulsion. In the precolonial periods in both Algeria and the region of Senegal, one finds a distinction between men of politics and men of religion. Men of politics were those who bore arms and could compete for political office. Men of religion did not normally bear arms (except against those who stood outside the moral community of Islam) or compete for political office (unless they deemed it necessary in order to bring their society back into the moral fold of Islam).[19]

In early nineteenth-century Algeria, political and military affairs were dominated by the Ottoman janissaries, professional soldiers of mainly Turkish origin. At the local level, the Ottoman rulers delegated power to chiefs, the most important of whom were drawn, in the east, from the *juwad,* or military nobility, and in the west, from the makhzan tribes, the Duwair and Zmala.[20] The Senegal region, on the eve of the colonial conquest, was dominated by numerous royal dynasties, each in control of a limited area. They drew their military strength on the right bank (present-day Mauritania) from *hassani* warriors of putative Arab descent, and on the left bank (Senegal) from slave warriors known as *tieddo*.[21]

Religious affairs were the realm of groups with a specifically religious vocational identity, be they 'ulama' families in cities such as Algiers or Constantine, or clerical lineages or communities in the countryside, known by such terms as Sayyid, sharif, zawaya, or *torodbe,* or by the catch-all French term, marabout. Besides teaching, ministering to spiritual needs, and mediating disputes, religious groups often engaged in such peaceful and peace-requiring pursuits as commerce and agriculture. One might well ask if these pursuits made religious specialists better adapted than military ones for survival under the colonial regime.[22]

Against this background of a politics-religion dichotomy, the qadi took on an ambiguous coloring whether, as in much of Algeria, he was long familiar as a local judge or, as in Senegal, he was known more as a religious figure in the entourage of the king. Though he came from a religious group, the qadi was appointed by the political authority, and such judgments as he made could be backed up by force. He was bound to encounter political pressures and often to succumb to them, if only in the interest of his own survival. But a particularly influential and eloquent qadi could become a focus of opposition to the local political chief or a significant force in urban politics.[23]

From the point of view of the country dweller, the qadi was usually associated with urban ways and interests. He represented a potential threat to the authority of communal leaders, particularly when his justice proved attractive to the malcontents of rural society—women seeking divorce, slaves seeking freedom, or orphans seeking inheritance shares from miserly uncles. In colonial Algeria in the last half of the nineteenth century, with the development of the domestic market and the rapid extension of private ownership of land, the qadi came to be associated with the class of city and small-town notables who managed, in some cases, to prosper from these developments.[24]

Within the city, the status of different judges and the rules of jurisdiction were guideposts of intercommunity relationships. In Algeria, the precedence of the Hanafi qadi indicated the superiority of Turks and mixed-blood Kurughlis over the indigenous Moors, who followed the Maliki rite. The Jews had their rabbinical courts, the Europeans their consular courts, and the rural immigrants of various origins had *amins* or syndics. In Saint-Louis, the establishment of a qadi's court under the

French was to mark the recognition that the Muslims of that town were a distinct community, as opposed to being considered simply as dependents of French or mulatto residents. Within such a framework, a change of rules or judges meant a change in the ordering of relationships between communities and potentially a change also in the rules applicable to the circulation of goods and money between communities.

The First Phase—Official Recognition

The histories of colonial Muslim judicial policy in Algeria and Senegal have their beginnings in the mid-1850s, when the French, having secured their urban bases, were concerned with extending their domination into the rural hinterland. It was a time at which the pendulum of French colonial policy had swung well into the Islamophile phase of its arc. The French army was fighting in Crimea for the Ottoman sultan, and it was widely believed among French colonial officers that Islam would prove compatible with ideas of progress.

In Algeria, the French had only just succeeded in pacifying the regions to the north of the desert and, as many of the resistance leaders had also been religious figures, the French now saw a need to assuage the religious elite. The granting of wide powers to the Muslim courts was one way to do this, since it was from this elite that the judges were drawn.

The period from 1854 to 1865 was a turbulent one for Algerian Muslim judges, buffeted as they were by political clashes within Muslim society, by bewildering new standards and procedures imposed upon them by the administration, and by the hostility of the colons, who saw the qadi as an obstacle to easy land transactions.[25]

In the wake of a major rebellion in 1864–65, it was recognized that a stronger, more effective Muslim judicial system had to be organized to meet these pressures. The solution devised by a combined French-Muslim commission was embodied in a new decree issued in 1866. Its principal features were the bureaucratization of the Muslim judiciary—recruitment and promotion on the basis of examinations—and the centralization of jurisdictions. Many of the old tribal qadiships were eliminated, and with them the deadwood who, in the words of a prominent Muslim member of the commission, "were incapable of understanding the sense of expressions and turns of phrase in judicial documents, assuming they [could] manage to read them."[26]

The enlarged new *circonscriptions* quite often had their centers in new colonial towns that, though hardly more than military outposts in the 1850s, had by the 1870s begun to take over many of the functions formerly served by rural markets where the tribal qadis once held forth. For the majority of Algerians, the focus of economic and political life was to be in these new towns, where the qadi was the most visible Muslim official and a leading figure in what there was of a class of Muslim provincial town notables. At the same time, the rural tribal chiefs, who had once overshadowed and dominated the qadis, were fading in power and importance.

In Senegal, politics and commerce were often closely intertwined, and such was the case with the establishment of the Muslim court at Saint-Louis in 1857. In Saint-Louis, commercial relations with the hinterland were largely in the hands of Christianized mulatto traders, many of whom had close ties with various local chiefs in the Senegal valley. The Muslim population of the town was, to a large extent, composed of former slaves, who had been employed as craftsmen and laborers. With the abolition of slavery in 1848, many of them began working for wages.[27] But as the capital of an expanding colonial territory in a largely Muslim environment, Saint-Louis also came to support a small number of Muslim government employees, mainly in the capacities of interpreters or scribes. Literacy in Arabic, the language of government correspondence with the chiefs, was essential for these posts.

The Muslims of Saint-Louis had first petitioned for the establishment of a Muslim court in 1843, citing French Algerian policy (at that time, limited to formal recognition of the Muslim courts with no endeavor to intervene in procedure or organization) as a precedent.[28] Only with the accession of Faidherbe to the governorship in 1856 did the basic demand receive strong official backing. But the Muslim community's conception of the court clashed significantly with that of Faidherbe. The Muslims called for the election of the qadi and for an appeals court composed of twenty-two notables. One has the impression that the Saint-Louisiens wanted a qadi who would be a sort of Muslim mayor, and that their appeals court was a counterpart to the electoral assemblies of the French and mulatto residents of Saint-Louis and Gorée. (That of Gorée had precisely twenty-two members.) In contrast, Faidherbe had in mind the Algerian conception of a Bureau Arabe qadi, a loyal, progressive-minded judge, from an influential family, handpicked by the administration, handsomely salaried, and closely supervised, who would act as both judge and Muslim affairs adviser to the local Bureau Arabe officer.[29]

It was Faidherbe's conception of the court that prevailed, and so the nineteenth-century qadis of Saint-Louis were men like Ahmadou Hamet and Bou El Moghdad, who also served the government at times as interpreters or diplomatic emissaries to chiefs in the interior. It is worth noting that these men were drawn from the Qadiriyya brotherhood, the major rivals in West Africa of the Tijaniyya, brotherhood of Faidherbe's arch foe, al-Hajj Umar.[30]

The Qadiriyya connection was important with respect to the situation in southern Mauritania, a Qadiri stronghold, where the zawaya clerics chafed under the oppression and exactions of the dominant *hassani* warriors. It was the zawaya who supervised the gum collection and encouraged followers to carry on sedentary agriculture along the river banks. It was the *hassani*s who controlled the trading posts along the river, running the trade in collaboration with the mulatto traders of Saint-Louis. The major Bordeaux traders wanted to break the *hassani*-mulatto stranglehold on commerce, and to encourage the development of new crops, especially groundnuts, and they found a supporter in Faidherbe. The zawaya clerics stood as possible allies in the fight against the *hassani*-mulatto axis.[31]

In order to break the long-standing control of the mulattos in local Saint-Louis politics, Faidherbe reorganized the municipal government, appointing a French mayor and, along with two mulatto *adjoints,* a Muslim one, none other than the qadi.[32] So while the petition seemed to have called for a qadi as a leader of a Muslim community government, the one that emerged was closely linked to the colonial administration and owed his position in the municipal government to the French governor rather than to the Muslim community. These close ties of the qadi to the colonial state were typical of Algeria, but in Senegal that pattern remained limited to Saint-Louis.

Toward Elimination of the Muslim Courts

In 1865, al-Makki Ben Badis, qadi of the city of Constantine and a major figure in the restructuring of the Muslim judicial system in the late 1860s, lashed out against a proposal to codify Islamic law. He explained to the Conseil Général of Constantine:

Three sorts of things can be detrimental to man: an attack on his wordly goods; an attack on his physical person; an attack on his religion. The first is the lightest, the second intermediate, and the third most terrible of all, for it attacks what conscience respects the most.[33]

The basic thought expressed here is important to an understanding of how an articulate urban notable saw the early phase of the colonial situation. He valued above all his religion, here identified with Islamic law and hence the pattern of exchanges and relationships within the Muslim community. The denial of political power was resented, but seen as less important. Within the framework of the Muslim city, where there had been no municipal government in the European sense, but only communities articulated by religious schools and courts, the proposition is understandable. Men of politics were men of the state, standing outside the urban community, acting upon it, sometimes for the better, sometimes for the worse, but not acting in it.

Though such an understanding could be applied under the paternalistic regime of the Second Empire, in neither Algeria nor Senegal could it withstand the return to electoral politics after 1871. Politics now took on a new significance. The city could no longer be viewed simply in terms of communities, where magistrates played the key role in regulating relationships within and between groups. Rather, it now had to be seen in terms of constituencies competing for the control of municipal institutions. And state policy was no longer to be formed by the sort of ad hoc Franco-Muslim commission that had framed a new judicial policy in 1865, but in the national parliaments, seats that were the preserve of the Europeans, as was the position of mayor. Municipal and provincial council seats were dominated by Europeans (including assimilated groups, the Algerian Jews and Senegalese mulattoes).

There were, however, two important differences between Algeria and Senegal. Eligible Algerians voted for municipal council candidates in a separate college, and had no say in the election of the mayor and his deputy, a privilege reserved for French citizens. The Africans of the communes in Senegal voted for the same *listes* as the French and mulattoes, but were impeded in attempts to gain office by a combination of literacy requirements for officeholders and their own lack of political organization and skill. So while the Algerians had more representatives on the municipal council than did the African *originaires* in Senegal, they had fewer potential ones, since they could not compete for French-held seats.[34]

As electoral democracy was taking hold in France, so was thirst for *revanche* against Germany, and hence there was a need for military manpower to offset Germany's ever-increasing numerical superiority. France's closest and most assimilated colonies seemed a logical source for additional soldiers.[35] Already, in 1870, the Algerians had seen the Jewish population of their country granted citizenship rights by the Crémieux Decree, which also imposed on them military conscription and French law. This seemed to indicate that the question of conscription was linked to political rights and religious law. In this connection, the assumptions about politics, soldiering, and religion of the precolonial period should be recalled. Military roles were the preserve of the political elite, and of particular groups with a strong military tradition, such as the Kabyles in Algeria (one tribe of whom were the namesake of the Zouaves) or the Bambara in West Africa, while religious specialists were noncombatants.

The mechanism that set off the campaign against the Muslim courts in Algeria was a complex one. Its origins go back to the early 1870s, when the French adopted as a priority the preservation of Kabyle culture as a bulwark against Islamic influence. The Kabyles became enmeshed in a sort of Rousseauian myth with a positivist twist: their democratic and secular nature, it was argued, made their region a particularly apt pilot zone for French intervention in social and cultural life.[36] Following a decree of 1874, French *juges de paix* were appointed to the Kabylia and, with a three-volume compendium of Kabyle customs at the ready,[37] they took charge of administering justice, until then in the hands of village assemblies.

In the wider context, the late nineteenth century was a period of growing tension between France and the Muslim world. It was the era of Sultan Abdulhamid, a proponent of Pan-Islam as a counterforce to European colonial expansion. When these elements were combined with French fears of Abdulhamid's friend, the Kaiser, the French found themselves in a quandary in Algeria. Pursuit of a policy based on selective assimilation of marginal groups, while possibly effective in stemming Islamic influence in a limited area, might also work to alienate the Arabic-speaking Muslim majority. Further, in order to tap the colony's full manpower potential, it was necessary to devise a policy of full-scale assimilation. But this was a path involving considerable risk.

An important step down that path was taken in the late 1870s, when the French judicial authorities proclaimed that the experiment with the *juges de paix* in the Kabylia had been a resounding success, and cited it as proof that Muslims would enthusiastically accept the supposed wise and incorruptible French judges. The statistical evidence proffered was seriously questioned,[38] but this seems to have had little effect on the momentum toward the unification of jurisdictions. Curiously, judicial policy in Algeria at this time appears to have been linked to a sort of judicial purge in France, launched by the republicans to cleanse the system of clerical and monarchist stalwarts.[39] A brief tour in Algeria helped to qualify loyal republicans for advancement into the metropolitan hierarchy.

By this time, important changes had taken place within the Muslim judicial system. It had become increasingly bureaucratized and town centered. The average qadi had had considerable experience with French administration and politics; several had some proficiency in the French language. Yet virtually all of them came from families with a clerical tradition, often claiming descent from a local saint. The rule of avoidance, which had been applied in the 1870s and which assigned magistrates to posts away from their home districts, was relaxed during the 1880s because the financial rewards of the Muslim magistracy had declined with its loss of competence over land and commercial disputes. Thus, at the time of the crisis, the qadis had a mixed character. They usually had long experience as judges, were well integrated into a centralized judicial bureaucracy, and, hence, could not easily be subordinated to a local French mayor. The mayor of the colonial town owed his position to the French voters alone, and so felt no direct pressure to build up a set of reciprocal obligations with the Muslim community, in contrast to the situation in Senegal. Yet, since the qadis were often men of considerable wealth and local prestige and influence, a mayor could ill afford to ignore them.

In Senegal, electoral politics came to Saint-Louis and Gorée in 1872, to Rufisque in 1880, and to Dakar in 1887. Elections were dominated by French and mulatto politicians, but the African *originaires,* because of their votes, collected election-time handouts, and the politicians took their views and interests into consideration on certain issues.[40] Since there were no formally recognized African institutions in the communes, the office of qadi became a focus of political competition.

This was especially noticeable in Dakar, a town that had formed after the days of Faidherbe and developed its institutions in the intensely political atmosphere of the early Third Republic. The office of qadi in Dakar quickly became ensnarled in politics, as part of the patronage system that linked the Lebou, who were the original inhabitants of the site and held the largest block of votes, to the city's politicians.

On November 30, 1890, just three years after Dakar's promotion to municipal status, an election for qadi was held, in which Massemba Coky defeated Dial Diop by 250 votes to 171. The election took place at the town hall, with the blessings of the mayor, although the post of qadi had not yet received official recognition from the central colonial administration. In the ensuing debate, a subsequent mayor proclaimed that Coky, a grand marabout of the Lebou (and, one suspects, a supporter of the mayor's rivals), was "un homme dont la hardiesse n'a d'égale que la nullité."[41] Only in 1895 did the Muslim court of Dakar gain official recognition, thanks to the efforts of Senegal's deputy in Paris. Officially recognized or not, however, the qadi of Dakar was widely acknowledged to be an electoral agent.[42]

An interesting comparison with the situation in Dakar can be found in the Algerian town of Miliana, a town of precolonial origin best known for its pleasant mountain climate. By the 1880s, it was declining in importance relative to neighboring new towns in the Chélif Valley. In the late 1880s, the qadi of the town, a member of one of Miliana's illustrious old clerical families, came under fire from the local mayor, apparently for failing to favor one of the mayor's Muslim protégés in an inheritance case, and for suggesting to the rabbi that his congregation vote for the mayor's opponent in an election. Through the whole affair, which included a detailed scrutinization of all of the qadi's records, his imprisonment, exile, and subjection to every conceivable sort of accusation, the qadi maintained a steadfast defense of religious dignity and bureaucratic correctness. He made use of all the connections acquired in the course of his judicial service since 1864, in the French army, the Government General, and the Ministry of Justice. Eventually, he was resoundingly vindicated in the French Senate, and the mayor was denounced in the liberal French metropolitan press as a crass and vulgar small-town politician.[43]

Definitive Recognition

The qadi of Miliana was often mentioned in arguments for terminating the campaign of the 1870s and 1880s to eliminate the Muslim courts.

His case was effective material for the French political arena, for the qadi emerged as steadfastly apolitical, a wronged but loyal *vieux serviteur.* While Miliana was an important reflection of the situation in Algerian provincial towns, however, the first and most direct impetus for a reversal in policy came from Constantine, where colon political leaders combined with Muslim notables in 1887 to make a joint protest against the proposed elimination of the qadis, as well as against compulsory military service.

This joint protest was forged in the heat of crisis, in the wake of the first serious outbreak of urban Muslim collective violence, which occurred in Constantine in late June of 1887. It thus involves two partially independent questions; the position of urban Muslim notables in city and provincial politics, and the social and economic tensions that led to the violence.

The notables of Constantine were emerging, in the 1880s, as a coherent and self-conscious group under articulate leaders such as al-Makki Ben Badis, leading Constantinois political spokesman until his retirement from the Conseil Général in 1882, and Abd al-Qadir al-Majjawi, the first significant Islamic modernist in the country.[44] The influence of these leaders, who stressed the defense of Islamic institutions, seems to have radiated fairly effectively to the outlying provincial towns. There was also emerging a more secular group, strongly influenced by French democratic ideals. In 1882, they published, together with a radical French journalist, a short-lived bilingual weekly newspaper, *al-Muntakhib (The Elected).*[45]

But as Constantine urban notables became more assertive, their meager political rights came under attack. Most striking was an 1886 measure that deprived all Muslim patented merchants of the right to vote. According to the leading French historian of the period, Charles-Robert Ageron, this decree was aimed primarily at the numerous and overtly independent merchants of Constantine, causing that city's Muslim electorate to shrink from 2,000 to 500.[46] Unfortunately, it is not clear whose initiative lay behind the decree.

Lacking effective representation, the Constantine notables carried on in a well-established tradition of petitions to put forward their demands: increased representation at all levels, an end to the attack on the Muslim courts, and no military conscription or mass naturalization.[47]

The violent incident in question was a brawl *(rixe)* pitting popular elements of Constantine Muslim society against the Mzabis, immigrant merchants from an oasis complex at the edge of the Sahara, who followed the puritanical Ibadite rite of Islam. The only figure mentioned as playing a prominent role in the former group was a dissident leader of the Tijaniyya brotherhood. The followers can be only loosely described as laborers and artisans. Muslim municipal councillors reportedly made efforts to restore calm. As for outside agitators, the most likely candidates are the colon radical politicians, for it is well known that they encouraged their European followers in similar outbursts against Algerian Jews.[48]

It is clear that the incident occurred at an important juncture in the history of Mzabi commerce. France had annexed the Mzab in 1884. The railway was pushing south from Batna to Biskra, and schemes were afoot to push on to the presumed fabulous markets on the banks of the Niger. Drawn by the improvement in security and transport, pushed by the decline of the trans-Saharan trade, and hard hit by the abolition of slavery, more Mzabi merchants came north. Annexation had changed their legal status from foreigner to subject, thus raising the question of whether they could retain their own separate court. This was a serious matter, for jurisdiction over Mzabi legal affairs meant having a controlling hand in the regulation of an extensive credit network. A recent Mzabi bankruptcy had served to underscore the importance of this issue.[49]

One suggestive piece of evidence appeared in the year after the altercation, when Mzabis in Constantine publicly disowned petitions by their coreligionaries in other northern towns to secure official approval for a separate Mzabi court.[50] The declaration, one suspects, was made under pressure. In any case, the Mzabis had been armed with truncheons, suggesting that they were not unfamiliar with intercommunal violence.

The crucial result of the brawls was that they apparently gave the colons a serious shock, and put at least some of the important politicians in a conciliatory mood toward the Muslim notables. The fact that a number of European houses had been attacked served as a reminder of the colons' vulnerability, and of the need to sustain a class of Muslim notables with genuine influence in the community. As soon as French troops managed to restore the peace, the Constantine municipal council issued a resolution endorsing the preservation of the Muslim courts, the rejection of conscription, and the widening of Muslim political rights through increased representation on the municipal council and through allowing Muslim councillors to participate in choosing the mayor.[51] (The then current mayor, one suspects, anticipated that the Muslims would support his party in the council.) On July 10, another petition on these issues, signed by 1,700 Muslim inhabitants of the city (a number strikingly close to the pre-1886 electorate) was sent to the Conseil d'État.[52] This was the first major step toward bringing an end to the war against the qadis.

However, when the matter came before the provincial Conseil Général in October, new divisions emerged. The Conseil passed a resolution that, in effect, linked judicial autonomy to the limitation of Muslim political rights. The majority of Muslim notables on the Conseil, led by Salah Ben Bu Shenak, proclaimed: "The only benefit we desire . . . is the maintenance of our religion and our law."[53]

Significantly, this was the first time that a Muslim councillor other than a Ben Badis had assumed the role of spokesman. The statement echoes that of al-Makki Ben Badis twenty-two years earlier, and it is an indication of the changes that had taken place in the political and social life of the city that it was his son, Hamida, who now provided the lone dissenting voice, refusing to give up the claim to increased political rights. Hamida reflected the views of the younger, more Westernized city notables who had earlier been involved with the publication of *al-Muntakhib*.

One way to explain this division between urban and provincial attitudes is to see rural and small-town notables as being mainly concerned with property rights, and thus with law, at a time when they were coming under strong pressure from colons to renounce any political ambitions. Educated city notables were more conscious of the importance of government services and regulatory powers, and less vulnerable to intimidation. One might, thus, see the Conseil Général's resolution as an expression of political forces coming from the provincial towns, where colons were adamant that Muslim courts and political rights constituted an either/or proposition.

The case of the qadi of Miliana shows to what great lengths a small-town Algerian mayor might go in victimizing his opponents, and it only foreshadowed the kinds of political pressures that would come into play once Muslim political rights were substantially broadened in 1920. At the same time, the tenacity of the qadi of Miliana was a reflection of the continuing importance of his office, due especially to his influence in cases of landed inheritance.

In Constantine, however, one has the impression that leading notables, such as al-Makki Ben Badis and his son Hamida, had shifted their attention to politics by the 1880s and were no longer content with the inadequate shelter that religious law had become. A substantial number

of colon politicians apparently saw increased Muslim political participation as acceptable, at least at the municipal level. But Constantine
and Algiers could not, as Saint-Louis and Dakar did, move faster than
the rest of the country. Rather than progressing themselves, they served
to curb regression in the provincial towns. The city notables, in acting
as political spokesmen and cultural models, helped to assure the survival
of the Muslim court as an institution and of the provincial Muslim
notables as a culturally and politically distinct class in the outlying towns.
In their absence, provincial town colons might have been able to insist
on a different proposition: neither Muslim courts nor political rights.

In Senegal, the crisis over the Muslim courts was precipitated by the
reorganization in 1902-3 of the French West African administration,
which was accompanied by the establishment of a uniform judicial policy
with the decree of November 10, 1903. The new decree was a product
of Governor General Ernest Roume's obsession with centralization and
uniformity. It established a hierarchy of courts dominated at the upper
levels by colonial administrators, while it provided for legal diversity
among the numerous ethnic groups of French West Africa. The Muslim
courts of Saint-Louis and Dakar were to be eliminated, since only French
courts were to have jurisdiction in the communes.[54] This reflected a
combination of doctrinaire assimilationism, suspicion of Islam, and contempt for the unprofessional, poorly educated judge cum electoral agent
who presided over the Muslim court of Dakar, hardly an appropriate
figure in Roume's new imperial capital.

The measure came at a time when the French and mulatto politicians
were increasingly courting the African vote, especially in Dakar, where
both of the rival mayoral candidates in 1903 placed Africans on their
tickets. It appears that the qadi of Dakar, Medoune Dieng, continued
to hear cases and issue judgments with the consent of local French
authorities. In justification, it was argued that he had received his inves-
titure from "village chiefs."[55] Moreover, he was named, at the insistence
of the mayor of Dakar, to the position of Muslim assessor on the French
Tribunal, with a salary of 4,000 francs, in spite of his not knowing
French—conceivably an irrelevant point, since he was also hard of hear-
ing. The mayor and the municipal government, it was reported, considered this nomination as a means "to facilitate their relations with their
native administrees."[56]

However, on April 7, 1905, the Court of Appeal of French West Africa
ruled against the concept of a chief-nominated qadi in the communes,

and proclaimed that the qadi of Dakar had no authority.[57] But even before this, the European mayors of Dakar and Saint-Louis had swung into action, extolling the traditional and democratic nature of the qadi's court. Less than two months after the Court of Appeal ruling, Muslim courts were officially reestablished at Dakar and Saint-Louis, and also at Kayes, a trading center on the upper Senegal River, in what is now Mali, where there was a major colony of traders from coastal towns.[58] In Senegal, the qadi was thus maintained as the man who delivered the votes, whereas in Algeria, he seemed to have become the man who delivered the abstentions.

Conclusion

Colonial societies are often depicted in terms of dualistic structures, in which contrasting social, economic, and political systems coexist and, through the artifices of colonial policy, achieve the minimum necessary articulation. While the concept of articulation within a colonial political system implies an unequal relationship, it also involves separation and the maintenance of hierarchical structures within the dominated society. The domination of the colonizer and the separateness of the colonized, in coexisting, necessarily qualify each other. Separation and the maintenance of an autonomous hierarchy require that the colonial authorities not intervene in certain areas of life, and that they listen to the leaders of the colonized community on certain issues. But those leaders, in turn, have to collaborate with the colonial authorities in other areas and on other issues.

In colonies with substantial European settler communities that control local government affairs, the problem of articulation could become quite complex, for it involved two different levels of authority: the central colonial government and the settler-dominated local government. In looking only at the Algerian case, one would be likely to focus on the failure to achieve effective articulation, for in modern Algerian history, all roads lead ultimately to the revolution. And such a focus can easily lead one to draw pessimistic conclusions about other colonies of settlement. Comparison with Senegal, however, where a similar situation existed and yet a relatively effective system of articulation was worked out, leads one to search for specific sources of the Algerian failure, and to ask if there were not some factors working in the other direction, toward genuine accommodation between European and Muslim society in Algeria.

A critical aspect of the problem of articulation was the problem of the Muslim courts, which were the institutional basis for the separateness of the Muslim community and which, in Algeria, became the rationale for its political inferiority. The most serious difficulties in Algeria arose at the local level, and one source of those difficulties was a remarkable achievement of the "indigenophile" period of the late Second Empire: the establishment of a centralized Muslim judicial bureaucracy. One can see in this achievement an effective system of articulation between Muslim society and the colonial state. Its very success helped to doom to frustration efforts to find a formula at the local level. Because the Muslim judges (and the urban notables that they, in effect, represented) had strong ties with the colonial administration in the capital, local colon politicians were limited in the influence that they could exercise over them.

The applause that the qadi of Miliana won from the French Senate and metropolitan press for defying the local mayor was a case in point. This was a principal reason for the settlers' insistence on linking issues of law and political rights. But it would be wrong to say that there was unanimity among colons on the linkage formula, or that the one ultimately imposed was unanimously accepted by the Muslim notables. There is evidence to suggest that both colons and Muslim notables in large cities were receptive to a more liberal formula, allowing for greater Muslim participation in municipal politics than was tolerable to small-town colons.

In Senegal, especially in Dakar, the qadi's links to the central government passed through the mayor, and the qadi, in turn, was one of the mayor's principal links to his Muslim constituents. Hence, in Senegal, full political rights for the *originaires* were quite compatible with maintenance of the Muslim courts.

The respective absence and presence, in Algeria and Senegal, of effective articulation at the local level, was paralleled in economic relationships between colons and natives. Many of the Senegalese *originaires* played an essential role in the European economic penetration of the interior. Their connections with European trading houses made possible a basic harmony of interests among Europeans and Africans, giving allowance for quarrels over the distribution of profit and the division of control. Separate Muslim courts for family law cases posed little threat to European commercial interests, since commercial cases and cases involving debts of Muslim traders to Europeans were under the jurisdiction of French courts.

In Algeria, however, the dominant interest of the Muslim urban elite was not commerce but land, as was the case with their counterparts in the Ottoman Empire and Egypt, where minority groups dominated commerce.[59] This gave the Muslim courts a special importance, for family law was intricately involved in questions of land ownership. Some urban families were involved in commerce, but their disenfranchisement points to an antagonism with some powerful colon interests.[60] If any group in Algeria had a role similar to that of the Senegalese *originaires* in commercial penetration of the interior, it was the Mzabis. They may be seen as a sort of intermediate type between the minority-group traders of the Mediterranean and the Muslim traders of West Africa.

The crisis of 1887 weaves together these seemingly disparate political and economic strands. At the time, the central administration in Algiers was becoming increasingly preoccupied with southward expansion and commercial penetration of the Saharan interior. The cooperation of the Mzabis seemed essential to this task. Meanwhile, the affairs of the coastal region were left increasingly to the colons, who sought to reduce the cultural and political autonomy of the Muslim population, notably by suppression of the Muslim courts. For the urban Muslim notables, the prospect of privileged treatment for the Mzabis by the central administration made the colons' project of assimilating and subordinating the Muslim population all the more galling. And it helped to make them realize that they could no longer hope for an occasional gesture of paternalistic benevolence from the central government, as they could have under the Second Empire. Ironically, the Mzabis, rather than constituting themselves into the Saharan vanguard of the Marseille Chamber of Commerce, were becoming increasingly involved in the dry goods trade within the coastal region, and it is this that probably best explains the friction between them and the popular classes of Constantine.

The disturbances of 1887 made many colon politicians recognize that the existing form of articulation through the Muslim courts was preferable to either brute subordination or absolute equality, which seemed to be the major alternatives. The compromise, which linked maintenance of the Muslim courts with denial of political rights, seemed, for a brief while, to be effective. During World War I, the government was able to call upon the "official clergy" (Muslim judicial officials and Sufi leaders) to mobilize Algerian opinion for the war effort. And they managed to meet the call fairly effectively. Some 173,000 Algerians volunteered for or accepted induction into the French army during the war, while there were only two serious but localized rebellions in the north of Algeria.[61] In the case of the judicial officials, their strong historical links to the central government help explain their wartime loyalism.

With the end of the war there came a wide extension of the suffrage for Algerian Muslims in local elections. At this point, the qadis, along with other traditional notables, had to be drafted into the service of the administrative electoral machine. Their success in the war effort, along with an emphasis on pageantry imported from Marshal Lyautey's Morocco,[62] seemed to help conceal from the French the declining prestige of men who were now obliged to use their power and influence to help smother currents of Muslim opposition to colon domination at the local level.

Nevertheless, there were some striking signs of change, particularly in the Algerians' perceptions of religious legitimacy. The most prestigious religious leader to emerge in the interwar period was Abd al-Hamid Ben Badis, leader of the reformist 'ulama'. He came from a highly influential family in Constantine with a tradition of service in the judiciary. Indeed, it was his grandfather's leading role in the judicial reforms of the late 1860s that helped to cement the relationship between the official clergy and the state. But Abd al-Hamid openly scorned the official clergy, and he saw a judicial career as a sure path to the torments of public vilification in this world, to say nothing of those in the hereafter. He devoted his own career to the activities of an Islamic cultural association and to the establishment of independent Islamic schools. The wide popularity of Ben Badis's attack on the official clergy suggests that the French had overexploited the influence of religious offices, and thus ultimately sapped them of their prestige. The result was a major transformation of Algerian Islam.[63]

In the communes of Senegal, the Muslim courts were of more limited importance than those in Algeria. But their position in the early twentieth century illustrates a pattern of widespread importance in Senegalese politics, where Sufi leaders, beginning with Ahmadou Bamba in the early 1900s, played a critical role as election brokers. Later on, prominent Sufi leaders, most notably Ibrahim Niass, linked their religious orders with nationalist political parties. To this day in Senegal, political and spiritual efficacy have gone hand in hand, while in Algeria, lack of political efficacy gradually eroded the spiritual powers of the official clergy, giving rise to the religious anticlericalism of Ben Badis and the socialist messianism of Messali Hajj.

NOTES

1. On Nigeria, see David D. Laitin, *Hegemony and Culture: Politics and Religious Change among the Yoruba* (Chicago, 1986). On Sudan, see Safiya Safwat, "Islamic Laws in the Sudan," in *Islamic Law: Social and Historical Contexts,* ed. Aziz al-Azmeh, 231–49 (London, 1988).

2. On Muslims in England, see "Setting Themselves Apart," *Economist,* July 22, 1989, 49–50. In Europe today, the main focus of debate is on education. In North Africa, there was a shift of emphasis from law to education in the 1920s and 1930s.

3. Bryan S. Turner, "State, Religion, and Minority Status," *Comparative Studies in Society and History* 27, no. 2 (April, 1985): 311. Turner sees this as a problem common to all three Abrahamic religions. Certainly more than "spiritual credentials" is involved, since religious law stands as the foundation for the pattern of relations within a community—and hence for its cohesiveness—and also for its internal distribution of power.

4. Allan Christelow, "Three Islamic Voices in Contemporary Nigeria," in *Islam and the Political Economy of Meaning,* ed. William R. Roff, 220–53 (London, 1987). See especially the section on Ibraheem Suleiman, 237–44.

5. Slimane Chikh, *L'Algérie en armes ou le temps des certitudes* (Algiers, 1981); Mahfoud Kaddache, *Histoire du nationalisme algérien: Question nationale et politique algérienne, 1919–1951* (Algiers, 1980); Tony Smith, *The French Stake in Algeria, 1945–1962* (Ithaca, N.Y., 1978).

6. Patrick Manning, *Francophone Subsaharan Africa, 1880–1985* (Cambridge, 1988).

7. Assimilationist policy in Senegal was limited to the *quatre communes*—Saint-Louis, Gorée, Dakar, and Rufisque. Their African inhabitants were referred to as *originaires*. Gorée, the old island trading post just off Dakar, was small and had few Muslims, and thus plays no role in this study. Until 1907, Rufisque was included in the jurisdiction of the Dakar Muslim court. In Algeria, only the territory of the Sahara, which had a military administration, escaped the influence of assimilationist policy.

8. On the concept of the Muslim city, see Ira Lapidus, *Muslim Cities of the Middle Ages* (Cambridge, Mass., 1967). On the initial differentiation of the

Muslim madina from the polis of the classical age in the Mediterranean, see Hugh Kennedy, "From Polis to Madina: Urban Change in Late Antique and Early Islamic Syria," *Past and Present* 106 (February, 1985): 3–27. For a long-term study of an Algerian city with a strong Islamic identity, see Richard I. Lawless and Gerald H. Blake, *Tlemcen: Continuity and Change in an Algerian Islamic Town* (London, 1976), which concentrates on geographic and economic aspects of the city's development. A social anthropologist's approach to the North African city can be found in Kenneth L. Brown, *People of Salé: Tradition and Change in a Moroccan Society* (Manchester, England, 1976).

9. For colonial settlers, the potential leveling effects of native conscription were clear. On the original model, see Isser Woloch, "Napoleonic Conscription: State Power and Civil Society," *Past and Present* 111 (May, 1986): 101–29.

10. See Allan Christelow, *Muslim Law Courts and the French Colonial State in Algeria* (Princeton, 1985). Research on Senegal was carried out in Aix-en-Provence, France, and Dakar in the summer of 1979.

11. This study focuses mainly on the city of Constantine, since it had a crucial role in the Muslim court crisis. I do not deal with Oranais cities (Oran, Tlemcen, Mascara, Mostaganem) because of the complications this would introduce. They suffered severe disruptions during the resistance period (1830–47) and were more strongly colon dominated than Constantine.

12. These towns have been mainly the province of geographers. On the region of Orléansville, see Xavier Yacono, *La colonisation des plaines du Chélif* (Algiers, 1955). On patterns of land ownership, see A. Prenant, "La propriété foncière des citadins dans les regions de Sidi Bel Abbès et de Tlemcen," *Annales algériennes de géographie* 2, no. 1 (1967): 2–108. Paralleling the rise of new centers was the decline of small, precolonial hill towns; this is covered by Djilali Sari, *Les villes précoloniales de l'Algérie Occidentale: Nédroma, Mazouna, Kalâa* (Algiers, 1970).

13. A leading representative of the Islamophile tendency in Algerian policy was Ismail Urbain, a French–West Indian mulatto, Saint-Simonian, and convert to Islam. With a number of other Saint-Simonians, he had gone on a mission to the Orient in the 1830s, teaching French in the Egyptian military academy.

14. Faidherbe went through his apprenticeship in colonial administration in Algeria and went on to become governor of Senegal in 1856. On Algerian influence, see Roger Pasquier, "L'influence de l'expérience algérienne sur la politique de la France en Sénégal (1842–1869)," in *Perspectives nouvelles sur le passé de l'Afrique Noire et le Madagascar—Mélanges offerts à Hubert Deschamps* (Paris, 1974), 263–84.

15. Islamophobia bred by insecurity tended to be most prevalent along the frontiers of Morocco and Tunisia and in the south, particularly at times of political turmoil—for instance, in the East Constantinois in 1881 during the

invasion of Tunisia. Colons often found vague accusations of fanaticism a useful tool in local political quarrels, as in the case of the qadi of Miliana, discussed subsequently.

16. On French Islamic policy in Senegal, see David Robinson, "French 'Islamic' Policy and Practice in Late Nineteenth Century Senegal," *Journal of African History* 29 (1988): 415–35. On Algeria, see Peter von Sivers, "Les plaisirs du collectionneur: Capitalisme fiscal et chefs indigènes en Algérie (1840–1860)," *Annales: Économies, sociétés, civilisations* 35 (1980): 679–99.

17. For a critique of codification efforts, see D. Penant, "De la condition juridique des indigènes en matière civile et commerciale dans les colonies françaises," *Recueil Penant* 15, pt. 2 (1906): 1–40; Alphonse Gouilly, *L'Islam dans l'Afrique Occidentale Française* (Paris, 1952), 251–53. For an in-depth study of the economic effects of legal change within a limited region in Senegal, see Francis Snyder, *Capitalism and Legal Change* (London, 1981). The leading judicial figure in the Algerian campaign for the unification of jurisdictions was Édouard Sautayra. With Arabist Eugène Cherbonneau, he published *Le droit musulman: Du statut personnel et des successions,* 2 vols. (Paris, 1873), which can be seen as the opening volley in the campaign. Captain Nicolas Seignette's virtually incomprehensible translation of Sidi Khalil's treatise on the Maliki rite of Islamic law, the Mukhtasar, was significantly titled *Code musulman* (Algiers, 1878). On the contrast between French and British approaches, see M. G. Smith, "The Sociological Framework of Law," in *Corporations and Society* (London, 1974). For an insightful analysis of the role of customary law in colonial British Africa, see Martin Channock, *Law, Custom, and Social Order: The Colonial Experience in Malawi and Zambia* (Cambridge, 1985).

18. The earliest representative of this trend was Abd al-Qadir al-Majjawi, who began teaching in Constantine in 1869. The phenomenon was officially celebrated with Abduh's visit to Algiers in 1903. An excellent study of French Islamic policy in West Africa is Jean-Louis Triaud, "La question musulmane en Côte d'Ivoire (1893–1939)," *Revue française d'histoire d'Outre-Mer* 61, no. 4 (1974): 542–71.

19. On the Senegal region, see Lucie G. Colvin, "Islam and the State of Kajoor: A Case of Successful Resistance to Jihad," *Journal of African History* 15, no. 4 (1974): 587–606; Ahmad Baba Miske, *"Al-Wasit* (1911)—Tableau de la Mauritanie à la fin du XIXème siecle," *Bulletin de l'Institut Fondamental de l'Afrique Noire* 30, pt. B, no. 1 (1968): 117–64; Christian Coulon, *Le marabout et le prince: Islam et pouvoir au Senegal* (Paris, 1981). On Algeria, see Allan Christelow, "Saintly Descent and Worldly Affairs in Mid-Nineteenth-Century Mascara, Algeria," *International Journal of Middle East Studies* 12, no. 2 (1980): 139–55; Fanny Colonna, "Saints furieux et saints studieux dans l'Aures," *Annales: Économies, sociétés, civilisations* 35 (1980): 642–62; Ernest Gellner, *Muslim Society* (Cambridge, 1980).

20. Augustin Berque, "Esquisse d'une histoire de la seigneurie algérienne," *Revue de la Méditerranée* 7, no. 1 (1949): 18–34, and 7, no. 2 (1949): 168–80.

21. On *hassani*s, see Miske, *"Al-Wasit"*; C. C. Stewart, *Islam and Social Order in Mauritania: A Case Study from the Nineteenth Century* (Oxford, 1973). On *tieddo,* one should, in the following order, read V. Monteil, *Esquisses Sénégalaises* (Dakar, 1966) (the stereotype of the *tieddo* as drunken brute); see Ousmane Sembene's film, *Ceddo* (the antithesis: the chivalrous, brave, and fearless warrior who saves the princess); and read Colvin, "Islam and the State of Kajoor." Berque's "Esquisse d'une histoire" also needs to be read in the light of Colvin's comments on the stereotyping of nobilities.

22. This has been suggested by Berque for Algeria and Colvin for Senegal.

23. The difficulties of a precolonial Algerian qadi are detailed in E. Cherbonneau, "Notice biographique sur Mohammed Ben Bou Diaf, Muphti de Constantine," *Journal Asiatique,* 4ème Serie, 5 (1850): 275–89.

24. A theoretical framework for understanding this process is developed in Ilya F. Harik, "The Impact of the Domestic Market on Rural-Urban Relations in the Middle East," in *Rural Politics and Social Change in the Middle East,* ed. R. Antoun and I. Harik (Bloomington, Ind., 1972).

25. See Allan Christelow, "Inquiry into the Origins of the Algerian Medjlis Crisis of 1858," *Revue d'histoire maghrebine,* no. 15–16 (July, 1979): 35–51.

26. Al-Makki Ben Badis, in Conseil Général, Constantine, September 21, 1865. In the early 1860s, the French had attempted to impose a requirement of attendance at one of the three official madrasas, to which Ben Badis strongly objected.

27. For a general history of the town, see Camille Camara, *Saint-Louis de Sénégal* (Dakar, 1968).

28. Pasquier, "L'influence de l'expérience algérienne," 268.

29. On the history of attempts to create a Muslim court in Saint-Louis, see Faidherbe's 1856 report on the Muslim court question, in Archives du Gouvernement Général de l'Afrique Occidentale Française (hereafter cited as AGGAOF), M 8. The tendencies found in the Sant-Louis Muslim community show similarities to those of the colonial British West African port cities of Freetown and Lagos: see Peter Clarke, *West Africa and Islam* (London, 1982), 170–71, 179.

30. The creation of the Muslim court figured in propaganda against al-Hajj Umar. See Claudine Gerresch, "Judgments du Moniteur du Sénégal sur al-Hajj Umar de 1857 à 1864," *Bulletin de l'Institut Fondamental de l'Afrique Noire* 35, pt. B, no. 3 (1973): 571–73. For a complete treatment of al-Hajj Umar, see David Robinson, *The Holy War of Umar Tal* (Oxford, 1985).

31. Leland Conley Barrows, "The Merchants and General Faidherbe: Aspects of French Expansion in the 1850s," *Revue française d'histoire de'Outre-Mer* 61 (1974): 275.

32. Francois Zuccarelli, "Les maires de Saint-Louis et de Gorée de 1816 à 1872," *Bulletin de l'Institut Fondamental de l'Afrique Noire* 35, pt. B, no. 3 (1973): 551–73.

33. Al-Makki Ben Badis, in Conseil Général, Constantine, October 3, 1865.

34. On Algerian politics, see Charles-Robert Ageron, *Les algériens Musulmans et la France (1871–1919)* (Paris, 1968); Jean-Claude Vatin, *L'Algérie politique: histoire et société* (Paris, 1974). On Senegal, see G. Wesley Johnson, *The Emergence of Black Politics in Senegal, 1900–1919* (Stanford, Calif., 1971); H. O. Idowu, "Assimilation in Nineteenth-Century Senegal," *Bulletin de l'Institut Fondamental de l'Afrique Noire* 30, pt. B, no. 4 (1968): 1422–47.

35. On conscription in Algeria, see Ageron, *Les Algériens,* chap. 38. On Senegal, see M. Michel, "Citoyenneté et service militaire dans les quatre communes de Sénégal au cours de la première guerre mondiale," in *Perspectives nouvelles,* 299–314.

36. On Kabyle policy, see Ageron, *Les Algériens,* chap. 10. On the educational aspect of intervention, see Fanny Colonna, *Instituteurs algériens (1883–1939)* (Paris, 1975).

37. A. Hannoteau and A. Letourneux, *La Kabylie et les coutumes kabyles,* 3 vols. (Paris, 1872–73). It is important to note that this work was published at the same time as Sautayra and Cherbonneau's *Le droit musulman,* pointing to a unity of purpose behind the two works.

38. V. Mallarmé, "La brochure 'L'Administration de la justice en Algérie' et ses conclusions," *Bulletin judiciaire de l'Algérie* 1 (May, 1877): 129–34.

39. On the purge in France, see Georges Picot, "Les magistrats et la démocratie," *Revue des deux mondes* 62 (March 15, 1884): 288–315. See also Benjamin F. Martin, "The Courts, the Magistrature, and Promotions in Third Republic France," *American Historical Review* 87, no. 4 (October, 1982): 977–1009. The connection with Algerian policy is made clear in the speech by Procureur Général Pompei, in Conseil Supérieur du Gouvernement, Algérie, November 16, 1883.

40. Johnson, *Emergence of Black Politics,* 44–55.

41. Maire, Dakar, to Gouverneur, Senegal, July 22, 1892, in AGGAOF, M 8. The mayor, Charles de Montfort, was probably French, according to H. O. Idowu, and was married to a mulatto woman. He served on the Conseil Général, as mayor, and as leader of the bar of Senegal. He spoke fluent Wolof, and claimed to be a defender of Lebou interests in the land question. See H. O. Idowu, "Café au Lait: Senegal's Mulatto Community in the Nineteenth Century," *Journal of the Historical Society of Nigeria* 6, no. 3 (December, 1972): 272.

42. For instance, see the Lieutenant Governor's remarks in Extrait des délibérations de la Commission Coloniale, Conseil Général, Senegal, Session de 1903, in AGGAOF, M 241.

43. The case is discussed by Ageron in *Les Algériens,* 443–45. A full report appears in Sénat (France), *Documents,* Annexe 136, June 19, 1891.

44. On al-Majjawi, see Allan Christelow, "Hawl bidaya al-nahda al-jazairiyya: katib li Abd al-Qadir al-Majjawi" (Concerning the Beginning of the Algerian Cultural Revival: A Pamphlet by Abd al-Qadir al-Majjawi), *Al-Thaqafa* (Algiers) 46 (September, 1978): 55–64. On al-Makki Ben Badis, see Christelow, "al-Makki Ben Badis wa ba'd nawahi al-haraka al-wataniyya al-jazairiyya fi-l-qarn al-tasi' 'ashar" (al-Makki Ben Badis and Some Aspects of the Algerian Patriotic Movement in the Nineteenth Century), *al-Thaqafa* 11, no. 61 (1981): 41–51; Christelow, "al-Makki Ben Badis," *Parcours: L'Algérie, les hommes et l'histoire* 5 (1985): 14–21.

45. A similar sort of collaboration between an independent-minded French journalist and aspiring native politicians can be found in Dakar, with Jean d'Oxoby's *La démocratie du Sénégal,* beginning in 1913. See Johnson, *Emergence of Black Politics,* 103–4, 148–53.

46. Ageron, *Les Algériens,* 360.

47. *Mémoire adressée à la Commission Sénatoriale par les conseillers municipaux indigènes et notables de Constantine* (Constantine, 1891). In the National Archives in Algiers, I have also seen a number of manuscript petitions protesting the municipal government's hostile attitude toward the city's mosques.

48. The only surviving account of which I know is that in *L'Indépendant de Constantine,* June 24–28, and July 1, 1887. For French radicals, the political logic behind instigating the violence, if they had any such role, might have been based on the ties between Mzabi merchants and Jewish wholesalers. In any case, the radicals had set an example of violence to be imitated in their election-time assaults on Algerian Jews. More important factors, in my view, were social and economic changes within the Muslim community, which I discuss in the conclusion.

49. *L'Indépendant de Constantine,* March 23, 1886. The debtor had fled to the Mzab, and the Mzabi community of Constantine tried to settle the matter out of court, but one major commercial house refused to settle, so they initiated a boycott of it throughout the province. One finds strikingly similar problems involving personal status jurisdiction and European credit to native merchants in Saint-Louis at the same time. See Rapport de la Commission sur la Réorganisation de la Justice Musulmane, April 1, 1889, in AGGAOF, M 8.

50. *Le temps* (Paris), November 3, 1888, and January 15, 1889. A noteworthy supporter of separate Mzabi courts was the native affairs expert, Commandant Louis Rinn, who probably saw it as an application of divide-and-rule tactics and as a way of winning influence in the south.

51. *Le Républicain de Constantine,* July 4, 1887. The mayor was Arabist Ernest Mercier, who produced a number of studies on the history of the city.

Ironically, he had been one of the first to call for the abolition of qadis—in *Des abus du régime judiciarie en Algérie* (Constantine, 1870).

52. *Mémoire addressée à la Commission Sénatorial de l'Algérie par les conseillers municipaux indigènes et notables musulmans de Constantine* (Constantine, 1870), 1.

53. Conseil Général, Constantine, October 9, 1887.

54. Reports and correspondence on the decree are in AGGAOF, M 79 and M 244.

55. Lieutenant Gouverneur, Senegal, to Gouverneur Général, AOF, April 14, 1904, in AGGAOF, M 244.

56. Maire, Dakar, to Lieutenant Gouverneur, Senegal, December 26, 1903, in AGGAOF, M 244.

57. Cour d'Appel, AOF, April 7, 1905 (Alphan Toure *v.* Maman Diaware) in *Recueil Penant* 14 (1905). For other details, see Procureur Général, Senegal, to Gouverneur Général, AOF, April 8, 1904, in AGGAOF, M 244.

58. Decree of May 22, 1905. An interesting reaction to the decree was a reported "exodus" of Muslims from Senegal—see *La quinzaine coloniale,* June 10, 1905. Presumably their destination was The Gambia, where the British had just established a Muslim court. See Governor, The Gambia, to Gouverneur Général, AOF, June 22, 1903, in AGGAOF, M 241.

59. For an instructive comparison, see Joel S. Migdal, *Palestinian Society and Politics* (Princeton, 1980), 12–16. On the Algerian case, see Prenant, "La propriété foncière."

60. Little is known of Algerian Muslim commerce in this period. The antagonism may have stemmed from the fact that the merchants were involved in trade with Tunisia and the Middle East and were bringing back Pan-Islamic ideas from their commercial travels. Peirre Bardin, *Algériens et Tunisiens dans l'Empire Ottoman de 1848 à 1914* (Paris, 1979), covers only the diplomatic aspects of this question, but he does make it clear that the late 1880s were a period of severe tension between France and the Ottoman Empire over the status of Algerians.

61. The most serious of these occurred in the Aurès region; a smaller outbreak occurred in the region of Mascara. The French also faced a Sanusiyya-Ottoman inspired rebellion in the far south of Algeria and in Niger, but this was essentially a Saharan, not an Algerian, affair.

62. The pageantry is strikingly illustrated in some of the photographs of the period reproduced in Françoise Renaudot, *L'histoire des Français en Algérie* (Paris, 1979).

63. For a theoretical treatment of this theme, see Fanny Colonna, "Cultural Resistance and Religious Legitimacy in Colonial Algeria," *Economy and Society* 3, no. 3 (1974): 233–63.

The Intellectual, Islam, and Modernization: Haykal and Shari'ati

Charles D. Smith

Past studies of modernization assumed that intellectuals adhering to Western values would be conduits of rational, scientific norms deemed necessary to the structuring of modern, complex societies. Little consideration was given to the attitudes of these intellectuals toward the social change presumably resulting from the distribution of rational values. Modernization theorists supposed a positive relationship between rationalism, as a mode of thought, and social change, a supposition reflecting their own expectations of a progressive and relatively predictive evolution of traditional societies toward more modern and intricate social systems.[1]

Now, however, the transformation of traditional societies has become more problematical than certain. Greater attention is paid to those historical and cultural factors germane to a particular society's experience and its potential receptivity to stimuli for change. In this chapter I wish to question the assumption that Western-oriented intellectuals are necessarily willing agents of change in premodern societies. Examining Egypt and the career of Muhammad Husayn Haykal (1888–1956), I will show how men who were ardent supporters of the transference of Western rational values to Egypt were also committed to the preservation of the social status quo and traditional relationships. Their conceptions of their roles as intellectuals and landowners prevented their approach to the Egyptian masses, whose lives they proposed to transform as part of Egypt's advancement into the modern world. Committed to rationalism as the basis of Egypt's modernization, they feared its spread beyond their control and responded to social problems in light of their self-images as leaders. The result was a situation on the eve of Nasser's coup in 1952 where the Muslim Brotherhood, a repository of supposedly traditional religious values, could perceive and respond to Egypt's socioeconomic problems far more readily than could a Westernized elite such as the Liberal Constitutionalist party, of which Haykal was president.

In this context, I will argue that intellectuals' self-images are bound to their perceptions of society and the relationships they envisage therein. It is this conception of ideal social relationships, often derived from a rural experience, that can place them in opposition to modernization as a social process. Indeed, the adoption of rationalist thought in defiance of traditional socioreligious beliefs may reinforce feelings of elitism and a need to be separate from society rather than encouraging social change. Or, in the case of an Iranian intellectual whom we will consider, Ali Shari'ati, he felt himself estranged from both Western rational values and Muslim traditionalism, a position that justified his separate stance as the guide of a revived Muslim society that rejected modernization in any form that suggested Western inspiration. These distinctions separate our consideration of the self-conscious intellectual from the functionalist assessment of intellectuals in light of the tasks they perform. The former are created by their self-awareness, the latter by fulfillment of social needs through their education and chosen professions, which are derived from the modernization process itself.

The failure to separate these two groups adequately as different types of intellectuals is clear in the work of Edward Shils, who has argued that there "would be intellectuals in society even if there were no intellectuals by disposition."[2] Shils's discussion of Indian intellectuals indicates the problems of his approach. He views India as the model for the path taken by most colonies. Initial leadership of rationalist movements by creative, self-conscious intellectuals, motivated by their dispositions, gave way to their later "disillusioned withdrawal" from politics once popular movements appeared with their "indispensable organizational machinery and functionaries."[3] Though correctly noting intellectual despair at mass involvement in politics, Shils confuses the issue by associating organizational machinery and functionaries, bureaucracy, with popular movements. In both of his studies of Indian intellectuals, however, he links them, as a group, with bureaucratic posts without distinguishing between those created by disposition or by society and its needs. He thus ignores his own inference that a basic difference between these two types of intellectuals rests in their aversion to or willingness to serve popular movements.[4]

On the other hand, Shils abstracts self-conscious intellectual sensibilities from social contexts. He notes that Indians associated with the Liberal party withdrew from the independence movement once Gandhi induced mass participation in politics. He links Liberal withdrawal to dislike for the mundane in life, politics, which he identifies with the masses, rather than to dislike for one type of political activity that included, rather than isolated, the populace. Shils furthermore associates this wish for separation with an Indian Liberal concern for the cosmic, separate from material concerns, and fails to note that this ideal reflected traditional sociopolitical status in Hindu society. Only Brahmins could assume the possibility of such separation. In this regard, the self-consciousness of Indian intellectuals blended an identification with universal ideas, rationalism, with a sense of elite status derived from their social standing, which should be preserved.[5]

Egyptian liberal intellectuals held similar attitudes but expressed them differently. Instead of withdrawing from politics out of distaste for mass contact, they strove to preserve the social status quo through political involvement. At the same time, they considered contact with the masses and acceptance of mass opinion a derogation of their purpose. In Haykal's case, we can examine these feelings and his reaction to social change in his novels and short stories as well as in his public pronouncements and activities. Haykal wrote several controversial studies on Egyptian literature and Islam's role in modern society, a by-product of his position as a prominent journalist of the interwar period and editor of the two newspapers most closely associated with the call for modernization after World War I. Here, and in later life as a politician who gained the leadership of his party and aspired to become prime minister, he continuously assessed Egypt's progress and his own opportunities to influence its direction. That he would express his social attitudes and evaluation of Egypt's development with greater consistency in his fiction than in his other writings suggests the utility of fictional expression as a self-conscious index of social change.[6]

In addition, Haykal's experience encourages broader consideration of the intellectual's conception of modernization, social change, and the introduction of rational values. Using Max Weber and Karl Mannheim as examples of the reaction of self-conscious intellectuals to the impact of modernization on Germany, I will suggest that similarities exist among such intellectuals in developing societies undergoing stress imposed by the rapidity of change, although different social and historical experiences must be taken into account.[7] These concerns have been far more a part of the European than the U.S. developmental process. They have inspired approaches by European and U.S. sociologists to social issues and change that reflect their different assessments of the positive or negative value of change itself and incorporate the distinctions between self-conscious and functional intellectuals noted above. I will return to a discussion of these issues in the conclusion, comparing the assumptions behind modernization found in the work of Weber and Mannheim with those of Shils and David Apter.

Muhammad Husayn Haykal was born in a village in the Egyptian delta to a "rural family with a tradition of local leadership" as well as of learning and piety, a group Albert Hourani rightly considers the creative class of Egypt at the turn of this century.[8] Haykal's family retained the post of 'umda (village headman). The sons were sent initially to al-Azhar, the great Sunni Muslim educational institution and mosque in Cairo, and to European schools once they appeared. Their awareness of the value of education indicated the desire of native Egyptians to replace Turko-Circassians as provincial administrators. As a product of a rural tradition and class that assumed power over villages as well as a sense of obligation for their well-being, Haykal and others like him would be conservative in their approach to democracy, however "Western" they might be intellectually. Their desire for democracy was based on its European origins. Opposed to this was their aversion to mass participation in government, which they saw as their province alone.

Haykal attended secular schools in Cairo from the age of seven. He spent three years in Paris studying law and received his doctorate from the Sorbonne in 1912. After World War I, Haykal abandoned his legal career for journalism and politics. In 1922 he became editor of *al-Siyasa,* which advocated reform along Western lines as the organ of the Liberal Constitutionalist party, a party that opposed the more popular Wafd and its national hero, Sa'd Zaghlul. Haykal and his fellow editors argued for the rule of the Western-educated elite they associated with the Liberals, those who were the most capable by virtue of their education, and condemned the Wafd's appeal to popular emotions. Their inability to defeat the Wafd in open elections led the Liberal Constitutionalists to seek alliances with the palace and the British during the 1920s in order to oust the Wafd and gain power. A particularly abrasive issue in the latter half of the decade was the charge of atheism hurled at the Liberals because of their attacks on Islamic authority and Islam's influence in Egyptian society. These charges caused the Liberals, Haykal in the lead, to gradually shift to an Islamic orientation in the 1930s whereby they gave up their open advocacy of Western ideas and secularism.

In responding to these accusations of atheism, the Liberals proclaimed themselves the true defenders of Islam. Haykal published *Hayat Muhammad,* an adulatory biography of the Prophet Muhammad that contained an apparent attack on Western values, in 1935. In reality, Haykal criticized Muslim conservatism far more sharply and ended by defending Western liberal ideals within an Islamic framework; he argued for an individualistic Islam that embodied those qualities he had previously associated with Western culture in opposition to Islam.[9] As a direct appeal to popular sentiment, *Hayat Muhammad* was a commercial success without benefiting Haykal or the Liberal party politically. Nevertheless, the popularity of *Hayat Muhammad* and later publications on early Islam circumscribed Haykal's public advocacy of Western ideals. He turned to politics, becoming head of the Liberal Constitutionalist party and president of the Egyptian Senate, but he never attained his real goal, the prime ministership.

Throughout his career, Haykal retained his belief that the intellectuals should rule. He became deeply alarmed by growing socioeconomic discontent in Egypt in the 1930s and viewed the impact of mass actions on public issues as a threat to his status as a landowner and intellectual. Concerned with the political chaos that enveloped Egypt after World War II, he saw the Officers' Coup of July 23, 1952, as an opportunity for him and the Liberals to gain power, unaware and unconcerned with the inspiration behind the overthrow of Faruq. He retained this illusion until Nasser abrogated parliamentary and constitutional life in April, 1954, an action that signified to him the ultimate victory of mass society.

Haykal's belief in the necessary leadership of the Western-oriented, intellectual elite was based on an amalgam of the views of Comte, Darwin, Spencer, and Mill. He accepted the positivist scheme of stages of social development leading to a scientific stage, which he and many of his contemporaries writing for *al-Jarida* (1907–14) thought Europe had reached. This in turn established proof of the law of the survival of the fittest, which demanded Egypt's adoption of Europe's scientific, rationalist techniques if she were to "survive." The means for placing Egypt on the path taken by Europe lay in the presence of those intellectuals educated according to European principles. Though a small minority, their superior knowledge required their leadership if Egypt were to achieve real independence.

Haykal linked these views to universal processes of history embodied not only in positivist schema, but also in his vision of the role of intellectuals. Throughout history, individuals possessing special awareness, geniuses, had acted against the prevailing sociocultural ethic to propel societies ahead. This was the basis of all great intellectual awakenings, whether religious in past centuries or secular in the present. Such awakenings reflected the insight of these special individuals into the true "spirit of the age," which enabled them to place society on the proper path. As the spirit of the modern era was scientific, Egypt had to accept the views of the Westernized elite. In this manner, Haykal saw himself and his colleagues as embodying the requisites of historical progress on a universal scale by assuming their right to lead, separate from the masses and the dominant Islamic ethic.[10] Conversely, this messianic attitude presupposed definite attitudes toward the people to be led. They should obediently follow the guidelines set down by the intellectuals, a view Haykal shared with, and likely borrowed from, Ahmad Lutfi al-Sayyid, editor of *al-Jarida*.[11] This conception of the masses contained a definite feeling of alienation in the positive sense of intellectual superiority, an assumption of the separation that should be maintained to preserve the intellectuals from harmful contact with the people. To become involved with the masses on their terms or level would signify becoming caught up in their irrationality. In so doing, the intellectual would be harming Egypt by harming himself, a conceptual framework in which the intellectual's obligation to isolate himself from the people was a duty benefiting Egypt, not merely a personal whim.

Initially presented in secular and individualistic terms, Haykal's arguments and expectations of leadership changed once religious opposition became a political factor, further weakening Liberal Constitutionalist political fortunes. *Hayat Muhammad* was both an intellectual and political response to these challenges. Haykal recognized his expediency, however, and considered his appeal to the masses on their terms a derogation of his role as an intellectual. Rather than leading from a distance, striving to elevate mass consciousness, he had stooped to their irrational level to seek their support, appealing to them on religious grounds, whatever his manipulation of the ideas themselves. Although he felt he had no choice given the circumstances, he believed he had compromised himself despite his continued political activity.

A factor of increasing importance for Haykal's continued involvement in Islamic publications in the 1930s was his growing concern over the emergence of class consciousness and of popular demands for greater socioeconomic equity. These developments threatened "chaos," the setting of different social groups against one another and particularly against the intellectual elite. It was a specter in sharp contrast to the harmony Haykal recalled from his childhood in the village, where the peasants both obeyed and loved his grandfather, the 'umda.[12] The 'umda provided a model of unquestioned paternalistic authority that he envisaged for Egypt as a whole, with the intellectuals in command. In the 1930s, he sought justification for such a system within Islam. In the second edition of *Hayat Muhammad,* Haykal advocated an Islamic socialism that would preserve property and inheritance. It guaranteed the spiritual equality of all men, but "as God had made some people above others and had distributed wealth to whom He wished, people have no choice but for the lowly to respect the great and the great to have [voluntary] compassion for the poor. . . . "[13] Acknowledging that his views were contrary to those of modern socialism, Haykal argued that his version preserved social harmony rather than introducing chaos through class conflict. It should be the model for all, not only Muslims, because it had originated at the time of the Prophet Muhammad, an apologetic technique used to claim universal validity for an idea intended to gain popular acceptance of the status quo through religious sanction.

What had begun as an attempt to inculcate Western scientific ideals as a means of elevating the level of the masses and achieving progress had now become a vehicle for preserving the position of the intellectual in the face of social change and by preventing that change if possible. Haykal's own awareness of the nature of his efforts and his growing despair at the likelihood of their success emerge not only in his articles and books, but perhaps more directly in his fiction. There, he constructed a dichotomy between rationality and irrationality in the form of love relationships and the individual's ability to comprehend true love that lasted, with changing emphases, from 1914 to 1955. His treatment of this dichotomy serves as a specific index of his consciousness of his role and the obstacles he confronted.

For Haykal, love served as a metaphor for his vision of the intellectual's relationship to mass society. The need to remain separate and to elevate the mass of Egyptians to a higher level applied to male-female relationships and the ability of the intellectual to find true love. Haykal, like Qasim Amin before him, saw the low status of women as the chief symbol of Egypt's backwardness. He went further than Qasim in believing, in his youth, that women should be entirely equal to men, their partners intellectually as well as emotionally and sexually. In this manner, women were identified with and epitomized the lower classes in general; they were irrational by virtue of their lack of education and their enslavement to the customs of the veil and arranged marriages.[14]

To liberate women would mean the achievement of freedom and progress for society as a whole because social acceptance of their emancipation would require a radical transformation of popular attitudes. Conversely, its realization would signal Haykal's gaining of personal happiness and success by fulfillment of his role as an intellectual. Only through the elevation of women could he find a woman equal to him and realize hubb, true love, which encompassed a sense of aesthetic appreciation, enjoyment of beauty, and the merging of two spirits rather than merely two bodies. Hubb could only be gained through the exercising of free will and choice, rights that Haykal did not believe existed in Egypt in his youth but that would have to be attained if he was to find fulfillment intellectually and, metaphorically, as a lover. Opposed to hubb was hawa, irrational, physical passion, which symbolized the low level of intellectual comprehension and appreciation of true love existing among the lower classes, especially clear when a member of the lower class entered into a relationship with a member of the elite. Hubb and hawa were not mutually exclusive: the ideal relationship would include passion. Rather, this juxtaposition embodied a set of class distinctions justifying the maintenance of separation between the intellectual and the lower classes (or women) until they achieved his level. Such a process might take generations of training because of Egypt's stagnation.[15]

Haykal portrayed attempts to bridge the gap between the intellectual and Egyptian women as both impossible and disastrous, lessons that dominate his novels *Zaynab* and *Hakadha Khuligat*. The former, published in 1914, depicted the futility of the Egyptian intellectual's efforts to find hubb, true love, with women beneath his status. They can respond to the intellectual only on an emotional and sexual level, whereas he seeks a more equal, intellectual relationship as well. When the peasant-intellectual Hamid, representing Haykal, approaches Zaynab to talk and flirt, she reacts by trembling, embracing him, and "acting as if madness had overcome her." He can control the passion he feels, but she (and peasant women in general) cannot, as it is the basis of their actions. When he does have intercourse with a peasant girl, who he claims forced herself on him, he later considers his response with alarm.

> Whatever her allure, how could he with his stature descend to that to which he descended, . . . from the high heavens to the level of people who do not think, a working girl. . . . Woman is a devil, a snare into which men fall. She is pure evil designed to bring man down to earth from his heights of pride and greatness.[16]

As Haykal did have a long and apparently happy marriage, the preceding quotations reflect more the class considerations noted previously than an innate aversion to women. They also indicate his despair at the possibility of finding a woman equal to him in Egypt, as shown by Hamid's decision to leave his homeland and search for his happiness elsewhere.

On the other hand, *Hakadha Khuliqat* (Thus She Was Created), published near the end of Haykal's life in 1955, was his commentary on his career following his decision to approach the masses on their irrational level by turning to Islam as the framework within which he addressed them. The heroine, representing Egypt, is controlled by blind passion, not so much sexually as in her material greed and need to dominate those around her. Though capable of recognizing her faults, she is not sufficiently educated to be able to use her mind to govern her needs; she cannot control the passions she feels, the same theme as advanced in contrast to the peasant-intellectual in *Zaynab*. She thus destroys all chances for love and wrecks the life of her first husband, a doctor of rural origins representing Haykal. Her hope of finding solace in Islam at the end of her life leads to her rejection of the opportunity to realize true love with her second husband without finding the happiness and peace in religion that she had sought. Explicit here, as in the short stories Haykal also published in 1955, was the lesson that the intellectual marrying beneath his level for love would be destroyed by the irrationality, hawa, in which he became involved, as the women could not react logically or loyally to the love offered to them. Under these conditions, true love, and recognition and acceptance of the intellectual, were unrealizable in Egypt.[17]

Haykal's deliberate use of these themes as a commentary on his own role in undermining his ideals is clear in a short story published in 1933, precisely the time when he shifted to Islamic themes and was engaged in writing *Hayat Muhammad*. "Kaffarat al-Hubb" (The Atonement for the Sin of True Love) presents a love affair in which the opportunity for fulfillment of the intellectual's ideal existed. The woman is both beautiful and intelligent, possessing that aesthetic sensibility nonexistent in the women of *Zaynab* or Haykal's later writing. Furthermore, once widowed from an unhappy marriage, she wishes to marry her lover, a judge from the countryside (again representing Haykal). Here, however, the judge rejects the idea of marrying her despite having longed for it previously. He now wishes to continue in the "role" of lover, a term repeated several times, and would be willing to have the heroine marry another. Stunned by his refusal to marry her, the heroine commits suicide, Haykal's commentary on the meaning of his choice to deal with mass instincts from within the guise of Islamic apologetics. His decision to play the "role" of intellectual in Egypt, commenting from within the texts he wrote that apparently defended Islam, signaled that he had abandoned his open commitment to secular reform in Egypt, just as the judge refused to commit himself openly to his beloved. Egypt, in the guise of women, would remain incompletely educated and therefore irrational, with results he felt obligated to describe in the first person in *Hakadha Khuliqat* twenty years later.

Nevertheless, although the judge rejected the ideal woman sought by the intellectual, Haykal did not condemn him outright, despite his own awareness of the meaning of his choice to turn to Islam. Life itself bore real responsibility. Whereas hawa had previously signified feminine irrationality associated with sexual passion, it now embodied the values of contemporary material life as well. The peasants of *Zaynab* could not fathom the meaning of hubb, but the "elegant people" of Cairo in 1933 viewed the idea of hubb with cynicism and pursued material gratification, hawa, indiscriminately, a theme carried over to Haykal's later fiction.

This change indicated Haykal's realization that the ideal society could not exist in Egypt. The alternative to the static and oppressive countryside representing the traditional past had been the city. Initially seen as the source of a Western education and escape from tradition, the city now reflected a chaotic influx of Western ideas, resulting in the pursuit of political and material gain. The intellectual was free in neither place, since the result of development and greater popular freedom was the growing assertiveness of the lower classes, a result that Haykal now contrasted to the stability and peace of the rural life of the past, whatever its intellectual and religious rigidity. There his family's status had been acknowledged unquestioningly. In seeking to assume a new role of intellectual leadership, Haykal felt he had sacrificed a sense of community, whose superimposition on the nation now seemed less possible. It was no accident that he could write an article in 1935 entitled "The Beloved Life" in which he harked back to the days of his childhood and the mutual respect on which relations between the 'umda and the villagers were based. It was a relationship based on hubb, which now signified a social framework in which the individuality of the elite was ensured by the villagers' passivity and gratitude at the former's fulfillment of its responsibilities to them.[18]

Haykal's treatment of love thus served as a metaphor for his career, a commentary on his hope of achieving his goals as an intellectual, given the impact of changing social relationships in Egypt. It also reflected the conflicting dualism of his approach to the problems of individualism and community. When discussing personal relationships, hubb meant the right of individual free choice in defiance of traditional norms, presumably only truly realizable and attainable by two persons of equally high levels of education. When presenting landlord-peasant relations, however, hubb signified the masses' acceptance of a static society and existing circumstances, the preservation of traditional bonds where leadership was unquestioned. In both cases, the particular and separate status of the intellectual would be recognized and secured.

Significantly, in the 1930s, Haykal could apply these distinctions only to a past image, the village of his youth. The milieu recalled in "The Beloved Life" was that found in *Zaynab,* where the intellectual could extol the validity of his ideal whatever the frustration of its realization at the moment. Nevertheless, his practical response, and that of colleagues, to change contained many elements of this rural model, even when introducing Western ideas and technologies. The rationale behind much of the impetus to industrialize among bankers and landowners after World War I, intensifying in the 1930s, was the preservation of order. An expansion of the economic base would provide jobs and lessen the likelihood of social unrest. Industrialization was seen more as a means of preserving the social status quo than as a response to opportunities arising within Egypt's socioeconomic structure.[19] Haykal's arguments for an Islamic socialism in *Hayat Muhammad* reflected this concern.

A more concrete example of Haykal's dualism in approaching issues of modernization and social reform was his motivation for supporting expansion of primary education among the peasantry. He claimed credit for its spread during his term as minister of education in 1938–39, noting it in his *Memoirs* as an example of his contributions to Egypt's progress.[20] On the other hand, his articles at the time indicated his long-standing concern and that of many landowners and politicians at increasing peasant migration to cities, which lent itself to political instability and deprived landlords of ready labor. Although this urban influx was due largely to increased landlessness and deprivation in rural areas, Haykal interpreted it as a result of a feeling of superiority among those peasants who had acquired literacy and thought themselves better than their illiterate compatriots; their newfound ambition caused them to wish to leave the countryside. If, however, "education becomes the rule and illiteracy the exception, the literate peasants would not be able to consider primary education a means of creating distinctions and would be forced to find a feeling of superiority, good character, and a lofty spirit" in their rural environment rather than by migration to the cities.[21] Haykal's intent in seeking educational reforms, therefore, was not simply or primarily to extend its benefits, as he claimed later. It was, in essence, a preventive measure designed to retain that social acquiescence he had attributed to peasants previously and postulated for social relations in general. It was part of his search for harmony and order, which he believed was also threatened by the demands of emerging labor unions and the rise of popular religious groups such as the Muslim Brotherhood and Young Egypt, whose appeals included calls for alleviation of economic ills.

These themes and the disillusionment of their realization recall two often disparate strands of nineteenth-century European, particularly German, romanticism: the ideal of the free individual and the wish for the organic community of the past.[22] Here, as then, they reflect apprehension at the erosion of these concepts of life by the emergence of the modern state. For Haykal, however, they were combined; his communal image of society sustained and reinforced his perception of his ability to retain his individuality, an association consistent with his response to the immediacy of change occurring in Egypt. In a similar manner, Haykal incorporated, in himself, characteristics of stages that Karl Mannheim considered successive when examining German social growth in the nineteenth century. Mannheim suggested that a sense of distance between elite and mass was held both by a landed aristocracy, representing conservatism, which saw society as an organic entity they had a right to lead and, later, by liberals who believed they embodied the "spirit of the age."[23] Haykal and many of his *al-Jarida* colleagues before World War I possessed both outlooks, consistent with their backgrounds, circumstances, and more immediate pressures for modernization. Most stemmed from landed traditions that included a belief in the responsibilities of village leadership that carried over to the Liberal Constitutionalists.[24] On the other hand, Haykal and friends such as Taha Husayn and 'Ali 'Abd al-Raziq believed they represented the spirit of the age of progress. Indeed, one of the legacies of the *al-Jarida* period was a belief that the rural elite was far more responsive to the need to modernize than Cairenes, a view openly expressed by Qasim Amin at the dedication of the site of the new Egyptian University in 1908.[25]

This fusion of an urge to transform Egypt while preserving existing social relationships was entirely logical to those who emerged from rural backgrounds as assertive intellectuals at the turn of the century. Haykal and his colleagues assumed their ability to lead Egypt on a new path of historical development. They also assumed that their success required that their leadership be recognized and secured. At the same time, these views form a basis of comparison with German sociological thought in confrontation with the realities of modernization. As Robert Nisbet has observed, "The social structure of the Middle Ages, real or imagined, . . . has provided a common point of departure . . ." for analysis of the transition from medieval to modern Europe.[26]

German thinkers, including Marx, looked back to the image of medieval social relations based on a feeling of shared community, *Gemeinschaft,* but believed it lost in the reality of their immediate circumstances and historical evolution. Tönnies, as well as Max Weber and, later, Mannheim, considered the changes occurring in Germany within a sociological matrix as part of a sequence of historical development. Given the forces set in motion, the transition seemed inexorable. The sociologist sought to interpret these events, part of the process yet separated by virtue of his knowledge, which might serve to establish some control through his ability to explain the factors at work.[27]

In a similar manner, Haykal looked back to a much more immediate past embodying the values of *Gemeinschaft* that he, in contrast to

German thinkers, sought actively to preserve. The differences in their views appear clearly in a comparison of Haykal's conception of the rationalization of society with those of Weber and Mannheim. Both Weber and Mannheim saw themselves as attempting to interpret historical forces over which they had no control. When considering the links forged between industry and bureaucracy, Weber deplored the increasing and apparently inevitable hold that bureaucracy, as the child of the capitalistic rationalization of socioeconomic relationships, would have on society and individuality. His primary fear was the increasing loss of individual freedom and choice in submission to the demands of efficiency and productivity required for the functioning of rational capitalism.[28]

Nevertheless, I must stress that, in practice, Weber and Mannheim did not simply accept bureaucratic rationalization, despite their assumptions of its historical inevitability. Weber, in particular, strove to delay this process while simultaneously protecting Germany from mass upheaval and was quite willing to change his tactics to meet new circumstances. He actively backed German imperial expansion in the decade before 1914 because he believed that acquisition of colonies would encourage further economic growth that would delay social stultification and bureaucratic rationalization. He also thought this expansion would contribute to the consolidation of German national power, which was the chief consideration behind his theoretical as well as his more clearly political writings. Likewise, he conceived of the charismatic leader not simply as a buffer against bureaucracy, but primarily as a means of establishing strong leadership in an unstable postwar Germany, and swiftly attributed to him much greater power than originally intended once strikes broke out at the end of the war. Instead of being responsible to parliament as initially conceived, Weber granted the charismatic leader broad powers that should permit him to attract mass support while remaining independent of mass control. This would ensure "complete subservience and 'blind obedience'" of the people, precisely the idea of the people being "led unawares" that Haykal's mentor, Ahmad Lutfi al-Sayyid, postulated for Egypt.[29]

Mannheim shared with Weber his feeling of helplessness in the face of social changes threatening individuality, particularly the freedom of the intellectual, but he saw bureaucracy ultimately as a savior, not a villain. Faced with the specter of postwar Soviet revolutionary communism, fascism, and social crisis in Europe, bureaucratic rationalization seemed, to him, the sole means of saving society from dissolution. Strong bureaucracy could give order and efficiency to social relations, thereby resolving the conflicts arising out of the social stratification created by bourgeois capitalism, with resulting tensions between different classes and utopias. This bureaucratic efficiency might well endanger individual freedoms, but its alleviation of social stress was necessary. In addition, its threat to freedom could be minimized by society's acceptance of intellectuals as a separate group having a powerful contributory role as critics of those who governed, apart from considerations of class as well as bureaucratic regimentation. Such separateness would originate in their education, an inculcation of universal values enabling them to rise above particularistic concerns and their own class origins, thus establishing them as the only truly disinterested group in society. In this manner, their guidance would assist the restoration of social order, resolving the apparently unmanageable course of recent European history while preserving a separate function and identity for the intellectual.[30]

Weber and Mannheim both reflected, in these conceptions, specific historical circumstances in which they felt personally involved and threatened. Similarly, Haykal emphasized freedom of thought for the individual and sought to guarantee social order, but true individuals were Westernized intellectuals; social order could be maintained only by their active leadership while preserving a traditional framework of authority opposed to social stratification, even if modern structures of interchange such as parliamentary government were established. Weber and Mannheim saw rationalization as an imposition of rational and efficient values derived from capitalism to be used by an expanding bureaucracy to control and direct social relations. Haykal perceived rationalization in a literal and personal sense. It meant the introduction of rational, secular ideas by an elite whose supremacy would be undermined by the rise of classes with necessarily different visions, whether religious or economic. He opposed, albeit ineffectually, that process of social stratification already existing in Europe that Weber and Mannheim accepted as a given factor whose excesses might be controlled. What Weber and Mannheim saw as unstoppable, Haykal, in a premodern situation, assumed he could prevent—namely, the process of modernization in its social, as opposed to its intellectual, ramifications. What seemed in later nineteenth-century Europe to be only a lost ideal, the image of communal society and values now replaced by the reality of capitalism and mass society, a "necessary historical development," was, to Haykal, a necessary prerequisite of development with the inroads of mass society a threat to, rather than a concomitant of, progress.[31]

That this could be so rested, in part, on the meaning of modernization to the individuals considered. In viewing social developments with such pessimism, Weber and Mannheim saw themselves confronted with the results of a progressive constriction of their ideals and freedom because of the inevitable slowing of capitalistic expansion. There was little if any choice involved in these changes, whether bureaucratic rationalization or the growing potential for social instability. For Haykal and his colleagues, however, choices did seem to exist and to be required of them in light of historical development as well as immediate social concerns. What was crucial was to decide how to respond to the challenge and appeal of the West, not least in considering the colonial occupation of their homeland. The issue, in its most basic terms, was a matter of survival, whether in Darwinian or Islamic terms, with the modernist choice of secularization as much, if not more, a matter of envisioned necessity than a positive step willingly taken. Modernization was required if Egypt was not to stagnate and remain subjected to European control. At the same time, practical steps were required to preserve the leadership of the intellectuals and to maintain social order. These two goals would remain paramount for Haykal throughout his life. His changes of orientation to meet the demands of new political trends in Egypt were in keeping with Weber's own practical responses to the threats he perceived to German national stability both before and after World War I.

These questions, especially that of the search for an ideology that would achieve national survival, reappear in the thought and activity of a young Iranian intellectual, Ali Shari'ati (1933–77), whose writings attracted many members of the younger generation to the Islamic revolution that overthrew the shah in 1979. Shari'ati's father was a Shi'ite cleric and his initial education was steeped in Islamic history and thought. He came of age during the tumultuous period after World War II, when Iranian nationalists strove to free themselves of the threat of Soviet occupation in Azerbaijan and the ongoing British control of Iranian oil production. He later went to Paris, where he took his doctorate in medieval Iranian philology, but it is clear that he became familiar with Western sociological theory and with non-Western revolutionary sociology, especially the writings of Franz Fanon.[32]

A devout Muslim, Shari'ati absorbed elements of European thought while also being attracted to reformist thinkers who strove to revive Muslim societies against both cultural stagnation and foreign occupation, especially Jamal al-Din al-Afghani and Muhammad Iqbal. This dual influence of Western theory and Muslim reformist tenets had a particular impact on Shari'ati because of his view of Iranian society. He saw its future stranded between the polar opposites of the Shi'a Muslim clergy, steeped in traditionalism, and a younger generation educated in Europe and the United States that was totally secularistic and that linked its hopes to the shah's regime. Each represented oppression, religious or political, each demanded submission to a regime of thought or governance, and both seemed to ignore the social and religious deprivation of the mass of Iranian society.

In response, Shari'ati developed a corpus of writings, often published speeches, that mirrored his experience. He strove to ensure intellectual freedom as the path to personal and social salvation. Like Haykal, he advocated a return to original Islam where ijtihad was open to all and where no entrenched class interests existed, unlike later and current periods where vested interests competed and the clergy, itself, constituted a class. Shari'ati's writings suggest that the Islamic clergy was superfluous, that one should return to an era of total personal freedom whose example, if emulated, would lead to the overthrow of religious and political tyranny.

Here Shari'ati clearly differs from Haykal and those like him who abhorred the thought of social upheaval, but he is very similar in his argument that those who would lead this revolution and the subsequent resurgence of Islam as a symbol of religious harmony in a world of strife would be the "true intellectuals." Such individuals were clearly distinct from the people (al-Nas) who should practice ijithad as best they could to signify personal responsibility rather than reliance on clerical authority. True intellectuals understood both the essence of Islam and the real value or shortcomings of Western thought, thereby distinguishing them from those rooted in either an Islamic or totally Western intellectual tradition. Moreover, despite the lack of systematic development of his ideas, it seems clear that Shari'ati foresaw the leadership of Iranian society in the hands of such intellectuals, who resemble Plato's philosopher-king. Shari'ati considered himself to be part of a historic and historical evolution that would eventually lead to the fusing of spiritual and rational elements in man, whose potential could best be realized in a revitalized Islam that had thrown off the shackles of traditional thought while simultaneously escaping the materialistic appeal of Western ideas, be they liberal or Marxist in origin.[33]

The forcefulness of Shari'ati's arguments, though often expressed obliquely to avoid censorship and imprisonment, had a major impact on a rising generation that sought escape from Iran's stagnation within its own cultural tradition. He is quite different from the European or Egyptian intellectuals discussed in that his self-image as an intellectual does not prevent him from calling for social revolution. On the contrary, that revolution would apparently be the means whereby true intellectuals would achieve power. Also, unlike Haykal, Shari'ati rejects the idea of modernization outright, just as he rejects the idea of Western rationalism as a necessary basis of social renewal and national survival. What remains constant is the role of the self-conceived intellectual as leader, directing society along the path that, for Shari'ati, God, rather than history, deems both necessary and inevitable.[34]

The nature of the choices made or conceived as available and the intellectual's sense of futility at the course of Egyptian or Iranian development challenge David Apter's assumption that modernization, despite its costs, is or was desired eagerly throughout the world. Of particular interest is Apter's statement that "to be modern means to see life as alternatives, preferences, and choices," self-conscious choices implying rationality.[35] This assertion confirms Joyce Appleby's judgment that "the expectation that modernization will promote rationality as a mode of thought is more tautological than descriptive. . . ."[36] Conversely, the expectation that rationality, as a mode of thought, will promote modernization when its proponents, in her words, confront "the unfamiliar territory of a radically altered future" reflects the projection of the theorist rather than awareness of the actual choices perceived as available or preferable by the individual considered.

Expectations such as Apter's appear, as Bramson notes, peculiarly American.[37] They contain a belief in unlimited progress and the free role of the individual to act without the fear of mass behavior evidenced among European sociologists and, as indicated, much closer to Haykal's experience and that of Indian liberal politicians. It would seem, therefore, that an understanding of modernization would be aided by adding to functional analysis an awareness of the meaning of modernization and progress to those directing the process and believing themselves to be its guides. Their conceptions of their roles and the relationship of these roles to an ideal social structure, as opposed to a fluid one, can easily clash with the ideals and institutions through which they strive to achieve their goals.

These tensions can exist in U.S. analyses of the purpose of intellectual leadership as readily as in Egyptian. In a different context, Apter carries his notion of intellectuals as a special group deservedly apart from irrational whims hindering their efforts to the point where the term applies only to social scientists. In his view, meritocracy rewards the rational, those aware that the U.S. technological society requires "that power and prestige will be based on functional roles germane to modern industrial society in which science and efficiency go hand in hand." The gifted possess an integrity connected to a spirit of disinterested free inquiry in the scientific profession. They are alienated, but it is an alienation brought about by "superior wisdom" based on their "abilities to penetrate the ideologies of others and thereby emancipate themselves. In this group is the social scientist who is the objective observer. He penetrates all the disguises created by the untrained mind or the ideological mind and attaches himself to the image of the wise."[38]

Apter's social scientist thus becomes a true combination of Weberian and Mannheimian intellectual, guiding society by virtue of an ability to be "value free" through special rational knowledge, which disassociates the intellectual from all ideologies and belief systems. Apter strives to divorce the social scientist from irrationalism, which includes intellectual disciplines considered unscientific and emotional because they challenge the guidance of the objective observer, the social scientist, an assumption that is itself tautological rather than descriptive. Here Apter and Haykal are similar in their vision of the intellectual's or social scientist's role in social development. For both, positive alienation exists by virtue of knowledge and must be maintained to ensure proper guidance by the elite, more narrowly conceived by Apter. Their common dichotomy is between rationality and irrationality, the latter including the masses but also anyone disagreeing with them. For both, also, a tension exists in their need for unquestioning acceptance of their roles by the very people whom they consider inferior and from whom they feel it necessary to separate. Nevertheless, the differences are more significant and illuminate the problems of analysis referred to above. Apter, using U.S. society as the model, presumes social change and his role as arbiter of that change to be necessary for fulfillment of the conceived function of the social scientist. Haykal required the prevention of such change for fulfillment of his role as a rational intellectual.

With these comparisons, we can return to the problem of definitions raised at the beginning, between the self-conscious and functional intellectual. As J. P. Nettl has shown, the intellectual should be considered from "inside out" with his role defined on the basis of his perception of his intellectual identity and social context.

> The intellectual emerges from a cultural base and with a sociopolitical role (culture in this context is defined as a self-conscious concern with cultural dimensions). . . . Thus the intellectual can be defined from a triple set of dimensions: (1) a profession that is culturally validated, (2) a role that is sociopolitical, (3) a consciousness related to universals.[39]

Nettl rejects the functionalist identification of intellectuals with specific professions made by Shils and Lipset. He relates the consciousness of the intellectual to universalism, a feeling of conscience and awareness, a focus on "a single overriding idea contrasted not only with particularism as a system of thought, but with professionalism as a social category."[40] The definition of the intellectual should be "more a movement than a state." It is linked to certain culturally validated professions such as artists, writers, or lawyers, but corresponds more to their fulfillment of a social role using rationalist principles for critical judgments of society. Such intellectuals are critics by the fact of their universal awareness and conscience, qualities that distinguish them from the "technicians," engineers, planners, or administrators, who have no awareness of a global conscience; conversely, true intellectuals lack access to knowledge pertaining to diverse and limited specializations.

Nettl is unconcerned with modernization. He wishes to establish a conception of intellectuals linking their sense of self-validation with cultural acceptance, social tolerance of their right to possess and present critical ideas in a modern, technological society. Only with this tolerance can "structures of dissent" exist without fear of repression; the role of the dissenter is the special social function of intellectuals, given their perception of universal issues. True freedom can exist only where intellectuals are free to define their roles and express themselves without fear of reprisal rather than being accepted only by association with social or professional functions of a particular utility.

Nettl's conception of the intellectual is reminiscent of Mannheim's attempt to establish a separate, critical status for an intellectual elite in modern society. Though postulated with reference to developed states, it establishes criteria useful for examination of the intellectual's self-image and assumption of status in premodern contexts as well. It enables us to go beyond Shils's often blurred distinctions between creative and functional intellectuals to recognize a commonality of intellectual attitudes, European as well as non-European, toward change, its social impact, and the self-conscious intellectual's wish to remain separate from that process, if possible. Nettl's framework is broad enough, however, to permit recognition of different responses by these intellectuals based on their assumptions of their abilities or need to control society, assumptions that reflect particular sociohistorical contexts as well as levels of modernity. Such individuals can envision the impact of modernization on their lives and its implications for the future to conflict with their intellectual affinity for the culture they consider modern. They also wish to remain apart from, and possibly in confrontation with, mass society and its values, their critical stance justified by their superior awareness of the transformations occurring.

Opposed to this stance are functional intellectuals, the technicians. They are created by modernization and its demands, greater proliferation and specialization of tasks requiring expanded literacy and new, more narrowly defined skills. They are the product of development rather than its victim, their opportunities enhanced by the expansion of the functions available in modern society. From Nettl's perspective, Apter, as a social scientist, is a technician, not a true intellectual. He seeks separation from society to serve its needs more efficiently, not to act as critic of the ramifications of that efficiency; such critics are to him irrational. Apter also mirrors Bramson's distinction between European and U.S. sociologists, the former concerned with social relations in a total context, the latter with particular issues because they do not see themselves as threatened by behavior in a class construct. Using Nettl's criteria, Apter's assumption of the superior, disinterested role of the social scientist is itself particularistic and indicates his own sociohistorical experience. His claim that social scientists possess a higher, nonideological consciousness is the justification of his argument that they should perform specific, functional tasks.

Nettl's consideration of the intellectual from inside out is thus more germane to an analysis of the self-conceived intellectual in society than discussion of the functional roles with which they or literate persons are associated. Using Nettl's criteria in a more restricted framework than the realm of ideas per se permits an evaluation of Haykal's or Shari'ati's conception of universality as an extension of a particular social and personal experience in the same manner as Weber's, Mannheim's, Nettl's, or Apter's are a product of theirs; all seek to ensure the intellectual, as defined, the right to guide or criticize in what they perceive as a regimented environment. There is clearly a commonality of attitudes toward presumed roles apart from society and mass activity that stems from the intellectual's self-consciousness, whether Muslim or Western, despite the different nature of assumptions about how these roles should be fulfilled.

Awareness of these issues may help to assess the nature of change and different interpretations of its implications in developing countries, rather than attempting to measure such change in light of functional criteria alone. Eisenstadt's discussions of posttraditional societies reveals his dismay that expectations of progress toward more rational hierarchical structures of authority may have not been realized.[41] A more recent and very different interpretation of social development in the Middle East contains the same problem of projection, albeit from a different stance. Leonard Binder postulates the ultimate emergence of an "Islamic liberalism" when the bourgeoisie in Muslim countries expands sufficiently to conflate apparently conflicting tendencies found in conservative and liberal Islam.[42] The likelihood of this achievement rests on a growing tolerance of intellecutal freedom in the Islamic milieu, possible because both conservatives and liberals return to the same sources for their inspiration. But this fusion of interests between conservative and liberal Muslims will only come about when the bourgeoisie itself receives guidance from true intellectuals who feel at home in both Western and Muslim thought.

Despite Binder's extensive criticism of past approaches to the question of development, including that of Manfred Halpern, who envisaged the growth of a secularized bourgeoisie as the basis of a modern, rational state, Binder seems to provide an updated version of Halpern that takes into account the significance of various strands of Muslim thought on the question of society and the relevance or irrelevance of Western values to Muslim life. And despite Binder's wide-ranging foray into Western studies in hermeneutics and deconstruction, along with development theory, he returns, in the end, to the role of the intellectual as guide, mentioning in particular Abdallah Laroui, a Moroccan scholar at home in European as well as Muslim thought.[43] Laroui is important to Binder, I suggest, not simply because he himself has postulated the role independent intellectuals should play in directing society, but also, and perhaps primarily, because he ranges easily between Western and Islamic models of society. In short, Laroui is Binder's mirror image, a self-conceived intellectual fulfilling the goals of a liberal future to which both aspire. It is a future far more in keeping with the tenets of Western liberalism and rationalism than it reflects a concern for adherence to Muslim teachings, even though it must be based on Muslim bourgeois acceptance of its legitimacy. Just the opposite of that future envisaged by Ali Shari'ati for Iran, it is quite in keeping with Laroui's Franco-Moroccan background and his critical acceptance of Western ideas in contrast to Shari'ati's rejection of their underlying principles.

That Binder should choose Laroui as his model intellectual even though all the subjects of his analysis of different trends of Islamic thought have been Egyptian does not bother him. His projection of salvation through liberalism, to be achieved by the guidance of the Western-oriented intellectual, overrides his declared concern for the supposed integration of the intellectual with his environment. What he prefers is the ability of the intellectual to fuse various currents of Western and Muslim tradition in himself, a theoretical environment reflecting Binder's own interests. In this regard, Binder seems close to Apter, projecting his own sociohistorical background and career onto a different experience.

The expectations of these Western analysts indicate more the investigators' presumptions of the inevitability of certain structures emerging rather than their analyses of indigenous circumstances. Binder, like Apter, retains an optimism rooted in his own intellectual orientation for the triumph of Western, liberal values. The intellectuals I have considered strive to retain elements of their traditional societies they consider essential to social stability and that, in the more recent cases of Ali Shari'ati or Sayyid Qutb of Egypt, oppose the Western values Binder postulates as still attainable. These expectations, therefore, lack awareness of or interest in the desire for social continuity found in both Westernized or Muslim intellectuals. Their images of the ideal society may differ, but they all offer the hope of social order directed by individuals who assume they are truly rational by virtue of their educations.

In this regard, the utility of the *Gemeinschaft-Gesellschaft* dichotomy is not merely analytic, as Smith suggests, and as functionalists have stressed in order to examine how the ideal communal order has broken down and what restructuring of society has occurred.[44] The dichotomy can have an empirical reality to those who hope to direct the anticipated change, a change that, in Shari'ati's view, should reject Western values. Both Haykal and Shari'ati seek to preserve or restore a community, one in which social harmony is protected against the impact of Western precepts that cause social friction. For Haykal, his efforts explain the gap between his self-conscious rationalism and rejection of the religious legitimation of life and his continued adherence to the underlying social order linked to that basis of legitimacy. For Shari'ati, to be a true intellectual in Muslim terms meant to strive to create a new moral order embodied in a Muslim community free from clerical guidance and Western rationalism that remained obedient to the new form of leadership that he personified.

In Haykal's case, we can trace his impression of his changing relationship to Egyptian society as a result of social change through his fiction as well as through his public pronouncements, with his perception of his dilemma more consistently developed in the former. Though his beliefs cannot be generalized for all Egyptian intellectuals attracted to the West prior to 1952, they do reflect the attitudes of many of the self-conceived elite emerging out of the *al-Jarida* milieu who, as Liberal Constitutionalists, were often considered, by other Egyptians and the British as well as by themselves, those most capable of ruling because of their educations. That they could not do so or bring themselves to do so illuminates an attitude both understandable yet destructive and ultimately self-defeating for the intellectual and the society he envisioned.

NOTES

I wish to thank Joyce Appleby, Richard Steele, and Clement Henry for their criticisms of earlier versions of this chapter, and also the Comparative Studies in Society and History seminar participants, in particular Shahrough Akhavi and Juan Cole, for their suggestions.

1. For discussion and criticism of these issues, see Anthony D. Smith, *The Concept of Social Change: A Critique of the Functionalist Theory of Social Change* (London, 1973); S. N. Eisenstadt, "Studies in Modernization and Sociological Theory," *History and Theory* 13 (1974): 225–52.

2. Edward Shils, "The Intellectuals and the Powers: Some Perspectives for Comparative Analysis," in *On Intellectuals, Theoretical Studies, Case Studies,* ed. Philip Rieff (New York, 1969), 27.

3. Edward Shils, "Influence and Withdrawal: The Intellectuals in Indian Political Development," in *Political Decision Makers,* ed. Dwaine Marvick (Glencoe, Ill., 1961), 30.

4. Ibid. and Shils, "The Intellectual between Tradition and Modernity: The

Indian Situation," *Comparative Studies in Society and History,* supp. 1 (The Hague, 1961) (hereafter referred to as "Tradition and Modernity"). See, particularly, 9, 12, 16–18, 24–25 for association of the intellectuals with popular causes.

5. Shils's treatment of the Liberals' attitude toward Gandhi and their opinion of the people differs from "Tradition and Modernity" to his article "Influence and Withdrawal." In the former, the Liberals are treated in light of their development of a constitutional framework from which India's parliamentary system would arise, not with reference to their opinion of Gandhi; Shils merely mentions that the Liberals "were lost in the shadow cast by Gandhi's personality and the politics of the Indian National Congress . . . " ("Tradition and Modernity," 88). Furthermore, Shils presents most Indian intellectuals as being attracted by populism because they were alienated from British authority. This alienation made Gandhi attractive to the intellectuals as a symbol of their being Indian (74–75, 101). They were also attracted by his personality, despite their dislike of the Congress party, which he led. Although Shils incorporates material from his monograph (cf. "Tradition and Modernity," 101, and "Influence and Withdrawal," 41), his discussion of the intellectuals' antipathy to the masses and mass organization in the latter conflicts with his discussion of an intellectual attraction to Gandhi and populism in the former. His association of intellectuals with bureaucracy exhibits further confusion. He states that "the leaders of the States of Asia and Africa and the intellectuals who play such an important part in most of them aspire to transform their societies according to an ideal of modernity. . . . They wish to establish a far-flung system of modern bureaucratic administration. . . . " ("Tradition and Modernity," 12). He then notes that while many Indian intellectuals had played outstanding roles in public life and the civil service, intellectuals as a whole hated the "distant bureaucratic power" of the Indian Civil Service and its role in ruling the state (97–101). For a discussion of the Liberals in Indian politics, see Ray T. Smith, "The Indian Liberals and Constitutionalism in India," in *Studies in Indian Democracy*, ed. S. P. Aiyar and R. Srinivasan (New York, 1965), 27–39; R. T. Smith, "The Role of India's 'Liberals' in the Nationalist Movement, 1915–1947," *Asian Survey* 7 (July, 1968): 607–24. The similarities to Husayn Haykal and the *al-Jarida* group, discussed subsequently, are many, particularly in their sense of elitism and tutorial attitudes toward the masses that required the maintenance of distance from them if a rational approach was to be preserved. Egyptian and Indian liberal intellectuals shared the conviction they should lead their countries in the preparatory stages of education prior to gaining full independence. For a broader analysis of self-conscious elite attitudes toward modernization among nationalist radicals that did not entail a desire for social reconstruction, see J. H. Broomfield, *Elite Conflict in a Plural Society: Twentieth Century Bengal* (Berkeley, 1968), particularly the introduction and 131–62, 316–31.

6. See the call for the use of literature by historians in John V. Fleming,

"Historians and the Evidence of Literature," *Journal of Interdisciplinary History* 4, no. 1 (Summer, 1973): 95–106. I am calling attention more to the evidence of attitudes than artifacts and material evidence, which are Fleming's primary concern.

7. Norman Birnbaum suggests the particular impact of change on Germany in "Conflicting Interpretations of the Rise of Capitalism: Marx and Weber," *British Journal of Sociology* 4 (June, 1953): 126. See also Talcott Parsons, "Democracy and Social Structure in Pre-Nazi Germany," *Journal of Legal and Political Sociology* 1–2 (1942): 108–11.

8. Albert Hourani, *Arabic Thought in the Liberal Age* (New York, 1962), 130, 171, referring to Muhammad 'Abduh and Ahmad Lutfi al-Sayyid.

9. For a discussion of this controversy, see Charles D. Smith, "The 'Crisis of Orientation': The Shift of Egyptian Intellectuals to Islamic Subjects in the 1930s," *International Journal of Middle East Studies* 4 (October, 1973): 382–410; C. D. Smith, *Islam and the Search for Social Order in Modern Egypt: A Biography of Muhammad Husayn Haykal* (Albany, 1983).

10. These views were discussed frequently in Haykal's unpublished diaries for his years in Paris, 1909–12, and in articles published in *al-Jarida* during the same period.

11. Lutfi founded the newspaper *al-Jarida* (1907–14), which represented the Umma party. Hourani (*Arabic Thought*, 170–84) discusses Lutfi's career and ideas, while evidence of his view of the elite-mass relationship can be found in Charles Wendell, *The Evolution of the Egyptian National Image from Its Origins to Ahmad Lutfi al-Sayyid* (Berkeley, 1973), 275–90; Jamal M. Ahmed, *The Intellectual Origins of Egyptian Nationalism* (London, 1961), 91ff. For a discussion of the philosophical bases of this elite-mass distinction in medieval Islam, also see Nikki Keddie, *An Islamic Response to Imperialism: Political and Religious Writings of Sayyid Jamal al-Din al-Afghani* (Berkeley, 1968).

12. This longing for the rural past and its image of peace in contrast to present disorder was expressed vividly in Muhammad Husayn Haykal, "Al-Hayat al-Mahabba" (The Beloved Life), *al-Hilal* (April, 1934): 641–46.

13. Muhammad Husayn Haykal, *Hayat Muhammad* (Cairo, 1936), 543–44. These ideas were likely taken from Herbert Spencer, "Justice," in *Ethics*, pt. 2 (London, 1893), 40–46, where the inherent inequality of society and the right of man to hold property is supported. "Justice" was the only segment of Spencer's works Haykal read.

14. Hourani, *Arabic Thought*, 164–70.

15. These matters and their fictional examples are examined more fully in Charles D. Smith, "Love, Passion, and Class in the Fiction of Muhammad Husayn Haykal," *Journal of the American Oriental Society* 99, no. 2 (April-June, 1979): 249–61.

16. Muhammad Husayn Haykal, *Zaynab* (Cairo, 1964), 180–81.

17. In the collection, published as *Qisas Misriyya* (Egyptian Stories), only one story depicted a happy marriage containing true love. Significantly, the couple met and married outside Egypt, in Paris, and did not return to live in its stultifying environment.

18. Most explicitly stated in "al-Hayat al-Mahabba," but repeated in Haykal's articles on the need to stop peasant migration to the cities and its connection to social reform in general. See, for example, "Muhadirat Dr. Haykal Basha fi al-Islah al-Ijtima'i" (The Lecture of Dr. Haykal Pasha on Social Reform), *al-Siyasa al-Usbu'iyya,* February 10, 1940.

19. Robert Tignor, "The Egyptian Revolution of 1919: New Directions in the Egyptian Economy," *Middle Eastern Studies* 12, no. 3 (October, 1976): 50; Marius Deeb, "Bank Misr and the Emergence of the Local Bourgeoisie in Egypt," *Middle Eastern Studies* 12, no. 3 (October, 1976): 76. Cf. Eric Davis, *Challenging Colonialism: Bank Misr and Egyptian Industrialization, 1920-1941* (Princeton, 1983), in which attention is focused on local economic and world market factors that encouraged Egyptian landowners to support the creation of Bank Misr. Consequently, Davis's excellent study does not consider broader social attitudes.

20. Haykal devoted a chapter of his *Mudhakkirat fi al-Siyasa al-Misriyya* (Memoirs of Egyptian Politics) (Cairo, 1951-53), to his tenure as a minister of education (2: 92-133).

21. See Muhammad Husayn Haykal, "Hijrat al-Rif ila al-Mudun" (The Migration of the Countryside to the Cities), *al-Siyasa al-Usbu'iyya,* March 1, 1930; and several articles in the same paper between 1938 and 1940.

22. Leon Bramson, *The Political Context of Sociology* (Princeton, 1961), 30-32ff. See also Arthur Mitzman, "Anti-Progress: A Study in the Romantic Roots of German Sociology," *Social Research* 33 (1966): 65-85. As Bramson notes, these strands did come together in sociological romanticism, the idealization of *Gemeinschaft* linked with the "emphasis on the isolated, unhappy and alienated individual, liberated from the traditional society and thrust into the impersonal and abstract world of the city," a theme also found in Haykal's alienation from what he saw as the materialistic ideals of Egyptian politics, which he identified with city life.

23. Karl Mannheim, *Ideology and Utopia* (New York, 1968), 106-8, 127; Mannheim, "Conservative Thought," in *Essays on Sociology and Social Psychology,* ed. Paul Kecskemeti (New York, 1953), 80-83.

24. For a discussion of the 'umda in Egypt, see Gabriel Baer, "The Village Shaykh in Modern Egypt, 1800-1950," in *Studies in the Social History of Modern Egypt,* ed. Gabriel Baer (Chicago, 1961), 30-61.

25. See *al-Jarida,* April 18, 1908. Two references by Haykal to the *ruh al-'asr* (spirit of the age) are in his diaries, August 13, 1909, and "al-Harb wa Harakat al-Tajdid fi al-Sharq" (The War and the Movement for Regeneration in the East), *al-Siyasa al-Usbu'iyya,* February 25, 1928.

26. Robert Nisbet, The Quest for Community (New York, 1970), 79.

27. See, for example, Mitzman, "Anti-Progress"; Werner J. Cahnman, "Tön-nies and Social Change," Social Forces 4 (1968): 136–44.

28. A good summary of these issues with bibliography is Wolfgang I. Mommsen, The Age of Bureaucracy: Perspectives on the Political Sociology of Max Weber (New York, 1974), particularly 47–71, 95–115; see also Mitzman, "Anti-Progress."

29. See Wolfgang Mommsen, Max Weber and German Politics, 1890–1920, trans. Michael S. Steinberg (Chicago, 1984), esp. 82–83, 182–89, 340, 409ff; Peter Struve, Elites Against Democracy: Leadership Ideals in Bourgeois Political Thought in Germany, 1890–1933 (Princeton, 1973), 143. For Lutfi al-Sayyid, see Ahmed, Intellectual Origins, 91.

30. Mannheim's hope of establishing the intellectuals as a "classless stratum" guiding society is presented in Ideology and Utopia, 137–46. His despairing of this approach ever succeeding and his feeling of the need for institutional restraints through bureaucratic safeguards, still retaining the intellectuals as advisors if possible, emerges in Karl Mannheim, Man and Society in an Age of Reconstruction, 1st English ed. (New York, 1940), where the specter of mass irrationality arising out of the disintegration of liberal society is a central issue. A good discussion of these and other issues can be found in Colin Loader, The Intellectual Development of Karl Mannheim: Culture, Politics, and Planning (Cambridge, 1985).

31. Bramson, Political Context, 29–31.

32. I rely on the following works for my discussion of Shari'ati: Shahrough Akhavi, "Shari'ati's Social Thought," in Religion and Politics in Iran: Shi'ism from Quietism to Revolution, ed. Nikki R. Keddie (New Haven, 1983), 125–44; John L. Esposito, Islam and Politics (Syracuse, 1984), 182–87; Ervand Abrahamian, Iran between Two Revolutions (Princeton, 1982), 464–73; Abdulaziz Sachedina, "Ali Shari'ati: Ideologue of the Iranian Revolution," in Voices of Resurgent Islam, ed. John L. Esposito (Oxford, 1983), 191–213; Edward Mortimer, Faith and Power: The Politics of Islam (New York, 1982), 335–38. In addition, I have used two of Shari'ati's own works, Marxism and Other Fallacies: An Islamic Critique, trans. R. Campbell (Berkeley, 1980); and On the Sociology of Islam, trans. Hamid Algar (Berkeley, 1979). Although most sources agree on Shari'ati's commitment to Islam, Abrahamian argues that he saw himself as "a radical theorist who found his inspiration in Shi'ism and his tools of political analysis in Western social science—especially in Marxism. . . . [He wished to create] a secular religion that would appeal to the modern intelligentsia without alienating the traditional bazaaris and the religious masses" (467). This interpretation contradicts most others, especially that of Sachedina. I accept Shari'ati's religiosity at face value while realizing that no final verdict can be given.

33. For the "true intellectual" and his role, see Shari'ati, Marxism, 95–96.

For the masses and their individual responsibility, see Shari'ati, *Sociology of Islam*, 49–50. Akhavi, "Shari'ati's Social Thought," 137–43, has a good discussion of Shari'ati's idea of the enlightened intellectual and his political responsibilities.

34. Shari'ati declares that the "ideal man" should lead the "ideal society." This person is the "Viceregent of God [who,] because he has accepted [God's] heavy trust . . . is a responsible and committed being with the free exercise of his will" (*Sociology of Islam*, 123, and the broader discussion, 119–25). It seems likely that Shari'ati was influenced here not only by Shi'ite precepts but also by Thomas Carlyle's *Heroes, Hero Worship, and the Heroic in History* (London, n.d.), especially Carlyle's first chapter, "The Hero as Divinity." There the heroic individual receives divine inspiration that guarantees his freedom of action, "his free force direct out of God's hand" (15), a statement resembling Shari'ati's. Furthermore, both Carlyle and Shari'ati state that the great or ideal man forms his environment or age rather than being a product of it (Carlyle, *Heroes*, 15–16; Shari'ati, *Sociology of Islam*, 123). Shari'ati knew of Carlyle's study and called him a "great scholar" (*Sociology of Islam*, 46) but he distinguished himself from Carlyle's heroes because they separated themselves from society rather than seeking to influence it directly, precisely what Shari'ati hoped to do. Likewise, Haykal was influenced by Carlyle but saw himself as the product of a secular heroic era, whereas Shari'ati sought to improve on Carlyle's conception of the hero as divinity, a new prophet.

35. David E. Apter, *The Politics of Modernization* (Chicago, 1969), 1, 9–11.

36. Joyce Appleby, "Modernization Theory and the Formation of Modern Social Theories in England and America," *Comparative Studies in Society and History* 20 (April, 1978): 261.

37. Precisely because U.S. sociologists did not see themselves as threatened by behavior in a class construct and were more concerned with specific social problems than with society as a whole; see Bramson, *Political Context*, 47–55ff. Thus, the idea of man on his own, alienation to Europeans viewing it within the framework of community and social order, is celebrated as true individualism and liberation in the United States (67–70).

38. David E. Apter, "Ideology and Discontent," in *Ideology and Discontent,* ed. David E. Apter (Chicago, 1964), 37–38. It is ironic that while Apter argues that "ideology reflects the suppositions of its observers" (16), he ignores the implications of this statement for his own arguments, presumably because social scientists are beyond ideology; nevertheless, social science "has become the ultimate ideology . . ." as opposed to "nonrational, vulgar ideologies" (41).

39. J. P. Nettl, "Ideas, Intellectuals, and Structures of Dissent," in Rieff, ed., *On Intellectuals*, 81. Nettl's argument here is based on Edgar Morin, "Intellectuels: critique du mythe et mythe du critique," *Arguments* 4, no. 20 (October, 1960): 34–40.

40. Nettl, "Ideas," 82–83.

41. See the overview by S. N. Eisenstadt, "Post-Traditional Societies and the Continuity and Reconstruction of Tradition," *Daedalus* (Winter, 1973): 1–28; also see Eisenstadt, *Tradition, Change, and Modernity* (New York, 1973). I have not been concerned with the retention of traditional social structures or the growth of more modern "institutional or organizational frameworks" (Eisenstadt, *Tradition,* 102) as such. Rather, I wish to note an intellectual's impression of these structures and frameworks and his changing relationship to them.

42. Leonard Binder, *Islamic Liberalism: A Critique of Development Ideologies* (Chicago, 1988).

43. Manfred Halpern, *The Politics of Social Change in the Middle East and North Africa* (Princeton, 1963); Binder, *Islamic Liberalism,* 77–80. See also Binder, *Islamic Liberalism,* 9, for his perception of the importance of an Islamic bourgeoisie for any future liberal society in Muslim countries; especially 316–38 for his treatment of Abdallah Laroui.

44. A. D. Smith, *Concept of Social Change,* 94.

45. A British assessment is found in Foreign Office 371/21948/1197., dated November 7, 1938, which views the Liberals particularly and non-Wafdists in general as the best administrative talents in Egypt. An Egyptian view is that of Muhammad Zaki 'Abd al-Qadir, *Aqdam 'ala al-Tariq* (Steps Along the Way) (Cairo, 1967), 355–57. Al-Qadir admired the Liberals for their individual talents, intellectual and administrative, and was appalled at their cynical manipulation of political life in violation of their stated principles.

Part 3
States and Social Structures

Smashing Idols and the State: The Protestant Ethic and Egyptian Sunni Radicalism

Ellis Goldberg

Recent scholars of the Middle East have implicitly and suggestively noted similarities between contemporary Muslim activists and sixteenth-century Protestant reformers.[1] A more explicit and rigorous argument comparing Protestantism and contemporary Sunni movements in Egypt can yield insights into both movements.

Both Calvinism and contemporary Islamist Sunni movements in Egypt are discourses on the nature of authority in society. Historically both movements arose as central state authorities made absolutist claims to political power and, in the process, sought to dominate transformed agrarian societies in new ways. Ideologically, both movements asserted that the claims of sweeping power by nominally religious secular central authorities were blasphemous egotism when contrasted with the claims of God on the consciences of believers. Socially, both movements transferred religious authority away from officially sanctioned individuals who interpret texts to ordinary citizens. Institutionally, both movements create communities of voluntary, highly motivated and self-policing believers that yield greater degrees of internal cohesion and compliance than the absolutist authority can achieve, and they therefore can become the basis for postabsolutist political authority in an authoritarian and antidemocratic fashion.

Although the use of the word *fundamentalist* is awkward and raises questions relevant primarily to Christian doctrine, it does convey something important about Protestant Christian and Sunni radical movements. Both early Protestantism and the Islamist movement seek to force believers to confront directly the authority of the basic texts of revelation and to read them directly, rather than through the intervening medium of received authority. Both believe that Scripture is a transparent medium for anyone who cares to confront it.

If both movements contain arguments about who can read and interpret Scripture, it behooves us to listen carefully to those arguments. The agenda they set forth is not economic but profoundly political: How do human beings cooperate and what role does coercion have when free consent is not forthcoming? It seems to me, therefore, that the fundamental question in post-Lutheran Protestant movements and in contemporary Sunni Muslim movements is an argument about public authority and the state rather than—as Max Weber would have had it—an argument about capitalism.

Weber and a Research Agenda for Religious Change

In *The Protestant Ethic and the Spirit of Capitalism,* Max Weber argued that shifts in religious doctrine have sociological as well as theological implications. In Weber's original formulation, Calvinism helped to forge the "spirit of capitalism," and thus the economic structure of modern capitalist Europe, through the doctrinal features of one specific form of Protestantism (Calvinism) in regard to transcendence and human predestination.[2] It was a new and powerful form of Christianity that "placed a premium on the individual's disposition to organise coherently and control consciously his own conduct."[3]

Modern scholars of Islam pursue the Weberian research agenda but focus on the 'ulama (authoritative interpreters whose role and socialization will be defined below), who are dismissed as likely Protestants. Most of these attempts to expand the Weberian thesis, or even test it in non-European contexts, keep largely to the theological dimensions of the argument.[4] Weber had also argued that Protestants were institutional innovators. He recognized that there was an institutional "Protestant ethic," insofar as the organization to which Protestants were typically partial was the small group or sect through which they associated.

Pursuit of institutional and ideological arguments were not long in coming and have largely transcended arguments about Protestantism based on doctrine.[5] All share an understanding of Protestantism as a cohesive community of equal and cooperating individuals. Sheldon Wolin has argued that organization through sects carried the "potentially explosive idea that a community rests on an active membership" and included the anarchist principle that human society could be "at once well organized, disciplined, and cohesive and yet be without a head."[6]

Michael Walzer's study of Puritan saints has found echoes in the contemporary literature on the Middle East.[7] Walzer defines Protestantism not as a doctrine but as a voluntary grouping of equals with a zealous commitment to engage in methodical and systematic struggle (including violence if need be) in order to attack customary social structures. Members who have a zealous commitment to ideologically oriented action are called "saints" by Walzer. These saints need not be religious, but are any individuals forming voluntary associations that engage in ideologically directed collective action. Thus, Walzer transforms Weber's arguments regarding sect organization to argue that Calvinism was historically important not only by means of sectarian organization but because of it. For Walzer, sect organization and radical political doctrine emerge in periods when social order breaks down and state structures become weak. Predictable ideological and organizational responses to disorder will, however, generate distinctive social outcomes depending on the real historical situation.

The Calvinist saints were the first of these bands of revolutionary magistrates who sought above all control and self-control. In different cultural contexts, at different moments in time, sainthood will take on different forms and the saints will act out different revolutions.[8]

It makes sense to Walzer to compare Puritan saints, French Jacobins, and Soviet Leninists because of their ideological and organizational similarities despite historical differences. His focus on institutions allows him to see a "Protestant" ethic in many more movements than does a strictly Weberian formulation.

I propose to look at contemporary Sunni activism to see if there are significant institutional and ideological similarities providing a useful comparison to Protestantism. Despite the many contextual and historical differences, such a comparison has at least two advantages. First, we are at least comparing Puritan saints with Muslim activists who both believe in a personal, all-powerful and all-knowing God—something not true of Jacobins or Bolsheviks. Second, we are comparing movements confronting not (as did Jacobins or Bolsheviks) weakened states but, on the contrary, strengthened states in which heads of state claimed unrestricted authority for themselves (which is somewhat more true of the Calvinists).

Why is authority important? Arguments about Protestantism hold it helped to destroy personal monarchies and absolutist regimes in Western Europe that emerged coeval with Protestant movements. In absolute regimes, the monarch rules as the sole source of law by means of a permanent, professional, and dependent bureaucracy and army.[9] Absolutism was a state in transition between two historical periods: one in which landed magnates possessed preponderant political power and another in which urban industrial capitalists possessed such power. Protestantism destroyed the absolutist monarch's claim to power because it destroyed the mystical base for civil authority, insisting that the interpretation of Scripture was the responsibility of all believers, not just officials bound by the classical corpus, and sanctioned methodical and ascetic behavior.

Given a tendency of some writers to make facile distinctions between Christianity and Islam on the basis of a supposed categorical separation of church and state in the former, a word of caution is in order.[10] Radical Protestantism worked not because it furthered the separation of church and state, but precisely because it did not. In Wolin's reading, Scripture and scriptural dispute provided believers with a standard by which the action of political authority could be judged. The merger of church and state became necessary in Calvinist thought because "political and religious thought form a continuous realm of discourse."[11] Calvinism created new ideological communities of activists endowed with a theory that allowed them to withdraw their allegiance from an institutional order that was only nominally Christian:

> But in the obedience which we have shown to be due to the authority of governors, it is always necessary to make one exception, and that is entitled to our first attention—that it do not seduce us from obedience to him, to whose will the desires of all kings ought to be subject, to whose decrees all their commands ought to yield, to whose majesty all their sceptres ought to submit.... If they command any thing against him, it ought not to have the least attention; nor, in this case, ought we to pay any regard to all that dignity attached to magistrates.[12]

Calvin's words resonate with earlier Christian thought, and we can find a similar note in the classical Islamic hadith literature, although it formed a minor note. Ibn 'Umar reported that "to hear and obey [the authorities] is binding so long as one is not commanded to disobey (God); when one is commanded to disobey (God), he shall not hear or obey."[13]

What we wish, then, to look at is twofold. First, have contemporary "fundamentalist" groups made the same kind of break with customary and received religious authority that the Puritans did? Second, if so, what are the implications of this break? I propose to look first at how some Protestant believers looked at authority and community in the context of earlier Christian thought and then to do the same for contemporary Egyptian Muslims. As a form of religious authority, Calvinism will be defined as a refusal to accept received interpretations of the texts of revelation and a refusal to accept the authority of the old interpreters as well.

The Protestant Paradigm

For Christian and Muslim believers there is a fundamental dilemma regarding the institutional stability of a visible community of believers. This dilemma arises because humanity once had direct contact with an omnipotent and omniscient divinity who continues to hold fallible men and women responsible for their actions despite the partial, imperfect, and limited nature of their understanding. Believers are the legatees of an institutional framework that claims historical continuity with revelation but that seems to lack the emotional basis to make its claims binding.

Between the institutional and intellectual task of maintaining historical continuity and the emotional task of creating anew the reception of revelation lies a significant religious space. To paraphrase Abdul Hamid el-Zein, the late anthropologist and student of Islam, the analyst cannot privilege the intellectual activity of systematic interpretation over that of "direct insight" into the order of the world.[14] We can only investigate how believers carry out these tasks. For my purposes, Protestantism involves the development of earlier Christian thought around four dimensions (which I shall later elaborate in terms of Islam). Protestantism brought new answers to four old questions inherent in Christianity (and perhaps any monotheism) and Protestants found themselves in a state of tension—if not war—with human society. Mastering themselves and society required thinking about four issues: (1) the claims due a single and all-powerful God by believers; (2) the recognition of the danger that there exist loyalties antagonistic to God; (3) the nature of education, socialization, and authority required to interpret the Scripture and determine what actions validly fulfill divine claims; and (consequently) (4) the relation of revealed Scripture to received interpretations of it. The emergent themes in Protestantism and contemporary Sunni radicalism recapitulate and transform earlier conflicts in their respective thought. Calvin's position on God's claims over man was simple enough in outline: "The purpose of creation is for man to know God and to glorify him by worship and obedience."[15] In Calvin's own words, "the worship of God is therefore the only thing which renders men superior to brutes, and makes them aspire to immortality."[16] What is worship? It is not merely a practice but the direct confrontation of God and His Word as the apostles or prophets or saints had done. When this occurs, the meaning of Scripture becomes apparent without institutional mediation.

> How shall we be persuaded of its divine original, unless we have recourse to the decree of the Church? This is just as if any one should inquire, How shall we learn to distinguish light from darkness, white from black, sweet from bitter? For the Scripture exhibits as clear evidence of its truth, as white and black things do of their color, or sweet and bitter things of taste.[17]

For the Reformers, the Reformation was not a social movement with mundane goals, but the reemergence of the spirit that men felt who had lived when God's presence was manifest.

> [T]he Reformation is not to be confused with any earlier worthy attempts which men undertook to put right the faults in the church or in Christendom. It is rather the work of Christ himself ... the reformation message is identical with the preaching of Jesus and his disciples, and actually transports us into the situation faced by the early church.[18]

The Reformation and Calvinism recapitulated some doctrinal and institutional forms of earlier Christian movements. The sixteenth century was not the first time Christians had turned to the Apostles for models. In the twelfth century, devout European Christians viewed the *vita apostolica* as a framework for "the return to the primitive life of the church, to the life of the Apostles ... [which] by inspiring new states of life, inspired as well a new awareness of the ways that grace could take root in nature."[19] In the Middle Ages, an

> evangelical awakening took place not by a revision of existing institutions but by a return to the gospel that bypassed those institutions . . . [whose] dynamics had to be: witness to the faith, fraternal love, poverty, the beatitudes—all these were to operate more spontaneously and sooner among laymen than among clerics, who were bound within an institutional framework. The risk could be great—and in this case it was great—that laymen would grossly abuse their evangelical liberty, for once on the way to imitating the apostles, they would claim the right to teach derived from that liberty.[20]

In the twelfth century the church could avoid this risk; in the sixteenth it could not.

In the Reformation, the Apostles ceased to be men whose lives were to be emulated; collectively they became models for a new form of governance that allowed the evangelical movement to re-create a community receiving a Scripture rather than one without it. The systematic emulation of the Apostles was coupled with congregational activity that allowed constant collective scrutiny to create high levels of individual compliance with religious norms.

Why was it so necessary to link congregationalism to the systematic following of the call of Jesus? Because, although salvation was granted to individuals, human social activity created the possibility of error and damnation.[21] The Protestants were not concerned that the visible church might fail to lead people to salvation; they were more concerned that it might systematically lead them away.[22] Obedience to the letter and form of revelation could easily become submission to idolatrous and nondivine claims. Men and women tended almost invariably, it seemed, not to worship God's truth and authority but human law and human power.

Norms arising from human law and power are idolatrous, because idolatry is the interposition of human and humanist values between the believer and the divine. The struggle against idolatry was not limited to iconoclasm; images were only one form of idolatry. Another form was manifest in the government of the Catholic church itself, in which Calvin saw "chaplains, canons, deans, provosts, and other idlers . . . [who] falsely usurp the honour, and thus violate the sacred institution of Jesus Christ."[23] If idolatry could be found within the church itself, it was possible that people who appeared to be good Christians actually were not and that figures of religious or civil authority were not entitled to respect.

For early Protestants like Ulrich Zwingli, *the* critical question of the age was whether or not customary religiously sanctioned practices were in accord with the revealed word of God. "The question for Zwingli was no longer one of rejecting the misuse of 'good and honorable customs'... but rather of separating human customs from divine ordinances."[24] The church and its received doctrines derived from interpretation of the Bible were not merely inefficient or ineffective customs to be cast off; rather they were themselves symbols of idolatry. Calvin certainly developed this aspect of Protestant thought to an extreme degree in the *Institutes* and asserted that "Scripture settles all questions and describes the truth [in]... detail."[25] At stake was not nominal controversy but the very essence of monotheist religion: "As often as the Scripture asserts that there is one God, it is not contending over the bare name, but also prescribing that nothing belonging to his divinity be transferred to another."[26]

Once the Scripture itself becomes the basis for decisions about ethics, morality, and what is required of Christians rather than a received body of interpretations, a significant decentralization of authority occurs. The logic of argument then discards not only that received interpretation of Scripture (that is, canon law and the entire range of church discourse built up in the medieval period) but also implies that interpreters no longer need socialization in the old educational institutions.

Socialization and education into the priesthood is a threat to the Protestant community and a derogation of the principles upon which it is built. For Calvin, the very preparation for entry into the priesthood marks the deformation of the intended function of the pastorate; the role of canons marks the deformation of the presbytery; and the dictatorship of the bishops and the Pope marks the extinction of the active participation of the Christian in the church. Calvin's critique of church government is far more scathing than his critique of civil government. Priests, Calvin tells us, do not know Scripture; they know only canon law.[27]

Protestantism was a directly powerful and compelling doctrine in the sixteenth and seventeenth centuries. Congregationalism and the possibility of a direct reading of the Scriptures gave legitimacy to lay theology and the pamphlet explosion that began as early as the first decades of the sixteenth century. City dwellers demanded religious reforms in order to preserve social community and sought an apostolic vocation, which implied that believers entered society and engaged in "admonishing one's brother against sin and warning him to repent."[28] Along with his fellow communicants, the believer henceforth was engaged in a constant struggle against idolatry and to obey the word of God in ways that required ever-increasing levels of knowledge of Scripture and a willingness to renounce received interpretations of it. To paraphrase Ulrich Zwingli, the believer was henceforth in a company of soldiers whose captain was Christ.

The Muslim Official Consensus: The Historical Background

Although there is no Islamic church, we can nevertheless identify a potential tension between the "visible community of believers" and the "invisible" or eternal community of believers. It is possible to identify a set of religious concepts in contemporary Sunni Islam that at least make it possible to examine a correspondence with Puritanism. I would like to suggest that these concepts are (1) jihad (the nature of the activity to which believers are called), (2) taghut (the existence of competing claims over the behavior of believers), (3) ijma' (a relationship between Scripture and received interpretations of it), and (4) the role of the 'ulama (the nature of the socialization and education required for interpreting the Scripture). The role of the 'ulama differs from that of the priesthood in many ways, not least of which is the absence of an established orthodoxy that they were to uphold.[29]

Although Sunni Islam lacks a charismatically endowed hierarchy, Sunni Muslims have developed a sophisticated methodology for understanding Scripture, for evaluating it, and for extending the logic of its arguments. The science of Scripture is called 'ilm. Those who practice 'ilm are known as 'ulama, that is, those who know. In general, the methodology mastered by these men (and they are all men) is jurisprudential knowledge.

Without a single, well-defined hierarchy with clear disciplinary capacities (such as found in the Catholic church), 'ulama could all arrive at different interpretations of Scripture. Only cooperation can avert the absolute fragmentation of the legal corpus whose mastery defines the 'ulama. Thus, the doctrine developed that "where ... conclusions were the subject of general agreement by the scholars, they then become incontrovertible and infallible expressions of God's law."[30] This general agreement is called ijma'. Over time, the mastery of the methodology and content of ijma' itself outweighs by far the effort required to master the Scripture.[31]

Historically, Sunni Muslims were enjoined as individual Muslims to the performance of five acts: the witness to the faith or shahadah (recognition of one God and Muhammad's prophecy), prayer, a ritual fast, the payment of alms, and pilgrimage. These essentially formal requirements establish the bounds for membership in a visible community of believers. Those who perform these rituals are members of a visible community and, possibly, members of the "invisible" community of Muslims who achieve Paradise. Historically, jihad was not considered to be a duty incumbent on all believers; it usually referred to relations between the Muslim community and other communities rather than within the Muslim community itself.[32]

Jihad has become a critical concept for contemporary Sunni Egyptian activists and may well be *the* critical concept for them. To the degree that these activists are like the Protestant reformers, their concepts of jihad should be markedly different from earlier understandings. Constant recognition of the supremacy of God and methodical service to Him should merge with a growing sense of antagonism to a purely nominal adherence to Islam. In succeeding sections I shall present some arguments that this is, indeed, the case.

Jihad is no longer thought of as a particular act or event, but it is the positive pole in a continuum in which believers orient themselves to action. Such a definition of jihad entails another concept: that of a negative pole in the continuum. There must be a competing and antagonistic claim regarding the behavior of believers.[33] Evil, the danger of a competing claim, should be understood in terms of a theology of human egoism rather than in naturalist terms. Idolatry is the principle of moral orientation that competes with God rather than the physical presence of Satan. One of the few studies of jihad as a concept in development affirms precisely such a differentiation over time—namely, that for contemporary fundamentalists, "The important objects of jihad are . . . : an end to the domination of man over man and of man-made laws, the recognition of Allah's sovereignty alone, and the acceptance of the shari'a as the only law."[34] Human egoism expressed in ordinary politics is designated by the Sunni activists as taghut—idolatry. Succeeding sections will show that the growing reliance on the concept of taghut is a "quasi-Protestant" shift in Muslim thought. The choice of the word *taghut* to refer to idolatry, rather *sanam* or *iblis* (which would refer to Satan), will be adduced to support this view.

Before doing so, let me briefly pursue the logic of the argument. Concern with jihad and taghut is not only a concern with the nature of the relationship of the egotistical individual to God, but it also challenges the received meaning of these concepts and implies a radical redefinition of the present Muslim community to its past and to the guardians of received knowledge from that past. Redefining what is required of the community of believers necessitates redefining the requirements for interpreting Scripture. It suggests that the monopoly over received interpretations must be broken.

Contemporary Sunni radicals attack the well-developed and sophisticated consensus of the 'ulama on two levels. First, they deny that the prior meanings are correct; and second, they deny the very right of such scholars to determine the meanings. This double attack on the 'ulamas' interpretations and their right to define them makes contemporary Sunni activism comparable to the Protestant impulse in Europe. A refusal to accept received interpretations means a return to the origins: Scripture. Denying the institutional integrity of the established religious elite challenges the kind of education, socialization, and authority required to interpret the Scripture.

To argue that the contemporary Islamic movement mounts a radical attack on received Islam requires the establishment of two prior arguments. We must first show that the ideas being discussed have an earlier provenance. Without prior dialogue, we might be looking at an imported idea rather than a conceptual break. Second, we must demonstrate that this break had not already occurred, even though contemporary activists were intellectually nourished by earlier debates. What follows is an attempt to trace the origins of the "Protestant" break with the immediate past and to provide a context for understanding the nature of contemporary Egyptian Islamist discourse.

Nearing the Edge

In his sermons and written work, Hasan al-Banna, founder of the Society of Muslim Brothers *(Al-Ikhwan al-Muslimun)* discussed many of the questions that concerned Sunni radicals in the 1930s and 1940s. Al-Banna's Brotherhood was the historic cradle of contemporary Islamic activism, and the personal connections between him and the present activists obscure the critical difference between them. Al-Banna was not a "Protestant," although this has been suggested.[35]

Al-Banna was concerned that Qur'anic inspiration enter the daily life of Muslims. He perceived a widespread flagging of emotional commitment to Islam but expected a solution from the existing political elite. He specifically addressed this problem in the sermon "Nazrat fi islah al-Nafs" (Remarks on Self-reform), with its striking central image of electricity.

> Why did the Noble Qur'an have such an impact on our worthy ancestors and why was it so beneficial to them but not to us? Why did the verses [of the Qur'an] affect our minds in so weak a fashion? Let me direct your attention to someone who creates electricity and must feel the electric current. This effect will vary with the force of the current, and if it is strong enough will put someone who comes into contact with it into the hospital and if it is stronger yet will put him in the grave [he then discusses similar physical effects on early converts to Islam]. . . . [I]f the effect of Qur'an is not the same in us as it was in our ancestors then we are like an electrician who has put insulation between himself and the current so that he is not affected by it, and our task is to break down this insulation so that we can feel the Noble Qur'an so that our hearts will be in communication with it and we will taste its sweetness.[36]

For al-Banna, modern Muslims were emotionally insulated from the Qur'an, but he did not connect this insulation with an institutional foundation. Commitment could increase primarily through practical activity rather than through a sweeping act of faith. Even those who were only nominal Muslims could, by integration into the works of an Islamic organization, play a role in creating an Islamic society. This was so because, for al-Banna, the community of Muslims was (in Wilfred Cantwell Smith's expression) orthoprax rather than orthodox.[37]

Without naively believing in the likelihood that all would become better, al-Banna nevertheless seems to have believed that men could affect not only their mundane but their eternal destinies.

> Regarding the Islamic spirit and the Islamic personality, 90 out of 100 never fully develop it. Thus it occurred to me to give this talk

on the role of self-reform and clearly explicate what it means to say if the character is changed everything will be changed "for God only changes [events] for those who change themselves." Now it is said that this is a characteristic aim of the Sufis and we are a Brotherhood of activists not masters of mysticism [shuyukh al-turuq]. I say we must fear lest Satan put a veil over our spirits so that we will not reach our goal.[38]

Clearly, for al-Banna, it was quite possible for character to be changed through action, but action was not all. Human frailty was understood to be man's choice to listen to "the power that opposes God in the hearts of men . . . [and] whispers his insidious suggestions in their ears and makes his proposals seductive to them."[39] Nevertheless, the most dangerous enemies were the colonial political power: foreign, non-Muslim rulers who controlled Muslim societies and ruled without reference to Islamic law. For al-Banna, the most dangerous characters remain foreign; they are not to be found lurking within the community of nominal believers to confound the virtuous.

Al-Banna was assassinated in 1949. For the next fifteen years, the elaboration of his ideas about the nature of human community and governance fell to Sayyid Qutb. A literary critic by training and a moderately secular liberal, Qutb returned to Egypt from a yearlong stay in the United States a committed Islamic activist. From 1949 until his execution in 1966, Qutb elucidated an Islamic vision of society, governance, and community. If al-Banna was the product of the ancien régime and the colonial era, Qutb focused far more sharply on the nationalist state in the postcolonial era. Qutb's understanding of community and agency was profoundly conditioned by the experience of watching a powerful but nationalist state intrude into society as the colonial regime had never been capable of doing.

Qutb evokes evil as an active and insidious force identified as taghut: "deception that cannot endure the mere existence of truth . . . for even if truth wished to live in isolation from deception—leaving victory to the decision of God—deception cannot accept this situation."[40] To describe human political power, Qutb conflates two words, taghut and tughyan. Although given as separate forms in classical dictionaries, the two words are easy to relate in meaning. Tughyan has to do with overstepping boundaries (including "going beyond in disbelief"), whereas taghut seems to be associated with "that which is worshipped other than

God."[41] The arbitrary power of the state symbolized by the Pharaoh is evoked in this conflation.

Pharaoh is, of course, as familiar a figure to Muslims as he is to Jews and Christians. In the Qur'an he usually appears in direct contrast to the prophet Moses. Pharaoh tries constantly to overstep established normative boundaries, whether by the infliction of cruelty, the use of illusive magic, or the direct appropriation of divine status.[42] For Qutb, the moment in which Moses challenges Pharaoh exemplifies the situation of real persons torn between allegiance to God and the seductions of idolatry. The essence of Islam is in this conflict.

> The confrontation between Moses and Pharaoh and his retinue reveals the reality of the struggle between the entirety of the religion of God and the entirety of ignorance [*jahiliyyah*]. It shows how taghut regards this religion and how it feels the threat to its existence even as it reveals how the faithful understand the conflict between themselves and taghut.... If God is the lord of the world then no servant of his—even haughty and tyrannical Pharaoh—can make them subject to him for they are subject to no one except the lord of the world, and return of divinity to God means the return of all government to him ... [thus Moses's] call to the lord of the world can only have one meaning, namely withdrawal of power from the servants—*tawaghit* [plural form of taghut]—and return of it to its Master and this means (in the eyes of such people) wickedness! Or as is said today in the *jahili* ordinances in response to this same call: this is an attempt to overturn the established order! And indeed from the point of view of ignorant idols [*al-tawaghit al-jahiliyyah*] that have usurped the power of God—that is that have usurped His divinity even if they do not say it directly—this [i.e., this same call] is an overthrow of the established order.[43]

Here, state power and the established order (*nizam al-hukm*) are assimilated to a set of loyalties in opposition to God. Qutb's argument is not that politics as a vocation implies choices at odds with the ultimate ethic of Islam, nor does he argue that the political is necessary but corrupting. His argument is more radical.

Qutb is arguing that the state and its leadership constitutes a glorification of human needs and desires that is idolatrous, and that the leaders of the state demand the kind of uncritical loyalty due only to God. For the state to demand such loyalty and to insist on such authority strikes a blow at the foundation of revealed monotheism and restores premonotheistic idolatry. In premonotheistic Egypt, religion and politics were one and the same; their unity was cemented in the divine or quasi-divine character of the human ruler who had a theoretical right to rule unhindered. Such a ruler places himself outside law and is an absolute ruler because he rules only "from himself."[44]

Qutb's vision of the law-governed community of Moses, in contradistinction to the unconstrained coercive power of Pharaoh, analyzes (in religious terms) the state structure erected by Gamal Abdel Nasser in the 1950s, which still stands. After 1952, Egypt was a powerfully concentrated administrative regime, with Nasser himself wielding extraordinary powers unconstrained either by law or by any normal political process. Even local decentralization aided the concentration of power in Nasser's hands.[45] It was also during Nasser's liftime that Egypt moved from being a society in which the landed elite controlled the state to one in which the urban professionals and capitalists gained significant political power.[46]

Qutb represents the point of departure for the present generation of Islamic militants, whom we have yet to discuss. The state ruled by Anwar Sadat was still a Nasserist state, even if the policies sometimes differed. No matter how Sadat appeared to the West, in Egypt he often seemed to be at least as dictatorial as Nasser. He was frequently more arbitrary, even if he relied less on coercion. His speech to the Israeli Knesset, which broke the war deadlock, only occurred because Sadat could disregard any normal political or constitutional restraints. Sadat also used his power to ban the sale of meat in Egypt for a month in 1980, to enforce rigid and unrealistic laws regarding business hours, and even to suggest allowing Israel access to Nile water.

Qutb's originality lies in his uncompromising vision of the Prophet's mission in Mecca rather than Medina. Qutb's Prophet does not make a new order until he has broken with the old. In this view, Islam

is neither an Arab national program nor social, military, legal or even ethical movement. The Meccan Qur'an is nothing other than a revolution (*thawra*) of consciousness and beliefs necessary for all that followed: ethics, state, law, and social order. But this revolution of the heart was aimed at the very heart of the powers already in place: priests, tribal shaykhs, princes and local political powers, and not only at distant Persian and Byzantine despots.[47]

The Prophet and his Companions destroyed the foundations of political power in Mecca, just as Moses destroyed Pharaoh's pretensions *from within* ancient Egyptian society and only then turned to building a new one. The message is clearly that contemporary monotheists must be willing to oppose shaykhs, princes, and pharaohs within their own societies before a new order can be built.

Qutb's focus on Pharaoh gave him a vocabulary, moreover, with which to reach a much wider audience for a politics of religious criticism than any earlier thinkers did. Moses and Pharaoh have an extremely deep resonance in Egyptian folk proverbs. Almost any contemporary collection of Egyptian proverbs offers *illi ma yirda bi-hukm Musa yirda bi-hukm Fir'awn* (who will not accept the rule of Moses must accept that of Pharaoh).[48] This particular bit of folk wisdom, distinguishing a coercive from a normative order, is by no means recent. We have it in almost exactly the same words in a collection almost 175 years old.[49] It also appears in Ahmad Taymur's compendium recording usage in the early part of the twentieth century, with an explication identical to Burckhardt's and followed by another proverb with similar grammatical structure and similar meaning.[50] Historically the proverb has been taken to mean that one should accept that which is; to the extent that Qutb has enriched the meaning of the popular contrast between Pharaoh and Moses (both of whom, after all, are products of Egypt), followers of Moses were now to see themselves on the offensive.[51]

For Qutb, the partisans of Moses would still be aided in their struggle against Pharaoh by the breadth and depth of the classical Islamic heritage. Some 'ulama might be wrong in their interpretation of classical discourse, but their discourse would remain necessary for a new polity to be built. Qutb had claimed that a new approach to the sources of Islam and its interpretation were needed. His great life's work, *Fi zilal al-Qur'an,* was written in part with the desire to reclaim for intellectuals such as himself a greater familiarity with the Islamic sciences and intellectual resources of the 'ulama. Qutb may have created a new approach to the relationship of man to God and a new approach to the governance of the community of the Muslims. What he did not develop was a theory of the kind of socialization necessary to pursue the new kind of governance or the relationship between past and present interpretations of the Law.

I now turn my attention to those who radically reject the old socialization required for interpretation and the entire canon of received interpretation. This radical rejection creates the possibility of imagining a new form of governance for the community and for bringing that new form into being: the creation of the sect. Before doing so, however, I wish to dispose briefly of the idea that we can explain the emergence of this break with classical Islamic doctrine merely by reference to the social background of those who join such groups.

Social Origins and Personal Attributes

The arguments about the effect of social and economic changes creating the Islamist trend seem compelling in regard to the very recent past. Egypt has experienced inflation, stagnation, low productivity, crowding, and increased income inequity in the very recent period. Gilles Kepel and Eric Davis argue that the Islamist program arises from the declining economic situation of group members or (in Davis's words) "pressurization."[52] Such arguments link up neatly with Walzer's approach to Puritanism as a response to social and economic disorder, although they unfortunately do not explain the development of this ideology in the 1950s and 1960s, when the economic situation was improving for all Egyptians. It also cannot explain the militants' manifest and self-conscious understanding that their movement is the result of Nasserism's political victory rather than its economic failure.

We do have a fairly good idea of the Islamist groups' membership. What stands out for all the groups is the degree to which members and leaders alike were middle class, well educated in science and technology, upwardly mobile, and possessed of strong personalities. Salih Siriyya, founder of an Islamist group that attacked the Military Academy in 1972, had a Ph.D. in science education. Shukri Mustafa, leader of a group that kidnapped a leading 'alim, had a bachelor's degree in agricultural science.

The followers resembled the leaders. Although research on membership has been based on those arrested rather than random sampling, most scholars consider the results to be impressionistically representative of active members. Saad Eddin Ibrahim found twenty-nine of thirty-four members "were university graduates or university students who were enrolled at the time of their arrest." Seventeen of the eighteen students were in scientific programs, rather than programs in humanities or social studies; and most of those members who were employed seem to have also been heavily oriented to the hard sciences. The members were also decidedly middle class in origin and prospects. As graduates of technical or professional schools, they either had or could look forward to professional employment. Only one member of the group was a worker. Only two of thirty-four had working-class fathers, and only another three had fathers who were peasants. "With regard to fathers' occupation, about two-thirds (twenty-one out of thirty-four) were government employees, mostly in middle grades of the civil service." Even people who know very little about Egypt will realize how restricted this social group is in a country in which half the population is still rural.

Although many members appear to have been immigrants from small towns, they seem not to have carried much of the culture of deference from the small towns with them. They were not awed by political authority, nor do they seem to have had intense personal grievances traceable to their rural backgrounds for which the state was a convenient target. They mostly came from stable families and, as Ibrahim notes, are quite the opposite of the "alienated, marginal, anomic" individuals often presumed to be the basis for social movements such as theirs. It may be that the social groups from which these members were drawn were "pressurized" by the development of the Egyptian economy in the last decade as Davis and Kepel suggest, but there is little reason to believe that these individuals directly experienced such pressures.[53]

The economic picture that Davis and Kepel draw does not apply well to the late 1960s, when the Islamist groups first formed. The 1950s and 1960s saw significant economic progress and redistribution. Between 1951–52 and 1969–70, we know wages as a proportion of agricultural gross domestic product increased from 17 percent to 30 percent, although after 1970 they did drop back to 25 percent.[54] The relative shares of the lowest 60 percent of households in overall consumption increased between 1958–59 and 1974–75. The relative income share of the top 10 percent, rather than the middle class, declined between the 1950s and 1976.[55]

Davis and Kepel have also misunderstood some aspects of internal migration. Immigrants to Cairo and Alexandria were more likely to see their share in the national income increase simply by moving, because urban governorates had a disproportionately high share of income, wages, and consumption relative to population.[56] It is unlikely that many of the young people in these groups were adversely affected during the Nasser years; to the extent that some were, it is more remarkable that their families bounced back under Sadat.[57] These young people were affected far more by the increasingly centralized authority of the state. Far from acceding to authority, these young people challenged it, although we cannot say whether they enjoyed challenging it. They were not raw bumpkins disoriented by the relatively greater freedom of the cities, for that freedom had drawn them to the cities—namely, the "desire by the younger members of the rural community to break away from the rigid sociocultural traditions prevailing in the village."[58] The young militants in the Islamist groups were more likely to have disliked both the authority structures of their rural homes and the prevailing norms of the urban elites. They became hostile to two distinct strands of contemporary Egyptian life: the enhanced power of the state and the monopoly of the 'ulama over assessing the moral dimensions of the state in terms of Islamic norms.

These young militants sought the freedom to engage in open religious discussion and in action. Middle-class youth are attracted to activism in self-denying groups. They have been drawn to what are essentially groups of equals in which discussion over questions of ethics and morals are fairly wide ranging. The organizational structure and the membership of such groups are of a piece with an equal association of "saints." The self-abnegation, rectitude, and discipline of these groups, coupled with their moral certainty and self-assurance, seem favorably related to the demands on middle-class youth if they are to succeed. It therefore seems to me to make less sense to argue that these groups respond to social or economic "pressure" than that they responded—as did the early Protestant groups—to the process of political centralization that enhanced the arbitrary power of the political elite and especially the head of state. To make this argument, however, we must examine the actual concerns of the Sunni radicals as they themselves expressed them and pay attention to the institutional innovations they introduced into everyday life for members.

The New Puritans

The Puritans broke not only with a prevailing understanding of the relationship between man and God, they also broke with a previously accepted theory of the governance of the Christian community—the church. In so doing, the Puritans created not only a theory of calling but a theory of the socialization necessary to interpret Scripture. Protestants substituted ministers for priests not merely for ceremony: They presumed that "the most important knowledge of all, that which God imparts to his people, is... supremely and exclusively practical... [because] 'it affects the whole man with a hundred times more efficacy than the frigid exhortations of philosophers.'"[59] Contemporary Islamist groups have made a similar and equally significant break: They have received and developed a theory of jihad and taghut to address the relation of the human community to Revealed Law. They have also developed a theory of socialization and education that substitutes the practical experience of voluntary associations of lay intellectuals for the abstract *'ilm* of religious professionals.

The groups with which I am primarily concerned are the so-called Jihad group, the Flight and Repentance group, and the Military Academy group.[60] The most important single source for my purposes is the text of *Al-Faridah al-Gha'ibah* (The Neglected Duty), an internal document of the Jihad group, whose members assassinated Anwar Sadat in 1981.[61] Western scholars widely agree that it is the most important single document presenting Egyptian Islamist positions and Egyptian intellectuals alike.[62] There are numerous commentaries on this work, including a fatwa or jurisprudential judgment issued by the highest institutional Islamic authority in Egypt, Shaykh al-Azhar, Jad al-Haqq Ali Jad al-Haqq.[63]

The "neglected duty" to which the pamphlet refers is jihad. The pamphlet was written to define jihad, an issue that consumed the internal discussions of the group. Of special interest was the relation of group members to nominal Muslims in political authority, such as Sadat, who called himself the "believing President." The pamphlet, written by 'Abd al-Salam Faraj, paints a picture of Muslims in a world of idolatry and ignorance. Idolatry and ignorance are not spatially and temporally apart from modern Egypt but found even within nominally Muslim society. For Faraj, true Muslims cannot view Islam as orthopraxis: the performance of acts. Islam requires the believer to take a stand; and this stand, jihad, is the struggle for that enjoined by God. Not to struggle for that which is enjoined by God is to give allegiance to idols (taghut). To establish the validity of this nonreceived concept of jihad, Faraj must negate received interpretations of it and deny a privileged interpretive role to the 'ulama.

For Faraj, believers live in a situation of extreme tension. A distant and all-powerful God sends them down paths of salvation or error, acts alone, and cannot guarantee them salvation.[64] At the same time, the world constantly forces believers to accept the idols of state power as the source of law. Such "idols of this world can only be made to disappear through the power of the sword."[65] Contemporary idolatry is revealed primarily by the intrusive structure of the state, which enforces the law of unbelief.[66] Rulers of the state are members of the nominal community of Muslims. They have Muslim names, pray, fast, and claim to be Muslims, but they are actually apostates.[67]

The God evoked here is quite similar to the God in whom Weber argued the Protestants believed. The logic of Faraj's argument is that believers must ceaselessly strive in the path of God to be considered true Muslims. In this regard, Faraj has made a critical break with all the received understandings of Islam. Jad al-Haqq (representing the 'ulama) and social critics, such as Jamal al-Banna and Muhammad 'Amara, all agree that Muslims are those who recite the shahada or statement of belief in the unity of God and the prophecy of Muhammad. All three critics of Faraj agree that the recitation of the shahada is sufficient to place one within the community of Muslims, regardless of other sins of omission or commission. The only acceptable way to place someone who has recited the shahada outside the visible community of Muslims would be if that same person expressly recanted. Insofar as Islam is a religion of orthopraxy, as suggested in the earlier discussion of al-Banna, it is impermissible to distinguish between segments of the visible community.[68]

The core of the pamphlet is an argument about jihad in the so-called *ayat al-sayf* (Verse of the Sword) in the Qur'an: Is it historically specific to the situation of the Prophet at a particular moment of his mission, or does it have wider implications?[69] The Islamists argue for a broader interpretation—a need to continue to struggle until God is recognized as supreme throughout human history. The argument becomes somewhat technical, but the intent of the author is plain. Faraj wants to use the Verse of the Sword to argue that those who nominally accept Islam but become renegades commit a greater sin than those who never accept Islam at all. When linked to the rejection of Islam as orthopraxy, any nominal members of the community of Muslims are liable to be renegades in the eyes of the Islamists. The details in which the argument is couched thus do not detract from its basic nature: Those nominal Muslims who manifestly betray the community by the standards of the religious virtuosi commit the most heinous ethical and moral delinquency imaginable.[70]

The political rulers of Egypt are apostates because they do not rule in accord with revelation. They impose some, but not all, of the Islamic laws. More remarkable is the way the argument is made: It contrasts politics as an inherently arbitrary activity with the divine rules that should be used to administer a well-ordered society. Contemporary rulers are like the Mongols, whose king, Genghis Khan, ruled by means of arbitrary and self-interested decrees (*siyasat*—the word that in contemporary Arabic means policies or politics): "It contains many legal rulings which he simply made up himself because he liked them."[71] Evil resides in the arbitrariness as much as in the substance of the state, and the state, in Faraj's sights, is the nationalist, postcolonial state, not Western liberalism.

Jad al-Haqq presents the 'ulama's criticism of Faraj, but there is another current critical of his work sustained primarily by intellectuals long associated with the older Islamic movements. Jamal al-Banna, brother of Hasan al-Banna, has been a Muslim activist in the trade union movement for almost forty years. He has written extensively on an Islamic approach to trade union and labor problems. Muhammad 'Amara has fought strenuously to renew a lay tradition of Islamic political argument for over two decades and, in the process, has contributed significantly to Egyptian political and intellectual dialogue. Writers such as al-Banna and 'Amara abhor the idea that the entire postcolonial process of state building must be rejected as idolatrous and error ridden. Such a blanket condemnation is presented as impermissibly naive by those who attack the Jihad group from within the Islamist movement. For them, politics remains the art of the possible within an anticolonial framework.

> In any case, we must distinguish between rulers who furthered colonialism in our country and between those who headed toward national independence **in a secular framework or did not apply the shar' of God totally;** struggle against the former is immediate and direct . . . but with the latter insofar as they move toward independence they bring closer the day when Islam and its state return to the countries of the Muslims.[72]

Such critics hold to an incrementalist Islamist strategy and view the Nasser period as positive. For these authors, human frailty enhances the attractiveness of gradual and incremental politics.

The knowledge of human frailty and a sense of predestination need not inspire withdrawal; it can inspire absolute certainty in the effort to master the world. Such a vision can be profoundly antihumanist. Just how much it opposes a contemporary Islamic humanism can be seen in the reponse by Jamal al-Banna to the doctrines of *Al-Faridah al-Gha'ibah*. Al-Banna asserts that justice is the distinguishing feature of Islam as a monotheist religion, even as love (*mahabbah*) and the singleness of God (tawhid) are the distinguishing features of Christianity and Judaism respectively.[73]

At this point there appears to be an obvious and important distinction between Calvinism and Sunni fundamentalism. Islamists can identify the source of idolatry occurring in human activity. The West is that source, and colonial history gives weight to their claims.[74] Unfortunately, this may be a distinction without much of a difference. Calvin himself believed the Turkish conquests of Europe in his day had brought "filthiness and defilement."[75] Early Protestantism and Sunni radicalism have significant affinities not only in conceptualizing sin in terms of tyranny but in exemplifying arbitrary tyranny in the ruling institutions of other cultures. It would be a mistake to assume that the denunciations of the West rest on any great familiarity with Western society and culture.[76] As analysts, we might do better to conceptualize Sunni antagonism to the West as a metaphor for antagonism to the "world," the human condition in which believers are tempted and tested every day and duped by error and idolatry. The West is not only a source but a symbol for the place in which idolatry has reached its logical extreme and established its kingdom.

We should recall that early Protestants often projected what they thought to be most evil to the little-known countries of the East. Protestant poets could even conflate the symbols of Catholicism and Islam to draw a generalized picture of tyranny. In Protestant imagery, it was Spenser's very "Oriental" Pope (and Milton's Satan) who appear as beguiling tyranny.

A goodly lady clad in scarlet red,
Purfled with gold and pearle of rich assay,
And like a Persian mitre on her hed
She wore, with crowns and owches garnished,
The which her lauish louers to her gave;
Her wanton palfrey all was ouerspred.[77]

The conflation of tyranny and idolatry in the work of Sayyid Qutb and in *Al-Faridah al-Gha'ibah* reminds us of John Calvin's own understanding of tyranny: the ruler who has no self-restraint.[78]

Such arguments make little sense to Jad al-Haqq or a humanist layman such as 'Amara. In 'Amara's words, to say that the ruler of Egypt is an apostate "contradicts reality: for prayers are being said, and mosques are open and being built, and there are alms that Muslims give, and they go on pilgrimages, and the verdicts of Islam are effective in the state except in certain areas such as the *hudud* punishments and *riba* and other concerns that are the object of positive legislation."[79]

Beside the authority of the state lies the authority of interpretation. Both 'Amara and Jad al-Haqq point out the ludicrous and acontextual readings the pamphlet makes of Ibn Taymiyyah and the Qur'an respectively. Jad al-Haqq parses the syntax of the Qur'an verses regarding "those who refuse to rule by what God has sent down" to show it does not conform with Faraj's reading. 'Amara draws on fourteenth-century history to show that Islamist militants not only take words out of context but willfully misread them.

By insisting on their interpretations of the Qur'an in direct contradiction to received meanings, however, the Sunni militants openly defy the control of a small elite over these texts. As long as discussions about what the Qur'an means remain technical, rulers have little need to worry about Islamic critiques of political actors finding wide audiences. To the degree that the Islamist militants have found a language that is evocative in such everyday terms as proverbs and that remains rooted in a sophisticated ethical critique of state power, they become a danger. Only from the perspective of a fundamental critique of state power and coercion does it make sense to say that Egypt is today governed worse than the East under the Mongols. As 'Amara points out, it otherwise makes no sense at all.

From this perspective, Mongol law means improvised decisions by human beings, and that implies, for Faraj, rulers who cannot restrain themselves and must therefore be restrained. From this rationale, the young fundamentalists draw revolutionary and almost Maoist implications: There is no need to fight the distant enemy (such as Israel) until the near one is vanquished. For older Islamic activists, such as 'Amara, this reasoning resembles that of the the Communists who argue that class struggle supersedes national struggle.[80] For 'Amara, the danger of such reasoning lies in its implicit approval of the politics of the putsch: It was precisely such thinking, he points out, that impelled the Free Officers to take power after the 1948 Palestine War.

Faraj and the ideas he presented to the Jihad group must be seen in the context of a much broader movement. The Jihad group not only had to develop its own ideas but also to defend them in competition with other groups for a larger audience of interested listeners and potential adherents. Therefore, Faraj differentiates his approach for establishing the *hukm allah* (rule of God) from other strategies: mysticism, partisan politics, "burrowing from within," or withdrawal into closed communities. The pamphlet clarifies, to some degree, the existence of a growing movement in which these ideas are routinely debated.[81]

The final section of the pamphlet concerns intragroup relations. Almost the entire conclusion deals with issues of intention, motivation, and compliance. Jihad is not presented merely as another form of works but as a higher instance of faith, for the actions of jihad will yield a nullity without "complete devotion . . . forgetting the outward appearance of things created by looking uninterruptedly towards the Creator."[82] How would one know what is in people's hearts, however? How can one be sure that people—even in groups like Jihad—are not saying one thing but thinking another? The only way to come close is through unrelenting examination of motives and behavior accomplished in small groups in which everything can be scrutinized. It is not surprising that the pamphlet ends by calling on those who are *not* up to the task of *jihad fi sabil allah* (struggle in the path of God) to "declare outright their true motive."[83] Blind obedience is not enough. Such obedience in this instance would be less than total and would reveal unreliable human emotions: friendship or familial ties that would be more harmful than outright enmity.[84] Members of the group must cut themselves off from their pasts and refuse to tolerate the regrowth of other loyalties within the group.

In this regard, the Jihad group recapitulates internally what it has already proclaimed externally: the existence of a constant danger that human emotions and the condition of man lead to a loss of commitment to God. The only way to guard against this likelihood is to limit radically membership in the sect and guard at every moment against leakage from the world at large. Coupled with the incipient definition of the need for members to express, or one might say confess, constantly, the small group creates a new atmosphere of heightened individual dedication that is not mystical at all. Here we can see the creation of a new cultural norm at odds with received Islamic thought, although well known within Christianity: the use of confession to bind followers to an institution. I shall return to this later.

The Jihad group is not the only fundamentalist group. We also have some sense of the ideas of at least one of the others, the so-called *Al-Takfir wa al-hijrah* group, which generally prefers to call itself the Association of Muslims (*Jama'at al-Muslimin*). This group was responsible for the kidnapping and murder of the former minister of Religious Endowments, Shaykh Dhahabi, in 1977. Although different in nuance, much of what the Flight and Repentance group believed was similar to Jihad. The five main points around which Flight and Repentance formed were:

1. all existing societies are in a state of ignorance and apostasy;
2. all decisions by ijma' must be rejected, including the "idols" of "*qiyas*" or analogical reasoning;
3. only members of the *jama'at al-muslimin* are good Muslims because all others submit [*aslamu*] to taghut, governance by other than what God sent down, and they consider as Muslims all those who recite the shahada;
4. Islam is not merely a recitation of the shahada but determination [*iqrar*] and action [*'amal*];
5. only the Prophet and his companions are to be accepted as a true group or congregation, and all other congregations established so far must be rejected.[85]

The radical rejection of all previous interpretations in Islam and of the socialization required to enter into the interpretative discussion with the 'ulama is pronounced. We can see another form of this rejection of the authority of the 'ulama in the precis of Shukri's declarations before a Military Court of State Security on November 6–8, 1977:

> The interpretive works of the four imams, Shukri argued, were unnecessary. The Koran was delivered in Arabic; it is therefore clear, and the only tool that may be needed for explaining the meaning of some of its terms is a good dictionary. In what way do the glosses of the imams make its meanings more accessible? And why do the glosses of the imams themselves not need to be glossed? . . . After thus appealing to the common sense of his interlocutors, Shukri told them why the imams have closed the door of ijtihad: so that they had indeed become idols (*asnam*) worshipped like the deities of a pagan pantheon.[86]

As a technical legal issue, ijtihad has to do with whether the 'ulama are seen as giving independent and original decisions of principle or following existing ones. In terms of power, the issue of ijtihad has to do, as Shukri realized, with the kind of education needed to make valid judgments on Islamic law: Does one need an elite socialization or does one simply need to be able to take out a dictionary?

The truly radical nature of Shukri's rejection of the visible community of Muslims since the fourth century *hijri* led him to a position regarding the goals of the Islamist movement somewhat different from that of the Jihad group. The distinction between the Jihad group and Shukri's group may not be obvious and might even seem minor.

Jihad members tend, as do the Muslim Brothers and other activists, to identify the goal of the Islamic movement as the institution of real Islamic law, *al-hukm bi-ma anzala allah*. The Jihad group rejected the notion that the president of Egypt was really a Muslim, despite his nominal membership in the visible community, and seems to have implicitly assumed that other nominal Muslims could be brought (if not to salvation) at least to compliance with appropriate norms of behavior by a state led by a member of the invisible community. Shukri's group distinguished themselves from the Brotherhood (and presumably other Islamist groups) by their insistence that their program envisaged a prior stage: getting nominal Muslims to accept Islam as their real religion (*idkhal al-nas fi din allah*). Islamist groups, like Protestants, disagree with each other as much as they disagree with the tradition from which they come.

Shukri's group was far more intensely directed toward its leader and closed than any other group. In prison, the group members refused any contact with members of other groups or with former members of their own group; even the Communists were more acceptable to them than other Islamists.[87] The nature of attachment to the group was varied. Shukri, of course, was an extraordinarily powerful, perhaps even charismatic, personality. The focus of loyalty for group members nevertheless appears to have remained the group rather than Shukri and remained so even as members disagreed with Shukri. Abu al-Khayr, in his memoirs of the group, affirms a rejection of ijma' and passive membership in the Muslim community, freely admits his dislike for the kidnapping and subsequent murder of the former Minister of Religious Endowments, and does not seem completely at ease with the idea that all Islamic history from the death of the Prophet to Shukri is one of apostasy.

Summary

Islamist groups appear to share a common core of beliefs despite their disputes. This common core of beliefs allows militants to move within the framework of a larger dialogue that clearly is more than the mere search for the latest and most fashionable guru.[88] When one looks especially at the Jihad group and the *Jama'at al-Muslimin,* several aspects of their beliefs appear to be shared among themselves and in common with early Protestantism.

1. Belief in a single and implacable being who chooses our destiny after life (the "double decree,") and belief that, as a consequence, men and women must persevere actively in the way of God intellectually because we can have no knowledge or assurance of salvation.
2. Belief in a principle of order that, by the nature of human existence, subverts our faith in God and converts our faith into idolatry.
3. Rejection of the socialization and education that form into an elite those who would interpret Scripture.
4. Rejection of all or almost all received commentary on Scripture and a preference for reading Scripture directly.

From this common ground with Puritanism flow two important features of the lives of the members of these groups. First, they exist in a state of war with society; and second, they adopt congregational innovations that strengthen the cohesion of their small group, even if such innovations fall outside the realm of normal Islamic practice.

Members of these groups conceive of themselves as the only real Muslims living in what is essentially an apostate society. War becomes a duty for every one of them, not just a duty for some against an external enemy. Abu al-Khayr twice alludes to his own belief that groups like "TH" and others were at war with society, although he would have preferred a long period of struggle within society (*idkhal al-nas fi din allah*) to a sharp confrontation with the state, because he "saw that the group [TH] was in need of long years of peace during which it could manage its struggle [jihad, in the original] of a type that I like to think of as 'struggle with social appearances.'"[89] When Salih Siriyya was executed, Abu al-Khayr's feelings of social and ideological warfare intensified.

Silence overtook me with the inner secret feeling in the depths of my being, that of incessant war against Islam. For Salih Siriyya and his group met the same fate as the Muslim Brotherhood which had been beaten down because they dared to make the victory of Islam on the earth their aim. . . ."[90]

Shukri's testimony during his trial certainly attests also to his sense of being at war with state and society. He even refused to allow his followers to pray in state-supported mosques.[91]

The belief that Muslims inside the Muslim community are at war with their own society is a significant break with the received Muslim thinking on jihad. The conclusions the Islamists draw for constructing the institutions of their own congregational and communal life are equally at odds with the received doctrine about how Muslims ought to deal with each other. The perception of social war provides the context for the major institutional innovation of these sectarian congregations: They spy on and constrain the behavior of each other. The militants are engaged in constant oversight of each other and constant reporting on each other; they are also engaged in constant discussion of their own behavior and that of others. This is a striking feature of their normal activity and one that clearly makes an impact on more popular circles.

The Friday religion page in the daily newspaper *Al-Ahram* provides some insight into how innovative this sectarian behavior is. Islam has traditionally opposed the idea of "spying out" or *tajassus*. What then, one reader writes, is the verdict of religion on overseeing one's comrades at work? Although it is acceptable to oversee one's comrades in the sense of supervision, "snitching" is frowned on. Even worse would be the routine and public discussion of one's own shortcomings and those of others; yet this is precisely the activity so highly regarded by saints and virtuosi. Whether the name is public confession or criticism and self-criticism, the activity is quite familiar.

The young people in both the Jihad group and in the TH group were especially concerned with the problems of what it meant to "bare one's heart." Yet this concern was something the 'ulama found contradictory to received Islam because it would turn the religion into one of "spying out." Most of the young people in these groups found society to be wholly corrupt and thus were inclined to flee from it, whether by retreating to living in the circle of the group within urban society or by leaving urban society altogether for the oases. Muhammad 'Abd al-Nur, dean of the Women's College at Al-Azhar University, ridiculed the idea of revolt against state authority. Relying on classical compilations and consensus, 'Abd al-Nur said that "the original sources such as Al-Bukhari and Muslim make clear what the relationship [between ruler and ruled] is and in these sources we find agreement that it is not permissible to combat the ruler nor to attack him when that would lead to widespread anarchy [*ihdath al-fitan*] or bloodshed [*safk al-dima'*] or splitting the community [*tamziq shaml al-umma*]." Even if the members of the Islamic community do not like a ruler's policies, he must be patiently borne as long as he does not commit an act of outright apostasy. "Rebellion," he said, "against the ruler and strife with him are forbidden [*haram*] by the received consensus [ijma'] of Muslims."[92]

'Abd al-Nur also suggests that ordinary Muslims cannot clearly evaluate state policies in the light of religious injunctions. Judgments about the character of a ruler as a good Muslim are also to be avoided. Thus, 'Abd al-Nur suggests we must be careful about judging anyone, because judgment is reserved to God. Perhaps someone ought to look at the relation of policies to religion and hold officials accountable, but it is not a task to be left to the uninitiated and certainly not one to be decided by civil strife.

Conclusion

The sixteenth century is not the twentieth century, and Islam is not Christianity. That much is obvious. If mere statements that times or doctrines differed were sufficient to have any real meaning, then most of the literature surveyed at the beginning of this essay would not have been written, nor would there be a discipline of comparative politics. What is most striking about many post-Lutheran Protestant views of the state and those of the contemporary Egyptian Islamists studied here is how similar they are in their distrust of a state in which policies directly reflect the personal preferences of rulers. The Egypt of Nasser and Sadat was not dynastic or wholly absolute, but state policies grew out of their personal preferences to a greater degree than is true in the states of the advanced industrial economies. *L'état,* to paraphrase Louis XIV, *était presqu'eux.*

We look at polities today as if the categories of corporatism, pluralism, and authoritarianism exhausted the conceptual framework available for analysis. These categories suggest less variety in politics than citizens experience. Absolutism was not a lasting form of the European state, but it may be helpful in understanding contemporary state building in the Third World. It certainly allows us to escape from the pluralist-corporatist dichotomy.

Absolutism and Puritanism were competing strategies for building powerful postagrarian states. The dominant theme in absolutist state building was the monarch's enhanced persona at the administrative center, but the dominant theme in Puritanism was society's enhanced compliance through service to a just political order. Puritan communities and absolutist rulers form a stable antagonism. If Puritan communities remain indigestible during the period of absolutist state building, then some form of liberal and plural regime may emerge, as in England. If Puritan communities become integrated into the machinery of government, then an effective and pervasive authoritarian state is built. Fundamentalism (whether Calvinist or Islamic) represents a challenge to absolutist regimes. Puritanism can be the basis for resistance to one kind of state and for dogged acquiescence in another.

The doctrinal and ideological arguments about Calvinism and capitalism emerge in comparative perspective as less important then Calvinism and the ideology of governance—whether governance of the individual, the society, or of any particular institution. Walzer and Wolin seem on firmer ground than other analysts of the Puritan experience when they argue that it was primarily an argument about politics and the state. The state in my argument, unlike theirs however, appears to be getting stronger not weaker. The question that then logically arises is why should either Calvinism or Sunni fundamentalism emerge as an ideology of governance? What is the reason for talking about power and governance in terms of predestination, calling the socialization required for interpretation jihad, taghut, or ijma'?

The central question of fundamentalism is how men and women live together: whether they can cooperate freely or whether they must be coerced into cooperation. In Calvin's words, civil polity is required for human existence and "to entertain a thought of its extermination is inhuman barbarism; it is as necessary to mankind as bread and water, light and air, and far more excellent."[93] The need for a civil polity that provides secure property, guards against fraud, and ensures modesty and religion arises, in Calvin's analysis, because men are wicked and egoistic and because fallen men (and women) cannot triumph on their own over their own instincts. Civil society's excellence, however, arises not from wickedness and egoism but as an act of divine grace: "The authority possessed by kings and other governors over all things upon earth is not a consequence of the perverseness of men, but of the providence and holy ordinance of God, who has been pleased to regulate human affairs in this manner; forasmuch as he is present, and also presides among them, in making laws and in executing equitable judgments."[94]

Calvin was aware that kings might act cruelly and, indeed, considered the likelihood of monarchy degenerating into tyranny to be great. His argument is, however, that the Christian community (however sinful its members might be in a theological sense) can thus only form a viable society by submitting to the rule of God. If everyone acted in accord with the manifest rules of God, then presumably coercion—and especially the likelihood of arbitrary, self-interested coercion—would decline.

The arguments about divinely established norms are not only about salvation but also about the formation of cooperative human societies in which members police themselves and each other. Creating such a society was not an aim of Protestant thinkers, but they did consider the existence of such societies a valuable background condition for the pilgrimmage of the soul on earth. For contemporary Muslims (and indeed perhaps for the Islamic tradition as a whole), it may be that the creation of such a rule-governed society in accord with the laws of God is a more desirable end than in sixteenth-century Europe.

Calvin himself, like most sixteenth-century divines, was unwilling to recognize a right of generalized rebellion. Calvinist theory, which did develop with Pierre Viret and Theodore Beza, promptly moved in the direction of opposing not only churchly authority but civil authority as well.[95] Its development did not include any squeamishness with regard to the use of violence of the kind we would call terrorism. As Walzer notes, Calvinists such as John Knox rapidly developed a theory of civil office in which "[m]agistrates and noblemen had no rights beyond the performance of their godly duty and no rights at all short of that."[96] Mary, Queen of Scots, "that Jesabel" to John Knox, ought to have been punished with death; and Walzer is probably correct that Knox would have been quite content had an individual accomplished the punishment.[97] That Islamist movements resort to violence against individual rulers does not necessarily differentiate them from early Protestants.

Is it possible to employ an argument about Sunni radicalism similar to that just developed for Protestantism? For example, is Sunni radicalism an argument about the state, rather than merely a response to a particular set of social conditions? Most attempts to explain Sunni radicalism begin with the particular nature of contemporary Egypt: its confusion, poverty, crowding, and the failure of Nasserism.[98] Many of Egypt's current problems no doubt stem from the failures of Nasserism. It still seems plausible to suggest that not a few also arise from Nasser's successes in transforming the state and society. The recruits to Islamist movements not only confront the vastly enhanced power of the colonial state, but they are themselves the result of the social change and educational opportunities Nasser created.

Attraction to Puritanical doctrines, however, seems to occur not among those who are downwardly mobile but the reverse—it occurs among those who will find the concerted and methodical use of their talents rewarded. It may well be that immersion in the Islamist movement in general helps people to succeed rather than excuse their failures to themselves.

One of the very few microstudies of nonarrested members of Islamist movements involves women. There are certainly economic benefits to joining groups, but these may be side effects rather than causes of their existence. Young women have been attracted to Islamist movements and veiling for a variety of reasons, including the economic habits of dress they inspire. The willingness to forego being fashionable by keeping up with imported designs may stem from strengthened identities in a variety of areas.[99]

Certainly Egypt and most of the Islamic countries today are in situations reminiscent of the period of change to territorial state building and economic consolidation from an older order that was ideologically universalist but institutionally localist and cosmopolitan. Everywhere, Puritanism aided in the transition to state-defined societies, and it is easy to see in contemporary Islamic activism the same kind of commitment to activities that would strengthen the state, should a leader actually allied to or at least sympathetic to Islamist currents appear.[100] The contemporary Islamist movement will grow due, in part, to the way it inculcates methodical discipline in its adherents and any consequent prosperity they experience, but such prosperity remains an effect, not a cause. Religion continues to exist; and Islam, like Christianity, will not go away but will remain the preeminent factor in "ethics and ritual . . . [n]either capitalism, nationalism, nor later forces such as socialism have effective means of linking the family, its life cycle, and death to the macrosocial forces they embody."[101] Perhaps today, as well, we appreciate the role that the family and its life cycle play, for life and death are among the few experiences universally shared: We are all born, and we all die.

An explanation of Puritanism as merely a response to the interests of particular groups tends rapidly to functionalism. Those whose "interests" are met by being Puritans become Puritans because otherwise those interests would never be met.[102] A historical explanation of the success of those who happen to accept such doctrines, as given by Walzer for Puritanism and Davis for Islamism, makes more sense; but, as I hope I have shown, we need to bring the state rather than the capitalist market into the explanatory picture. A fully historical analogical explanation is, however, not completely sufficient, though it might be satisfying to separate "us" from "them." Such an explanation makes Puritanism only an atavistic ideology of transition through whose doors all cultures and civilizations pass, once and in only one direction.

The most compelling conclusions from comparing Sunni fundamentalists has to do with the rescue of the term *fundamentalist* and a deeper understanding of its meaning. If the argument presented here is valid, and if Sunni radicalism and Protestantism are two variants of a single transformation of a prior classical religious tradition, then that transformation has more to do with state building than with capitalism. Protestantism has been presented either as the midwife of capitalism or of modern politics. It might be more fruitfully conceived of as the unintended progenitor of the modern state. Thus, there may still be room to rethink the Protestant ethic in terms of its role in the process of building states that have pushed the competing powers of religion and community to the side.

The importance of thinking about fundamentalism as a movement that presents a powerful critique of arbitrary absolutist power and one that presents a model for church and lay government that draws more than any predecessor on the voluntary compliance of members should not blind us to the negative nature of fundamentalism. If a single ruler can be arbitrary as he presides over the transition of a pluralistic (and to use Weber's word, polytheist) society from an agricultural to an industrial base, then contemporary democracy may also appear arbitrary, pluralistic, and polytheist.

NOTES

The author would like to acknowledge the encouragement and help received from Kenneth Jowitt, Kevin Reinhart, Farhat Ziadeh, and Ahmad Sadiq Sa'd.

1. For an extremely early and suggestive insight to this problem, see Clement Henry Moore, "On Theory and Practice among Arabs," *World Politics* 24, no. 1 (1971): 106–26. Moore's concern is primarily with the Egyptian Muslim Brothers. Looking at contemporary Sunni activists, Fouad Ajami refers to them as having "[t]he perseverance of reformers and 'saints' we can admire" in *Islam in the Political Process,* ed. James Piscatori (Cambridge: Cambridge University Press, 1983), 34. The reference is, of course, to Michael Walzer's *Revolution of the Saints* (Cambridge: Cambridge University Press, 1965), a study of Protestantism, of which more below. Nazih Ayubi argues that "[a]s in Protestantism, the importance of discarding the church's teachings and 'going back to the sources' is the egalitarian and participatory ethos that makes everybody capable of understanding and interpreting the word of God without barriers based on clerical ranks or theological education." See Ayubi, "The Politics of Militant Islamic Movements in the Middle East," *Journal of International Affairs* 36, no.2 (1982): 272. Said Amir Arjomand has also tried to relate the Shi'i-led revolution in Iran to this paradigm. See Arjomand, "Iran's Islamic Revolution," *World Politics* 38, no. 3 (1986): 384–414; especially the argument that the Shi'ite 'ulama are the equivalent of Calvinist preachers (390). The most sustained arguments are by Ernest Gellner. See especially "Flux and Reflux in the Faith of Men" in *Muslim Society* (Cambridge: Cambridge University Press, 1983).

2. Weber was vague regarding the possibility of non-Christian religions undergoing a shift toward Protestant ethics. On the one hand, see Max Weber, *The Protestant Ethic,* trans. Talcott Parsons (New York: Scribner's, 1958), especially 227: "Because the Mohammadan [*sic*] idea was that of predetermination, not predestination, the most important thing, the proof of the believer in predestination, played no part in Islam. Thus only the fearlessness of the warrior (as in the case of moira) could result, but there were no consequences for rationalization of life; there was no religious sanction for them." On the other hand, the logic of some Weberian formulations reinforces a possible comparison of Calvinism and Islam on several dimensions, including that of predestination. See Weber, *Economy and Society,* ed. Guenther Roth and Claus Wittich (Berkeley: University of California Press, 1978), 522. Weber's knowledge of Islam was weak in comparison to his knowledge of other religions. See Bryan Turner, *Weber and Islam* (London: Routledge and Kegan Paul, 1974), 140–41. A good selection on various approaches to the problems raised by Weber is S. N. Eisenstadt, *The Protestant Ethic and Modernization: A Comparative View* (New York: Basic Books, 1968). Also worth looking at is Ernest Gellner, "Trust, Cohesion, and the Social Order," in *Trust,* ed. Diego Gambetta (London: Basil Blackwell, 1988), 152.

3. Gianfranco Poggi, *Calvinism and Capitalist Spirit: Max Weber's Protestant Ethic* (London: Macmillan, 1983), 78.

4. The major contribution to this extension is Maxime Rodinson, *Islam and*

Capitalism (New York: Pantheon, 1973), which explicitly confronts the issue at several points (notably pp. 7–9). Other contributions in the area of Islam include Ernest Gellner, "Sanctity, Puritanism, Secularization, and Nationalism," in Eisenstadt, *Protestant Ethic,* 289–308.

5. For the most recent summation of this argument, see Michael Mann, *The Sources of Social Power* (Cambridge: Cambridge University Press, 1986), 465, regarding the tensions in Christianity as a system of meanings faced with emergent capitalism. For an older but still useful summary of the problems regarding the causal mechanisms involved, see Sidney A. Burrell, "Calvinism, Capitalism, and the Middle Classes: Some Afterthoughts on an Old Problem," in Eisenstadt, *Protestant Ethic,* 135–54.

6. See Sheldon Wolin, *Politics and Vision* (Boston: Little, Brown, 1960), 191.

7. Walzer, *Revolution of the Saints.*

8. Ibid., 310–11.

9. See Mann, *Sources of Social Power,* 476.

10. See, for example, Bernard Lewis, *The Political Language of Islam* (Chicago: University of Chicago Press, 1988), 2: "Throughout the history of Christendom there have been two powers: God and Caesar . . . always there are two, with its own laws and jurisdictions, its own structure and hierarchy."

11. Wolin, *Politics and Vision,* 179.

12. John Calvin, *Institutes of the Christian Religion,* trans. John Allen (Philadelphia: Presbyterian Board of Christian Education, 1936), IV, 20, xxxii. (The numbers for Calvin's *Institutes* in this and subsequent citations represent, in order, the particular book, chapter, and paragraph.)

13. See Maulana Muhammad Ali, *A Manual of Hadith* (London: Curzon Press, 1944), 396; the hadith is from Bukhari, 56:108. In Arabic, the word for disobeying (*ma'siyyah*) has overtones of revolt, sin, and seduction somewhat similar to Calvin's wording. (Imam Bukhari's *Sahih* is widely considered to be an important classical edition of hadith, and Maulana's numbers refer to a book and chapter in which a particular hadith can be found.)

14. See Abdul Hamid el-Zein, "Beyond Ideology and Theology: The Search for the Anthropology of Islam," *Annual Review of Anthropology* 6 (1977):227–54; especially 248–52.

15. Carlos M. N. Eire, *War against the Idols* (Cambridge: Cambridge University Press, 1986), 197.

16. Calvin, *Institutes,* I, 3, iii.

17. Ibid., I, 7, ii.

18. Gottfried W. Locher, *Huldrych Zwingli's Concept of History* (Leiden: E. J. Brill, 1981), 102.

19. See M. D. Chenu, "Monks, Canons, and Laymen in Search of the Apos-

tolic Life," in *Nature, Man, and Society in the Twelfth Century,* trans. Jerome Taylor and Lester K. Little (Chicago: University of Chicago Press, 1968), 203.

20. Chenu, *Nature, Man, and Society,* 219.

21. Calvin, *Institutes,* I, iv.

22. Calvin, *Institutes,* IV, i, iv–v, and IV, ii, ii–iii; especially: "The communion of the Church was not instituted as a bond to confine us in idolatry, impiety, ignorance of God, and other evils; but rather as a means to preserve us in the fear of God, and obedience of the truths."

23. Calvin, *Institutes,* IV, 5, x.

24. Eire, *War against the Idols,* 54.

25. Ibid., 202.

26. Calvin, *Institutes,* I, 12, i.

27. Calvin, *Institutes,* IV, v, ii.

28. Paul Russell, *Lay Theology in the Reformation: Popular Pamphleteers in Southwest Germany, 1521–1525* (Cambridge: Cambridge University Press, 1986), 222. Russell himself quotes Hans Sachs, an early sixteenth-century pamphleteer.

29. Wilfred Cantwell Smith, *Islam in Modern History* (Princeton: Princeton University Press, 1957), 20.

30. Noel Coulson, *A History of Islamic Law* (Edinburgh: Edinburgh University Press, 1964), 78.

31. See *The Shorter Encyclopedia of Islam,* ed. H. A. R. Gibb and J. H. Kramers (Leiden: E. J. Brill, 1974), s.v. "Idjma'."

32. Ibid., s.v. "djihad."

33. Gustave von Grunebaum argued that an inherent complementarity of good and evil could be found in classical Islamic theology that "conceived of evil as the *muqabal* of good, that is, its correlative opposite, and hence possessed of equal ontological reality." Today's militants take the existential implications of such a position quite seriously. See Gustave von Grunebaum, "Observations on the Muslim Concept of Evil," *Studia Islamica* 31 (1970):117–34.

34. Rud Peters, *Islam and Colonialism: The Doctrine of Jihad in Modern History* (The Hague: Mouton, 1979), 130. Peters uses the terms *modernist* and *fundamentalist* to distinguish those who might also be differentiated as humanist and fundamentalist.

35. See the articles by Moore and others cited above.

36. Hasan al-Banna, "Nazrat fi islah al-Nafs" (Remarks on Self-reform), *Al-'Itisam* (Cairo), June, 1944.

37. Smith, *Islam in Modern History,* 19.

38. al-Banna, "Nazrat fi islah al-Nafs."

39. *Encyclopedia of Islam,* s.v. "shaitan."

40. Sayyid Qutb, *Fi zilal al-qur'an* (Beirut: Dar al-shuruq, 1974), 3:1306.

41. See *Taj al-arus* (Cairo ed., 1306 A.H.), s.v. "taghut"; *Concordance et indices de la tradition musulmane,* ed. A. J. Wensinck and J. P. Mensing (Leiden: E. J. Brill, 1962), 4:4–5, especially the reference to Abu Da'ud.

42. See especially XX: 43–72 and XXVIII: 32–40 in the Qur'an.

43. Qutb, *Fi zilal al-qur'an,* 1330–31.

44. For a discussion of Calvin's own approach to the problem of *princeps legibus solus* and insight into developing Protestant thinking on the subject, see Harro Hopfl, *The Christian Polity of John Calvin* (Cambridge: Cambridge University Press, 1982), 13–18.

45. See Tariq al-Bishri, *Al-Dimuqratiyyah wa al-nasiriyyah* (Cairo: Dar al-Thaqafah al-Jadidah, 1975), 22–24, especially the description of Nasser's use of the power to appoint and remove high officials.

46. See Leonard Binder, *In a Moment of Enthusiasm* (Chicago: University of Chicago Press, 1978), 376–77.

47. Olivier Carré, *Mystique et politique: Lecture revolutionnaire du Coran* (Paris: Presses de la Fondation Nationale des Sciences Politiques, 1944), 47.

48. See, for example, Wafa' al-Khanajri, *Al-Amthal al-Sha-'biyyah fi hayyatina al-yawmiyyah* (Cairo: Al-Maktabah al-Qawmiyyah Al-Hadithah, 1982), 10, entry 26.

49. John Lewis Burckhardt, *Arabic Proverbs, or the Manners and Customs of the Modern Egyptians,* 3d ed. (1817, rpt. London: Curzon Press, 1972), 237, entry 671. See also 275, entry 761 for indications of other proverbs regarding Pharaoh as an embodiment of the state.

50. See Ahmad Taymur Basha, *Al-Amthal al-'ammiyyah,* 4th ed. (Cairo: Al-Ahram Center for Translation and Publication, 1986). See nos. 371 and 372 (pp. 61–62). See also no. 3080 (p. 512) with the explication again that the word *pharaoh* implies oppression and coercion, and counterposes Moses to Pharaoh, asserting the need for active opposition to those who assert that they are "the highest lord." The text of the proverb is the well-known "Ya, fir'awn, min far'anak qal ma laqitsh hadd yiraddini" (Oh, Pharaoh, how did you become Pharaoh? No one opposed me).

51. Although there is no doubt that Qutb's vision of secular authority as idolatrous grew during the Nasser years, it is quite possible that something of the populism of Nasserism has actually encouraged the opposition to the state by privileging popular and nonofficial feelings of resistance to that oppression, even if the state did not allow people to act on such feelings. Compare the treatment of the proverb "Oh Pharaoh, how did you get to be Pharaoh? No one opposed me" in Al-Khanajri, *Al-Amthal al-sha'biyyah,* 191, entry 1591, and in Taymur, *Al-Amthal al'ammiyyah,* with Muhammad Ibrahim Abu Sina, *Falsafat al-mithl al-sha'bi* (Cairo: Dar al-katib al-arabi, 1968), in which it is closely joined with a discussion on the need to resist tyranny (*al-tughyan*) and the proverb "Silence in the right is like eloquence in the wrong" (61).

52. See Gilles Kepel, *Muslim Extremism in Egypt* (Berkeley: University of California Press, 1986); Eric Davis, "Islamic Radicalism in Egypt," in *From Nationalism to Revolutionary Islam,* ed. S. Arjomand (New York: Macmillan, 1984), 147.

53. There is certainly reason to believe that Davis is correct in his general proposition. Some survey research data indicate that children of clerical and sales workers were more likely to experience downward than upward mobility. See Saad Eddin Ibrahim, "Social Mobility and Income Distribution," in *The Political Economy of Income Distribution in Egypt,* ed. Gouda Abdel-Khalek and Robert Tignor (New York: Holmes and Meier, 1982), 403. Those drawn into the movements do not seem to have been directly downwardly mobile; see Davis, "Islamic Radicalism," 147; Kepel, *Muslim Extremism,* 217.

54. See Ibrahim Hassan al-Issawy, "Income Distribution and Economic Growth," in Abdel-Khalek and Tignor, eds., *Political Economy,* 90.

55. Ibid., 100–101.

56. Ibid., 119.

57. See, for example, John Waterbury, *The Egypt of Nasser and Sadat: The Political Economy of Two Regimes* (Princeton: Princeton University Press, 1983), 274, for an account of the Zumr family, two members being arrested for participation in the assassination of Sadat.

58. See Mahmoud Abdel-Fadil, *Development, Income Distribution, and Social Change in Rural Egypt (1952–1970),* University of Cambridge Department of Applied Economics Occasional Paper 45 (Cambridge: Cambridge University Press, 1975), 114.

59. William J. Bouwsma, *John Calvin: A Sixteenth-Century Portrait* (New York: Oxford University Press, 1988), 150.

60. None of these groups call themselves by the names commonly used for them. The use of these common names is necessary, however, if this chapter is to establish a dialogue with other scholars in the field. The so-called Flight and Repentance group referred to themselves as the *jama'at al-muslimin* (Community of Muslims); the so-called Military Academy group called themselves the *munazzamat al-tahrir al-islami* (Islamic Liberation Organization).

61. This particular work is so important that it has been translated into English.

62. See the translation and commentary by Johannes J. G. Jansen, in *The Neglected Duty* (New York: Macmillan, 1986), xvii–xviii; and Jamal al-Banna, *Al-Faridah al-Gha'ibah: jihad al-sayf am jihad al-aql?* (Cairo: Dar Thabit, 1983), 5.

63. See Ali Jad al-Haqq, *Al-Fatawa al-Islamiyyah* (hereafter *FI*) (Cairo: Dar al-Ifta' al-misriyyah, 1983), 10: no. 29, 3726–92, for the fatwa and an Arabic text of the booklet itself. See also Muhammad 'Amarah, *Al-Faridah al-Gha'ibah: 'ard wa-hiwar wa-taqyim* (Cairo: Dar Thabit, 1982).

64. See Jansen, *Neglected Duty,* 160 and 162: "If God sends someone on the right path, no one can send him astray. If God sends someone astray, no one can guide him." See also 223, §130 and 131. In *FI,* see 3762 and 3789–90. This is, of course, the "double decree" whose absence Weber found in conflict with a developed Protestant ethic. All translations are from Jansen. Citations will be to both Jansen and *FI* to allow general readers, as well as those who read Arabic, to pursue the argument.

65. Jansen, *Neglected Duty,* 161, §4; *FI,* 3762. The word for idols here is *taghut.*

66. Jansen, *Neglected Duty,* 167, §21; *FI,* 38.5.

67. Jansen, *Neglected Duty,* 169, §25; *FI,* 38.5. Cf. Calvin, *Institutes,* II, xv, i: "Thus the Papists in the Present age, although the name of the Son of God, the Redeemer of the world, be frequently in their mouths, yet since they are contented with the mere name, and despoil him of his power and dignity [Christ] is not their foundation."

68. For support for such a position from the Qur'an, see III: 87 and LXIV: 2. The sticky issue of intentionality intrudes here, and what led the 'ulama to orthopraxis is an important and subtle argument. I hope to deal with issues of community and intentionality in the classical Islamic tradition in other works.

69. For a lucid presentation of the arguments here, see Peters, *Islam and Colonialism,* 128–29, especially whether the question of the verse to "slay the unbelievers" should be interpreted in the context of earlier verses regarding treaty breaking. *Ayat al-sayf* is IX: 5 in the Qur'an.

70. That apostasy is the only unforgiveable sin is agreed by everyone writing in this controversy. The question is over what constitutes apostasy: Does it need to be an express and intended repudiation of Islam, or not.

71. Jansen, *Neglected Duty,* 168, §22; *FI,* 3865. See Kepel, *Muslim Extremism,* 195–96. Compare Zwingli's "A Christian Town Is the Same as a Christian Congregation," in Lochner, *Huldrych Zwingli's Concept,* 228–29.

72. 'Amarah, *Al-Faridah al-Gha'ibah,* 47.

73. See al-Banna, *Al-Faridah al-Gha'ibah,* 122, regarding justice (*'adl*) and an exposition of the need for free discussion of religion.

74. This is a staple of writing on Islamist movements. One of the most eloquent examples would be the chapter "The Question of Authenticity and Collaboration," in Fouad Ajami, *The Arab Predicament* (Cambridge: Cambridge University Press, 1981), but also see R. H. Dekmejian, "The Anatomy of Islamic Revival," *Middle East Journal* 34, no. 1 (Winter, 1980): 1–12. An early and still useful approach is Smith, "Islam in Recent History," in *Islam in Modern History.*

75. Bouwsma, *John Calvin,* 64.

76. This is fairly well recognized among Arab researchers of the phenomenon and Muslim official figures. See "Nadwat al-sahwah al-islamiyyah wa humum al-watan al-'arabi," *Al-Watan,* April 15, 1987.

77. Edmund Spenser, *The Faerie Queene*, book 1, canto 2, stanza 13. See also John Milton, *Paradise Lost*, 1:330–50, in which Satan is perceived by the fallen angels as "their great Sultan," and 2:1–10, for the description of the Satanic "Throne of Royal State, which far / Outshone the wealth of Ormus and of Ind...."

78. As Hopfl puts it in *Christian Polity*, for Calvin, "the absence of restraint seems to have been of the essence of tyrannical rule..." (16).

79. *FI*, 3743; 'Amarah, *Al-Faridah al-Gha'ibah*, 48–50, and especially the comparison of the Mamluks governing Egypt as described by Ibn Taymiyyah, to whose juridical rulings the members of the Jihad group referred in comparison to contemporary Egypt.

80. 'Amarah, *Al-Faridah al-Gha'ibah*, 46.

81. Jansen, *Neglected Duty*, 8–15.

82. Ibid., 222, §130; *FI*, 3789.

83. Jansen, *Neglected Duty*, 225, §134; *FI*, 3791: *"wa yad'uhum ila al-ifsah 'amma sataruhu."*

84. Jansen, *Neglected Duty*, 228, §138; *FI*, 3792.

85. See 'Abd al-Rahman Abu al-Khayr, *Dhikrayati ma'-a "Jama'-at al-Muslimin" (Al-Takfir wa al-hijrah)* (Kuwait: Dar al-Buhuth al-'ilmiyyah, 1980), 9–10. This is essentially a statement of Shukri's at a court proceeding published in the press on October 21, 1977. The word for idols in paragraph 2 is *asnam*.

86. Kepel, *Muslim Extremism*, 79.

87. Abu al-Khayr, *Dhikrayati*, 137–39.

88. Kepel, *Muslim Extremism*, 204.

89. Abu al-Khayr, *Dhikrayati*, 78.

90. Ibid., 98.

91. Kepel, *Muslim Extremism*, 80–82.

92. "Uslub al-ta'amul bayna al-hakim wa al-mahkum" (Modes of Interaction between Ruler and Ruled), *Al-Ahram*, November 5, 1982.

93. Calvin, *Institutes*, IV, 20, ii.

94. Calvin, *Institutes*, IV, 20, iv.

95. Eire, *War against the Idols*, 294–98.

96. Walzer, *Revolution of the Saints*, 105.

97. Ibid., 108–9.

98. Kepel, *Muslim Extremism*, 234–35; Michael M. J. Fischer, "Islam and the Revolt of the Petty Bourgeoisie," *Daedalus* 111, no. 1 (1982): 112–13; Abd al-Moneim Said Aly and Manfred Wenner, "Modern Islamic Reform Movements: The Muslim Brotherhood in Contemporary Egypt," *Middle East Journal* 36, no. 3 (Summer, 1982): 347–48.

99. Valerie Hoffman-Ladd, "Polemics on the Modesty and Segregation of Women," *International Journal of Middle East Studies* 19, no. 1 (1987): 23–50, 44.

100. Mann, *Sources of Social Power,* 470–71.

101. Ibid., 472.

102. For a good critique of functionalist explanations, from which this section is drawn, see Jon Elster, *Making Sense of Marx* (Cambridge: Cambridge University Press, 1985), 27–29.

Women, Islam, and the State:
A Comparative Approach

Deniz Kandiyoti

Analyses of gender relations and ideologies in Muslim societies have been dominated by a persistent preoccupation with the role of Islam. A considerable output of both feminist and antifeminist writing debates the compatibility of Islam with the emancipation of women. Positions within this debate range from apologias for divinely ordained inequalities between the sexes to more progressive readings of religious texts and early Islamic history. The latter suggest that the initially egalitarian message of Islam was variously subverted through the rise of class systems, the victory of patriarchal interests, or the defensive cultural entrenchment prompted by imperialism and colonial domination.[1] Some argue that Islam is intrinsically patriarchal and inimical to women's rights.[2] A new wave of cultural criticism in the Arab world further contends that both attachment to an unchanging, frozen conception of Islam and the continuing subordination of women in the name of cultural authenticity are interrelated symptoms of a broader syndrome of cultural stagnation. The latter is purported to emanate from deep-seated authoritarian tendencies in Arab society that are ultimately inimical to any kind of emancipatory project.[3]

What these approaches share is the analytic primacy of culture and ideology and the privileged place assigned to Islam, though evaluations of its role may vary, in understanding the condition of women. This tendency has been criticized for its ahistoricism, its monolithic conception of Islamic ideology and practice, and the lack of class perspectives in the debate on gender.[4] This critique has, however, not yielded alternative ways of acknowledging and engaging with the specificity of Islam, leaving some of the justifiable political and practical concerns of feminists and cultural critics unaddressed.[5] It is indeed hard to overlook both the prevalence and resilience of practices such as veiling, female seclusion, polygyny, and easy male divorce in Muslim societies, which, although they may predate Islam and are variable in their actual incidence and application, nonetheless ultimately derive their legitimation from a divinely inspired text that forms the basis for actual legislation.

Part of the difficulty stems from the fact that references to Islam have largely lacked analytic precision. Any attempt to move beyond this state of affairs must, therefore, start by questioning the use of the term *Islam* as a unified and self-evident analytic category. In studies about gender, Islam is most commonly evoked with reference to at least three overlapping but analytically distinct levels of social reality: (a) to describe patriarchal gender arrangements in the family and society that, though religiously sanctioned, can be shown to have an autonomous existence that may not be conflated with the workings of any one religion; (b) to designate bodies of Islamic jurisprudence that inform the legal apparatuses of modern states and, to varying degrees, impinge upon the legal and citizenship rights of women; and (c) to denote more diffuse ideologies about women's appropriate place and conduct couched in an Islamic idiom that may be encountered in contemporary discourses about cultural authenticity and in pronouncements by modern Islamic political movements.

I have argued elsewhere that a serious weakness in our current analyses stems from a conflation of Islam, as ideology and practice, with patriarchy.[6] I have suggested the possibility that many of the uniformities we observe with respect to gender may be due to the workings of a generic system of male domination that I characterized as "classic patriarchy," and that Middle Eastern societies share with most of South and East Asia. Further, I have argued that distinct systems of male domination, evident in the operations of different kinship systems, exercise an influence that inflects and modifies the actual practice of Islam as well as ideological constructions of what may be regarded as properly "Islamic." The fact that the core areas of Islamic civilization have historically coincided with areas of classic patriarchy has deepened the confusion between the assumed workings of Islam and those of a specific type of gender hierarchy.

The aim of this chapter is not to search for possible sources of uniformity but, on the contrary, to highlight the deep and significant variations in the condition of women resulting from the different political projects of contemporary nation-states in the Middle East and South

Asia. Studies of women in Muslim societies have tended to neglect the role of the state and the extent to which the place of Islam, itself, is mediated through various aspects of state practice.[7] The first part of the chapter, therefore, documents variations in the deployment of Islam in relation to different nationalisms and state-building projects and assesses their impact on legislation and policies affecting women. The second part examines the effects of the expansion of modern state apparatuses and the nature and limitations of state interventions in the realm of women and the family. The final section situates contemporary policies and ideologies concerning women in the context of the contradictory pressures governments face from different factions of their internal constituencies as well as from their international political and economic relations.

Islam, Nationalism, and the "Woman Question"

The turn of the nineteenth and the beginning of the twentieth century has witnessed the emergence of reformers of women's condition in the Muslim world from the ranks of an educated, nationalist, and predominantly male elite. This elite's concern with women's rights centered around issues of education, seclusion, veiling, and polygyny and coincided with a broader agenda about "progress" and the compatibility between Islam and modernism. Positions on the "woman question" mirrored the splits on this problematic issue. Liberals and reformists favored the emancipation of women, which they generally justified through a modernist reading of Islam, while conservatives perceived such reformism as both an attack on the integrity of the Islamic polity and a capitulation to Western cultural imperialism. In the case of Egypt, Cole pointed out that this controversy was characterized by fairly clear class divisions.[8] Whereas the champions of women's emancipation, such as Qasim Amin, tended to be members of the new, upper-middle class who were integrated both economically and culturally into the Western orbit, the opposition emanated from petit bourgeois intellectuals, such as Talat Harb, who felt threatened by the encroachment of the West. Similarly, the cleavages between the Ottoman modernizers, whose reforms also acted as an instrument for the smooth integration of the Ottoman state into a Europe-dominated world economy, and the groups and classes that were excluded from the new, "modernized" structures found expression in a resistance by the latter that often invoked Islamic authenticity and the defense of traditional Ottoman mores.

However, presenting Western hegemony as the midwife of both modernist reformism and conservative reaction inevitably simplifies a more complex picture. Benedict Anderson draws our attention to the process of transition from sacred communities and dynastic realms to the "imagined community" of nation-states, a transition achieved under varied circumstances and at different time periods by the modern nation-states of the Middle East and South Asia.[9] Diverse processes of nation creation in the Muslim world have produced a spectrum of distinct, shifting, and actively contested syntheses between cultural nationalism and Islam. The terms of the "woman question" were forged in this process of search for new ideologies to legitimize and support emerging forms of state power.

In Turkey, where the process of secularization went furthest, the shift from the multiethnic Ottoman empire to an Anatolia-based nation-state involved a progressive distancing between cultural nationalism and Islam culminating in Kemalist secular republicanism. Turkish nationalism, which found its earliest expression in the Turkist currents of the Second Constitutional Period (1908–18), introduced new elements into the debate about women's emancipation that had so far remained caught between the terms of Westernism and Islam. Cultural nationalism began to present, as indigenous Turkish features, items that were admired in the West, such as equality of conjugal partners in a nuclear and monogamous family. However, the decisive break came with Mustafa Kemal Ataturk, who not only dismantled the central institutions of Ottoman Islam by abolishing the Caliphate and secularizing every sphere of social life, but took additional measures to heighten Turkey's "Turkish" national consciousness at the expense of a wider Islamic identification; the compulsory romanization of the alphabet, the new dress code, and an elaborate rereading of Turkish history stressing its pre-Islamic heritage were consistent elements of the cultural mobilization in the service of the new state. The fact that the Istanbul government headed by the Sultan-Caliph had reached an agreement with the powers of occupation in the aftermath of World War I to supress the Ankara government's struggle for national liberation compromised the Islamic establishment, making it vulnerable to the charge of abetting imperialist designs and acting treasonably. Although the nationalist alliance that brought Kemal to power included men of religion, his ability to confront the theocratic institutions of the Ottoman state appears to have been heightened by this disjunction between the goal of national independence, supported by a nascent indigenous middle class, and the vested interests of the Ottoman ancien régime. The introduction of a secular Turkish Civil Code in 1926 and the enfranchisement of women in 1934 were thus part of the broader struggle to liquidate the theocratic institutions of the Ottoman state and to establish a republican notion of citizenship.[10] The republican establishment has since undergone several transformations following the transition to a multiparty democracy that saw the rise of new classes and interest groups, some with pro-Islamic leanings, competing for state power.[11] At present, the Kemalist legacy is being actively contested and reappropriated by conflicting political tendencies. The current debate on women's rights mirrors these tendencies and includes the positions of more recent Islamist currents.[12] However, the state has not, to date, moved to reverse legislative reforms introduced by the early republican regime, although these may become arenas of renewed struggle between secular and pro-Islamic political forces in coming years.

A comparison of Turkey and Iran is particularly pertinent in view of the fact that Reza Shah openly derived at least part of his inspiration from the example of Mustafa Kemal. Indeed, his move to ban the veiling of women in 1936 was more drastic than Kemal's more indirect, propagandistic approach to this issue. However, in Iran, the clergy, although enfeebled under Reza Shah, was none the less able to resist cooptation into the institutions of the Pahlavi state.[13] Unlike the Ottoman clerical establishment, the Shi'a clergy of Iran did not suffer a loss of legitimacy and remained strong enough economically and in its mass-based networks to reenter the political arena from the early 1960s onward. The organization and structure of the Shi'a clergy, which was in any case quite different from its Ottoman Sunni counterpart, was not radically transformed. Almost an adjunct of the state in the Ottoman case, the clergy retained a measure of organizational and financial autonomy in Iran, with profound consequences for the shape of things to come. In addition, the fact that Reza Shah's power was consolidated not on the basis of a social movement but a military coup resulting in a military-based monarchy provided a weak basis for legitimacy that was further eroded under the "sultanic" rule of his son. Afsaneh Najmabadi points out that the transition to the Islamic Republic brought about a radical shift, discarding all previous discourses about progress and modernity in favour of a complete "moralization" of questions pertaining to women.[14] The

Islamic state proceeded to enforce the norms of female domesticity and modesty through a wide array of policies in the areas of employment, education, marriage, divorce, and women's dress and mobility.[15]

Commenting on the problems facing women in the contemporary Arab world, Nawal El Saadawi points to inherent contradictions in laws and values whereby women are defined as equals in citizenship rights by national constitutions yet are denied equality in marriage and the family by personal status laws derived from the Shari'a.[16] She lays responsibility for this state of affairs at the door of imperialists who selectively modified whichever aspect of indigenous legal systems they found expedient to further their own designs; "They aimed to create a schizophrenic split in the laws in order to modernize some sectors of society at the cost of others, to open the upper classes to the civilization of the West, and to lock the overwhelming majority—especially the rural population—into the ancient heritage."[17] Nadia Hijab, who also notes the resistance of Arab states to breaking with Shari'a law in the case of personal status codes—even when secular laws have been adopted in every other area of social life, invokes a total interpenetration between Islam and Arab cultural identity and the need to protect the latter from imperialist onslaughts.[18] Fatima Mernissi looks to the Arab heritage itself for an explanation of the stubborn conservatism in the sphere of women and the family. She suggests that Arab culture was unable to bridge the gap between religious belief and modern notions of citizenship, between absolute obedience and human rights. In this context of cultural stagnation, women, she suggests, "were delegated the obedience role in the engineering of the Arab-Islamic identity."[19]

There is no doubt that a complicated mix of endogenous and exogenous influences have been at work. In Egypt, for instance, the disjuncture between national and personal status laws that was present in the Wafdist constitution of the 1920s and continued thereafter can more readily be derived from the agenda of nationalist politicians of landlord extraction than from British influence. In other parts of the Ottoman periphery, such as Lebanon, the resilience of religious laws in the area of personal status can be traced to the influence of the Ottoman *millet* system, although sectarian fragmentation was subsequently bolstered and exploited by both foreign and local interests. The degree of political autonomy and leverage retained by local sectarian communities vis-à-vis the central state is also germane to the issue of family legislation and personal law and will be examined in some detail in the next section.

Therefore, invoking either the agency of imperialist designs or the attributes of an essential Arab-Muslim identity can only yield partial and possibly misleading insights, particularly if analyses result in lumping together modern states with significantly different political trajectories.

It could be argued with some justification that the interpenetration between Islam and cultural nationalism has been most pronounced in the Arab world.[20] Indeed, whatever the different emphases of nationalist movements with respect to the links between Arabism and Islam, the former, at the very least, co-opted the latter, as is evident in the doctrine of Arab socialism in its Nasserite or Baathist versions.

Nonetheless, in the Arab world as elsewhere there have been shifting definitions of nationhood and different variants of nationalism. Mernissi points out that, in Morocco, opting for "Arabness" was convenient in terms of finding a place and identity in the Arab world, just as the French colonizers had found it expedient to stress the divisions between Arabs and Berbers for their own purposes.[21] Leila Hamamsy presents Egyptian national sentiment as a complex amalgam involving a dissociation from alien (albeit Muslim) Turkish rulers, pride in the pharaonic past, and a connection to a broader Arab cultural heritage crystallizing around a common language and history, that of Islam itself.[22] Beth Baron shows how different stands on the "woman question" in early twentieth-century Egypt reflected the positions of different nationalist camps, namely those of religiously inspired Egyptian Ottomanists and territorially grounded, secular nationalists.[23] These cleavages were reflected in women's nationalist discourses and predilections. Women who were the followers of the leading Egyptian Ottomanist, Mustafa Kamil, denounced the spread of Westernization and immorality and urged a return to Islamic law, endorsing all the strictures this implied for women. However, the defeat of the empire at the end of World War I signaled the demise of the Ottoman option and encouraged a shift to a territorial and secular definition of nationhood in a bid to achieve independence. Liberal nationalists looked for indigenous models of women's emancipation and turned to the pharaonic past to prove that such models need not come from the West (much as the Turkish nationalists had turned to central Asiatic origins). Women's education and emancipation were justified as requirements for the advancement of the nation, confirming the broader association Kumari Jayawardena makes between secular nationalisms in the Third World and the rise of feminist movements.[24] The inherent limitations of "nationalist" feminisms will receive separate attention. Suffice it to point out here that local feminisms took varied forms and created different symbolic universes in different parts of the Arab world.

The countries of the South Asian subcontinent constitute a particularly fertile ground for the exploration of the juxtapositions between Islam and national identity, especially since their fates were so intimately intertwined. In prepartition India, Islam was a communally based religion that served as an ethnic marker. Pakistan emerged after partition as a state claiming its separate identity on religious grounds, so that Islam was integral to nationhood itself. Unlike Turkey, where severing broader, multiethnic, Islamic imperial connections was instrumental to its emergence as a nation-state, Pakistan had to affirm and capitalize upon its Muslim identity in the struggle for a separate homeland. However, Pakistan under Jinnah originated as a state for the Muslims in India rather than an Islamic state, and it was not until 1956 that Pakistan was declared an Islamic republic. Progressively, as the Pakistani state struggled to retain control in the face of regional and ethnic cleavages and strife, Islam was evoked as a legitimizing, if tenuous, ideology for Pakistani unity, culminating in the military rule of General Zia, who, lacking a popular mandate, claimed legitimacy through divine ordinance.[25] The Islamization package introduced by Zia-ul-Haq had women as its focal point. The Hudood Ordinance of 1979 often had the effect of giving legal sanction to sexual discrimination, and could even result in rape victims being tried and convicted for adultery. Under the qisas and diyat Ordinance of 1980, women victims were deemed worthy of half the compensation offered for a man in cases of injury or death, but were subjected to equal punishment in the case of an offense. The Law of Evidence aimed at reducing the weight of a female witness's evidence to half that of a man. Ayesha Jalal argues that this emphasis on the control of women as a means of establishing Islamic credentials has deep roots in the history of the subcontinent. The Muslim rulers of India had evolved a policy of accommodation and cooptation of members of other religious communities, on the one hand, and a social conservatism in the domestic sphere, on the other, as a means of preserving their identity "amid a sea of infidels."[26] This cultural reflex was further reinforced with the imposition of the British Raj, and entrenchment on the "woman question" lay at the heart of cultural resistance to both Hinduism and colonialism. Since the late 1970s, an Islamic idiom was favored by the Pakistani landed and industrial classes in order to attract the political support of the urban, lower-middle classes, whose class interests would otherwise be divergent, and as an insurance policy against more radical land reform or socialist nationalization policies. Ironically, the political alliance that Islamization policies aimed to forge between the Pakistani male elite and the lower middle classes threatened the interests of female members of the same elite, whose discontent fueled one of the most active women's movements in South Asia. The vitality of the Women's Action Forum is due, in no small measure, to Zia's Islamization policies and to the outrage they provoked among educated, elite women, even though, in practice, it was women of humbler extraction who were more likely to experience their full rigor.

Bengali Muslim identity in Bangladesh has been more ambivalent, not least by virtue of its problematic links with Pakistan. The quasi-colonial ties of domination by Pakistan and the fact that the latter appropriated the mantle of Islamic purity for itself enhanced the contradiction between Muslim and Bengali identity, a contradiction that was clearly apparent in the Bengali movement for national independence from Pakistan.[27] The protest demonstrations on the eve of independence witnessed Muslim Bengali women marching in the streets dressed in red and yellow festive saris, wearing *bindis* on their foreheads and chanting Bengali nationalist songs, including those of Tagore, banned by the Pakistan administration. The Bengalis were claiming the right to their own language, customs, and distinct cultural identity. After independence, Islam would increasingly be put to local political uses as successive regimes attempted to shore up their legitimacy.

Bangladesh emerged from the violence and dislocation of 1971 as a secular People's Republic. However, the successive military regimes after the assassination, in 1976, of Mujib-ur-Rahman, leader of the Awami League, proceeded to a progressive dismantling of state secularism that culminated in General Ershad's declaration of Bangladesh as an Islamic state in 1988. The regime's policies vis-à-vis women have, however, not matched the level of Islamic intransigence deployed by Zia's Pakistan or the Islamic Republic of Iran. The more tentative nature of the Islamization policies in Bangladesh have to be evaluated against the distinctive background of Bengali nationalism, the attempts of military regimes to achieve legitimacy by placating different sections of their internal constituencies, and the extreme dependence of this impoverished country on foreign-aid donors with different agendas and priorities, an important point to which I shall return in the final section of this chapter.

The predicament of Muslim women in India is closely tied to the minority status of Indian Muslims. The relationship between secular law and personal or religious law has always been a sensitive one in India, leading most of its rulers, including the British, not to tamper with the traditional laws of religious communities in personal matters relating to family and inheritance rights that remained uncodified for a long time. The Shari'a law passed in 1937 stipulated that Muslims in India would be governed by Muslim religious laws in matters of personal status. Although the personal laws of all religious communities are gender-discriminatory and the dual legal structure works to the detriment of women in general, the question of Muslim women's rights in India became the subject of renewed controversy and further legislation after the furor created by the case of Shah Bano. Shah Bano, a divorced Muslim woman, had pressed for her rights of maintenance from her husband under the Criminal Procedure Code. The Supreme Court dismissed the husband's appeal and ordered him to pay maintenance as well as legal costs. This led to mass demonstrations, strikes, and petitions by Muslims in protest against what they perceived as a violation of Muslim Personal Law, since the latter does not require husbands to pay alimony, but only short-term compensation (in the form of the 'idda). In 1986, the Indian Parliament passed The Muslim Women's Protection of the Right to Divorce Bill, which withdrew the right of Muslim women to appeal for maintenance under the Criminal Procedure Code.[28] Amrita Chhachhi situates this episode in the context of the construction of communal identities in India.[29] She notes the uneasy tension in Indian nationalism, from its very inception, between secularism and communalism. Although the Indian national movement was secular in its objectives, it capitalized upon Hindu communal sentiment and used the symbols and language of Hindu revivalism. Images of both Hindu and Muslim womanhood became central to the construction of not only distinct but antagonistic identities. The logic of communal politics thwarted any progressive attempts to redefine and expand Muslim women's rights, since this issue could readily be transformed into a confrontation of majority and minority rights and interests. This is precisely what happened in the case of Shah Bano.

Despite their remarkable diversity, it is possible to detect unifying strands among these cases. The question of women's rights is invariably part of an ideological terrain where broader notions of cultural authenticity and integrity are debated and where women's appropriate place and conduct may be made to serve as boundary markers. The content of discourses about authenticity are quite variable. Women's emancipation may be appropriated and endorsed as indigenous and legitimate by secular nationalisms or denounced as alien and impious by Islamic movements or state-supported fundamentalisms. Women and the family, nonetheless, retain a privileged place in the articulation of anxieties about integrity and difference. Commenting on the Mediterranean notion of honor in two different contexts, Paul Vieille and Victoria Goddard argue that the control of women is paramount among sociocultural groups who feel threatened and shield themselves from the intrusions of external, "predatory" centers of power such as the local state or foreign colonialists.[30] In Muslim societies, this threat has rather single-mindedly been presented as emanating from Western imperialism or the local bureaucratic or compradorial classes that are seen as its internal allies. In fact, the term representing the intrusive and threatening Other takes a multiplicity of forms and appears as the Hindu, the Levantine, the Copt, or the Jew in different contexts and easily extends to native Muslims who challenge existing patriarchal norms.

The fact that women represent the "privacy" of the group and the focal point of kinship-based solidarities against a more abstract and problematic allegiance to the state has therefore presented serious obstacles for the "modernizing" states of the Muslim world. Modern states have had to confront and, to some extent, eradicate local particularisms in order to create more universalistic loyalties and to liberate all the available forces of development, including the labor potential of the female citizenry. Depending on the nature of their political projects, central states have variously challenged, accommodated, or abdicated to local/communal patriarchal interests with important consequences for family legislation and more general policies affecting women. I shall now examine this facet of state practice, which has received relatively little attention in the study of Muslim societies.

The Expanding State: Women and Family Reform

The search for a modern family form in the Muslim world coincided with and was stimulated by the rise of nationalist movements discussed in the previous section. A nationalist/feminist alliance of progressive men and women produced a new discourse about women and the family that was markedly instrumental in tone. Women's illiteracy, seclusion, and the practice of polygyny were not denounced primarily because they curtailed the human rights of one half of the population, but because they created ignorant mothers, shallow and scheming partners, unstable marital unions, and lazy and unproductive members of society. In turn of the century Ottoman society, the traditional Ottoman family was attacked by modernizers as the root cause of multiple social ills, and family reform was presented as essential to the regeneration of state and society.[31] The nuclear family, based on stable monogamous unions, the free choice of spouses, and companionate relationships between conjugal partners was deemed to be the family form best suited to promote a healthier nation.

These and similar ideas remained in the realm of polemic for a long time in societies with small urban populations, weak industrial bases, and vast rural or tribal hinterlands with varying degrees of integration in national and international markets. The limited outreach of premodern states left many aspects of their citizens' lives untouched, especially in the regulation of marriage and family life, which remained firmly under local kin control. Suad Joseph notes the greater ability of Middle Eastern communities to resist the control of central states than their European counterparts;[32] invokes the absence of strong centralizing institutions, such as the Catholic church, competing for the control of alliances and family wealth;[33] and the greater interpenetration between the Muslim clergy and Islamic states. Indeed, neither the state nor the Muslim clergy acted to break the hold of local communities over the control of marriage alliances and women, and we witness the first attempts at deeper penetration of society by the state as late as the nineteenth century.

Judith Tucker's work on nineteenth-century Egypt points to the rather paradoxical consequences of the expansion of state power under the rule of Muhammed Ali.[34] On the one hand, interventionist state policies encouraged the recruitment of women into public works, state-run industries, and the expanding sectors of health and education, removing them from total and exclusive control by their families. On the other hand, the repressive apparatus of the state actually restricted the range of their more traditional activities and forms of association.

The first direct attempt at state intervention through family legislation in the Ottoman Empire, the 1917 Family Code, is noteworthy for its lack of success. This code aimed to replace the traditional Ottoman family with the nuclear, monogamous, "National Family" (*Milli Aile*) in line with the nationalist and regenerative ideals of the Committee for Union and Progress.[35] It attempted to curb polygyny by making its practice more difficult (by stipulating the consent of the first wife and imposing a conciliation procedure to discourage divorce) and had separate subsections applying to Muslim, Christian, and Jewish subjects. This law failed to satisfy either those who demanded fundamental changes in a family system considered to be in crisis or those who saw those changes as flagrant breaches of Shari'a law. Furthermore, minorities were also restive over what they perceived as a curtailment of the power of their own religious authorities. They demanded the repeal of the clauses pertaining to non-Muslim marriages from the Allied forces of occupation in Istanbul following the Ottoman defeat in the Great War. In short, the beleaguered Ottoman state was unable to wrest control from religious and communal interests by its timid moves toward secularization. The secular Civil Code of 1926 promulgated by the new Turkish Republic also remained essentially a dead letter for a long time, especially in parts of the Anatolian hinterland most weakly integrated in the national market and least affected by the administrative apparatus of the central authorities.

Despite these halting beginnings, this century has witnessed the dramatic expansion of state power in all Muslim societies. The attempts of postindependence states to absorb and transform kin-based communities in order to expand their control met with varying degrees of resistance or acceptance with important consequences for the formulation of policies and legislation affecting women and the family. In a comparative analysis of Tunisia, Morocco, and Algeria, Mounira Charrad argues, for instance, that variations in the balance of power between the national state and locally based communities during accession to independence in the three countries led to significant differences in their current family legislation.[36] Tunisia, which has the most progressive family legislation, with the 1957 Personal Status Law, is also the country where primordial communities appear to have had relatively less political autonomy and leverage and where the nationalist movement was led by a powerful party that was least reliant on these communities for political support.

In a comparative analysis of Iraq and Lebanon, Suad Joseph also demonstrates a close connection between elite strategies for state building and policies relating to women and the family.[37] In Iraq, where the Baath required the mobilization of women's labor in a context of continuing labor shortages and where the state party had an interest in wresting and transferring the allegiance of the population from particularistic loyalties to itself, women were recruited into state-controlled agencies and resocialized through public education as well as vocational training and political indoctrination. However, legislative reforms in personal status laws remained modest, and attempts to undermine the allegiance of the population to traditional kin-based groups came up against widespread mistrust of the state instilled by the pervasive climate of political repression.[38] In Lebanon, where the structure of the state incorporated the religious/ethnic heterogeneity of society in its formal institutions, governments formally relinquished matters of family and personal status to the religious authorities of existing communities. There has been no attempt to institute an integrated system of national education, and, in line with the communal fragmentation reflected in the state, such services were secured through public subsidies to the private sector, as a strategy by the ruling elite to maintain the balance of sectarian power in the state.

Even in the People's Democratic Republic of Yemen, where the state avowedly attempted to use family reform and the 1974 Family Law as a tool of socialist transformation, numerous concessions were made to Islamic law and local customs, both in the formulation and in the application of the law.[39] After unification with Northern Yemen, it remains to be seen whether the modest legal advantages gained by women will survive.

Clearly, marriage and the family constitute the area of greatest resistance to the acceptance of state laws, and we often witness a relative laxity in their enforcement if and when they confront patriarchal interests. Presenting this resistance as emanating from respect for Islam is somewhat misleading in view of the fact that local customs were often more notable for their breach rather than their strict adherence to Muslim law, selectively upholding its patriarchal privileges but failing to honor women's rights, most notably, and significantly, women's rights to inheritance.

It must be acknowledged, at any rate, that the interventionist measures deployed by postindependence states either through family legislation or broader education, employment, and population control policies have been quite limited in their emancipatory impact for several reasons. First, measures for the emancipation of women did not, as a rule, coincide with a drive for democratization and the creation of a civil society where women's gender interests could be autonomously represented. On the contrary, they were part of the general thrust of *dirigiste* and frequently authoritarian and repressive regimes. The same reformist governments that granted women new rights frequently proceeded to abolish independent women's organizations (where they existed) while setting up state-sponsored women's organizations that were generally docile auxiliaries of the ruling state party. This is true of the General Federation of Iraqi Women and its links with the Baath Party and the General Union of Yemeni Women established by the NLF. This was also the case during the single-party rule in Turkey, under Reza Shah in Iran, and under Nasser in Egypt. The latter, immediately after granting women's suffrage in 1956, outlawed all feminist organizations. In cases where rapid changes in women's condition became associated with the heavy hand of an interventionist state, as in Soviet Central Asia in the 1920s, the consequences for women were often disastrous and did not further their autonomous struggle. This was undoubtedly compounded by the fact that the holders of state power could be identified as foreign infidels by the ethnically and religiously distinct populations of the Central Asian Republics.[40]

Second, communal controls over women continued to flourish and, in some instances, became intensified. Although processes of capitalist penetration frequently eroded the material bases of patriarchal relations in the family,[41] primary groups and particularistic allegiances continued to play a crucial role in mediating citizens' access to resources such as jobs, schooling, health, and other social services. The failure of modern states to create and adequately redistribute resources has intensified cleavages expressed in religious, ethnic, and regional terms and, in many cases, nullified the secular pretensions of radical nationalistic projects. As the state increasingly uses local patronage networks and sectional rivalries in its distributive systems, citizens turn to their primary solidarities both to protect themselves from repressive states and to compensate for inefficient administration. This process tends to reinforce the stranglehold of communities over their women, whose role as boundary markers become heightened. The Shah Bano incident referred to earlier can only be fully appreciated in a context of the growing communalization of politics and civil life in India and against a background of heightened intercommunal tension and violence. At such junctures, governments may make the tactical choice of relinquishing the control of women to their immediate communities and families and may deprive their female citizens of full legal protection.[42] In those instances where we also witness the operations of state-sponsored religious fundamentalism, the exercise of patriarchal authority may be accorded to unrelated men who are given a free hand in monitoring women's dress and conduct in public places. Indeed, the clergy, the police, or even "concerned" male citizens in Pakistan or Iran may assume expanded functions of direct control over women's dress and deportment, control that is more habitually exercised within the confines of the household or the immediate neighborhood.

Some have argued that the very erosion of the traditional structures of patriarchy and the speed of social changes that have propelled women into the public arena and threatened existing thresholds of authority have created a favorable climate for the emergence of a conservative backlash against women's emancipation that is articulated in the idiom of religious fundamentalism.[43] While this may account for some of the popular appeal of conservative ideologies, it cannot explain their different degrees of incorporation into actual state policies. To elucidate these differences, we must turn to a final but crucial consideration, namely, an analysis of the complex field of forces, both local and international, that influence the formulation and implementation of policies affecting women.

Women, Development, and State Policies: The International Dimension

One of the more paradoxical phenomena of recent years has been the creation of local mechanisms in most countries of the Middle East and South Asia to channel development funds into projects designed to have empowering consequences for women against a background of proliferating conservative ideologies concerning their appropriate roles.

Regionally, the cleavages between oil-rich and resource-poor countries have had an important effect on the flow of migration, aid, and political influence between Muslim countries. Migrants have moved from poorer countries such as Egypt, Yemen, Pakistan, Bangladesh, and Turkey to the oil-rich countries of the Gulf, while a reverse flow of cash and political influence has left its imprint on their polities. This reverse flow has served to strengthen the cultural and political prominence of local forces and parties with Islamist platforms and prompted diverse accommodations with Islam in aid-dependent countries. This influence was achieved through the medium of internal Islamist constituencies that either received a measure of acceptance and favor from ruling parties and governments or pushed governments to declare their own commitment to orthodoxy as a means of upstaging more radical Islamist platforms.

At the same time, the international monitoring of local economies has reached unprecedented levels, from the structural adjustment packages of the World Bank, to stabilization measures imposed by the IMF, and development projects sponsored by myriad Western donor agencies. This has, in many instances, been accompanied by a drastic redefinition of priorities: departures from tight state control over the economy, extended access to private enterprise and foreign investment, and an emphasis on export-led strategies of development. Although the gender effects of such policies, which have been the subject of heated polemics under the rubric of "women and development," must remain outside the scope of this chapter, the international institutional framework within which these debates were carried out and their effects on government policies must be noted.

Since the International Women's Year in 1975 and the subsequent United Nations Decade for Women, the women and development lobby has exerted pressure on national governments to recognize the role of women in combating poverty, illiteracy, and high birth rates. Governments have also been invited to eliminate all forms of legal discrimination based on sex.[44] In 1973, the Percy Amendment to the U.S. Foreign Assistance Act required that U.S. bilateral aid should promote projects integrating women into development efforts. Monitoring bureaucracies were set up within the U.S. Agency for International Development, the World Bank, and within foreign aid departments of the main European and Scandinavian donor nations. Although these structures are still peripheral to mainstream development funding, they are indicative of the ways in which the growing vitality of women's movements in both industrialized and Third World countries has put gender issues on the policy agenda. The "official" feminist rhetoric that had been the hallmark of the modernizing, postindependence state has now been appropriated by supranational monitoring bodies that have contradictory results at the local level.

The case of Bangladesh is particularly pertinent in this respect because of its high level of dependence on foreign aid. The coup that brought Zia ur-Rahman to power coincided with the 1975 declaration of the United Nations Decade for Women. At the time, Zia accumulated considerable political capital by championing the causes of the women and development lobby. However, he also needed the support of right-wing elements in society, including the army, to counter the opposition of the Awami League. Meanwhile, oil-rich states such as Saudi Arabia joined the ranks of major aid donors and subsequently increased their political leverage considerably. Zia embarked on a progressive Islamization policy that culminated in his successor's declaration of Bangladesh as an Islamic state in 1980. At the level of state policies, both Zia's and later Ershad's strategies constituted a delicate balancing act between the conflicting gender ideologies implicit in different aid packages; the development projects encouraged women's participation in the labor force and in public life while aid from the wealthier Muslim countries strengthened the madrasas and the proreligious parties advocating stricter controls on women. Thus, the government now finances the Islamic Foundation— which publishes tracts condemning family planning—while supporting U.S. funded attempts at population control. Meanwhile, women's movements in Bangladesh appear to have capitalized upon the spaces created by development projects and women's Nongovernmental Organizations (NGOs) were able to experiment with innovative forms of organization and mobilization such as the creation of rural-based consciousness-raising and action groups.[45]

Ironically, in Pakistan, the establishment of a Women's Division as part of the Cabinet secretariat to safeguard women's interests and promote development programs coincided with the passage of the discriminatory Islamization laws discussed in the earlier part of this chapter. Parallels to these cases may be found in many countries where policies and bureaucracies purportedly promoting women's advancement coexist with legal systems, ideologies, and social movements emphasizing their subordinate status in society.

The apparent contradiction between these facts disappears upon closer inspection. Donor governments and funding agencies attempt to harness women directly to their vision of a more effective, though not necessarily more equitable, international economic order. The very manner in which the recipients of aid are integrated into that order encourages the rise of unstable or repressive regimes, most of which are caught up in a corrosive cycle of foreign debt. The development policies favored by such regimes have, by and large, led to more visible disparities in wealth that fuel widespread resentment and discontent, often in the absence of democratic channels of expression. The legitimacy crises engendered by these processes have favored the rise of organized opposition movements with Islamist platforms as well as attempts at social control by governments emphasizing their own commitment to orthodoxy. The arena in which these political projects can most easily be played out and achieve a measure of consensus is, for reasons spelled out throughout the text, the control of women.

However, women are not merely the passive victims of such projects. They are political actors who have their own, frequently divergent, agenda and vested interests. Women's movements, to the extent that they are able to exercise any autonomy, may favor strategic alliances with different factions of national and international power structures in pursuit of their own objectives.[46] Women's organizations span the whole political spectrum in more pluralistic societies such as Turkey and Egypt, or appear as co-opted structures in single-party states. Their degrees of elaboration and autonomy are generally an accurate reflection of the extent of development of civil society in their respective countries. The fate of women's movements will, therefore, remain closely linked to broader struggles for democratization and social justice that are likely to follow distinctive paths and achieve diverse outcomes in the countries I have examined in this chapter.

Conclusion

The aim of this chapter was to offer a comparative analysis of the fluid and complex landscape of social forces affecting gender relations and ideologies in the Muslim societies of the Middle East and South Asia. One of the most persistent and controversial issues in this area involves the variations in the role assigned to Islam, which, depending upon the theoretical predilections of any particular author, is given a more or less central or peripheral place. References to Islam have, however, lacked analytic precision, resulting in a confusion between different levels of social reality through which Islam, as ideology or practice, is assumed to affect women's lives. The patriarchal features of marriage and kinship in Muslim communities, aspects of legal systems of contemporary states, and modern political ideologies employing an Islamic idiom have all been interchangeably evoked under the rubric of "Islam" with little regard for their overlapping yet distinct geneses, dynamics, and domains of influence.

This chapter has set itself the specific task of examining ways in which the role of Islam may be mediated through various aspects of state practice. I attempted to show how variations in the deployment of Islam in relation to different nation-building projects could have important consequences for legislation and policies affecting women. However, I also argued that the formal emancipation of women, which generally arose in conjunction with nationalist/secularist state projects, had little direct impact on the operations of patriarchy in rural and tribally based Muslim communities where the maintenance of existing kinship arrangements is, in fact, central to the reproduction of the social system as a whole. Invoking the resilience of Islamic traditions and laws to explain this resistance is totally misleading, given their selective application and frequent breach. A better understanding of this dynamic appears to lie in an analysis of the material conditions lending life and substance to a specific form of patriarchy that, in fact, transcends the boundaries of Islam.[47]

Modern states have also made numerous incursions into the realm of women and the family in pursuit of various developmental and political objectives. The aims underlying these interventions have ranged from population control and ensuring an adequate labor supply to restricting the autonomy of local, kin-based communities in order to create a more homogenous, modern citizenry, thereby deepening central governmental control. The consequences of such interventions have been far from uniform and, at times, deeply paradoxical. Processes of capital penetration and integration in national and international markets have led to a destructuring of local communities and substantially eroded the material bases of patriarchy in its tribal and peasant domestic forms. However, as traditional hierarchies based on age and gender came under increasing pressure from changing social and economic realities, the attractions of compensatory ideologies promising a more stable social and moral order appear to have increased. Furthermore, the perceived failure of modern states in the Muslim world to create and adequately redistribute resources has intensified social cleavages expressed in religious, ethnic, and regional terms. The role of primary groups and particularistic allegiances in mediating citizens' access to resources and services has remained critical. In this context, women have not emerged as full-fledged citizens but often remained members of religious/ethnic collectivities whose control is relinquished by the state to the patriarchal interests of their communities.

Finally, in the realm of ideology, the place and conduct of women has been and remains a metaphor for deeper concerns about cultural authenticity and integrity. Whether these concerns center around the encroachments of an imperialistic West or the internal threats posed by religious or ethnic diversity and class cleavages, the stability of the

Muslim family and the role of women as the guarantors of such stability have continued to occupy their historically prominent place. It is small wonder that modern Islamic movements use this powerful idiom to signal their political intent and denounce changes in the position of women as the hallmark of corruption and imperialist infiltration. However, the deeper attractions of these ostensibly anti-Western and antiimperialistic discourses reside in a populist ideology that attempts to both negate and heal the wounds opened up by the erosion of domestic patriarchy and the deepening of class, regional, and ethnic cleavages in society.

NOTES

I would like to thank Nikki Keddie for her incisive comments on an earlier draft of this paper and Juan Cole for his helpful editorial advice.

1. See Nawal al-Saadawi, "Women and Islam," in *Women and Islam,* ed. Azizah al-Hibri (Oxford: Pergamon Press, 1982); Azizah al-Hibri, "A Study of Islamic Herstory," in al-Hibri, ed., *Women and Islam;* Fatima Mernissi, *Le harem politique* (Paris: Albin Michel, 1987).

2. For a more finely modulated approach, see Leila Ahmed, "Women and the Advent of Islam," *Signs* 11 (1986): 665–91. For a more critical view, see Mai Ghoussoub, "Feminism—or the Eternal Masculine—in the Arab World," *New Left Review* 161 (January-February, 1987): 3–13.

3. See Hisham Sharabi, *Neopatriarchy: A Theory of Distorted Change in Arab Society* (Oxford: Oxford University Press, 1988); Fatima Mernissi, "Democracy as Moral Disintegration: The Contradiction between Religious Belief and Citizenship as a Manifestation of the Ahistoricity of the Arab Identity," in *Women of the Arab World,* ed. Nahid Toubia (London: Zed Books, 1988).

4. See Nikki R. Keddie, "Problems in the Study of Middle Eastern Women," *International Journal of Middle East Studies* 10 (1979): 225–40; Judith E. Tucker, "Problems in the Historiography of Women in the Middle East: The Case of Nineteenth-Century Egypt," *International Journal of Middle East Studies* 15 (1983): 321–36; Reza Hammami and Martina Rieker, "Feminist Orientalism and Orientalist Marxism," *New Left Review* 170 (July-August, 1988): 93–106.

5. The debate between Ghoussoub (n. 2) and Hammami and Rieker (n. 4) is indicative of the unresolved questions with respect to the place of Islam. Similar concerns are echoed in Mervat Hatem, "Class and Patriarchy as Competing Paradigms for the Study of Middle Eastern Women," *Comparative Studies in Society and History* 29, no. 4 (October, 1987): 811–18.

6. See Deniz Kandiyoti, "Islam and Patriarchy: A Comparative Perspective," in *Shifting Boundaries,* ed. Nikki Keddie and Beth Baron (New Haven: Yale University Press, forthcoming).

7. This neglect occurred against a background of growing feminist scholarship on the state; see Ann Sassoon, ed., *Women and the State* (London: Hutchinson, 1987); Nira Yuval-Davis and Floya Anthias, eds., *Woman-Nation-State* (London: Macmillan, 1989); Carol Pateman, *The Sexual Contract* (Oxford: Polity Press, 1988).

8. Juan R. Cole, "Feminism, Class, and Islam in Turn of the Century Egypt," *International Journal of Middle East Studies* 13 (1981): 387–407.

9. Benedict Anderson, *Imagined Communities* (London: Verso, 1983).

10. See Deniz Kandiyoti, "End of Empire: Islam, Nationalism, and Women in Turkey," in *Women, Islam, and the State,* ed. Deniz Kandiyoti (London: Macmillan, 1991).

11. Caglar Keyder, "Class and State in the Transformation of Modern Turkey," in *State and Ideology in the Middle East and Pakistan,* ed. Fred Halliday and Hamza Alavi (London: Macmillan, 1988).

12. Deniz Kandiyoti, "Women and the Turkish State: Political Actors or Symbolic Pawns?" in Yuval-Davis and Anthias, eds., *Women-Nation-State.*

13. Shahrough Akhavi, "The Ideology and Praxis of Shi'ism in the Iranian Revolution," *Comparative Studies in Society and History* 25, no. 2 (1983): 195–221.

14. Afsaneh Najmabadi, "Hazards of Modernity and Morality: Women, State, and Ideology in Contemporary Iran," in Kandiyoti, ed., *Women, Islam, and the State.*

15. Haleh Afshar, "Behind the Veil: The Public and Private Faces of Khomeini's Policies on Iranian Women," in *Structures of Patriarchy,* ed. Bina Agarwal (London: Zed Books, 1988).

16. Nawal El Saadawi, "The Political Challenges Facing Arab Women at the End of the 20th Century," in Toubia, ed., *Women of the Arab World.*

17. El Saadawi, "Political Challenges," 12.

18. Nadia Hijab, *Womanpower* (Cambridge: Cambridge University Press, 1988).

19. Fatima Mernissi, "Democracy as Moral Disintegration," in Toubia, ed., *Women of the Arab World,* 40.

20. For an argument against a simplistic conflation of the two, see Aziz al-Azmeh, "Arab Nationalism and Islamism," *Review of Middle East Studies* 4 (1988): 33–51.

21. Fatima Mernissi, *Beyond the Veil* (London: Al Saqi Books, 1985).

22. Leila Hamamsy, "The Assertion of Egyptian Identity," in *Arab Society,* ed. N. S. Hopkins and S. Ibrahim (Cairo: American University in Cairo Press, 1985).

23. Beth Baron, "Women's Nationalist Rhetoric and Activities in Early Twentieth-Century Egypt," in *The Origins of Arab Nationalism,* ed. R. Khalidi and L. Anderson et al. (New York: Columbia University Press, forthcoming).

24. Kumari Jayawardena, *Feminism and Nationalism in the Third World* (London: Zed Books, 1988).

25. Hamza Alavi, "Pakistan and Islam: Ethnicity and Ideology," in Halliday and Alavi, eds., *State and Ideology.*

26. Ayesha Jalal, "The Convenience of Subservience: Women and the State of Pakistan," in Kandiyoti, ed., *Women, Islam, and the State,* 80.

27. Naila Kabeer, "The Quest for National Identity: Women, Islam, and the State in Bangladesh," in Kandiyoti, ed., *Women, Islam, and the State.*

28. For a sensitive account of the different phases of this episode, see Zakia Pathak and Rajeswari Sunder Rajan, "Shah Bano," *Signs* 14, no. 3 (1989): 558–82.

29. Amrita Chhachhi, "Forced Identities: The State, Communalism, Fundamentalism, and Women in India," in Kandiyoti, ed., *Women, Islam, and the State.*

30. Paul Vieille, "The State of the Periphery and Its Heritage," *Economy and Society* 17, no. 1 (1988): 52–89; Victoria Goddard, "Honour and Shame: The Control of Women's Sexuality and Group Identity in Naples," in *The Cultural Construction of Sexuality,* ed. Pat Caplan (London: Tavistock, 1987).

31. Kandiyoti, "End of Empire," 24.

32. Suad Joseph, "Family, Religion, and the State: Middle Eastern Models," in *Dialectics and Gender: Anthropological Approaches,* ed. R. Randolph, D. Schneider, and M. Dias (Boulder, Colo.: Westview Press, 1988).

33. On the role of the church in Europe, see Jack Goody, *The Development of Family and Marriage in Europe* (Cambridge: Cambridge University Press, 1983).

34. Judith E. Tucker, *Women in Nineteenth-Century Egypt* (Cambridge: Cambridge University Press, 1978).

35. Zafer Toprak, "The Family, Feminism, and the State during the Young Turk Period (1908–1918)," in *Colloque international sur la Turquie contemporaine* (Istanbul: Isis, forthcoming).

36. Mounira Charrad, "State Formation and Women's Rights: The Case of North Africa," paper presented at the conference on Family Law and Change in the Middle East, SSRC-ACLS Joint Committee on the Near and Middle East, Tuxedo, New York, 1983.

37. Suad Joseph, "Elite Strategies for State Building: Women, Family, Religion, and the State in Iraq and Lebanon," in Kandiyoti, ed., *Women, Islam, and the State.*

38. In fact, relinquishing the control of women to individual men and denying women protection by the state may serve as a sop to an otherwise subjugated male population. The government's newly announced legal exemption for Iraqi men, entitling them to kill women members of their family if they suspect them of adultery, may be one such example. See Fred Halliday, "A State Based on Butchery," *Guardian,* March 16, 1990, 23.

39. See Maxine Molyneux, "The Law, the State, and Socialist Policies with Regard to Women: The Case of the People's Democratic Republic of Yemen," in Kandiyoti, ed., *Women, Islam, and the State.*

40. I am indebted to Nikki Keddie for pointing out (contra Gregory Massell, *The Surrogate Proletariat* [Princeton: Princeton University Press, 1974]) that the main dynamic in the central Asian case may have revolved around the issue of intrusion by infidels rather than state intervention per se. I nonetheless feel that even indigenous rulers may become tainted with the charge of being infidels if they seriously tamper with patriarchal privileges, although admittedly they are less easy targets.

41. Kandiyoti, "Islam and Patriarchy."

42. Roushan Jahan, "Hidden Wounds, Visible Scars: Violence against Women in Bangladesh," in Agarwal, ed., *Structures of Patriarchy.* Also see Kandiyoti, "Islam and Patriarchy."

43. Fatima Mernissi, "Muslim Women and Fundamentalism," *MERIP Reports* no. 153 (July-August, 1988): 8–11. Also see Kandiyoti, "Islam and Patriarchy."

44. An informative account of the resistance of Arab states to fall in line with this UN recommendation may be found in Hijab, *Womanpower.*

45. Kabeer, "Quest for National Identity."

46. The Women's Action Forum in Pakistan attempted to resist Zia's Islamization policies by invoking their un-Islamic nature and appealed to some progressive 'ulama' to endorse their position. Feminists in Turkey used the ratification of the proposals of the United Nations Forum in Nairobi in 1985 by the Turkish government as the occasion for a campaign to eliminate the remaining discriminatory clauses of the Turkish civil code, without success so far. In Egypt, women's movements put pressure on the government to reconsider the cancellation of the 1979 decree law revising the Personal Status Law and giving women greater equality just before the Egyptian delegation was due to attend the Nairobi Forum. This effort was met by partial success, since a new law was passed restoring most, but not all, of the benefits for women of the 1979 law. For details, see Margot Badran, "Competing Agenda: Feminists, Islam, and the State in Nineteenth- and Twentieth-Century Egypt," in Kandiyoti, ed., *Women, Islam, and the State.*

47. Kandiyoti, "Islam and Patriarchy."

Shi'ism, Corporatism, and Rentierism in the Iranian Revolution

Shahrough Akhavi

The Iranian revolution of 1979 presents a case in which religion played a key role in generating profound social change, rather than serving only as a basis for social integration. For a long time, sociologists of Islam had emphasized the integrative characteristics of that religion in the context of order and stability of the social system. Given the upsurge in Islamic movements in the late 1970s and in the 1980s, however, some observers may have overstressed the revolutionary characteristics of that great world religion, as though "Islam" is a monolithic actor in international history. Yet it is difficult to exaggerate the force and depth of feeling generated by Shi'ites in Iran, motivated as they were by apocalyptic impulses of their messianic faith to overthrow the monarchy and establish an Islamic, if not necessarily a clerical, regime.

This chapter will compare and contrast the role of the state, the economic foundations of that state, and the uses of Shi'ite ideology and values by actors in the pre- and postrevolutionary periods in Iran. It concludes that corporatism is an appropriate model for analyzing both the Pahlavi and Khomeini states. It emphasizes the relevance of the rentier state model and discusses its implications for each period. Finally, it shows the significance of Shi'ite doctrine and values both for mobilizing collective protest and for institutionalizing clerical power.

Models for the Study of the State

The literature on the historical and political sociology of Iran has generated several models that may be useful in helping us to understand the role of the state in the country's social evolution. Soviet scholars surveying the various eras of Iranian history have tended to apply class analysis based on changes in the mode of production.[1] A second attempt to provide an appropriate model for the study of the Iranian state centers on the application of the concept of patrimonialism. This effort stresses the absence of feudal forms and structures in an otherwise basically medieval authoritarian system.[2] A third model, directed more specifically at the nineteenth-century Iranian state but with important implications for its twentieth-century counterpart, focuses on the concept of oriental despotism. This last effort is more satisfying than that listed first because the analyst brings greater sensitivity to the empirical evidence.[3] Somewhat along the same lines, other specialists have directed attention to the phenomenon of the rentier state, "whose sudden acquisition of enormous revenue sources leads to its hypertrophy...."[4] More recently, dissatisfaction with existing models in the literature has led one observer to advance "bourgeois monarchical capitalism" as a substitute, believing it to have greater explanatory value.[5]

One is struck by the usefulness of most of these models. The Soviet interest in identifying different stages in the evolution of modes of production has the advantage of reminding us that the subject matter can best be approached within the framework of political economy. The stress on patrimonialism, in its turn, is of great interest inasmuch as it suggests the absence of intermediate autonomous groups with legal prerogatives of their own to defend and promote their interests, even if that conflicts with state interests. Oriental despotism, especially in the amalgamation of both variants (Marx's stress on "weak society" and Engels's emphasis on the "strong state"), is important for the analysis of the Pahlavi state—even though observers overestimated the latter's strength. The concept of the rentier state suggests excessive growth in one sector— here, petroleum—at the expense of others and the evolution of a brittle and fragile sociopolitical and economic infrastructure that appears deceptively intact until fundamentally challenged.

Theoretical Considerations on Corporatism

I will return to rentierism and its pertinence to both the pre- and the postrevolutionary Iranian state. I hope to show its significance in a causal explanation of the Iranian revolution. But I would like, at this point, to introduce the notion of corporatism. At bottom, corporatism is a system for representing interests in society. A key difference with liberalism is corporatism's stress upon the state's role in organizing the representation of these interests.

State elites, mindful of the importance of securing legitimacy and acknowledging demands for participation, may choose corporatist arrangements for the purpose of addressing these issues. If they do so, they may opt for either of two options, as discussed by Stepan: (1) inclusionary corporatism, or (2) exclusionary corporatism.[6] In both cases, interests are organized and represented according to occupation. However, in inclusionary corporatism, the state—albeit playing an active role—is more of a facilitator and guarantor of arrangements. Inclusionary corporatism, as the term suggests, involves the meaningful involvement of the various social forces in society in the political game. This kind of corporatism features a bargain that is struck between the state (which, to be sure, is the senior partner in the bargain) and these social forces. Usually, this means that the state offers various services and the social forces, in turn, acknowledge the primary role of the state in public affairs, particularly in the economy.

In contrast, exclusionary corporatism is a system by which the state maintains its privileged position in society through at least implicit coercion and denies meaningful participation to the social forces of society. Exclusionary corporatism has been a vehicle for state elites to prevent such forces from institutionally entrenching their interests in independent organizations. In the formulation of public policy, state elites pursuing strategies of exclusionary corporatism seek to maximize the population's support for the state by organizing them into highly dependent "corporations" that are incapable of channeling demands against the state.

It is undoubtedly the exclusionary form of corporatism that is encompassed by Schmitter's now famous defintion of the generic concept. His definition was that corporatism is a system in which interests are centered in units that are "singular, compulsory, noncompetitive, hierarchically ordered, functionally differentiated." The state creates such units and licenses them to provide a monopoly of representation in designated functional areas. There is, however, no possibility that such units, once brought into existence and chartered, could become autonomous from the state. In fact, they must observe limits upon their activity, limits that are set by the state through constitutional, statutory, or administrative codes.[7]

264 / Comparing Muslim Societies

Pahlavi Corporatism

Exclusionary corporatism, then, is arrantly authoritarian, whereas inclusionary corporatism is paternalistic. It would be a mistake, of course, to see all authoritarian systems as fitting the exclusionary corporatist mold. Thus, the Pahlavi state under Reza Shah (1925–41) was not corporatist, because state elites did not seek to organize the representation of interests in society. But after 1955, the Pahlavi state indeed appears to have followed the course of exclusionary corporatism, haltingly at first but, by the 1960s and 1970s more emphatically. Of course, corporatism is avowedly chosen only in cultures where it is known and understood—for example, the Iberian peninsula, certain Latin American countries, Italy, or Austria between the two world wars. In the case of Iran, state elites did not advocate a specifically corporatist model of rule; yet, the model they followed was corporatist in effect, even if they may not have been aware of the similarities between their path and that of classical corporatist regimes.

After the monarchy, with U.S. and British support, crushed the nationalist movement in the early 1950s, the Pahlavi state moved to prevent the expression of popular participation by orchestrating the activities of peasant, worker, and professional associations, unions, and syndicates. For example, although the Society of Merchants, Guilds, and Artisans (SMGA) had enjoyed autonomy in the late 1940s and early 1950s, it was dissolved by the shah and replaced with a compliant, government-controlled merchant's guild. The government controlled the guild until 1977, when growing internal protests against the Shah's autocracy led to the re-creation of the SMGA under the rubric of the Society of Merchants, Guilds, and Artisans of the Tehran Bazaar. Significantly, the new organization played an important role in mobilizing continuing protests against the regime until the shah's departure in January, 1979, and Ayatollah Khomeini's return to Iran in February.[8]

The same patterns may be discerned with respect to other social forces. As Bashiriyeh puts it, the state "extended its control to all employers' associations, trade unions, bazaar guilds, civil service associations, and rural cooperatives." Control was extended over the Syndicate of Textile Industry Owners, the Syndicate of Metals Industries, the Syndicate of Iranian Industries, the Chamber of Industries and Mines, the Chamber of Commerce, the Worker's Organization, and the Central Organization of Rural Cooperatives.[9]

Symbolizing the state's role in establishing and regulating these institutions was the practice of the shah in holding annual conferences for the various associations, chambers, unions, and syndicates and often presiding at their meetings. At other times, the heads of the various political parties established by the regime at different times since 1957 would preside at such meetings. Ultimately, Pahlavi exclusionary corporatism led to the bureaucratization of the state's power and heavy-handed efforts to suppress mass participation through systematic penetration of mass organizations. The regime's thinking, of course, was to prevent the emergence of class-based expressions of interest.

Particularly significant in this connection was the secret police's penetration of industrial unions, as in the late 1950s, when "SAVAK... created through the Labor Ministry an array of trade unions, and scrutinized anyone recruited into the university, the civil service, and the large industrial plants."[10]

There is consensus that the Iranian political system from the time of World War II took on the following forms: 1941–53, pluralist politics; 1953–63, authoritarian mobilization politics; 1963–79, monarchical absolutism and bureaucratization of power. Although the features of the last period had their origin and development in the earlier years, this discussion will focus on the last sixteen years of the shah's rule.

During these years the major institutions of the state were the monarchy, the intelligence services, the military, the central planning apparatus, and certain key ministries, such as interior and information. There was a party structure, but it remained an ancillary feature of the regime and failed in its purpose to mobilize the masses and intellectuals behind the shah's "White Revolution" reforms.

The central role of the monarchy is so obvious and has so often been cited that not much need be added here beyond noting that, whereas the country's constitution (1906–7) had stipulated that the shah reign—not rule—the actions of this shah since 1953 were in full disregard of these provisions.[11] Though his military-based monarchy may not have been an arrant "fascist-style totalitarian regime,"[12] his manipulation of politics resulted in the gross violation of the country's fundamental law.

The identification of the state with the monarchy, if not with the person of the shah, became the key objective of this ruler. He used the security services and the army to ensure his purpose, and the proliferation of agencies within the military-security establishment to accomplish his ends should cause less surprise than the fact that internal rivalries among chiefs of agencies did not surface more often than they did. Of the numerous intelligence organs, "four [were] in some ways overt police units, and the other four [performed] various intelligence and secret police functions."[13]

Since military power alone is insufficient and inefficient in the administration of society, the army, police, and intelligence services did not serve as day-to-day instruments of rule. The shah had to rely upon a socioeconomic program that government language characterized as progressive and even "revolutionary." Because the state, in many societies, can mobilize such extensive power and resources, it often becomes the paramount entrepreneur as well. The shah's third, fourth, and fifth development plans (1962–77) were the major instruments of national integration.

Since Iran under the shah was intended to be a capitalist state, the monarch required capitalist supporters. The requirement, however, was that they passively accept the benefits awarded to them by the state without taking initiatives to gain such benefits themselves. Many members of this capitalist class were former landowners who sold their lands to the state during the land reforms of 1962–71, investing the proceeds in capitalist enterprises in urban centers.

In fact, in 1962–73, private investment amounted to between two-thirds and three-quarters of state investments in the public sector.[14] The ratio of private to state investment in the first and last years of the fifth development plan (1973–77) was 79 and 74 percent, respectively.[15] The shah's strategy, thus, appeared to be working.

But, faced with high rates of inflation, a sudden decline in oil revenue due to oversupply in the markets, and mounting labor strikes, the very state that had long promoted the industrialists' interests eventually lost its nerve and launched a populist campaign in the summer of 1975. The most blatant effort came with the attacks against "price fixers" and "hoarders" (sometimes collectively called "economic terrorists"). The shah's 1963 "White Revolution" reforms provided for a modicum of profit sharing between factory owners and laborers. Now, in 1975, he imposed a "workers' share" scheme that allowed workers to purchase, with government assistance, up to 49 percent of the assets of enterprises that employed them. Although the plan never realized the goals set by the regime's rhetoric (a total of some 150 enterprises had sold about 20 percent of their shares by mid-1977 according to Looney), it did represent an effort to generate worker support for the regime. Further, workers' wages were increased in the 1971–75 period. In the process, the shah alienated members of both the bazaar and modern middle and upper-middle class.

The net effect was that real private investment in machinery declined from 63.4 percent in 1975 to − 1.7 percent in 1976 and − 17.9 percent in 1977. This was occurring while the sector's investment in construction was maintaining its expansion at 35.7, 32.6, and 14.9 percent per annum for 1975, 1976, and 1977 respectively.[16]

What this shows is that even exclusionary corporatism cannot permanently succeed without at least some gesture to acknowledge the corporatist bargain. It is clear that the shah felt his regime was losing its grip on the one group that he feared the most—the working class. He was less concerned with the disaffection of the traditional bazaar merchants and the modern industrial and financial bourgeoisie. The former he hoped would be destroyed by his modernization policies, while the latter he felt were so dependent upon him that their protests would not matter. As for the urban poor, still less did their situation cause him to doubt the wisdom of his policies. No, it was the specter of mounting *proletarian* dissatisfaction that was most troubling to him. Ironically, the industrial workers' disenchantment was ultimately less consequential for the success of the revolution than the actions of the bazaaris. Withal, the shah tried briefly and tentatively to transform the exclusionary corporatist policies into inclusionary ones. However, by the late summer and early fall of 1978, the workers finally rejected the shah's thinly veiled corporatist compact and went over to the opposition.

As for the urban masses more generally, the data show that their condition had deteriorated between the late 1950s and the mid-1970s. Patterns of urban household expenditures in Iran for these time periods are shown in table 1.

As can be seen, for the six lowest deciles of the population, the share of urban expenditures declined between the two benchmark years. While household expenditure is a telling statistic, income distribution is even more meaningful. Looney, summarizing Central Bank of Iran data, says that these "show the Gini coefficient of inequality increasing throughout most of the 1959–74 period: in 1959–60 the coefficient was 0.4552, increasing to 0.4945 in 1973–74. In 1971–72 the Gini value was exceptionally high at 0.5051."[17] Behdad corroborates pronounced skews in the concentration of wealth for the last years of the Pahlavi state, revealing the figures for 1977 to 1979 to have been 0.4687 and 0.4746 respectively.[18] While these figures show that the trends were not uniformly worsening insofar as income distribution is concerned, they do reveal long-term adverse patterns for the impoverished masses.

By themselves these economic trends would not necessarily have led to frontal assaults on the state. Perhaps the one stratum of society whose downward mobility under the shah was most consequential for the collective social action that led to the revolution was the clergy. The bureaucratization of state power was accompanied by the seizure of the clergy's jobs, lands, revenue, madrasas (theological colleges), and administration of shrines. The process of declassing the clergy might have succeeded if the shah had not insisted upon appropriating the clergy's last remaining resource: "the cultural symbols which in the past [had] been so vital in inculcating among Iranians a sense of self, an explanation of the cosmos and social reality."[19]

The corporatism advanced by the Pahlavi state thus contained a critical weakness. In an area of the world where the religious basis of political legitimacy is of central importance, the Pahlavi state so excluded the religious institution of Shi'ism that it failed to gain religiously sanctioned moral acceptance. There was nothing inevitable about this state of affairs, although Khomeini's rhetoric in the 1970s suggested that this was so— that monarchy and Islam are fundamentally incompatible with each

TABLE 1. Distribution of Urban Household Expenditure in Iran by Population Decile

Decile (lowest to highest)	Percentage of Expenditure[a]	
	1959–60	1973–74
1	1.7	1.3
2	2.9	2.4
3	4.0	3.4
4	5.0	4.7
5	6.1	5.0
6	7.3	6.8
7	8.9	9.3
8	11.8	11.1
9	16.4	17.5
10	35.3	37.9

Source: Ervand Abrahamian, "The Structural Causes of the Iranian Revolution," *Middle East Research and Information Projects Reports* 87 (May, 1980): 23. See also Firouz Vakil, "Iran's Basic Economic Problems: A Twenty Year Horizon," *Economic Development and Cultural Change* 25, no. 4 (July, 1977), 723–25.
[a]Percentages do not total 100 percent due to rounding.

other. But Khomeini himself had written, in the 1940s, that the disenchantment of the clergy with secular governments historically lay in the failure of the latter to consult the jurists. Indeed, Khomeini had explicitly recounted cases where high clergy had cooperated with secular governments.

The Pahlavi state not only did not come even remotely close to meshing its corporatist structure with the salvationist yearnings of Iranian Shi'ites, it explicitly rejected such a possibility. Pahlavi corporatism, to its ultimate regret, ignored both the coextensiveness of the religious and political spheres in the perspective of many Muslims and the abiding determination of Iranian Shi'ites (after the 1963 protests) to withhold their approval of the shah's claim to legitimacy. This is not to say that Shi'ite doctrine categorically rejects the legitimacy of all temporal rulers. As already noted, Khomeini, for one, had earlier written about the cooperation of Shi'ite clergymen and Iranian shahs. In addition, doctrine is never crystallized forever; it evolves in accordance with the social-historical evolution of society.

However, at best, the authority of secular rulers is subject to review, and it may be denied entirely if it is determined and widely accepted that such rulers have violated the basic precepts of the faith.[20] The tenet that awards ultimate legitimate rule to the Imam alone has, at times, been utilized as doctrinal justification for rebellion against the policies of secular shahs in Iranian history.

Apparently in the belief that, in the modern period, the potential for such rebellion was nil, the shah at first (1953–61) made half-hearted attempts at corporate inclusion of the clergy. After the 1963 protests, he embarked on a strictly exclusionary path insofar as the religious groups were concerned. Thus was generated a system that permitted the emergence of a wide gap between the corporatist organization of the economy and sociopolitical life, on the one hand, and the continued, if for a time enfeebled, ability of the religious forces to oppose the monarchy. While not all religious groups followed an oppositionist course throughout the 1963–79 period, many ultimately did.

In summary, the Pahlavi state is appropriately analyzed as a corporate system according to which access to the levers of power was restricted to a small elite that established a hierarchical facade that purported to encourage public choice. Concomitantly, an ideology was fashioned that stressed distribution in its pronouncements but, as with most corporatist regimes, favored production in practice.

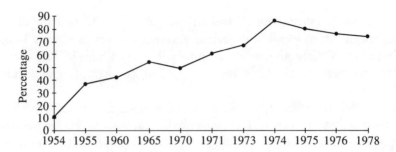

Fig. 1. Proportion of state revenue from oil sales. (Data from Najmabadi, "Depoliticization," 215; Clawson, "Islamic Iran's Economic Politics," 376. The figure for 1978 is actually for the period from March, 1977, through March, 1978.)

Some Considerations on the Rentier State

Although practically all economists studying the Iranian economy have focused on the overwhelming importance of its oil industry, fewer have consciously used the concept of rentierism. According to Mahdavy, "Rentier states are . . . those countries that receive on a regular basis substantial amounts of external rent."[21] These rents, in the form of revenue from the sale of oil in the case of petroleum-producing countries, "have very little to do with the production processes of [their] domestic economies."[22] Rentier states, in short, feature economies with undeveloped agricultural, industrial, and manufacturing sectors, the inputs from any such sectors being not significantly related to earnings from the sale of oil.

Figure 1 indicates the long-term trends of the Iranian state's reliance on the oil sector for revenue. The striking thing is that dependence on oil for such revenue increased precisely during the years of high economic growth. The sharpest jump (a 236 percent increase) occurred between 1954 and 1955 and reflects the resumption of oil sales after the British embargo of the Musaddiq period. Interestingly, the jump between the oil shock years, 1973–74, although in absolute terms rather striking, represented only a 28 percent increase, suggesting that it would be wrong to view Iran in terms of the ideal type of rentier state/rentier economy.

Mahdavy asks why it is that Iran, despite significant oil revenue, had such indifferent economic growth rates between 1950–65. His answer is that, for one thing, sociopolitical obstacles, such as an exploitative rural aristocracy and bureaucratic corruption and immobilism, hindered substantial growth. Additionally, he argues that the nature of government expenditure was unproductive, encouraging consumption of imported goods rather than of goods produced domestically. The government failed to "invest directly in well-planned industrial complexes," accompanied by "technological and labor force training programs...."[23] If government expenditure was directed toward industry at all, it was "not used to develop industries with the highest value-added per worker."[24]

Luciani goes even further and suggests that a rentier state "independent of the strength of the domestic economy, does not need to formulate anything deserving the appellation of economic policy; all it needs is an expenditure policy."[25] Indeed, Luciani insists that in rentier states, the fact that benefits from such expenditures may be unequally distributed in society is not a problem. For, in his view, it will always be easier for individuals to try to work within the system to maximize their interests than to try to overthrow the state.

Writing in the late 1960s, however, Mahdavy argued that prospects were not auspicious for Iran's future. Unless the government changed its policies, "the level of the economy's technology, the nature of its sociopolitical organization, and the standards of the people's general education and training" suggested poor future economic performance.[26]

Carrying forward some of these considerations about the rentier state, Delacroix distinguishes between coercive states, which are based on class relations, and "distributive" states, "where the political predominates over the economic and where benefit overweighs coercion; that is ... primary allocative, distributive states."[27] Although such states do not actually exist, Delacroix believes that certain oil-producing states, such as Kuwait before 1990, approximate them. The essential argument is that, in the absence of strongly developed productive structures, class conflicts are greatly attenuated, if they exist at all. On the negative side, such states typically lack strong taxation systems. Since taxation is, among other things, a method of integrating masses into the political system where they could participate and, through such participation, lend legitimacy to the regime, a weak taxation system can actually be politically costly, even if economically it may not be fatal. (Of course, it is true that a weak taxation system has its politically positive side—untaxed people may have fewer grievances against an otherwise intrusive state.)

Kuwait represented "an extreme instance of the distributive function of the state prevailing over the coercive/accommodating role attributed to the state by the hybrid Marxist-Weberian paradigm."[28] Opposition to the regime in the Kuwaiti-type distributive state cannot be class based, and so protest groups will base their opposition on an ideology of legit-imization that draws upon nonclass, moral themes, particularly religious myths.

But is Iran a rentier state like Kuwait? No. Iran under the shah, in Delacroix's view, was "a typical mixed, class-distributive state."[29] That is, it was partly based on prevailing class relations and partly typified by nonclass considerations. Collective protest against the shah prior to the revolution was definitely class based. Many political economists have shown how the private sector grew in the 1960s and 1970s, even though— as I have already noted—private capitalists remained highly dependent upon the state.[30] Along with growth in the private sector must come capitalist relations of production between employers and workers. Such workers, unlike the Kuwaiti and other gulf states, were mainly indigenous Iranians and not expatriate laborers. But rather remarkably, when the revolution came and continued, peasants and industrial workers (includ-ing those working in the oil fields) were relatively passive. Instead, it was the bazaar, "a clientelistically organized social formation," the urban poor lumpenproletariat, and national minorities that were the active forces. As Delacroix puts it, "The revolution unfolded in flagrant dis-regard of the most elementary rules of class struggle."[31] He fails to account for this pattern, although the implication is that Iran had enough of the rentier- and distributive-state characteristics to rule out class for-mations with strong social bases.

Theda Skocpol has come to roughly similar conclusions. She claims that the Pahlavi state was never really embedded in society, that the state "did not need to wrest taxes from its own people" because of oil revenue and lacked an alliance with any of the country's classes.[32] But "urban communal enclaves," as she puts it, consisting of poor strata of the population, many of whom had left rural Iran as a consequence of the state's socioeconomic modernization programs, comprised loci of poten-tial opposition. These urban poor were, in effect, orphans of Iran's rentier economy. Eventually, they were organized and mobilized by a coalition of religious leaders, who appealed for legitimacy to moral imperatives rooted in Shi'ite doctrines of authority and the state.

The Shi'ite Doctrine of Authority and the State

The Shi'ite position is based on the following beliefs: (1) Muhammad, the prophet of Islam, should be succeeded by his descendants, the Imams, through his daughter Fatima; (2) salvation is vouchsafed to those who believe in the restoration of God's justice, to be accomplished by the last Imam when he reappears on earth as the Mahdi; and (3) every historical period requires a "proof" of God, incarnate in the line of these Imams.

Iranian Shi'ites are known as Imamis or Twelvers, because they believe that the prophet's rightful heirs were twelve in number. Only the first in this line, 'Ali, actually ruled the entire Islamic community. The social mythos of Shi'ism suggests that blame for the deaths of their Imams must be placed at the door of the Sunni (majority) caliphs who ruled the Islamic world at that time, even though historical evidence exists to show that some Imams did not die a violent death.

Except for 'Ali and his younger son, Husayn, the practical role of the Imams consisted in spiritual guidance. The last Imam is believed, on God's command, to have disappeared as a child in 873/874 c.e. in order to escape assassination. The faithful anticipate his return as "the One Who Arises, the Master of the Age, the Mahdi." His reappearance will end injustice in the world and ensure the implementation of the religious injunctions.

The doctrine of the Imamate—or rule by the Imam—addresses itself to the occultation of the twelfth Imam. Shi'ites must accept the fact of his absence for an indefinite period of history; yet, the doctrine specifies that every historical age must feature a proof of God manifested in the Imam. It became a part of the doctrine, therefore, that the twelfth Imam maintained contact with his followers despite his phenomenal absence from the community.

The clergy argued that the occultation of the Imam did not mean that the proof of God did not exist. They maintained that God commanded the Imam into hiding because of fear that he would be killed. Because the Imam was obeying the will of God, and God meant that there need be a proof of Him for every age, then the proof must be construed to exist. The complex logic is captured in the following explanation.

The existence of the [proof] was necessary because the non-existence of the Imam . . . would have meant the . . . end of the religious injunctions, because the latter would have no protector. But if he . . . went into occultation by the command of God, and if he had the known means of mediation, then the proof continued on earth, because both he and the means of mediation were present. The state of occultation did not invalidate the presence of the proof.... [33]

But what role was assumed by the clergy apart from articulation of Imami doctrine? Gradually and indirectly, they became the transmitters of the sayings, traditions, and practices of the Imams and thus assumed the role of intermediary between the Imams and the faithful. The emphasis must be upon the word *indirectly,* because there is no doctrinal basis for arguing that the highest ranking clergymen, the mujtahids, received a categorical appointment from the Imams themselves in their lifetimes to be the Imams' replacements. Nevertheless, in a much later period, around the seventeenth century, tampering with the doctrinal principles appears to have occurred in order to make it seem as though a categorical, ex-ante, appointment of mujtahids had been granted by the Imams.[34]

The Imam's occultation also posed the dilemma of authority. If the community was to be organized, administered, and preserved according to a pattern that would be pleasing to God, then who was to lead? On this question, the Imamis may be said to have equivocated. As long as they lived under Sunni rule, they were absolved of the need for an answer. The absence of a requirement for an oath of allegiance (*bay'ah*) to the hidden Imam until his reappearance permitted Shi'ites to be faithful and yet also acknowledge the rule of the Sunni caliph. However, after 1501, Imami Shi'ism became the religion of a centralized Iranian state under the Safavid shahs (1501–1722). It became more and more urgent to discuss whether or not the clergy had doctrinal grounds for claiming the deputyship of the Imams as secular shahs began pressing such claims themselves.

Moreover, in the eighteenth century, an intraclergy dispute resulted in a key victory on the doctrinal side for those who wanted an assertive social role for the clergy. The victorious faction successfully argued that the mujtahids were entitled to use their independent judgment in interpreting the law. A doctrinal principle consequently came to be used as a lever for clerical activism in social matters beyond the narrow compass of ethical and pietistic concerns of the past. On this view, as against that which insisted that no room existed for independent judgment, authoritative opinions (fatwas) could now be used anathematizing secular policies. Empowered with this prerogative, the clergy became a corporate stratum whose leaders—the mujtahids—could expect imitation by the masses in practical and legal matters. The most distinguished of the mujtahids soon came to exercise great informal political influence. During the time of the Qajar shahs (1796–1925), the clergy began to claim that the eminent mujtahids of the age were, in fact, the proofs of the Imam. This doctrinal shift ensued from tampering with tradition, but the clergy mentally justified the sleight of hand, no doubt, on grounds of the increasingly intolerable acts of their secular rulers in the context of Western European imperialist behavior in Iran.

Interestingly, at the time the centralized state was created in sixteenth-century Iran, the clergy were the state's clients. The creation of Shi'ism as a state religion in the 1500s was not due to the influence of the mujtahids but, rather, to the decision of a Sufi leader responding to chiliastic expectations rife in northwestern Iran and eastern Turkey. Having conquered the territory of Iran, this individual then began to import Shi'ite mujtahids into Iran to serve in the administration of the state. Clearly, then, these clergy were dependent upon and vulnerable to the granting or withdrawal of the state's largesse and the maneuverings of the shah. In due course, many of the top-ranking clergymen, including those who were already inside the country, were brought into the state bureaucracy to serve as judges, notaries, financial administrators, scribes, Friday mosque prayer leaders, exchequers, and chancellors. Only a minority of the mujtahids in this period maintained an aloofness from state service.

Doctrinally, the religious leaders legitimated Safavid temporal rule by acquiescing in the claims made by the shahs to be the descendents of the seventh Imam, an acquiescence that added weight to the Safavids' claim to be rulers of the community. These shahs came to be known by the sobriquet appropriated by them, and not contested at the time by the clery, *zillullah,* the Shadow of God.

The increasing involvement of the clergy in politics in the last two centuries has had several causes, not all of them doctrinal. For instance, the increasing penetration of imperialism led the clergy to forge an alliance with intellectuals, artisans, and merchants. This political activism may be seen during the collective protests against the Reuters concession in 1871–73, the Tobacco Protest of 1890–91, the Constitutional Revolution of 1905–9, the oil crisis of 1949–53, and protests against the shah's White Revolution in 1961–63. This political activism by the clergy did not, however, amount to categorical challenges to the sovereignty of the shahs. The ruler continued to be regarded as an imperfect leader, and clerical protest was, for the most part, confined to very specific grievances against unjust decisions affecting local interests.[35]

Nevertheless, Shi'ite doctrine contains implicit justification for clerical assertiveness. First, they have the residual right to warn the community of the violation of the Imam's justice. Second, doctrinal justifications could be found for political action in the Qur'an, for example, "You are the best community sent forth among the people, commanding the good and enjoining from evil" (Q. III: 110) and "O you who believe, obey God, obey the prophet and those in authority among you" (Q. IV: 59). Enforcing good and preventing evil are seen as ultimately political acts that the entire community may undertake, sanctioning their leaders to implement the injunction. "Those in authority among you" are considered by Shi'ites to be the Imams, although a few, following Khomeini, believe that even the mujtahids qualify for this position.

In no sense, however, did the clergy historically advance doctrinal arguments for locating sovereignty in their own corporate group. When they perceived that their secular allies in the constitutional revolution were moving toward Western notions of popular sovereignty and republicanism, the clergy defected and ultimately sponsored the rise to the throne of a military officer who appeared to be willing to adhere to the cause of Shi'ism. It was thus ironic that this individual was to embark upon a series of policies that in fact led to the evisceration of the religious institution. Three generations later, however, the successors of these clergy would lead perhaps the most astounding revolution in modern times.

Collective Action in the Revolution

Is there an Islamic theory of collective action? From the Sunni perspective, the fundamental unit of social reality is the community of believers. Collective social action is conceived in terms of salvation, and the charisma of the community is the key to its attainment. The importance of community charisma and infallibility may be seen in the verse already cited—"You are the best community..."—and in the saying attributed to the prophet, "My community shall never agree upon error."

Collective social action against constituted authority is sanctioned only in the event of a ruler's arrant impiety, as, for example, his prohibition of prayer. Otherwise, unanimously accepted criteria by which to assess the rule of princes do not exist. Moreover, no machinery evolved for applying sanctions against impious rulers. There is only the general guideline in the Qur'an that "there is no duty of obedience in sin."[36]

In fact, revolution is considered ultimately a threat to the will of God. The community must be created and led in accordance with the holy law. Even if a ruler be impious, the danger to the community of revolution is so great that overriding certainty of dereliction is required before action is taken. In the absence of such certainty, inaction may be preferable, because a ruler cannot transcend the limits of his own mortality, and the situation can improve.

In the Shi'ite view of collective social action, the charisma of the community is replaced by that of the Imam. Salvation is guaranteed only through the implementation of the Imam's justice. The Imam "was entitled to political leadership as much as to religious authority, [although] his imamate did not depend upon his actual rule."[37] Moreover, the mujtahids, as a result of the eighteenth-century triumph noted above, have played a role that the Sunni clergy have forsaken; they exercise power to issue fatwas on crucial political issues, basing their pronouncements on independent reasoning.

Collective social action in the Iranian revolution, to put these considerations more concretely, is best seen in terms of both the ideal and material interests of those participating in it. The essentially Tocquevillean explanation of increasing general prosperity, combined with a sudden downturn in the fortunes of pivotal social forces (especially the capitalist middle-class, white-collar employees, and the urban poor) is very helpful in explaining the outbreak of revolution. Growing class conflict, too, can be seen in the increasing number of industrial strikes and incidents of labor turmoil in the 1970s over the previous decade.

But indispensable to a proper understanding of the Iranian revolution is the Weberian notion that, in gauging interests, ideas must be seen to play an autonomous role under certain circumstances. Yet it would be a mistake to believe that the revolution stemmed from mobilization through the doctrinal principles of official Shi'ism. Though the revolution was led by a grand mujtahid, Ayatollah Khomeini, due emphasis must be given to the popular or folk aspects in considering its religious aspect. On this dimension, the rituals, passion plays, and narrative accounts of the lives of the imams occupied a central place in the social drama. These rituals do not have inherent meanings. Instead, such meanings are attributed—as Weber argues—to the rituals by the actors in the drama. Within this framework, through Iranians were mobilized by one of Shi'ism's highest ranking official leaders, relying on the tactical power doctrine provided the mujtahids, many revolutionaries apparently construed the necessity to lay their lives on the line in order to redeem pledges to sacrifice themselves as part of a social order that calls for such martyrdom. The Iranian revolution culminated, of course, in armed overthrow of the shah's state, but until almost the very end, the revolutionaries lacked weapons.

One of the hallmarks of the revolutionary demonstrations was the passion plays. These enactments refer to the martyrdom of the third Imam, Husayn, on the battlefield at the hands of the forces of the Sunni caliph in 680 C.E. This Imam's cause was rebellion against impious tyranny. Present-day renditions of his story have clear implications for the legitimacy of the current Iranian regime, since the passion plays have allegorical value. People who are martyred for Husayn's cause are considered to be worthy of the Imam's primordial sacrifice themselves.

Such mass actions of collective social protest by demonstrators inspired by passion plays constituted efforts to be worthy of the Imam's trust on the part of the faithful, seeking status for themselves as members of an exalted community. To non-Shi'ites, these actions may appear irrational. If the sacrifices are deemed a means to actuate the mechanism of solidarity within the community, however, they appear as structurally essential in protecting loyalty groups against disintegration.[38]

Official, "high" Shi'ism has little to do with passion plays—a fact that did not deter Ayatollah Khomeini from utilizing them in mobilizing the masses. Michael Fischer is essentially correct in arguing that the collective action of Iranians from October, 1977, to February, 1979, comprised a giant morality play on the national level.[39] The climax, in such plays, is the Imam's martyrdom, but the triggering mechanism of martyrdom for participants is the repeated question: "May I be sacrificed in your stead?" In the Christian tradition, the sacrifice of one leads to the salvation of all. The Shi'ite tradition requires that the sacrifice be borne equally.

Thus, revolutionary mobilization stemmed not from ideational responses to abstract doctrinal elements. Instead, it derived from the conjunction of two factors: (1) the latitude the doctrine provided to the mujtahids to pronounce social criticism of impiety, and (2) the cathartic function of the passion play. The revolution occurred both because the masses wanted to improve their life's chances and because they were engaging in concrete, practical, and—for them—stable reactions to maintain the integrity of their community. Simultaneously, Khomeini's use of dramaturgical symbols and his own occultation from society as an exile for fifteen years provided additional powerful leverage for revolutionary action.

Shi'ite Praxis, Corporatism, and Rentierism

Factions and splits have characterized elite politics after the overthrow of the Pahlavi state. Such disagreements have not existed merely over means, but even over objectives. Perhaps the most significant split among the clergy has been over the concept of vilayat-i faqih itself—the custodial authority of the top jurist. Ayatollah Khomeini and his partisans eventually succeeded in the struggle to establish clerical rule by dint of this doctrinal innovation, but deep disagreements over its validity continue. Many top clergymen have rejected it on doctrinal grounds, arguing that there is no legal basis in Shi'ite law for the notion that the Imams appointed the clergy to rule society in their absence. The early struggle over this matter between Ayatollah Khomeini and Ayatollah Muhammad Kazim Shari'atmadari (d. 1986) is the most famous of these conflicts, but a number of grand mujtahids still dispute it.[40]

Major disagreements over elements of the new constitution pertaining to issues of national sovereignty, the powers of the faqih, the structure of government, and foreign policy also divided opinion among the clergy in the early revolutionary period. Even after the ouster of those clergymen and religiously minded secular leaders opposed to Khomeini's line, intraclergy factionalism remained significant, especially on economic matters.[41]

Given these disagreements, without denying, however, major areas of concord and cooperation, what sort of state has emerged in the post-revolutionary period? What is its relationship to the society and the economy? Evidence from the French, Russian, and Chinese revolutions shows that states become strengthened after a social revolution through the rationalization of their administrative, financial, and military structures.[42] Of course, this depends on what kind of time frame one uses. Certainly, states are weakened in the early period of revolution, but in the middle run these examples show the increasing power of the state.

In the Iranian case, the Pahlavi state seems to have been captured more than smashed. Of course, it became transformed, as judicial bodies and religious militias have replaced the monarchy and the army as the key organs of power. But scholars have observed that, since ruling classes did not join the state in a desperate effort to prevent its demise, the clergy's job of consolidating state power was greatly facilitated.

The revolutionaries transformed the monarchy into a hybrid, French-type presidential–prime ministerial system—an arrangement that has coexisted uneasily with Shi'ite institutions. As faqih, Khomeini chose not to be involved in the daily running of the government, unlike the shah's near total involvement in the country's security matters, oil affairs, and foreign policy generally. Yet the central role accorded by the constitution to the faqih very much echoes that of the monarchy's practice. Ironically, the old constitution indicated a titular role for the monarchy, but the Pahlavi shahs behaved otherwise. The faqih is not the executive, however. Instead, the executive, until August, 1979, consisted of the president and his cabinet, headed, in fact, by both the president and the prime minister.

The clergy also maintained the parliament, which, however, has been more assertive than its Pahlavi counterpart. Indeed, the debates in that body have been remarkably open, even though on occasion it has been an arena where threats against maverick speakers have been leveled by the leadership.

The judicial branch, not surprisingly, has been revitalized under the clergy, and it is a powerful branch of government. Such organs as the Guardian Council (a court exercising judicial review over parliamentary enactments), the Supreme Court (dissolved in 1989), the Supreme Judicial Council, and the various appellate, district, and local courts have served their functions. In 1989, a judicial innovation came with the creation of the office of the "head of the Judicial Branch." The state prosecutor-general is an important element of the judicial structure of the state. These civilian bodies have been augmented by the numerous revolutionary courts (extending also to the armed forces) and revolutionary prosecutors-general. The revolutionary courts were officially absorbed by the Ministry of Justice in early 1984, but they seemingly still function to mete out punishment to those judged guilty of moral offenses, such as drug smuggling.

Two revolutionary institutions of the Islamic state that have played an autonomous role have been the Revolutionary Guards (Pasdaran) and the Revolutionary Committees. Clerics were placed in charge of these organizations, but they initially remained separate from the Ministry of

Defense and the Ministry of Interior, their logical home bases. The Revolutionary Committees were officially merged into the Ministry of Interior in July, 1982, having served their purpose in helping the Khomeini clergy to eliminate their more moderate rivals. The merger, however, was not completed until 1984. As for the Pasdaran, they were created in May, 1979, and continue their separate existence as the military backbone of the clerical regime, even though officially the Pasdaran no longer have their own ministry and were presumably merged into the Ministry of Defense in 1988.

To orchestrate the representation of interests, the Khomeini regime founded the Islamic Republican Party (IRP), which apparently already existed embryonically in 1977. Early in the revolutionary period, observers were struck by the supposed struggle within the IRP of two opposing groups known as the hujjatis and the maktabis. The former had come into existence in the 1950s as an anti-Baha'i force dominated by economic conservatives, whereas the latter, dominated by Khomeini's former students, is putatively a child of the revolution with radical views on economic and cultural matters.

It is highly unlikely, however, that deeply rooted and institutionalized disagreements existed among those who nominally affiliated with one or the other of these organizations. What is known is that 'Ali Akbar Rafsanjani and 'Ali Khamanah'i—currently President of the Republic and faqih, respectively—were the IRP's leaders. Khomeini's heir apparent until March, 1989 (when Khomeini disgraced him), Ayatollah Husayn 'Ali Muntaziri, had constantly berated the IRP leadership for its lack of attention to the countryside. Eventually, the institution was dissolved in June, 1987, with the lame explanation that it had served its purpose of entrenching clerical power and was no longer required in the post-revolutionary period. It is not unlikely, however, that Rafsanjani and his allies feared that the IRP would somehow be converted into a militant, disciplined, cadre party with ambitions of playing a vanguard role on the Leninist model. Were this to have occurred, it would inevitably have strengthened the role of the secular left, whom the Khomeini people have always regarded as unreliable supporters of, and potential defectors from, the theory and practice of vilayat-i faqih.

Given that mobilization in the revolution itself had taken place through mosque networks dominated by the Friday prayer leaders, the IRP was, in fact, dispensable as far as the clergy was concerned. Arjomand persuasively argues that, in ridding themselves of the party apparatus, the clergy was clearly opting for a more autochthonous mobilizing institution, the mosques.[43]

Apart from all of these organizations, a raft of quasi-official bodies was created to absorb the energies of the masses without permitting them meaningful participation in the political process. These organizations, each headed by a reliable cleric, symbolize the dedication of the regime and the people to charitable and popular causes. In rare cases, as with the Reconstruction Crusade, they actually perform valuable services. In the main, however, such institutions as the Martyrs' Foundation, the Foundation for the Disinherited, the Housing Foundation, and the like have met with indifferent success. Some have been economically wasteful of resources entrusted to them. Yet, they have served the purpose of social and political mobilization and control.

Above all, it has seemed crucial to the upholders of the Khomeini model to deny representation of interests to workers, artisans, bazaaris, and other corporate groups. The regime's record on workers' organizations in the factories is instructive in this regard. Insisting upon the creation of so-called Islamic committees in the workplace, the clergy sought to preempt the rise of truly autonomous workers' councils. These workers' councils, in fact, were established in many locations and proved highly popular. Yet, clergy "truth squads" were sent to plant locations where they had mushroomed and the members of these organizations were persuaded, through a combination of blandishments and pressure, that the Islamic committees would do everything the workers' councils were meant to do, and more.

The regime's orientation to labor and to the professional syndicates, guilds, and women's associations is in the same mold as that of the monarchy: paternalistic-authoritarian control. As for peasant organizations, the noteworthy point is the regime's failure to implement consistent policies in the rural areas. Some regime figures have strongly endorsed major land-redistribution programs, but these efforts have been defeated by others who have upheld the categorical rights of property ownership.

The foregoing suggests, then, that the Khomeini clergy have continued the corporatist tendencies of the monarchy. It would be a mistake to equate the two models of rule and representation of interests, however, since the Islamic Republic is typified by inclusionary corporatism more than the Pahlavi state was. This said, it must be acknowledged that important social forces are not part of the corporatist bargain. The

Kurds, other enthnolinguistic minorities, the modern middle class, the professional bureaucratic intelligentsia, and even, at times, the bazaar have been disadvantaged by the regime. Yet, the populist policies that have been pursued seem to be more rooted in the country's social classes—especially the petite bourgeoisie and the lower class—than those of the shah in the 1960s and 1970s.[44]

Intriguingly, established legal doctrine regarding areas of public policy contradicts certain regime measures favoring the Iranian masses. The most important "carrot" available to the regime in regard to maintaining the support of the masses pertains to land expropriation from the wealthier strata and distribution to the needy. Yet the parliament has not been able to promulgate unambiguous legislation permitting such actions.[45] Consequently, the regime has had to resort to the so-called secondary principles of law, which are construed as supervening the primary principles during periods of extraordinary or emergency situations facing the community. Thus, the legal precept of *masalih mursalah* (the public interest) has been invoked frequently by the Khomeini clergy. It is also clear that one cannot make a strong legal case for basing economic transactions on the whole and in an everyday sense upon "secondary principles" of law, for by that reckoning, there would be no need for ever observing the "primary principles."

Rentierism since 1979

Despite the clergy's promises to transform Iran's economy to remove its exceptional dependence on oil revenue, going as far as to pledge the doubling of nonoil exports, the Khomeini clergy have been unsuccessful in this endeavor. In fact, nonoil exports by Fall, 1989, were only at the levels that existed in the late Pahlavi period.[46] According to one source,

Oil continues to be the mainstay of the Iranian economy because of the Islamic Republic's failure to diversify its economy and to harness its indigenous resources for a more self-reliant course.[47]

Figure 2 shows that high levels of dependence on oil revenues continued through the mid-1980s. The decrease in revenue between 1979–80 and 1981–82, unfortunately for Tehran, "was largely matched by the contraction of the industrial sector."[48] Moreover, the dramatic reduction in Iranian oil sales between 1983–84 and 1986–87 was not due to government

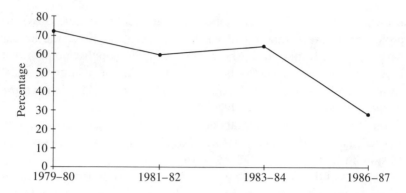

Fig. 2. Revenue from oil sales as a percentage of total revenue. (Data from Clawson, "Islamic Iran's Economic Politics," 376; the figure for 1986–87 is Clawson's projection from incomplete data.)

policy changes favoring nonoil sectors, but to the heating up of the war in the Gulf and Iraqi air strikes against Iranian oil platforms and tanker traffic.

The dilemma for the regime has always been that the chief means of surmounting overdependence upon oil is to have major growth in the private sector of the economy. But if the private sector does grow, then it would call into question the regime's strong commitment to defending the interests of the poor. Still, "government reluctance to see the private sector get rich"[49] has not prevented both President Rafsanjani and the faqih, Khamanah'i, from stressing the need, from mid-1989 onward, to tend to economic construction and to reject the idea that a truly Muslim society must disregard matters of economic prosperity. Indeed, the new five-year plan approved in 1990 suggests a major role for the private sector. Of course, it remains to be seen whether this will, in fact, be the case. Meanwhile, oil prices have made a recovery and, even before the crisis of Fall, 1990, were projected to increase by 50 percent by 1995. If such an increase occurs, the government will be tempted to revert to its traditional dependence upon oil revenue (as opposed to sales from the export of industrial goods and manufacturing).

The evidence is that the government has followed such unrealistic exchange rate policies (maintaining a value for the rial at the same level as in the prerevolutionary period) that it has been forced to cut development spending and to print money to pay for budgetary deficits. Meanwhile, an overvalued rial has led to rising levels of imports, as "the overvalued rial made imports a better buy compared to local products."[50] On the other hand, with the artificial exchange rate, certain merchants in the bazaar have benefited greatly. Given the high demand for imported goods, merchants selling them have generally charged high prices. Regime efforts to counter this through the imposition of price controls have not been fully effective, since these were goods for which some consumers have had an inelastic demand. Wealthy merchants in particular—that is, those who are able to bribe officials of the Islamic Republic to grant them import licenses—have done particularly well.[51]

Other merchants have complained about the regime's "socialist" policies, including the state's intervention to impose exchange controls and to regulate exports through the nationalization of foreign trade. Even with regard to internal trade, the governments of former Prime Minister Mir Husayn Musavi (1981–89) sought to control distribution by eliminating the merchant from the process. As noted before, there have been occasions when elements of the bazaar have clashed angrily with the regime over state interventionism in the economy.

The five-year plan adopted by the Majlis in early 1990 proposed to triple nonoil exports by 1995. President Rafsanjani indicated in a press conference that mining, cement, rubber, and paper would be the sectors favored for investment under the plan. At the same time, the minister of economics announced that factories and other enterprises seized by the government in the revolution would be sold back to the private sector.[52] Up to $27 billion in foreign credits and loans would be sought for investment as follows: $9 billion for agriculture, nonexport industries, and mines; $3 billion for dams and irrigation; $5 billion for natural gas and oil; and $10 billion for export industries.[53]

Rafsanjani's projection of the total foreign exchange needed for the five years of the plan was $112 billion.[54] This would mean that $85 billion would have to come from Iranian sources, once the $27 billion in foreign credits were factored in. At its November 25, 1989, meeting in Vienna, OPEC agreed to increase Iran's quota to 3.1 million barrels of oil per day (in fact, giving it parity with Iraq at that level). If oil prices hold at roughly $18.00 per barrel, this would mean total revenue from petroleum sales over the five years would be $101.8 billion—more than enough to meet the target. Since oil revenue is, in fact, projected to rise, rather than decline, in the next five years, given the increase in consumption in both Western and Eastern Europe, the United States, and East and Southeast Asia,[55] it appears that there is a good chance that the regime will meet its target. Of course, Tehran would wish to revitalize its nonoil export industries to be able to repay the foreign loans it will be contracting. Tehran's target for nonoil export earnings over the five years of the plan is $9 billion.[56] It is worth noting that in no previous year have nonoil export earnings been higher than $1 billion. Thus, whether the regime's goals will be met is, in fact, highly conjectural.

One thing is clear, however. Unless the private sector truly gains the necessary confidence to build up Iran's industrial and agricultural sectors, the society is likely to face the same economic dead ends of the Pahlavi period. That is, large amounts of oil revenue (some $20 billion a year) will be available, the country's industrial middle class will be prohibited from enjoying any autonomy and kept dependent upon the state, private sector investments will gravitate toward construction and housing, and agriculture will remain the orphan of the economy.

Shi'ism in Theory and Practice

The Iranian revolution has been a cultural revolution above anything else. Political ideology, the institutional structure of the state, education, male-female relationships, and the affairs of the nationalities have been arenas that have seen major changes since the Pahlavi period. Certainly the vocabulary and discourse of politics have been penetrated by Shi'ite symbols and concepts. The constitution, as well as the three branches of government, themselves, have witnessed the great impact of the Shi'ite clergy in molding the new state. The primary, secondary, and higher educational systems have all been purged of previous textbooks, teachers, and curricula. "Islamic" codes for social relationships between the sexes have been imposed. And the ethnolinguistic minorities have witnessed continued centralization of state power, although now rhetorically in the name of Islamic solidarity (cf. pre-Islamic notions of the sacred kingship). And, of course, the capstone of this, Khomeini's vilayat-i faqih (governance of the jurist) has provided the doctrinal grounding for the new dispensation.

Yet, how "Shi'ite" is this doctrine? On one level, one may say that it is a Shi'ite doctrine to the extent that doctrine evolves according to historical circumstances and cannot be regarded as carved in stone. Thus, innovations enter into the doctrine, whereupon future considerations must always take such innovations into account. On another level, though, vilayat-i faqih is distinctly counter to the classic traditions of the imamate, which holds that only the imams may rule.

Khomeini maintained that when the Imams encouraged their followers to practice *taqiyyah* (dissimulation of the faith for fear of persecution), they were doing so with regard to the rituals of the faith only—and not in political matters, regarding which he alleges they were advocates of jihad against despotic secular authorities. Yet this view is historically inaccurate, as the Imams withdrew into quietism and urged caution on their followers and, in the words of one observer, stressed purely "soteriological" concerns and, in another's view, comported themselves in such a way as to have achieved the "de facto depolitization" of Shi'ism.[57] Indeed, it is ironic that Khomeini has moved closer to the Sunni doctrine of leadership, since he argues that the just jurist who will exercise the authority of the Hidden Imam until his return will be selected by those qualified to do so. Such selection is in contrast to the Shi'ite tradition, where leadership is bestowed on the line of individuals descended from the Prophet through his daughter, Fatimah.

The 1979 constitution has ratified Khomeini's doctrinal innovations on the authority of the Imams by referring to the faqih (Khomeini) with the same sobriquet as that bestowed historically upon the Imams, namely, *vali-yi amr* (master of affairs) and *imam-i ummat* (the Imam of the community). Thus, Khomeini's argument has triumphed in making the faqih replace the Hidden Imam in his function as ruler of the community until he emerges from occultation.

These matters appear to have come full circle, however, with the constitutional changes introduced in mid-1989. The doctrine of vilayat-i faqih has been called into question as a consequence of political initiatives taken in 1989 after Khomeini's death. Realizing that no mujtahid exists who is as learned as Khomeini was and who also would ardently support the political system he had established, the post-Khomeini rulers have effectively removed the requirement that an individual of that stature guide society. Prior to his death, Khomeini had decreed the creation of the so-called Committee for the Discernment of Expediency. Its function was to reconcile differences between the parliament and the Guardian Council, whose vetoes of legislation in a variety of areas had created public policy immobilism. One of the members of this committee, 'Abdullah Nuri, later became Rafsanjani's minister of interior, but it was in his capacity as a member of the committee that he tried to explain the dropping of the requirement that the spiritual leader—the *rahbar*—

be a marja' al-taqlid (literally, source of imitation, the highest ranking position among the Shi'ite clergy).

Certainly, it is possible that at each period management, directorship, awareness of political and social issues and *marja'iyyat-i taqlid* [all co-exist in one person]. Although a *marja'*, because he is conversant with the *fiqh, usul,* mastery of the Qur'an and the *sunnah,* is capable in individual discussions of *fiqh,* this person [may] not have great capability in management and may not have strong political and social perspicacity in regard to the social affairs of the moment. In this case, restricting *vilayat-i amr* and *imamat-i ummat* in one *marja* naturally makes matters difficult for the Islamic system. Thus, it became necessary, in reviewing the constitution, to remove the requirement of *marja'iyyat* [for the office of *rahbar,* i.e., leader], since it is seen as a superfluous requirement.[58]

In late December, 1987, and early January, 1988, Ayatollah Khomeini issued a series of decrees that authorized the government to take certain initiatives that previously had been vetoed by the Guardian Council. These decrees sanctioned the state's disconnecting electricity and water to those businesses that refused to provide maternity leave for working mothers, for example. Appeals had been made that the state had no authority, under Islamic law, to take such actions, but Khomeini overruled these objections by invoking his powers as faqih.

Arguing that it was mandatory for the enterprises involved to take the actions designated, Khomeini was saying, in effect, that failure to do so would represent an unacceptable challenge to the Islamic revolution itself. In turn, that would be tantamount to disregard of Islam itself, since, in the words of a Khomeini clergyman, "obedience to vilayat-i faqih is an incumbent duty...and disobeying it is like disobeying the Islamic Sacred Law."[59]

Khomeini put it this way: "I want to say that the state, which has the full delegated authority of the prophet...takes precedence over other Islamic regulations, even prayer and pilgrimage." He added, "The state can unilaterally abrogate any legal agreement with the people if it is seen to harm Islam. The state can block anything...that contradicts the interests of Islam. It even has the power to temporarily prevent the pilgrimage—one of the most compelling of the divine obligations—if that is in the interests of the Islamic state."[60] This remarkable statement suggests that the Khomeini clergy equate obedience to its laws with the primary principles of the faith, including the five pillars of Islam.

Conclusions

This chapter has compared and contrasted phases of the Iranian revolution in terms of corporatist models of the state, economic rentierism, and Shi'ite culture and doctrine. It is abundantly clear that the original revolutionaries had varying interpretations of Shi'ite values, and that the Khomeini loyalists among the clergy established their control after much conflict. This conflict, documented at length in my original 1983 essay, has not been examined in detail here, but it did center on the most vital aspects of Khomeini's paradigm of vilayat-i faqih. Ironically, after Khomeini's death, the notion of faqih has been greatly devalued, so that while the office continues, the holder of the office is officially considered to be more of a public administrator than the deputy of the Hidden Imam.

Corporatism failed under the shah because he was never serious about the corporatist bargain. Although his state had secured the support of some strata of the peasantry that were grateful for the land they received under his land reforms, this was not a decisive group in the revolution. In the Khomeini period, the state has seemingly been more representative of the poorer masses and the petite bourgeoisie than its predecessor and is at least perceived by these constituencies to be less repressive and corrupt than the Pahlavi state.

But rentierism continues to bedevil the economy of this state, despite a decade of rhetoric that independence from an oil economy would be achieved. What is remarkable about the Khomeini regime is that it has been able to avoid foreign indebtedness, despite the mammoth costs of its war with Iraq. But such independence will be of little comfort if the state continues to rely on petroleum revenue for welfare distributions to its natural constituencies. More is needed than efforts to equalize disparities. Unless the regime commits itself to a balanced development of both the agricultural and industrial sectors, it will be faced with the same distortions of petroleum rentierism that Iran had confronted under the monarchy. In that event, it is not inconceivable that pressures would build once again, and that collective protests against the regime would eventually mount, even to the point of demands for full accountability. In that event, matters will have come full circle for a regime that originally came to power with the broadest support any Iranian regime has apparently ever had.

NOTES

1. Ahmad Ashraf, "Historical Obstacles to the Development of a Bourgeoisie in Iran," in *Studies in the Economic History of the Middle East,* ed. Michael Cook, 308–32 (London: Oxford University Press, 1970).

2. James A. Bill, "Class Analysis and the Dialectics of Modernization in the Middle East," *International Journal of Middle East Studies* 3, no. 4 (October, 1972): 417–34.

3. Ervand Abrahamian, "Oriental Despotism: The Case of Qajar Iran," *International Journal of Middle East Studies* 3, no. 4 (October, 1972): 317–34.

4. M. Crawford Young, personal communication. For the Iranian example, see Hossein Mahdavy, "Patterns and Problems of Economic Development in Rentier States: The Case of Iran," in Cook, ed., *Studies in Economic History,* 428–67; Afsaneh Najmabadi, "Depoliticization of a Rentier State: The Case of Pahlavi Iran," in *The Rentier State,* ed. Hazem Beblawi and Giacomo Luciani, 211–27 (New York: St. Martin's Press, 1987); Theda Skocpol, "Rentier State and Shi'a Islam in the Iranian Revolution," *Theory and Society* 11, no. 3 (May, 1982): 265–83.

5. Fred Halliday, *Iran: Dictatorship and Development* (Baltimore: Penguin Books, 1979), 38–63.

6. Alfred Stepan, *The State and Society: Peru in Comparative Perspective* (Princeton: Princeton University Press, 1978).

7. Phillip C. Schmitter, "Still the Century of Corporatism?" in *The New Corporatism,* ed. Frederick Pike and Thomas Stritch, 93–94 (Notre Dame, Ind.: Notre Dame University Press, 1974).

8. Misagh Parsa, *Social Origins of the Iranian Revolution* (New Brunswick, N.J.: Rutgers University Press, 1989), 141–44; Mohsen Milani, *The Making of Iran's Islamic Revolution* (Boulder, Colo.: Westview Press, 1989), 166–70; Hossein Bashiriyeh, *The State and Social Revolution in Iran* (New York: St. Martin's Press, 1983), 90–104; Halliday, *Iran,* 46–50.

9. Bashiriyeh, *The State and Social Revolution,* 30–31. The quoted passage is from p. 30.

10. Abrahamian, *Iran between Two Revolutions* (Princeton: Princeton University Press, 1982), 420.

11. See Leonard Binder, *Iran: Political Development in a Modernizing Society* (Berkeley: University of California Press, 1962); Marvin Zonis, *The Political Elite of Iran* (Princeton: Princeton University Press, 1971); James Bill, *The Politics of Iran: Elites, Classes, and Modernization* (Columbus, Ohio: Charles

Merrill, 1972); Richard Cottam, *Nationalism in Iran* (Pittsburgh: University of Pittsburgh Press, 1979).

12. Ervand Abrahamian, "The Structural Causes of the Iranian Revolution," *Middle East Research and Information Projects Reports* 87 (May, 1980): 23.

13. Halliday, *Iran,* 76.

14. Charles Issawi, "The Iranian Economy, 1925–1975: Fifty Years of Economic Development," in *Iran under the Pahlavis,* ed. George Lenczowski, 137 (Stanford, Calif.: Hoover Institution, 1978).

15. Robert Looney, *Economic Origins of the Iranian Revolution* (New York: Pergamon, 1982), 65–66.

16. Ibid., 217.

17. Ibid., 249.

18. Adapted from Sohrab Behdad, "Winners and Losers of the Iranian Revolution: A Study in Income Distribution," *International Journal of Middle East Studies* 21, no. 3 (August, 1989): 340, 343.

19. Shahrough Akhavi, *Religion and Politics in Contemporary Iran: Clergy-State Relations in the Pahlavi Period* (Albany: State University of New York Press, 1980), 183.

20. A debate has been taking place in the literature on the question of doctrinal principles and rule. Arguing in the tradition that the doctrine sanctions clerical assertiveness and revolutionary rejection of impious rule (*zulm*) have been A. K. S. Lambton, "Quis Custodiet Custodes?" *Studia Islamica* 5, no. 2 (1956): 125–48; 6, no. 1 (1956): 125–46; Nikki R. Keddie, "The Roots of the *Ulama's* Power in Modern Iran," *Studia Islamica* 29 (1969): 31–53; Hamid Algar, *Religion and State in Iran, 1789–1906* (Berkeley: University of California Press, 1969); Leonard Binder, "The Proofs of Islam," in *Studies in Honor of H. A. R. Gibb,* ed. George Makdisi, 118–40 (Leiden: Brill, 1965). Against the traditional view, the "revisionists" argue that Shi'ite doctrine does not support clerical activism in the political arena; see Said Arjomand, *The Shadow of God and the Hidden Imam* (Chicago: University of Chicago Press, 1985); Willem Floor, "The Revolutionary Character of the Shi'i *Ulama:* Wishful Thinking or Reality?" *International Journal of Middle East Studies* 12, no. 4 (December, 1980): 501–24; Joseph Eliash, "Misconceptions Concerning Shi'i Political Theory," *International Journal of Middle East Studies* 10, no. 1 (February, 1979): 9–25; Mangol Bayat, "Islam in Pahlavi and Post-Pahlavi Iran: A Cultural Revolution?" in *Islam and Development: Religion and Sociopolitical Change,* ed. John L. Esposito, 89–94 (Syracuse, N.Y.: Syracuse University Press, 1980); Bayat, "The Iranian Revolution of 1978–1979: Fundamentalist or Modern?" *Middle East Journal* 37, no. 1 (Winter, 1983): 30–42.

21. Mahdavy, "Patterns and Problems," 428.

22. Ibid., 429.

23. Ibid., 437.

24. Ibid., 465.

25. Giacomo Luciani, "Allocation vs. Production States: A Theoretical Framework," in Beblawi and Luciani, eds., Rentier State, 74.

26. Mahdavy, "Patterns and Problems," 465–66.

27. Jacques Delacroix, "The Distributive State in the World System," Studies in Comparative International Development 15, no. 1 (Fall, 1980): 9.

28. Ibid., 12.

29. Ibid., 17.

30. See Julian Bharier, Economic Development in Iran (London: Oxford University Press, 1971); Fereydoon Fesharaki, Development of the Iranian Oil Industry (New York: Praeger, 1976); Halliday, Iran; Homa Katouzian, The Political Economy of Modern Iran (London: Macmillan, 1981); Looney, Economic Origins; B. Mossavar-Rahmani, Energy Policy in Iran: Domestic Choices and International Implications (New York: Pergamon, 1981); Hossein Razavi and Firouz Vakil, The Political Environment of Economic Planning In Iran, 1981–1983 (Boulder, Colo.: Westview, 1984).

31. Delacroix, "Distributive State," 17.

32. Skocpol, "Rentier State," 269.

33. Abdulaziz A. Sachedina, Islamic Messianism: The Idea of Mahdi in Twelver Shi'ism (Albany: State University of New York Press, 1981), 105.

34. Eliash has shown that ex-ante appointment never occurred ("Misconceptions").

35. Algar, Religion and State; Akhavi, Religion and Politics, passim.

36. Bernard Lewis, "Islamic Concepts of Revolution," in Revolution in the Middle East, ed. P. J. Vatikiotis, 33 (London: Weidenfeld, 1972).

37. Wilfred Madelung, Encyclopaedia of Islam, n.s. (1971), s.v. "Imama."

38. Hans Kippenburg, "Jeder Tag Ashura, Jedes Grab Kerbala," in Religion und Politik im Iran: Mardom Nameh—Jahrbuch zur Geshichte und Gesellschaft des Mittleren Orients, ed. Kurt Greussing, 217–56 (Frankfurt am Main: Syndikat, 1981).

39. Michael M. J. Fischer, Iran: From Religious Dispute to Revolution (Cambridge, Mass.: Harvard University Press, 1980), 183.

40. Shahrough Akhavi, "The Ideology and Praxis of Shi'ism in the Iranian Revolution," Comparative Studies in Society and History 25, no. 2 (April, 1983): 212–13.

41. Shahrough Akhavi, "Elite Factionalism in the Islamic Republic of Iran," Middle East Journal 41, no.2 (Spring, 1987): 181–201; Akhavi, "Clerical Politics in Iran since 1979," in The Iranian Revolution and the Islamic Republic, 2d ed., ed. Nikki R. Keddie and Eric Hooglund, 57–73 (Syracuse, N.Y.: Syracuse University Press, 1986).

42. Theda Skocpol, States and Social Revolutions (New York: Cambridge University Press, 1979).

43. Said A. Arjomand, *The Turban for the Crown: The Islamic Revolution in Iran* (New York: Oxford University Press, 1988), 169.

44. Ali Farazmand, *The State, Bureaucracy, and Revolution in Modern Iran* (New York: Praeger, 1989), 182ff. Farazmand appears to exaggerate the "egalitarianism" of the Khomeini state.

45. On the question of land expropriation and distribution, see Shahrough Akhavi, "Clerical Politics," 68–69; Shaul Bakhash, "The Politics of Land, Law, and Social Justice in Iran," *Middle East Journal* 43, no. 2 (Spring, 1989): 186–201; Parsa, *Social Origins,* 263–65. Parsa wrongly says that "to date, land reform as a matter of principle has not been approved" (264). However, the parliament passed a land redistribution law in October, 1986, that was not vetoed by the Guardian Council.

46. *Iran Times* (Washington, D.C.), 31 Shahrivar 1368 H.Sh.

47. Michael G. Renner, "Determinants of the Islamic Republic's Oil Policies," in *Post-Revolutionary Iran* (Boulder, Colo.: Westview Press, 1988), 204.

48. M. H. Pesaran, "The System of Dependent Capitalism in Pre- and Post-Revolutionary Iran," *International Journal of Middle East Studies* 14, no. 4 (November, 1982): 518.

49. Patrick Clawson, "Islamic Iran's Economic Policies," *Middle East Journal* 42, no. 3 (Summer, 1988): 386.

50. Wolfgang Lautenschlager, "The Effects of an Overvalued Exchange Rate on the Iranian Economy, 1979-1984," *International Journal of Middle East Studies* 18, no. 1 (February, 1986): 38.

51. Ibid., 41.

52. *Iran Times,* 28 Mihr 1368 H.Sh.

53. *Iran Times,* 29 Day 1368 H.Sh.

54. *Iran Times,* 28 Mihr 1368 H.Sh.

55. *New York Times,* February 24, 1990.

56. *Iran Times,* 28 Mihr 1368 H.Sh.

57. Arjomand, *Shadow of God,* 32 and passim; Bayat, "Iranian Revolution," 35.

58. *Iran Times,* 3 Shahrivar 1368 H.Sh.

59. Cited in Arjomand, *Turban for the Crown,* 182.

60. *Iran Times,* 4 Day 1366 H.Sh.; 25 Day 1366 H.Sh.

Contributors

Shahrough Akhavi, professor of Government and International Studies at the University of South Carolina and author of *Religion and Politics in Contemporary Iran* (State University of New York Press, 1980), is editor of the Middle East Series for the State University of New York Press and has published widely on modern Iran.

Allan Christelow, associate professor of History at Idaho State University, has published journal articles and book essays on North and West Africa and is the author of *Muslim Law Courts and the French Colonial State in Algeria* (Princeton University Press, 1985).

Juan R. I. Cole is associate professor of History at the University of Michigan. He has written *Roots of North Indian Shi'ism in Iran and Iraq* (University of California Press, 1989), coedited *Shi'ism and Social Protest* (Yale University Press, 1986), and has just completed the manuscript of a book on the social and cultural origins of the 'Urabi revolution in nineteenth-century Egypt.

Dale F. Eickelman is Ralph and Richard Lazarus Professor of Anthropology and Human Relations at Dartmouth College. He has written *Moroccan Islam* (University of Texas Press, 1976), *The Middle East: An Anthropological Approach* (Prentice-Hall, 1989, 2d ed.), and *Knowledge and Power in Morocco* (Princeton University Press, 1985), and coedited *Muslim Travelers: Pilgrimage, Migration, and the Religious Imagination* (University of California Press, 1990).

Ellis Goldberg, associate professor of Political Science at the University of Washington, Seattle, is the author of *Tinker, Tailor, and Textile Worker* (University of California Press, 1986) and has written on Islamic political theory.

Deniz Kandiyoti, senior lecturer in the Social Sciences Division at Richmond College in Surrey, England, is author of *Women in Rural Production Systems* (UNESCO, 1985) and editor of the forthcoming *Women, Islam, and the State*. She has published widely on gender issues in the Middle East and has, since 1976, been an international correspondent for *Signs: Journal of Women in Culture and Society*.

Nikki Keddie, professor of History at the University of California, Los Angeles, is author of *Roots of Revolution: An Interpretive History of Modern Iran* (Yale

University Press, 1981) and numerous other books on Iranian history and has edited several volumes on the Middle East, including, most recently, a book treating gender issues, *Shifting Boundaries* (Yale University Press, forthcoming).

Charles Lindholm, University Professor and professor of Anthropology at Boston University, has written *Generosity and Jealousy: The Swat Pukhtun of Northern Pakistan* (Columbia University Press, 1982) and *Charisma* (Blackwell, 1990). He has also written a number of articles on politics and social structure in the Middle East.

Charles D. Smith is professor of History at San Diego State University. His books include *Islam and the Search for Social Order in Modern Egypt* (State University of New York Press, 1983) and *Palestine and the Arab-Israeli Conflict* (St. Martin's Press, 1988).

Glossary

'ālim. The Muslim equivalent of a clergyman, with a seminary or madrasa education. (Ar.)

diyāt. Blood money, wergild; indemnity for bodily injury. (Ar.)

faqīh. 1. A Muslim jurisprudent specializing in the corpus of Islamic law. 2. A tribal holy man. 3. In Iran, the supreme religious authority, as recognized by the constitution of the Islamic Republic. (Ar.)

fatwā. The considered opinion of a Muslim jurisconsult on an issue of law. (Ar.)

fqīh. See faqīh (North African colloquial transcription).

hadīth. An oral saying, later written down, said to derive from the Prophet Muhammad.

hāfiz. A Muslim who has memorized the Qur'an. (Ar.)

hawā. Base and selfish passion. (Ar.)

hubb. Love, especially romantic love. (Ar.)

hujjatī. Member of a clerical faction in Iran that opposed clerical rule.

hukūmat. Centralized government. (Persian, from Ar. hukūma.)

'idda. The legally prescribed period of waiting during which a woman may not remarry after being widowed or divorced, and during which her former husband is responsible for her support. (Ar.)

ijāza. The equivalent of a diploma in a Muslim seminary, certifying that a scholar has completed a particular set of readings with a master. (Ar.)

ijmā'. Most schools of Islamic law recognize four sources of law: the Qur'an, oral sayings from the Prophet (hadīth), reason, and ijmā' or consensus. In some instances, consensus refers to the majority opinion among great legal minds; in others, the consensus of the entire Muslim community is invoked. (Ar.)

ijtihād. The exertion of independent reasoning, applied to sacred Muslim texts, in an effort to determine the ruling of Islamic law in a particular case. Ijtihād is allowed in the majority school of Twelver Shi'ism, which predominates in Iran, and bestows great prerogatives on its practitioners, known as mujtahids. Many Sunni schools regard ijtihād as no longer appropriate to Muslim jurisprudents and as a preserve of the earliest founders of the legal rites. (Ar.)

Imām. In Shī'ite Islam, the Imām is the designated successor to and vicar of the Prophet Muhammad. The Twelver Shī'ites of Iran believe that 'Ali, the Prophet's cousin and son-in-law, was the first Imām, and that eleven of his lineal descendents held that position. They hold that the Twelfth Imām dis-

297

appeared into a supernatural realm from which he would one day return to restore the world to justice. (Ar.)

jihād. Holy war. According to most Muslim schools, jihād is not one of the five essential duties of a Muslim, but some fundamentalist groups make it a sixth, and even central, pillar of Islam. (Ar.)

jirga. A tribal council at which major decisions are made; important in Afghanistan and northern Pakistan. (Pushtu)

Kemalist. Adherent of the secularist principles of Kemal Ataturk, the founder of modern Turkey, who advocated a strict separation of religion and state and a banning of Islamic traditionalism and fundamentalism.

ma'rifa. Secular knowledge, as opposed to *'ilm* or religious knowledge. (Ar.)

madīna. The Arabic word for city, often referring especially to the complex of mosque, bazaar, and courthouse at the center of old Muslim cities.

madrasa. A Muslim institution of higher education. (Ar.)

maḥabba. Love. (Ar.)

mahdī. In Muslim thought about the last days, a descendent of the Prophet Muhammad is expected to arise and restore the world to justice. This mahdī is identified by Shī'ite Muslims with the return of the hidden, Twelfth Imām. Many Muslims have expected the mahdī to arise just before the return of Christ.

makhzan. The area of the country under central government control. (North African Arabic, literally "treasurehold.")

maktabī. In Iran, a clerical grouping faithful to the principals of Imām Ruhu'llah Khomeini, who held that clerics should play a leading role in the governance of society. (Persian, from Ar. maktab)

malang. A barefoot, bareheaded mystic given over to ecstatic religious practices. (Persian)

Mamlūk. A caste of slave-soldiers important at various times in medieval and early modern Egyptian history. (Ar.)

marabout. Term for Muslim holy men of various sorts. (French, from Portuguese *marabuto,* from Arabic *murābiṭ,* "a holy man or hermit.")

marja' al-taqlīd. The source to which a lay Twelver Shi'ite is supposed to look for guidance about religious practice. Such a source must be a mujtahid, capable of independently deriving the law. According to the Usuli school, all laypersons must choose a source for emulation and abide by his rulings. (Ar.)

mujtahid. A Muslim clergyman who is capable of independently deriving the law from the sacred texts and by use of reason and consensus. (Ar.)

mullah. English transcription of a colloquial term in Iran for a Muslim clergyman of the lower ranks, sometimes used pejoratively for all such clergy. (Persian, from Arabic *mawlā,* "master.")

pīr. Leader of a mystical confraternity or ṣūfī order. (Persian)

qāḍī. Muslim court judge who gives positive-law rulings. (Ar.)

qanāt. In Iran, underground irrigation canals of great technical sophistication. (Ar.)

qiṣāṣ. The Muslim law governing the penalty imposed on one party for injury to another; the equivalent of the lex talionis. (Ar.).

Ṣafavids. A dynasty that ruled over Iran (1501–1722).

SAVAK. Persian acronym for the dreaded security police established in Iran by Muhammad Reza Pahlavi (r. 1941–78).

Sayyid. One who asserts descent from the Prophet Muhammad. Sayyids are owed respect in most Muslim countries, and some schools require that they be given special charity. (Ar.)

shahāda. The witness a Muslim makes that there is no god but God, and that Muhammad is His Prophet. One of the five pillars of Islam. (Ar.)

shar'. The revealed, canon Law of Islam. Synonym of sharī'a. (Ar.)

sharī'a. The revealed, canon Law of Islam. (Ar.)

sharīf. Noble, often a term applied to Sayyids or descendents of the Prophet Muhammad.

shaykh. Literally, elder. Leader of a tribe or of a mystical confraternity. (Ar.)

Shī'ite. Adherent of one of the two main branches of Islam. Most Shī'ites believe the succession to the Prophet Muhammad should have been invested in 'Ali, the cousin and son-in-law of the Prophet, and in 'Ali's descendents thereafter.

shra'. North African colloquial transcription of sharī'a, q.v.

sība. The area of a country not under central government control, but rather left to the segmentary politics of tribespeople and nomads. (N. African Ar., from standard Arabic *sāba,* "to relinquish.")

ṣūfī. Muslim mystic, adhering to a form of Islam that stresses the attainment of ecstasy and feelings of oneness with God.

Sunnī. Adherent of the majority branch of Islam. Sunnīs accepted four orthodox caliphs after the death of the Prophet Muhammad: Abu Bakr, 'Umar, 'Uthman, and 'Ali.

tafsīr. Formal commentary on the Qur'an.

ṭāghūt. Originally a pre-Islamic idol, applied by contemporary Islamic activists to worldly things and attitudes that cause believers to depart from Islam.

ṭālib. Student, especially a Muslim seminary student seeking religious knowledge. (Ar.)

taqlīd. Emulation. The duty every Twelver Shī'ite of the Usuli school has to follow implicitly the rulings of a qualified clergyman on Islamic law and practices.

tarjama. The biography of a Muslim learned man, often written in a highly formal style employing numerous conventions to stress his piety and learning.

tawḥīd. Monotheism, the unity of God.

'ulamā'. Muslim clergy.

'umda. In Egypt, village headman.

vilāyat-i faqīh. The guardianship of the jurisprudent, the idea that a supreme religious authority ought to exercise some type of governance over the state. (Persian, from Ar. wilāya ["guardianship"] and faqīh ["jurisprudent"].)

yāghistan. The area of a country not under central government control, but rather left to the segmentary politics of tribespeople and nomads. (Pushtu, from Persian *yāgh,* "enemy.")

zawāya. Ṣufī centers, buildings for the meeting of mystical confraternities.

Bibliography

'Abd al-Qadir, Muhammad Zaki. *Aqdam 'ala al-Tariq* (Steps along the Way). Cairo, 1967.

'Abd ar-Raziq, Ahmad. *La femme au temps des Mamlouks en Egypte*. Cairo, 1973.

Abdel-Fadil, Mahmoud. *Development, Income Distribution, and Social Change in Rural Egypt (1952-1970)*. Cambridge, 1975.

Abdel Malik, Anwar. "Orientalism in Crisis." *Diogenes* 44 (Winter, 1963).

Abrahamian, Ervand. *Iran between Two Revolutions*. Princeton, 1982.

――――. "Oriental Despotism: The Case of Qajar Iran." *International Journal of Middle East Studies* 3, no. 4 (October, 1972).

Abu-Lughod, J. *Cairo: 1,001 Years of City Victorious*. Princeton, 1971.

Abu Sina, Muhammad Ibrahim. *Falsafat al-mathal al-sha'bi*. Cairo, 1968.

Adams, Robert McC. *The Evolution of Urban Society*. Chicago, 1966.

――――. *Land behind Baghdad: A History of Settlement on the Diyala Plains*. Chicago, 1965.

Afshar, Haleh. "Behind the Veil: The Public and Private Faces of Khomeini's Policies on Iranian Women." In *Structures of Patriarchy*, ed. Bina Agarwal. London, 1988.

Ageron, Charles-Robert. *Les algériens Musulmans et la France (1871-1919)*. Paris, 1968.

Ahmad, Imtiaz, ed. *Caste and Stratification among Muslims in India*. New Delhi, 1978.

――――. *Family, Kinship, and Marriage among Muslims in India*. New Delhi, 1976.

――――. *Ritual and Religion among Muslims in India*. New Delhi, 1981.

Ahmed, Akbar. "Islam and the District Paradigm." *Contributions to Indian Sociology* 17 (1983): 155-83.

――――. *Millenium and Charisma among Pathans*. London, 1976.

――――. *Pukhtun Economy and Society*. London, 1980.

Ahmed, Jamal M. *The Intellectual Origins of Egyptian Nationalism*. London, 1961.

Ahmed, Leila. "Women and the Advent of Islam." *Signs* 11 (1986).

Ajami, Fouad. "The Question of Authenticity and Collaboration." In *The Arab Predicament*. London, 1981.

Ajmal, Mohammad. "A Note on *Adab* in the *Murshid-Murid* Relationship." In *Moral Conduct and Authority: The Place of Adab in South Asian Islam,* ed. Barbara Daly Metcalf. Berkeley, 1984.

Akhavi, Shahrough. "Clerical Politics since 1979." In *The Iranian Revolution and the Islamic Republic.* 2d ed., ed. Nikki R. Keddie and Eric Hooglund. Syracuse, 1986.

———. "Elite Factionalism in the Islamic Republic of Iran." *Middle East Journal* 41, no. 2 (Spring, 1987).

———. "The Ideology and Praxis of Shi'ism in the Iranian Revolution." *Comparative Studies in Society and History* 25, no. 2 (April 1983): 195–221.

———. *Religion and Politics in Contemporary Iran: Clergy-State Relations in the Pahlavi Period.* Albany, N.Y., 1980.

———. "Shariati's Social Thought." In *Religion and Politics in Iran: Shi'ism from Quietism to Revolution,* ed. Nikki Keddie. New Haven, 1983.

Alavi, Hamza. "Pakistan and Islam: Ethnicity and Ideology." In *State and Ideology in the Middle East and Pakistan,* ed. Fred Halliday and Hamza Alavi. London, 1988.

Algar, Hamid. *Religion and State in Iran, 1789–1906.* Berkeley, 1969.

'Amarah, Muhammad. *Al-Faridah al-Gha'ibah: 'ard wa hiwar wa taqyim.* Cairo, 1982.

Anderson, Benedict. *Imagined Communities.* London, 1983.

Anderson, Lisa. *The State and Social Transformation in Tunisia and Libya, 1830–1980.* Princeton, 1986.

Andrews, P. A. "The Felt Tent in Middle Asia: The Nomadic Tradition and Its Interaction with Princely Tentage." D. Phil. thesis, University of London, 1980.

Apter, David E. *The Politics of Modernization.* Chicago, 1969.

Arjomand, Said A. "Iran's Islamic Revolution." *World Politics* 38, no. 3 (1986).

———. *The Shadow of God and the Hidden Imam.* Chicago, 1985.

———. *The Turban for the Crown: The Islamic Revolution in Iran.* New York, 1988.

Arminjon, Pierre. *L'Enseignement, la doctrine et la vie dans les universités musulmanes d'Égypte.* Paris, 1907.

Asad, Talal. "Market Model, Class Structure, and Consent: A Reconsideration of Swat Political Organization." *Man* 7 (1972): 74–94.

Ashraf, Ahmad. "Historical Obstacles to the Development of a Bourgeoisie in Iran." In *Studies in the Economic History of the Middle East,* ed. Michael Cook. London, 1970.

Ashton, T. H., and C. H. E. Philipin, eds. *The Brenner Debate: Agrarian Class Structure and Economic Development in Pre-Industrial Europe.* Cambridge, 1984.

Ashtor, E. *A Social and Economic History of the Near East in the Middle Ages.* London, 1976.

Aubin, Eugène [Descos]. *Morocco of To-Day.* London, 1906.

Ayalon, David. *Gunpowder and Firearms in the Mamluk Kingdom.* 2d ed. London, 1978.

Ayubi, Nazih. "The Politics of Militant Islamic Movements in the Middle East." *Journal of International Affairs* 36, no. 2 (1982).

Al-Azmah, Aziz. "Arab Nationalism and Islamism." *Review of Middle East Studies* 4 (1988).

Badran, Margot. "Competing Agenda: Feminists, Islam, and the State in Nineteenth- and Twentieth-Century Egypt." In *Women, Islam, and the State,* ed. Deniz Kandiyoti. London, forthcoming.

Baer, Gabriel. *Studies in the Social History of Modern Egypt.* Chicago, 1969.

Bahadori, M. N. "Passive Cooling Systems in Iranian Architecture." *Scientific American* 238, no. 2 (1978): 144–54.

Bailyn, Bernard. *Education in the Forming of American Society.* New York, 1960.

Bakhash, Shaul. "The Politics of Land, Law, and Social Justice in Iran." *Middle East Journal* 43, no. 2 (Spring, 1989).

Banani, A., ed. *State and Society in Iran. Iranian Studies* 11 (1978).

Al-Banna, Jamal. *Al-Faridah al-Gha'ibah: Jihad al-sayf am jihad al-'aql?* Cairo, 1983.

Bardin, Pierre. *Algériens et Tunisiens dans l'Empire Ottoman de 1848 à 1914.* Paris, 1979.

Barkan, Ömer Lutfi. "The Price Revolution of the Sixteenth Century: A Turning Point in the Economic History of the Near East." Trans. Justin McCarthy. *International Journal of Middle East Studies* 6, no. 1 (January, 1975): 3–28.

Baron, Beth. "Women's Nationalist Rhetoric and Activities in Early Twentieth-Century Egypt." In *The Origins of Arab Nationalism,* ed. R. Khalidi and L. Anderson. New York, forthcoming.

Barrows, Leland Conley. "The Merchants and General Faidherbe: Aspects of French Expansion in the 1850s." *Revue française d'histoire d'Outre-Mer* 61 (1974).

Bartha, Fredrik. *The Last Wali of Swat.* New York, 1985.

———. *Political Leadership among Swat Pathans.* London, 1965.

———. "Segmentary Opposition and the Theory of Games: A Study of Pathan Organization." *Journal of the Royal Anthropological Institute* 89 (1959): 5–21.

Basha, Ahmad Taymur. *Al-Amthal al-'ammiyyah.* Cairo, 1986.

Bayat, Mangol. "The Iranian Revolution of 1978–1979: Fundamentalist or Modern." *Middle East Journal* 37, no. 1 (Winter, 1983).

———. "Islam in Pahlavi and Post-Pahlavi Iran: A Cultural Revolution?" In *Islam and Development: Religion and Sociopolitical Change,* ed. John L. Esposito. Syracuse, N.Y., 1980.

Beck, Lois. *The Qashqa'i of Iran.* New Haven, 1986.

Beck, Lois, and Nikki R. Keddie, eds. *Women in the Muslim World.* Cambridge, Mass., 1978.

Beckett, P. "Qanats-Persia." *Journal of the Iran Society* 1 (1952): 125–33.

Behdad, Sohrab. "Winners and Losers of the Iranian Revolution: A Study in Income Distribution." *International Journal of Middle East Studies* 21, no. 3 (August, 1989): 327–58.

Bernstein, Basil. *Class, Codes, and Control.* Vol. 3, 2d ed. London, 1977.

Berque, Augustin. "Esquisse d'une histoire de la seigneurie algérienne." *Revue de la Mediterranée* 7, no. 1 (1949); 7, no. 2 (1949).

Berque, Jacques. "Dans le Maroc nouveau: Le rôle d'une université islamique." *Annales d'histoire économique et sociale* 10 (1938): 193-207.

——. "Lieux et moments du réformisme islamique." In *Maghreb: Histoire et sociétés.* Paris, 1974.

——. *Structures sociales de Haut Atlas.* Paris, 1955.

——. "Ville et université, aperçu sur l'histoire de l'école de Fès." *Revue historique de droit français et étranger* 27 (1949): 64-117.

——. *Al-Yousi: Problèmes de la culture marocaine au XVIIème siècle.* Paris, 1958.

Bharier, Julian. *Economic Development in Iran.* London, 1971.

Bill, James A. "Class Analysis and the Dialectics of Modernization in the Middle East." *International Journal of Middle East Studies* 3, no. 4 (October, 1972).

——. *The Politics of Iran: Elites, Classes, and Modernization.* Columbus, Ohio, 1972.

Binder, A. *Iran: Political Development in a Modernizing Society.* Berkeley, 1962.

——. *Islamic Liberalism: A Critique of Development Ideologies.* Chicago, 1988.

——. *In a Moment of Enthusiasm.* Chicago, 1978.

——. "The Proofs of Islam." In *Studies in Honor of H. A. R. Gibb,* ed. George Makdisi. Leiden, 1965.

Birnbaum, Norman. "Conflicting Interpretations of the Rise of Capitalism: Marx and Weber." *British Journal of Sociology* 4 (June, 1953).

Al-Bishri, Tariq. *Al-Dimuqratiyyah wa al-nasiriyyah.* Cairo, 1975.

Black, Jacob. "Tyranny as a Strategy for Survival in an 'Egalitarian' Society: Luri Facts Versus an Anthropological Mystique." *Man* 7 (1972): 614-34.

Bloch, Maurice. "Introduction." In *Political Language and Oratory in Traditional Society,* ed. Maurice Bloch. London, 1975.

Bonnie, M. E. "Aridity and Structure: Adaptation of Indigenous Housing in Central Iran." In *Desert Housing: Balancing Experience and Technology for Dwelling in Hot Arid Zones,* ed. K. N. Clark and P. Baylore. Tucson, Ariz., 1980.

——. "The Morphogenesis of Iranian Cities." *Annals of the Association of American Geographers* 69, no. 2 (June, 1979): 208-24.

——. "From Uruk to Casablanca: Perspectives on the Urban Experience of the Middle East." *Journal of Urban History* 3, no. 2 (February, 1977): 141-80.

Bosworth, E. "Armies of the Prophet." In *The World of Islam,* ed. Bernard Lewis. London, 1976.

Bourdieu, Pierre, and Jean-Claude Passeron. "Cultural Reproduction and Social Reproduction." In *Knowledge, Education, and Cultural Change,* ed. Richard Brown. London, 1973.

——. *Reproduction in Education, Society, and Culture.* Beverly Hills, 1977.

———. "Systems of Education and Systems of Thought." *International Social Science Journal* 19 (1967): 338–58.

Bouwsma, William J. *John Calvin: A Sixteenth-Century Portrait.* New York, 1988.

Bowering, Gerhard. "The *Adab* Literature of Classical Sufism: Ansari's Code of Conduct." In *Moral Conduct and Authority: The Place of Adab in South Asian Islam,* ed. Barbara Daly Metcalf. Berkeley, 1984.

Bramson, Leon. *The Political Context of Sociology.* Princeton, 1961.

Braudel, F. *Capitalism and Material Life.* Trans. M. Kochan. New York, 1973.

Brenner, Robert. "Agrarian Class Structure and Economic Development in Pre-Industrial Europe." *Past and Present,* no. 70 (1976): 30–75.

Brett, M. "Mufti, Marabout, Murabit, and Mahdi: Four Types in the Islamic History of North Africa." *Revue de l'Occident Musulman et de la Mediterranée* 29 (1980): 5–15.

Briggs, L. *Tribes of the Sahara.* Boston, 1960.

Broomfield, J. H. *Elite Conflict in a Plural Society: Twentieth-Century Bengal.* Berkeley, 1968.

Brown, Kenneth L. "The Impact of the Dahir Berbere in Salé." In *Arabs and Berbers,* ed. Ernest Micaud and Charles Micaud. London, 1973.

———. *People of Salé: Tradition and Change in a Moroccan City, 1830–1930.* Cambridge, 1976.

Brown, Leon Carl. "The Religious Establishment in Husainid Tunisia." In *Scholars, Saints, and Sufis,* ed. Nikki R. Keddie. Berkeley, 1972.

Brown, Leon Carl, ed. *From Madina to Metropolis.* Princeton, 1973.

Bujra, A. *The Politics of Stratification.* Oxford, 1971.

Bulliet, Richard W. *The Camel and the Wheel.* Cambridge, Mass., 1975.

———. *The Patricians of Nishapur.* Cambridge, 1972.

Burckhardt, John Lewis. *Arabic Proverbs: Or, the Manners and Customs of the Modern Egyptians.* London, 1972.

Burke, Edmund, III. *Prelude to Protectorate in Morocco.* Chicago, 1976.

Burrel, Sidney A. "Calvinism, Capitalism, and the Middle Classes: Some Afterthoughts on an Old Problem." In *The Protestant Ethic and Modernization,* ed. S. N. Eisenstadt. New York, 1968.

Cahen, C. *L'Islam: Des origines au debut de l'Empire Ottoman.* Paris, 1970.

———. "Le service de l'irrigation en Iraq au debut du XIe siècle." *Bulletin d'études orientales* 13 (1949–51): 117–43.

Cahnman, Werner J. "Toennies and Social Change." *Social Forces* 4 (1968).

Calvin, John. *Institutes of the Christian Religion.* Trans. John Allen. Philadelphia, 1936.

Camara, Camille. *Saint-Louis de Sénégal.* Dakar, 1968.

Carlyle, Thomas. *Heroes, Hero Worship, and the Heroic in History.* London, n. d.

Caroe, Olaf. *The Pathans.* London, 1965.

Carre, Olivier. *Mystique et politique: Lecture revolutionnaire du Coran.* Paris, 1984.

Cenival, Pierre de. "La légende du Juif Ibn Mech'al et la fête du sultan des tolba à Fès." *Hesperis* 5 (1925): 137–218.

Channock, Martin. *Law, Custom, and Social Order: The Colonial Experience in Malawi and Zambia.* Cambridge, 1985.

Charrad, Mounira. "State Formation and Women's Rights: The Case of North Africa." Paper presented at the conference on Family Law and Change in the Middle East, SSRC-ACLS Joint Committee on the Near and Middle East, Tuxedo, N.Y., 1983.

Chenu, M. D. "Monks, Canons, and Laymen in Search of the Apostolic Life." In *Nature, Man, and Society in the Twelfth Century.* Trans. Jerom Taylor and Lester K. Little. Chicago, 1968.

Cherbonneau, E. "Notice biographique sur Mohammed Ben Bou Diaf, Muphti de Constantine." *Journal Asiatique* 4ème Serie, 5 (1980).

Cherbonneau, Eugène. *Le droit musulman: Du statut personnel et des successions.* Paris, 1873.

Cherkaoui, Mohamed. "Socialisation et conflit: Les systèmes educatifs et leur histoire selon Durkheim." *Revue française de sociologie* 17 (1976): 197–212.

Chhachhi, Amrita. "Forced Identities: The State, Communalism, Fundamentalism, and Women in India." In *Women, Islam, and the State,* ed. Deniz Kandiyoti. London, forthcoming.

Chikh, Slimane. *L'Algérie en armes ou le temps des certitudes.* Algiers, 1981.

Christelow, Allan. "Hawl bidaya al-nahda al-jaza'iriyya: katib li 'Abd al-Qadir al-Majjawi." *Al-Thaqafa* (Algiers) 46 (September, 1978).

———. "Inquiry into the Origins of the Algerian Medjlis Crisis of 1858." *Revue d'histoire maghrebine,* no. 15–16 (July, 1979).

———. "al-Makki Ben Badis." *Parcours: L'Algérie les hommes et l'histoire* 5 (1985).

———. "al-Makki Ben Badis wa ba'd nawahi al-haraka al-wataniyya al-jazairiyya fi-l-qarn al-tasi' 'ashar." *Al-Thaqafa* 11, no. 61 (1981).

———. *Muslim Law Courts and the French Colonial State in Algeria.* Princeton, 1985.

———. "Saintly Descent and Worldly Affairs in Mid-Nineteenth-Century Mascara, Algeria." *International Journal of Middle East Studies* 12, no. 2 (1980).

———. "Three Islamic Voices in Contemporary Nigeria." In *Islam and the Political Economy of Meaning,* ed. William R. Roff. London, 1987.

Cipolla, Carlo M., ed. *The Fontana Economic History of Europe: The Middle Ages.* N.p., 1972.

Clarke, Peter. *West Africa and Islam.* London, 1982.

Clawson, Patrick. "Islamic Iran's Economic Policies." *Middle East Journal* 42, no. 3 (Summer, 1988): 371–89.

Cole, Juan R. "Feminism, Class, and Islam in Turn of the Century Egypt." *International Journal of Middle East Studies* 13 (1981).

Cole, Michael, with John Gay, Joseph A. Glick, and Donald W. Sharp. *The Cultural Context of Learning and Thinking.* New York, 1971.

Colin, G. S. "La noria marocaine et les machines hydroliques dans le monde arabe." *Hesperis* 14 (1932): 22–60.

Colonna, Fanny. "Cultural Resistance and Religious Legitimacy in Colonial Algeria." *Economy and Society* 3, no. 3 (1974).

———. *Instituteurs algériens, 1883–1939.* Paris, 1975.

———. "Saints furieux et saints studieux dans l'Aures." *Annales: Économies, sociétés, civilisations* 35 (1980).

Colvin, Lucie G. "Islam and the State of Kajoor: A Case of Successful Resistance to Jihad." *Journal of African History* 15, no. 4 (1974).

Combs-Schilling, M. E. *Sacred Performances: Islam, Sexuality, and Sacrifice.* New York, 1989.

Coon, Carlton. *Caravan: The Story of the Middle East.* New York, 1953.

Cottam, Richard. *Nationalism in Iran.* Pittsburgh, 1979.

Coulon, Christian. *Le marabout et le prince: Islam et pouvoir au Sénégal.* Paris, 1981.

Coulson, Noel. *A History of Islamic Law.* Edinburgh, 1964.

Crapanzano, Vincent. *Tuhami: Portrait of a Moroccan.* Chicago, 1980.

Crone, Patricia. *Slaves on Horses.* Cambridge, 1980.

Damis, John. "Early Moroccan Reactions to the French Protectorate: The Cultural Dimension." *Humaniora Islamica* 1 (1973): 15–31.

Davis, Eric. *Challenging Colonialism: Bank Misr and Egyptian Industrialization, 1920–1941.* Princeton, 1983.

———. "Islamic Radicalism in Egypt." In *From Nationalism to Revolutionary Islam,* ed. S. Arjomand. New York, 1984.

Deeb, Marius. "Bank Misr and the Emergence of the Local Bourgeoisie in Egypt." *Middle Eastern Studies* 12, no. 3 (October, 1976).

Dekmejian, R. H. "The Anatomy of Islamic Revival." *Middle East Journal* (Winter, 1980).

Delacroix, Jacques. "The Distributive State in the World System." *Studies in Comparative International Development* 15, no. 1 (Fall, 1980): 3–21.

Delphin, Gaetan. *Fas, son université et l'enseignement supérieur Musulman.* Paris, 1889.

Digard, J.-P. *Techniques et culture des nomades baxtyari d'Iran.* Paris, 1981.

Dore, Ronald P. *Education in Tokugawa Japan.* Berkeley, 1965.

Douglas, Mary. *Natural Symbols.* New York, 1973.

Downing, T. E., and M. Gibson, eds. *Irrigation's Impact on Society.* Tucson, Ariz., 1974.

Dresch, Paul. "The Significance of the Course Events Take in Segmentary Systems." *American Ethnologist* 13 (1986): 309–24.

Duby, Georges. *The Early Growth of the European Economy.* Trans. Howard B. Clarke. Ithaca, 1974.

Dumont, Louis. *Homo Hierarchicus: An Essay on the Caste System.* Chicago, 1970.

Durkheim, Emile. *The Elementary Forms of the Religious Life.* Trans. Joseph Swain. London, 1915.

———. *The Evolution of Educational Thought*. Trans. Peter Collins. London, 1977.

———. *Moral Education*. Trans. Everett K. Wilson. New York, 1973.

Eickelman, Dale F. "The Art of Memory: Islamic Knowledge and Its Social Reproduction." *Comparative Studies in Society and History* 20 (1978): 485–516.

———. "Ideological Change and Regional Cults: Maraboutism and Ties of 'Closeness' in Western Morocco." In *Regional Cults*, ed. Richard P. Werbner. London, 1977.

———. "Islam and the Impact of the French Colonial System in Morocco." *Humaniora Islamica* 2 (1974): 215–35.

———. *Knowledge and Power in Morocco: The Education of a Twentieth-Century Notable*. Princeton, 1985.

———. *The Middle East: An Anthropological Approach*. Englewood Cliffs, N.J., 1981.

———. *Moroccan Islam: Tradition and Society in a Pilgrimage Center*. Austin, Tex., 1976.

———. "National Identity and Religious Discourse in Contemporary Oman." *International Journal of Islamic and Arabic Studies* 6 (1989): 1–20.

———. "Time in a Complex Society: A Moroccan Example." *Ethnology* 16 (1977): 39–55.

Eire, M. N. *War against the Idols*. London, 1986.

Eisenstadt, S. N. "Post-Traditional Societies and the Continuity and Reconstruction of Tradition." *Daedalus* 102, no. 1 (Winter, 1973).

———. *The Protestant Ethic and Modernization: A Comparative View*. New York, 1968.

———. "Studies in Modernization and Sociological Theory." *History and Theory* 13 (1974).

———. *Tradition, Change, and Modernity*. New York, 1973.

El Saadawi, Nawal. "The Political Challenges Facing Arab Women at the End of the 20th Century." In *Women of the Arab World*, ed. Nahid Toubia. London, 1988.

Elster, Jon. *Making Sense of Marx*. Cambridge, 1985.

English, P. *City and Village in Iran: Settlement and Economy in the Kirman Basin*. Madison, Wis., 1966.

English, P. W. "The Origin and Spread of Qanats in the Old World." *Proceedings of the American Philosophical Society* 112, no. 3 (1968): 170–81.

Esposito, John L. *Islam and Politics*. Syracuse, 1984.

Evans, Peter B., Dietrich Rueschemeyer, and Theda Skocpol, eds. *Bringing the State Back In*. Cambridge, 1985.

Evans-Pritchard, E. *The Nuer*. Oxford, 1940.

———. *The Sanusi of Cyrenaica*. London, 1949.

Farazmand, Ali. *The State, Bureaucracy, and Revolution in Modern Iran*. New York, 1989.

Fernea, Richard. *Shaykh and Effendi*. Boston, 1970.

Fesharaki, Fereydoon. *Development of the Iranian Oil Industry*. New York, 1976.

Fischer, Michael M. J. *Iran: From Religious Dispute to Revolution*. Cambridge, 1980.

―――. "Islam and the Revolt of the Petty Bourgeoisie." *Daedalus* (1982).

Fleming, John V. "Historians and the Evidence of Literature." *Journal of Interdisciplinary History* 4, no. 1 (Summer, 1973).

Floor, Willem. "The Revolutionary Character of the Shi'i Ulama: Wishful Thinking or Reality." *International Journal of Middle East Studies* 10, no. 1 (February, 1979).

Foucault, Michel. *The Order of Things: An Archaeology of the Human Sciences*. New York, 1973.

French Protectorate, Morocco, Direction Générale de l'Instruction Publique. *Historique (1912–1930)*. Rabat, 1931.

Galdieri, E. *Isfahan: Masgid-i Gum'a*. Rome, 1972-74.

Garthwaite, Gene R. *Khans and Shahs*. Cambridge, 1983.

Gaube, Heinz, and Eugen Wirth. *Der Bazar von Isfahan*. Wiesbaden, 1978.

Geertz, Clifford. *Islam Observed*. New Haven, 1968.

―――. *Local Knowledge*. New York, 1983.

―――. "Suq: The Bazaar Economy in Sefrou." In *Meaning and Order in Moroccan Society*, ed. Clifford Geertz, Hildred Geertz, and Lawrence Rosen. Cambridge, 1979.

Geertz, Hildred. "A Statistical Profile of the Population of the Town of Sefrou in 1960: Analysis of the Census." In *Meaning and Order in Moroccan Society*, ed. Clifford Geertz, Hildred Geertz, and Lawrence Rosen. Cambridge, 1979.

Gellner, Ernest. *Muslim Society*. Cambridge, 1980.

―――. "Political and Religious Organization of the Berbers of the Central High Atlas." In *Arabs and Berbers*, ed. Ernest Gellner and Charles Micaud. Lexington, Mass., 1972.

―――. *Saints and Sufis*. London, 1969.

―――. "Sanctity, Puritanism, Secularization, and Nationalism." In *The Protestant Ethic and Modernization*, ed. S. N. Eisenstadt. New York, 1968.

―――. "Trust, Cohesion, and the Social Order." In *Trust*, ed. Diego Gambetta. London, 1988.

Gerber, Haim. *The Social Origins of the Modern Middle East*. Boulder, Colo., 1987.

Gerresch, Claudine. "Jugements du moniteur du Sénégal sur al-Hajj Umar de 1857 à 1864." *Bulletin de l'Institut Fondamental de l'Afrique Noire* 35, pt. B, no. 3 (1973).

Ghoussoub, Mai. "Feminism—or the Eternal Masculine—in the Arab World." *New Left Review* 161 (January-February, 1987).

Gibb, H. A. R., and Harold Bowen. *Islamic Society and the West*. Vol. 1, part 2. London, 1957.

Gibb, H. A. R., and J. H. Kramer, eds., *The Shorter Encyclopedia of Islam*. Leiden, 1974.

Gimpel, Jean. *The Medieval Machine*. Harmondsworth, 1977.

Glick, Thomas F. *Irrigation and Society in Medieval Valencia*. Cambridge, Mass., 1970.

————. *Islamic and Christian Spain in the Early Middle Ages.* Princeton, 1979.
Gluck, J., and S. Gluck, eds. *A Survey of Persian Handicrafts.* Tehran, 1977.
Goblot, Henri. *Les Qanats: Une technique d'acquisition de l'eau.* Paris, 1979.
Goitein, S. D. *A Mediterranean Society.* 5 vols. Berkeley, 1968–88.
————. *Studies in Islamic History and Institutions.* Leiden, 1966.
Goodard, Victoria. "Honour and Shame: The Control of Women's Sexuality and Group Identity in Naples." In *The Cultural Construction of Sexuality,* ed. Pat Caplan. London, 1987.
Goody, Jack, ed. *The Development of Family and Marriage in Europe.* Cambridge, 1983.
————. *The Domestication of the Savage Mind.* Cambridge, 1977.
————. *The Interface between the Written and the Oral.* Cambridge, 1987.
————. *Literacy in Traditional Societies.* Cambridge, 1968.
————. *The Logic of Writing and the Organization of Society.* Cambridge, 1986.
Gouilly, Alphonse. *L'Islam dans l'Afrique Occidentale Française.* Paris, 1952.
Grabar, O. "The Architecture of the Middle Eastern City." In *Middle Eastern Cities,* ed. Ira Lapidus. Berkeley, 1969.
————. "Islamic Art and Archaeology." In *The Study of the Middle East,* ed. L. Binder. New York, 1976.
Green, Arnold. "Political Attitudes and Activities of the Ulama in the Liberal Age: Tunisia as an Exceptional Case." *International Journal of Middle East Studies* 7 (1976): 209–41.
Guilmartin, J. F., Jr. *Gunpowder and Galleys.* Cambridge, 1974.
Gulick, J. *Tripoli: A Modern Arab City.* Cambridge, Mass., 1967.
Halliday, Fred. *Iran: Dictatorship and Development.* Baltimore, Md., 1979.
————. "A State Based on Butchery." *Guardian,* March 16, 1990, 23.
Halpern, Manfred. *The Politics of Social Change in the Middle East and North Africa.* Princeton, 1963.
Hamamsy, Leila. "The Assertion of Egyptian Identity." In *Arab Society,* ed. N. S. Hopkins and S. Ibrahim. Cairo, 1985.
Hammami, Reza, with Martina Rieker. "Feminist Orientalism and Orientalist Marxism." *New Left Review* 170 (July-August, 1988).
Hammoudir, Abdullah. "Sainteté, pouvoir, et société: Tamgrout aux XVII et XVIII siècles." *Annales: Économies, sociétés, civilizations* (1980): 615–41.
Hannoteau, A., and A. Letourneux. *La Kabylie et les coutumes kabyles.* Paris, 1872–73.
Hardy, Peter. "The Authority of Muslim Kings in Mediaeval South Asia." In *Islam and Society in South Asia,* ed. Marc Gaborieau. Paris, 1986.
Harik, Ilya F. "The Impact of the Domestic Market on Rural-Urban Relations in the Middle East." In *Rural Politics and Social Change in the Middle East,* ed. R. Antoun and I. Harik. Bloomington, Ind., 1972.
Hart, David Montgomery. "Les Ait 'Atta du Sud-Centre Marocain: Elements d'analyse comparative avec les Pakhtuns (Afridi) du Nord-Ouest Pakistanais." In *Islam, société et communauté,* ed. Ernest Gellner. Paris, 1981.
————. *The Aith Waryaghar of the Moroccan Rif: An Ethnography and History.* Tucson, Ariz., 1976.

———. "Clan, Lineage, Local Community, and the Feud in a Rifian Tribe." In *Peoples and Cultures of the Middle East*. Vol. 2, ed. Louise Sweet. New York, 1970.

———. *Dadda 'Atta and His Forty Grandsons: The Sociopolitical Organisation of the Ait 'Atta of Southern Morocco*. Outwell, 1981.

———. *Guardians of the Khaibar Pass: The Social Organisation and History of the Afridis of Pakistan*. Lahore, 1985.

Hatem, Mervat. "Class and Patriarchy as Competing Paradigms for the Study of Middle Eastern Women." *Comparative Studies in Society and History* 29, no. 4. (October, 1987).

Haykal, Muhammad Husayn. "al-Harb wa Harakat al-Tajdid fi al-Sharq" (The War and the Movement for Regeneration in the East). In *al-Sharq al-Jadid*. Cairo, 1962.

———. "Al-Hayat al-Muhabba" (The Beloved Life). *al-Hilal*, April, 1934.

———. "Hijrat al-Rif ila al-Mudun" (The Migration of the Countryside to the Cities). *al-Siyasa al-Usbu'iyya*, March 1, 1930.

———. *Mudhakkirat fi al-Siyasa al-Misriyya*. (Memoirs of Egyptian Politics). Cairo, 1951–53.

———. "Muhadirat Dr. Haykal Basha fi al-Islah al-Ijtima'i" (The Lecture of Dr. Haykal Pasha on Social Reform). *al-Siyasa al-Usbu'iyya*, February 10, 1940.

Hess, Andrew. *The Forgotten Frontier*. Chicago, 1978.

Heyworth Dunne, J. *An Introduction to the History of Education in Modern Egypt*. London, 1968.

Al-Hibrih, Azizah. "A Study of Islamic Herstory." In *Women and Islam*, ed. Azizah al-Hibrih, Oxford, 1982.

Hijab, Nadia. *Womanpower*. Cambridge, 1988.

Hodges, R., and D. Whitehouse. *Mohammad, Charlemagne, and the Origins of Europe*. Ithaca, 1983.

Hodgson, Marshall. *The Venture of Islam*. Chicago, 1974.

Hoffman-Ladd, Valerie. "Polemics on the Modesty and Segregation of Women." *International Journal of Middle East Studies* 19, no. 1 (February, 1987): 25–50.

Holod, Renata, ed. *Studies on Isfahan*. Boston, 1974.

Hopfl, Harro. *The Christian Polity of John Calvin*. Cambridge, 1982.

Hourani, A. *Arabic Thought in the Liberal Age*. New York, 1962.

Hourani, A., and S. M. Stern, eds. *Middle Eastern Cities*. Oxford, 1970.

Hussein, Taha. *The Stream of Days*. Trans. Hilary Waymont. London, 1948.

Ibn Khaldun. *The Muqaddimah*. 3 vols. Trans. Franz Rosenthal, 2d ed. Princeton, 1967.

Ibrahim, Saad Eddin. "Social Mobility and Income Distribution." In *The Political Economy of Income Distribution in Egypt*, ed. Abdel Khalek and Robert Tignor. New York, 1982.

Idowu, H. O. "Assimilation in Nineteenth-Century Senegal." *Bulletin de l'Institut Fondamental de l'Afrique Noire* 30, pt. B, no. 4 (1968).

———. "Café au Lait: Senegal's Mulatto Community in the Nineteenth Century." *Journal of the Historical Society of Nigeria* 6, no. 3 (December, 1972).

Inalcik, Halil. "Bursa and the Commerce of the Levant." *Journal of the Economic and Social History of the Orient* 32, no. 2 (1960).

Issawi, Charles. "The Iranian Economy, 1925–1975: Fifty Years of Economic Development." In *Iran under the Pahlavis,* ed. George Lenczowski. Stanford, 1978.

al-Issawy, Ibrahim Hassan. "Income Distribution and Economic Growth." In *The Political Economy of Income Distribution in Egypt,* ed. Abdel Khalek and Robert Tignor. New York, 1982.

Jahan, Roushan. "Hidden Wounds, Visible Scars: Violence against Women in Bangladesh." In *Structures of Patriarchy,* ed. Bina Agarwal. London, 1988.

Jalal, Ayesha. "The Convenience of Subservience: Women and the State of Pakistan." In *Women, Islam, and the State,* ed. Deniz Kandiyoti. London, forthcoming.

Jansen, J.G. *The Neglected Duty.* New York, 1986.

Jayawardena, Kumari. *Feminism and Nationalism in the Third World.* London, 1988.

Johnson, G. Wesley. *The Emergence of Black Politics in Senegal, 1900–1919.* Stanford, 1971.

Jones, E. L. *The European Miracle: Environments, Economies, and Geopolitics in the History of Europe and Asia.* Cambridge, 1981.

Joseph, Suad. "Elite Strategies for State Building: Women, Family, Religion, and the State in Iraq and Lebanon." In *Women, Islam, and the State,* ed. Deniz Kandiyoti. London, forthcoming.

———. "Family, Religion, and the State: Middle Eastern Models." In *Dialectics and Gender: Anthropological Approaches,* ed. R. Randolph, D. Schneider, and M. Dias. Boulder, Colo., 1988.

Kabeer, Naila. "The Quest for National Identity: Women, Islam, and the State in Bangladesh." In *Women, Islam, and the State,* ed. Deniz Kandiyoti. London, forthcoming.

Kaddache, Mahfoud. *Histoire du nationalisme algérien: Question nationale et politique algérienne, 1919–1951.* Algiers, 1980.

Kandiyoti, Deniz. "End of Empire: Islam, Nationalism, and Women in Turkey." In *Women, Islam, and the State,* ed. Deniz Kandiyoti. London, forthcoming.

———. "Islam and Patriarchy: A Comparative Perspective." In *Shifting Boundaries,* ed. Nikki Keddie and Beth Baron. New Haven, forthcoming.

———. "Women and the Turkish State: Political Actors or Symbolic Pawns?" In *Woman-Nation-State,* ed. Nira Yuval-Davis and Floya Anthias. London, 1989.

Kane, Hamidou. *Ambiguous Adventure.* New York, 1963.

Katouzian, Homa. *The Political Economy of Modern Iran.* London, 1981.

Katz, J. "Deviance, Charisma, and Role-Defined Behavior." *Social Problems* 20 (1972): 186–202.

Kecskemeti, Paul K., ed. "Conservative Thought." In *Essays on Sociology and Social Psychology.* New York, 1953.

Keddie, Nikki R. *An Islamic Response to Imperialism: Political and Religious Writings of Sayyid Jamal al-Din al-Afghani.* Berkeley, 1968.

———. "Is There a Middle East?" *International Journal of Middle East Studies* 3 (July, 1973).

———. "Problems in the Study of Middle Eastern Women." *International Journal of Middle East Studies* 10 (1979).

———. "The Roots of the Ulama's Power in Modern Iran." *Studia Islamica* 29 (1969).

———. *Roots of Revolution.* New Haven, 1981.

Kennedy, Hugh. "From Polis to Madina: Urban Change in Late Antique and Early Islamic Syria." *Past and Present* 106 (February, 1985).

Kepel, Gilles. *Muslim Extremism in Egypt.* Berkeley, 1986.

Keyder, Caglar. "Class and State in the Transformation of Modern Turkey." In *State and Ideology in the Middle East and Pakistan,* ed. Fred Halliday and Hamza Alavi. London, 1988.

Khalil, Sidi. *Mukhtasar.* Trans. Nicolas Seignette. Algiers, 1878.

Khan, Ghani. *The Pathans: A Sketch.* Peshawar, 1958.

al-Khanajri, Wafa. *Al-Amthal al-Sha'biyyah fi hayatina al-yawmiyyah.* Cairo, 1982.

al-Khayr, "Abd al-Rahman." In *Dhikrayati ma'a "Jama'at al-Muslimin" (Al-Takfir wa al-hijrah).* Kuwait, 1980.

Kippenburg, Hans. "Jeder Tag Ashura, Jedes Grab Kerbala." In *Religion und Politik im Iran: Mardom Nameh—Jahrbuch zur Geshichte und Gesellschaft des Mittleren Orients,* ed. Kurt Greussing. Frankfurt am Main, 1981.

Krawczyk, J. L. "Environment, Constraints, and Technology: The Middle East and Europe in the Middle Ages." Manuscript.

Krenkow, F. "The Construction of Subterranean Water Supplies during the Abbaside Caliphate." *Glasgow University Oriental Society Transactions* 13 (1947–49): 23–32.

Lacoste, Yves. "General Characteristics and Fundamental Structures of Mediaeval North African Society." *Economy and Society* 3 (1974):1–17.

Laitin, David D. *Hegemony and Culture: Politics and Religious Change among the Yoruba.* Chicago, 1986.

Lambton, A. K. S. "Quis Custodiet Custodes?" *Studia Islamica* 5, no. 2 (1956).

Lane, Edward W. *The Manners and Customs of the Modern Egyptians.* London, 1871.

Lapidus, Ira. "Knowledge, Virtue, and Action: The Classical Muslim Conception of *Adab* and the Nature of Religious Fulfillment in Islam." In *Moral Conduct and Authority: The Place of Adab in South Asian Islam,* ed. Barbara Daly Metcalf. Berkeley, 1984.

———. *Muslim Cities of the Middle Ages.* Cambridge, Mass., 1967.

Laroui, Abdallah. *The Crisis of the Arab Intellectual.* Trans. D. Cammell. Berkeley, 1976.

———. *Les origines sociales et culturelles du nationalisme marocain (1830–1912).* Paris, 1977.

Lassner, J. *The Topography of Baghdad in the Early Middle Ages.* Detroit, 1970.

Lautenschlager, Wolfgang. "The Effects of an Overvalued Exchange Rate on the

Iranian Economy, 1979–1984." *International Journal of Middle East Studies* 18, no.1 (February, 1986): 31–52.

Lawless, Richard I., and Gerald H. Blake. *Tlemcen: Continuity and Change in an Algerian Islamic Town.* London, 1976.

Le Roy Ladurie, Emmanuel. *Times of Feast, Times of Famine: A History of Climate since the Year 1000.* Garden City, N.Y., 1971.

Le Tourneau, R. *Fès avant le protectorat.* Casablanca, 1949.

Leveau, Remy. *Le fellah marocain: Defenseur du Trone.* Paris, 1976.

———. "The Rural Elite as an Element in the Social Stratification of Morocco." In *Commoners, Climbers, and Notables,* ed. C. A. O. van Nieuwenhuijze. Leiden, 1977.

Levy-Provencal, E. *Les historiens des chorfa.* Paris, 1922.

Lewis, Bernard. "Islamic Concepts of Revolution." In *Revolution in the Middle East,* ed. P. J. Vatikiotis. London, 1972.

———. *The Political Language of Islam.* Chicago, 1988.

Lewis, Bernard, ed. *The World of Islam.* London, 1976.

Lienhardt, Godfrey. *Divinity and Experience: The Religion of the Dinka.* Oxford, 1967.

Lilley, S. *Men, Machines, and History.* London, 1965.

Lindholm, Charles. "Caste in Islam and the Problem of Deviant Systems: A Critique of Recent Theory." *Contributions to Indian Sociology* 20 (1986): 61–73.

———. *Generosity and Jealousy: The Swat Pukhtun of Northern Pakistan.* New York, 1982.

———. "Kinship Structure and Political Authority: The Middle East and Central Asia." *Comparative Studies in Society and History* 28 (1986): 334–65.

———. "Leatherworkers and Love Potions." *American Ethnologist* 9 (1981): 512–25.

———. "The Structure of Violence among the Swat Pukhtun." *Ethnology* 20 (1981): 147–56.

Loader, Colin. *The Intellectual Development of Karl Mannheim: Culture, Politics, and Planning.* Cambridge, 1985.

Locher, Gottfried W. *Huldrych Zwingli's Concept of History.* Leiden, 1981.

Looney, Robert. *Economic Origins of the Iranian Revolution.* New York, 1982.

Luciani, Giacomo. "Allocation vs. Production States: A Theoretical Framework." In *The Rentier State,* ed. Hazem Beblawi and Giacomo Luciani. New York, 1987.

McNeill, William. *The Pursuit of Power.* Chicago, 1982.

———. *The Rise of the West.* Chicago, 1963.

MacPherson, Charles. *The Political Theory of Possessive Individualism.* London, 1962.

Madelung, Wilfred. Q. v. "Imama." In *Encyclopaedia of Islam.* Leiden, 1971.

Mahdavy, Hossein. "The Patterns and Problems of Economic Development in Rentier States: The Case of Iran." In *Studies in the Economic History of the Middle East,* ed. Michael Cook. London, 1970.

Makdisi, George. "Hanbalite Islam." In *Studies in Islam,* ed. Merlin Swartz. New York, 1981.

————. *The Rise of Colleges: Institutions of Learning in Islam and the West.* Edinburgh, 1981.

Mallarme, V. "La brochure 'L'Administration de la Justice in Algérie' et ses conclusions." *Bulletin Judiciaire de l'Algérien* 1 (May, 1877).

Mann, Michael. *The Sources of Social Power.* Cambridge, 1986.

Manning, Patrick. *Francophone Subsaharan Africa, 1880–1985.* Cambridge, 1988.

al-Manuni, Muhammad. *Mazahir yaqza al-Maghrib al-hadith. Part 1.* Rabat, 1973.

Mardin, Serif. *Religion and Social Change in Modern Turkey.* Albany, N.Y., 1989.

Martin, Benjamin F. "The Courts, the Magistrature, and Promotions in Third Republic France." *American Historical Review* 87, no. 4 (October, 1982).

Marty, Paul. "L'université de Qaraouyne." *Reignseignements coloniaux, supplement de l'Afrique Française* (November, 1924): 329–53.

Marvick, Dwaine. "Influence and Withdrawal: The Intellectuals in Indian Political Development." In *Political Decision Makers,* ed. Dwaine Marvick. Glencoe, Ill., 1961.

————. "The Intellectual between Tradition and Modernity: The Indian Situation." *Comparative Studies in Society and History.* Supp. 1. The Hague, 1961.

Massavar-Rahmani, B. *Energy Policy in Iran: Domestic Choices and International Implications.* New York, 1981.

Mauss, Marcel. "Essai sur les variations saisonnières des sociétés eskimos: Etude de morphologie sociale." In *Sociologie et anthropologie,* ed. Marcel Mausse. Paris, 1966.

Meeker, Michael. *Literature and Violence in Early Arabia.* London, 1979.

————. "The Twilight of a South Asian Heroic Age: A Rereading of Barth's Study of Swat." *Man* 15 (1980): 682–701.

Mernissi, Fatima. "Democracy as Moral Disintegration: The Contradiction between Religious Belief and Citizenship as a Manifestation of the Ahistoricity of the Arab Identity." In *Women of the Arab World,* ed. Nahid Toubis. London, 1988.

————. *La harem politique.* Paris, 1987.

————. "Muslim Women and Fundamentalism." *MERIP Reports,* no. 153 (July-August, 1988).

Messick, Brinkley. "The Mufti, the Text, and the World: Legal Interpretation in Yemen." *Man,* n.s. 21 (1986): 102–19.

Metcalf, Barbara Daly. *Islamic Revival in British India: Deoband 1860–1900.* Princeton, 1982.

Michaux-Bellaire, E. "L'enseignement indigène au Maroc." *Revue du monde musulman* 15 (1911): 422–52.

Michel, M. "Citoyenneté et service militaire dans les quatre communes de Sénégal au cours de la première guerre mondiale." *Perspectives nouvelles sur le passé de l'Afrique Noire.* Paris, 1974.

Migdal, Joel S. *Palestinian Society and Politics.* Princeton, 1980.

Milani, Mohsen. *The Making of Iran's Islamic Revolution: The State and Social Revolution in Iran.* New York, 1983.

Miske, Ahmad Baba. "Al-Wasit (1911)—Tableau de la Mauritanie à la fin du XIXème siècle." *Bulletin de l'Institute Fondamental de l'Afrique Noire* 30, pt. B, no 1 (1968).

Mitzman, Arthur. "Anti-Progress: A Study in the Romantic Roots of German Sociology." *Social Research* 33 (1966).

Molyneux, Maxine. "The Law, the State, and Socialist Policies with Regard to Women: The Case of the People's Democratic Republic of Yemen." In *Women, Islam, and the State,* ed. Deniz Kandiyoti. London, forthcoming.

Mommsen, Wolfgang I. *The Age of Bureaucracy: Perspectives on the Political Sociology of Max Weber.* New York, 1974.

———. *Max Weber and German Politics, 1890–1920.* Trans. Michael S. Steinberg. Chicago, 1984.

Monteil, V. *Esquisses Sénégalaises.* Dakar, 1966.

Moore, Barrington, Jr. *Social Origins of Dictatorship and Democracy.* Boston, 1966.

Moore, C. H. "On Theory and Practice among Arabs." *World Politics* 24 (1971).

Morin, Edgar. "Intellectuels: Critique du mythe et mythe du critique." *Arguments* 4, no. 20 (October, 1960).

Morsy, Megali. "Arbitration as a Political Institution: An Interpretation of the Status of Monarchy in Morocco." In *Islam in Tribal Societies,* ed. David Hart and Akbar Ahmed. London, 1984.

Mortimer, Edward. *Faith and Power: The Politics of Islam.* New York, 1982.

Mosca, Gaetano. *The Ruling Class: Elementi di scienza politica.* Trans. Hannah D. Kahn. New York, 1939.

Mottahedeh, Roy. *Loyalty and Leadership in Early Islamic Society.* Princeton, 1980.

———. *The Mantle of the Prophet.* New York, 1985.

———. "Review of Bulliet, *The Patricians of Nishapur.*" *Journal of the American Oriental Society* 95 (1975): 491–95.

Moulieras, Auguste. *Le Maroc inconnu.* Vol. 1, *Exploration du Rif.* Paris, 1895.

———. *Le Maroc inconnu.* Vol. 2, *Exploration des Djebala.* Paris, 1899.

Muhammad Ali, Maulana. *A Manual of Hadith.* London, 1944.

Munson, Henry. *Islam and Revolution in the Middle East.* New Haven, 1988.

Najmabadi, Afsaneh. "Depoliticization of a Rentier State: The Case of Pahlavi Iran." In *The Rentier State,* ed. Hazem Beblawi and Giacomo Luciani. New York, 1987.

———. "Hazards of Modernity and Morality: Women, State, and Ideology in Contemporary Iran." In *Women, Islam, and the State,* ed. Deniz Kandiyoti. London, forthcoming.

Needham, Joseph. *Science and Civilization in China.* Cambridge, 1954.

Nettle, J. P. "Ideas, Intellectuals, and Structures of Dissent." In *On Intellectuals, Theoretical Studies, Case Studies,* ed. Philip Rieff. New York, 1969.

Noin, Daniel. *La population rurale du Maroc.* Paris, 1970.

Notopoulos, James A. "Mnemosyne in Oral Literature." *Transactions and Proceedings of the American Philological Association* 69 (1938): 465–93.

Novick, Peter. *That Noble Dream: The "Objectivity Question" and the American Historical Profession.* Cambridge, 1988.

Oberling, Pierre. *The Qashqa'i Nomads of Fars.* The Hague, 1974.

Parry, V., and M. Yapp, eds. *War, Technology, and Society in the Middle East.* London, 1975.

Parsa, Misagh. *Social Origins of the Iranian Revolution.* New Brunswick, N.J., 1989.

Parsons, Talcott. "Democracy and Social Structure in Pre-Nazi Germany." *Journal of Legal and Political Sociology* 1-2 (1942).

Pasquier, Roger. "L'influence de l'expérience algérienne sur la politique de la France en Sénégal (1842-1869)." *Perspectives nouvelles sur le passé de l'Afrique Noire et la Madagascar—Mélanges offerts à Hubert Deschamps.* Paris, 1974.

Pateman, Carol. *The Sexual Contract.* Oxford, 1988.

Pathak, Zakia, and Rajeswari Sunder Rajan. "Shah Bano." *Signs* 3 (1989).

Pehrson, Robert. *The Social Organization of the Marri Baluch.* New York, 1966.

Penant, D. "De la condition juridique des indigènes en matière civile et commerciale dans les colonies françaises." *Recuiel Penant* 15, pt. 2 (1906).

Peretie, A. "Les madrasas de Fès." *Archives marocaines* 18 (1912): 257-372.

Pesaran, H. "The System of Dependent Capitalism in Pre- and Post-Revolutionary Iran." *International Journal of Middle East Studies* 14, no. 4 (November, 1982): 501-22.

Peters, Rud. *Islam and Colonialism: The Doctrine of Jihad in Modern History.* The Hague, 1979.

Picot, Georges. "Les magistrats et la démocratie." *Revue des deux mondes* 62 (March 15, 1884).

Pipes, Daniel. *Slave Soldiers and Islam.* New Haven, 1981.

Piscatori, James, ed. *Islam in the Political Process.* London, 1983.

Planhol, Xavier de. *The World of Islam.* Ithaca, N.Y., 1959.

Poggi, Gianfranco. *Calvinism and the Capitalist Spirit: Max Weber's Protestant Ethic.* London, 1983.

Poni, Carlo. "Archeologie de la fabrique: La diffusion des moulins à soie." *Annales* 27, no. 6 (1972): 1475-96.

Pope, Arthur Upham, ed. *A Survey of Persian Art from Prehistoric Times to the Present.* 6 vols. London, 1938-39.

Prenant, A. "La propriété foncière des citadins dans les regions de Sidi Bel Abbès et de Tlemcen." *Annales algériennes de géographie* 2, no. 1 (1967).

Qutb, Sayyid. *Fi zilal al-qur'an.* Beirut, 1974.

Rabie, H. "Some Technical Aspects of Agriculture in Medieval Egypt." In *The Islamic Middle East, 700-1900: Studies in Social and Economic History,* ed. A. Udovitch. Princeton, 1981.

Rabinow, Paul. *Reflections on Fieldwork in Morocco.* Berkeley, 1977.

Ragin, Charles C. *The Comparative Method.* Berkeley, 1987.

Raymond, André. *Artisans et commerçants au Caire au XVIIIème siècle.* Damascus, 1974.

Razavi, Hossein, and Firouz Vakil. *The Political Environment of Economic Planning in Iran, 1971-1983*. Boulder, Colo., 1984.

Reath, N. A., and F. B. Sachs. *Persian Textiles and Their Technique*. New Haven, 1937.

Reid, Donald M. "Educational and Career Choices of Egyptian Students, 1882–1922." *International Journal of Middle East Studies* 8 (1977): 349–78.

Renaudot, Françoise. *L'histoire des Français en Algérie*. Paris, 1979.

Renner, Michael G. "Determinants of the Islamic Republic's Oil Policies." In *Post-Revolutionary Iran*. Boulder, Colo., 1988.

Rieff, Philip. "The Intellectuals and the Powers: Some Perspectives for Comparative Analysis." In *On Intellectuals, Theoretical Studies, Case Studies*, ed. Philip Rieff. New York, 1969.

Riesman, David, with Nathan Glazer and Ruel Denny. *The Lonely Crowd*. New Haven, 1961.

Rivet, Daniel. "Lyautey l'africain." *L'histoire* 29 (December, 1980): 17–24.

Robinson, David. "French Islamic Policy and Practice in Late Nineteenth-Century Senegal." *Journal of African History* 29 (1988).

———. *The Holy War of Umar Tal*. Oxford, 1985.

Rodinson, Maxime. *Europe and the Mystique of Islam*. Trans. Roger Veinus. Seattle, 1987.

———. *Islam and Capitalism*. New York, 1973.

———. *Mohammed*. Trans. Anne Carter. London, 1971.

Rosen, Lawrence. *The Anthropology of Justice: Law as Culture in Islamic Society*. Chicago, 1989.

———. "Social Identity and Points of Attachment: Approaches to Social Organization." In *Meaning and Order in Moroccan Society*, ed. Clifford Geertz, Hildred Geertz, and Lawrence Rosen. Cambridge, 1979.

Rosenfeld, Henry. "The Social Composition of the Military in the Process of State Formation in the Arabian Desert." *Journal of the Royal Anthropological Institute* 5 (1965): 75–86; 174–94.

Rosenthal, Franz. *Knowledge Triumphant: The Concept of Knowledge in Mediaeval Islam*. Leiden, 1970.

Roth, Geunther, and Claus Wittich, eds. *Economy and Society*. Berkeley, 1978.

Russel, Paul. *Lay Theology in the Reformation: Popular Pamphleteers in Southwest Germany, 1521-1525*. London, 1986.

Al-Saadawi, Nawal. "Women and Islam." In *Woman and Islam*, ed. Azizah al-Hibrih. Oxford, 1982.

Sachedina, Abdulaziz A. "Ali Shariati: Ideologue of the Iranian Revolution." In *Voices of Resurgent Islam*, ed. John L. Esposito. Oxford, 1983.

———. *Islamic Messianism: The Idea of Mahdi in Twelver Shi'ism*. Albany, 1981.

Safwat, Safiya. "Islamic Laws in the Sudan." In *Islamic Law: Social and Historical Contexts*, ed. Aziz al-Azmeh. London, 1988.

Said, Edward. *Orientalism*. New York, 1979.

Said Aly, Abd al-Moneim, and Manfred Wenner. "Modern Islamic Reform Movements: The Muslim Brotherhood in Contemporary Egypt." *Middle East Journal* 34, no. 3 (Summer, 1982).

Sari, Djilali. *Les villes précoloniales de l'Algérie Occidentale: Nedroma, Mazouna, Kalaa.* Algiers, 1970.

Sassoon, Ann, ed. *Women and the State.* London, 1987.

Schmitter, Philip C. "Still the Century of Corporatism?" In *The New Corporatism,* ed. Frederick Pike and Thomas Stritch. Notre Dame, Ind., 1974.

Schuyler, Philip D. "Music Education in Morocco: Three Models." *World of Music* (Berlin) 21 (1979): 19–31.

Seddon, David. "Economic Anthropology or Political Economy (II): Approaches to the Analysis of Pre-Capitalist Formation in the Maghreb." In *The New Economic Anthropology,* ed. John Clammer. New York, 1978.

Sergeant, R. B., and R. Lewcock, eds. *San'a: An Arabian Islamic City.* London, 1983.

Sharabi, Hisham. *Neopatriarchy: A Theory of Distorted Change in Arab Society.* Oxford, 1988.

Shariati, Ali. *Marxism and Other Fallacies: An Islamic Critique.* Trans. R. Campbell. Berkeley, 1980.

———. *On the Sociology of Islam.* Trans. Hamid Algar. Berkeley, 1979.

Shepard, William E. "Islam as a 'System' in the Later Writings of Sayyid Qutb." *Middle Eastern Studies* 25 (1989): 31–50.

Shepherd, Dorothy G. "The Textile Industry in Medieval Iran." Manuscript.

Skocpol, Theda. "Rentier State and Shi'a Islam in the Iranian Revolution." *Theory and Society* 11, no. 3 (May, 1982): 265–83.

———. *States and Social Revolutions.* New York, 1979.

Smith, A. "Qanats." *Journal of the Iran Society* 1 (1951): 86–90.

Smith, Anthony D. *The Concept of Social Change: A Critique of the Functionalist Theory of Social Change.* London, 1973.

Smith, Charles D. "The Crisis of Orientation: The Shift of Egyptian Intellectuals to Islamic Subjects in the 1930s." *International Journal of Middle East Studies* 4 (October, 1973).

———. *Islam and the Search for Social Order in Modern Egypt: A Biography of Muhammad Husayn Haykal.* Albany, N.Y., 1983.

———. "Love, Passion, and Class in the Fiction of Muhammad Husayn Haykal." *Journal of the American Oriental Society* 99, no. 2 (April-June, 1979).

Smith, M. G. "The Sociological Framework of Law." In *Corporations and Society.* London, 1974.

Smith, Ray T. "The Indian Liberals and Constitutionalism in India." In *Studies in Indian Democracy,* ed. S. P. Aiyar and R. Srinivasan. New York, 1965.

———. "The Role of India's Liberals in the Nationalist Movement, 1915-1947." *Asian Survey* 7 (July, 1968).

Smith, Tony. *The French Stake in Algeria, 1945-1962.* Ithaca, N.Y., 1978.

Smith, W. Cantwell. *Islam in Modern History.* Princeton, 1957.

Snouck Hurgronje, C. *Mekka in the Latter Part of the 19th Century.* Leiden, 1931.

Snyder, Francis. *Capitalism and Legal Change.* London, 1981.

Spence, Jonathan D. *The Death of Woman Wang.* New York, 1978.

Spencer, Herbert. *Ethics.* Pt. 2, "Justice." London, 1893.

Stepan, Alfred. *The State and Society: Peru in Comparative Perspective.* Princeton, 1978.

Stewart, C. C. *Islam and Social Order in Mauritania: A Case Study from the Nineteenth Century.* Oxford, 1973.

Stone, Lawrence, ed. *The University in Society.* Princeton, 1974.

Struve, Peter. *Elites against Democracy: Leadership Ideals in Bourgeois Political Thought in Germany, 1890–1933.* Princeton, 1973.

as-Susi, Mukhtar. *al-Ma'sul.* Casablanca, 1961.

Tignor, Robert. "The Egyptian Revolution of 1919: New Directions in the Egyptian Economy." *Middle Eastern Studies* 12, no. 3 (October, 1976).

Tocqueville, Alexis de. *Democracy in America.* Garden City, N.Y., 1969.

Toprak, Zafer. "The Family, Feminism, and the State during the Young Turk Period." In *Colloque international sur la Turquie contemporaine.* Istanbul, forthcoming.

Triaud, Jean-Louis. "La question musulmane en Côte d'Ivoir (1893–1939)." *Revue française d'histoire d'Outre-Mer* 61, no. 4 (1974).

Trimingham, J. *The Sufi Orders of Islam.* Oxford, 1971.

Tucker, Judith E. "Problems in the Historiography of Women in the Middle East: The Case of Nineteenth-Century Egypt." *International Journal of Middle East Studies* 15 (1983).

———. *Women in Nineteenth-Century Egypt.* Cambridge, 1978.

Turner, Bryan S. "State, Religion, and Minority Status." *Comparative Studies in Society and History* 27, no. 2 (April, 1985).

———. *Weber and Islam.* London, 1974.

Udovitch, A., ed. *The Islamic Middle East, 700–1900: Studies in Social and Economic History.* Princeton, 1981.

'Uthman, Muhammad ibn. *al-Jami'a al-Yusufiya bi Marrakush.* Cairo, 1935.

Valderrama Martinez, Fernando. *Historia de la accion cultural de España en Marruecos (1912–1956).* Tetouan, 1956.

Vatin, Jean-Claude. *L'Algérie politique: Histoire et société.* Paris, 1974.

Vieille, Paul. "The State of the Periphery and Its Heritage." *Economy and Society* 17, no. 1 (1988): 52–89.

Villard, Ugo Monneret de. *Introduzione allo studio dell'archeologia islamica: Le origini e il periodo omayyade.* Venice, 1966.

von Grunebaum, Gustave. "Observations on the Muslim Concept of Evil." In *Islam and Medieval Hellenism: Social and Cultural Perspectives.* London, 1976.

von Sivers, Peter. "Les plaisirs du collectionneur: Capitalisme fiscal et chefs indigènes en Algérie (1840–1860)." *Annales: Économies, sociétés, civilisations* 35 (1980).

———. "Riverine Realms: Iraq, Egypt, and Syria during the Classical Islamic Period." *Newsletter of the American Research Center in Egypt,* no. 124 (Winter, 1983): 12–18.

Waardenburg, Jacques. "Some Institutional Aspects of Muslim Higher Education and Their Relation to Islam." *Numen* 12 (1964): 96–138.

Wadud, A. *The Story of Swat as Told by the Founder.* Peshawar, 1962.
Wallerstein, Immanuel. *The Modern World System.* New York, 1974.
Walzer, Michael. *Revolution of the Saints.* Cambridge, 1965.
Waterbury, John. *The Egypt of Nasser and Sadat: The Political Economy of Two Regimes.* Princeton, 1983.
Watson, Andrew M. *Agricultural Innovation in the Early Islamic World.* Cambridge, 1983.
———. "The Arab Agricultural Revolution and Its Diffusion, 700–1100." *Journal of Economic History* 34, no. 1 (March, 1974): 8–35.
———. "A Medieval Green Revolution: New Crops and Farming Techniques in the Early Islamic World." In *The Islamic Middle East, 700–1900: Studies in Social and Economic History,* ed. A. Udovitch. Princeton, 1981.
Watt, W. M. *Muhammad at Mecca.* Oxford, 1953.
———. *Muhammad at Medina.* Oxford, 1956.
Weber, Max. *The Protestant Ethic.* Trans. Talcott Parsons. New York, 1958.
Wendell, Charles. *The Evolution of the Egyptian National Image from its Origins to Ahmad Lutfi al-Sayyid.* Berkeley, 1973.
Wensinck, A. J., and J. P. Mensing, eds. *Concordance et indices de la tradition musulmane.* Leiden, 1962.
Westermarck, Edward. *Ritual and Belief in Morocco.* Vol. 1. London, 1926.
White, Lynn, Jr. *Medieval Religion and Technology.* Berkeley, 1978.
———. *Medieval Technology and Social Change.* Oxford, 1963.
Wigley, T. M. L., M. J. Ingram, and G. Farmer, eds. *Climate and History.* Cambridge, 1981.
Wolf, Eric. *Peasant Wars of the Twentieth Century.* San Francisco, 1973.
Wolin, Sheldon. *Politics and Vision.* Boston, 1960.
Woloch, Isser. "Napoleonic Conscription: State Power and Civil Society." *Past and Present* 111 (May, 1986).
Wulff, H. E. *The Traditional Crafts of Persia.* Cambridge, Mass., 1966.
———. "The Qanats of Iran." *Scientific American* 218, no. 4 (1968): 94–105.
Yacono, Xavier. *La colonisation des plaines du Chélif.* Algiers, 1955.
Yuval-Davis, Nira, and Flaya Anthias, eds. *Woman-Nation-State.* London, 1989.
Zander, G. *Travaux de restauration des monuments historiques en Iran.* Rome, 1968.
Zonis, Marvin. *The Political Elite of Iran.* Princeton, 1971.
Zuccarelli, François. "Les maires de Saint-Louis et de Gorée de 1816 à 1872." *Bulletin de l'Institut Fondamental de l'Afrique Noire* 35, pt. B, no. 3 (1973).

Index